VERGIL'S *AENEID*

Sunt lacrimae rerum et mentem mortalia tangunt

PUBLIUS VERGILIUS MARO

known as *Vergil*

The Aeneid

AN EPIC POEM OF ROME

Translated by

L. R. LIND

MCMLXIII

INDIANA UNIVERSITY PRESS

BLOOMINGTON & LONDON

This translation is gratefully
dedicated to
BEN EDWIN PERRY

Contents

Vergil and the Meaning of the Aeneid

I

Of the three great classical epic heroes, Vergil's Aeneas is the most modern in his sense of responsibility, his social consciousness, and his serious moral purpose. He is committed to a cause that transcends personal ambitions, one in every way worthy of a hero's supreme efforts, for it is a cause in which selfhood is merged, to its greater glory, with the welfare of others. Vergil comes at the end of a long tradition ripe for innovation. The ideal of an interdependent humanity not identical with the Christian brotherhood of man was new in the Latin culture of his time; Cicero had spoken of it as *humanitas*.

The form in which Vergil left the epic tradition imposed itself on European literature for the next fifteen hundred years, in fact until epic ceased to be written, and the extent of the fundamental changes he brought about in that tradition must be understood in the light of later historical perspectives. Epic is now, of course, an extinct genre, but while it remained vigorous throughout the Middle Ages and the Renaissance most of its heroes continued to preserve the Vergilian pattern. Vasco da Gama is the hero of one of the most readable of post-Vergilian epics, the *Lusiads* of Camoens; he is also closer to Aeneas than any later hero.

It will not be difficult to demonstrate the validity of these statements. The tragedy of Achilles lies chiefly in his apparently unjustifiable irresponsibility. The cause of the Argives means almost nothing to him in comparison with his private resentment and grief. His cause is personal glory alone. When in the ninth book of the *Iliad* he replies to the generous offer of Odysseus, the actual chairman of the committee on reconciliation sent to Achilles by the Greek high command, all readers are impresssed with the shallowness of his thinking, the cold selfishness of his choice between long life and brief glory—for himself alone.

Odysseus, although a more complex and subtle personality, is similarly impelled by motives which cannot be called noble. Both he and Achilles went unwillingly to the war; both are stirred to their greatest efforts by revenge. Revenge is combined with a desire to return home after much fruitless fighting; but neither man seems quite sincere in his declared intentions. Achilles never goes home at all, and Odysseus does so only after ten years of aimless wanderings which include long stays in places whose attractions seem to outweigh both revenge and homesickness. One cannot say that Odysseus is really trying all the time. "Time out" is his frequent and characteristic response to difficult situations; before Troy, when Achilles is eager to go into battle, Odysseus urges that the fighters eat first and fight afterward.

Aeneas is also modern as a lover, strange as this may sound to those who dislike him for deserting Dido. Vergil makes it quite clear that the episode of the cave and the thunder storm was not a mere seduction, and that the love of Aeneas for Dido was genuine and his parting from her a great and sincere sorrow. Nothing in the history of love drama (for the Dido-book is really a magnificent play with many psychological overtones that chime with those of Racine) is more convincing: Aeneas is the first lover in ancient epic to be described more fully than Hector, his only rival, who displays a true tenderness matched by a willingness to sacrifice personal love for a larger purpose. Aeneas is a prototype of the chivalric lover of the Middle Ages, with more than a touch of the lover in the *Romance of the Rose*. Achilles and Agamemnon are schoolboys quarrelling for calf-love when compared with Aeneas; Achilles may even be regarded as insincere in love, considering his extremely close relations with both Patroclus and Briseis. Odysseus is by no means a faithful husband, and his infidelities are, moreover, those of a callous voluptuary who has made a habit of taking his pleasure where he finds it.

Nothing is more striking in the character and behavior of Aeneas than his almost obsessive ubiquity in the *Aeneid*. In startling contrast is the long absence of Achilles from the scene of action in the *Iliad*. Homer emphasizes in this way Achilles' indifference to the fate of his comrades, keeping his presence nevertheless keenly alive in the consciousness of the listener by many references to the absent hero and by the embassy to him. Aeneas, however, disappears from the center of the stage only in Book IX, where his absence is contrived by Vergil not in imitation of Homer but to allow Turnus his *aristeia* in the attempt to burn the Trojan ships, and to turn the spotlight upon Nisus and Euryalus. Elsewhere throughout the epic, Aeneas is constantly present to guide, console, and inspire his men, with a peculiar brooding tenderness, Vergil's own form of *humanitas,* a contribution to the character of Aeneas which neither

Ennius nor any other Roman predecessor achieved in handling the myth of Rome's founding.

The ancient Roman *virtus,* with its implied sense of duty, manly decision and courage, is combined with a new feeling of compassion and an attachment to his comrades which is more than the fellow-feeling men at war always have for each other· Not only are the survivors of Troy his only friends; they are the sole hope Aeneas has for founding the new state promised by the fates. His dependence upon them is heightened by his frequent deference, in true *pietas,* to the advice (once, at least, wrong) of his father, his outbursts of despair, and the constant doubts which assail Aeneas as to his destination, the route to it, and the will of the gods in respect to himself. *Virtus, pietas, humanitas* are the three dominant features in the hero's personality, a blending of the old, distinctively Roman moral qualities with a new element of culture ultimately Greek in origin. From its first formulation in the works of Cicero —and this is perhaps the solitary link between the thinking of Vergil and Cicero—*humanitas* was to reach its fullest expression as a philosophical concept in the ethical writings of the Silver Age. But it is in the figure of Aeneas that *humanitas* attained the glowing and satisfying embodiment which a truly creative imagination could give it.

There is more to the *Aeneid* than moral qualities, more than Aeneas. While he exemplifies a combination of moral values entirely new in ancient epic, his is a story in which he is only the principal character. The elements of style Matthew Arnold found in Homer apply as well to the *Aeneid:* Vergil is rapid, plain and direct in thought and expression, plain and direct in substance, and noble. It is absurd to speak of Vergil in the excessively laudatory words of Paul Claudel, who calls him "le plus grand génie que l'humanité ait jamais produit" and describes his book thus: "Il n'y a rien de plus divin au monde que les six premières livres [de l'Enéide]."[1] It is equally absurd for Simone Weil to say in her otherwise excellent essay, *The Iliad or The Poem of Force* that "the *Aeneid* is an imitation [of the *Iliad*] which, however brilliant, is disfigured by frigidity, bombast, and bad taste."[2] The *Aeneid* has always been popular because it is, first and foremost, a good story. The features of that story are a rapidly moving plot with a romantic background of love, adventure, and travel combined with both a high purpose and a magnificent his-

---

[1] "L'oiseau noir dans le soleil levant," in *Oeuvres complètes* (Paris: 1952), p. 312.

[2] Translated by Mary McCarthy, Politics Pamphlet No. 1 (New York: November, 1945), p. 27; also reprinted as Pendle Hill Pamphlet No. 91 (Wallingford, Pa.: 1956).

torical theme—the rise and grandeur of the Roman Empire. Self-preservation and the heroism to which this instinct can give way; the menace of both gods and elements; conflict on a national scale with a native population whose patriotism is a match for that of the Trojans; and the final conquest of a new land (*maior rerum mihi nascitur ordo, maius opus moveo*, VII. 44-5) which was to become the greatest ethnical melting pot of the ancient world—these are the main lines along which the *Aeneid* proceeds.

There is about the entire poem a compression and a rigorous selection of material which is remarkable but clearly perceived only by readers who realize how the essence of both the *Iliad* and the *Odyssey* has been poured into a new mold. The order of climax is in the order of greatness: first, the *Odyssey,* then the *Iliad,* both in a Roman setting; Vergil's admiration for the latter is implicit in the phrase *maius opus moveo* which opens the seventh book. The reversed chronologies were inevitable for Homer and Vergil, but only Vergil sees the obvious advantage of his. Perhaps the fifth book—the funeral games for Anchises—is the most disregarded of all the twelve; yet its narratives are among the best in the poem, and the most humorous, in a vein of hearty jocularity not found elsewhere in Vergil's works, for the humor of the *Eclogues* is of a different sort. The prize fight of Dares and Entellus is placed midway in the list of events—boat race, foot race, boxing, archery, and horsemanship—with careful purpose. The thundering, crashing impact of its blow-by-blow description is brought to its height by the victorious Entellus as he kills a bullock with one blow of his lead and iron-studded glove and then retires, an undefeated champion. The story of Hercules and Cacus in Book VIII, with the strong folktale flavor Vergil loved, is a story of another type, an action tale of gigantic proportions reminiscent of Paul Bunyan. The gruesome details, the quaint hero, and the clever integration of the tale with the primitive mythology of Rome's land site make this one of Vergil's most effective stories· More familiar are, of course, the tragic night raid of Nisus and Euryalus, Turnus' sortie against the Trojan ships, and the final combat of Aeneas and Turnus, with Juturna's intervention and its marvellous simile of the swallow's flight (paralleled by that of the sparrow in the Venerable Bede's *Ecclesiastical History of the English People,* II .13). But even these narratives, absorbing as they are in themselves, are subordinated to the total effect of the poem more carefully than are the episodes ot the *Odyssey.*

Much has been written about the defects of Latin literature. It has been called inferior not only to Greek literature but to more than one of the modern literatures which have sprung from Latin. Rhetoric and emphasis on external form have been declared the chief characteristics of

Latin literature; it has been charged with lack of imagination and, above all, of originality. There is, of course, more than a little truth in these statements. Yet when one reads the greatest Latin writers, especially Vergil, one can grant all this and still remain convinced that no adverse criticism can deprive the *Aeneid,* among many other Latin poems, of its peculiar charm and appeal, or explain these attractions as mere borrowings.

Vergil borrowed from Homer a great many items: his verse form, the division into twelve books, mythology, many episodes and similes. In the *Aeneid* Venus doubles for Nausicaa, Dido for Calypso and Circe (with a very great difference, of course), and Drances for Thersites. The funeral games, the descent into Hades, where Aeneas meets Dido as Odysseus met Ajax, the prophecy of Anchises, the catalogue of ships, Turnus' attempt to burn them, a broken truce, a Doloneia[3] more full of pathos than that of Odysseus and Diomedes, an embassy to Diomedes, a quarrel between two Italian leaders, the slaying of Patroclus (though he is named Pallas), and a final single combat, Aeneas against Turnus, are all taken from Homer and put to new uses. Dido and her suitors recall Penelope and her suitors, although Dido is not Penelope. The parade of sea nymphs in Book V recalls the parade of mythological beauties in *Odyssey,* II or the list of nymphs in *Iliad,* XVIII. Palinurus is a Roman Elpenor. Juno creates a false Aeneas to draw off Turnus in a boat, as the false Deiphobus tricked Hector in the *Iliad.* Aeneas kills Lausus with the same pity, less the scorn, with which Achilles killed Lycaon. The horse of Pallas weeps for him as did the horses of Achilles for their charioteer, Patroclus.

But the Roman motivation toward historical fact in many of these correspondences with Homer is unmistakable. Venus is the founder of the Julian line, Dido is the embodiment of Roman-Carthaginian enmity, the prophecy of Anchises is one of Rome's future history, the catalogue of the Italians is a roll call of the primitive peoples whom Rome amalgamated under her rule; even Turnus swims the Tiber like the semi-historical Horatius. Each borrowing, even when not thus motivated, has its integral use and purpose and is not mere epic decoration. The theme of fate which rings from first book to last is interwoven with a constant symbolism which, if not quite so concentrated and omnipresent as Cruttwell's little book implies,[4] is certainly abundant everywhere, from the golden bough of mistletoe (the parasite which symbolizes death in life) to the sows with their litters and the cutting of the ship's cable by Aeneas

---

[3] The ancient name of *Iliad, X.*
[4] R. W. Cruttwell, *Virgil's Mind at Work* (Oxford: 1926).

as he leaves Carthage, severing the thread which held him to Dido and inaugurating the centuries of hatred between Rome and Carthage, amid the echoes of Dido's curses.

Homer's epics live in a glow of Greek sunlight. The *Aeneid* moves through gloom from dusk to dawn, from storm to peace, through a complex chiaroscuro of motion and quiet, peace and war, history and idyll, changing from book to book, at least eight of them brought to a close with the piercing sorrow of a haunting death: Creusa, Anchises, Dido, Palinurus, the historical Marcellus, Lausus and Mezzentius, Camilla, and Turnus. The atmosphere of the poem is one of mystery and religious awe; the friendly Hermes of Homer is replaced by a chthonic Hermes, the Homeric monsters yield to Pan, the Fauns, Picus, and Cacus. Fate brings Aeneas to Italy, although the outer and inner journeys, his physical movement and his growing decisiveness and resolution, are never quite plain to him, his destiny never clear as are the destinies of Achilles and Odysseus from the very beginning of their poems. The exile from Troy gradually loosens all family ties but one as his sorrowful love accompanies each of his dear ones in their passing. As Dido and Hades are tests of his courage and enduring purpose to discover the goal of the oracle, they are also the symbols of his love: and he must lose all but a handful of faithful followers before his triumph begins to swell in Italy. To lose all is to gain all, as the summoning, the preparation, and the confirmation of his bravery mark the three divisions of the poem. Reluctant to leave Troy, to leave Dido, to leave Anchises, to kill the Latins, he presses on to the end because there is no other course he can take; while his destination, the route, and the exact will of the gods are all left undetermined.

The journey of life made by a hero amid good and evil is the theme of much great literature and of the best epic. The goal varies: brief glory for Achilles, welcome home and revenge for Odysseus, a new state in the western wilderness for Aeneas, who comes not as the white god Cortes with bloody invasion to the Aztecs and Montezuma, but as a man who seeks to land in peace and takes up war only when forced to do so. The blend of allegory and history which sets the *Aeneid* apart from earlier epic and provides a model for later epic must have been obvious to Vergil as he wrote the story of the first true culture-hero in Western literature. John Heath-Stubbs has recently pointed out the amazing resemblances between the Old Testament story of the Exodus from Egypt and the *Aeneid*.[5] In each tale a leader obedient to a divine command leads his

    [5] "Tasso's Gerusalemme Liberata as Christian Epic," *Nine*, 7 (1951), 138-152.

people, often protesting, to a land which not only has been promised them but was the original home of their forebears. Midway through the journey the leader reaches a point (Sinai, Cumae) where his mission is strengthened and furthered by divine agency (Moses and the Tables of the Law, the Sibyl with her books of oracles).

Self-knowledge through suffering, the full realization of one's own strength and weakness through a deep and tragic emotional experience, is another of the great themes in world literature. It appears in the first great book we have, Homer's *Iliad:* Achilles in his willful pride sends his best friend out to die and then must die himself, not in atonement but because his code allows him no other choice. The scene with Priam, where he accepts the old man's ransom for Hector, does not for all its demonstration of a common humanity between them indicate a real change of heart. Achilles weeps as he recalls his old father and the dead Patroclus, and he pities Priam, but he is still fierce enough to inspire fear in the old man. He has, however, come closer to a knowledge of tragedy.

We find this theme again in the *Agamemnon* of Aeschylus in the key phrase *pathei mathos,* "learning through suffering," surely a formulation which applies to many plays of Aeschylus and Sophocles· Agamemnon, too, has erred and his suffering and death result from the abuse of his responsibilities as a leader; it is keen irony that an adulterous wife should bring him to his doom. In the intellectual drama of Lucretius, *On the Nature of Things,* knowledge itself provides the salvation of man from the superstition and fear created by ignorance; Epicurus does not seem quite as heroic to us as he does to Lucretius. In *Don Quixote,* the tragi-comic hero comes to his senses upon his death-bed after suffering many ridiculous, painful, and humiliating experiences in defense of his ideals and illusions. Goethe's *Faust* shows us a man who has paid for his insatiable lust for experience and knowledge by the ultimate consciousness of sin against man and God; only his altruism, within a medieval framework of behavior, saves him for heaven at the end of Part II. In all of these books it is some form of excess, a grave lack of proportion and balance in the hero's wishes and conduct, which brings him to his sorrow.

It is in Vergil's *Aeneid* that this pattern of learning by suffering is exemplified most fully in ancient epic; and it is probably his comparative freedom from excess which makes a less colorful hero of Aeneas. However, like Faust he brings ruin upon a woman who loved him; like Don Quixote, his chivalry toward his people brings him through many painful and dangerous experiences; like Achilles, he feels, but even more deeply, the common tragedy of mankind upon the battlefield, in the lower world, or in the lonely fastnesses of the Italian forest. Vergil has fashioned his story so that self-realization comes slowly and with difficulty; it is not yet complete even when the soul of Turnus goes moaning into the shadows. The ending of the poem leaves us with the impression that Aeneas has found himself at last but that the full growth of his self-knowledge will be attained only through many more years of struggle and mastery in Italy. His ripeness is yet to come.

What, then, is the meaning of the *Aeneid?* Vergil spoke of his last six books as the "greater work"; evidently the importance of the poem for himself lay in the *Iliad*-half. Servius, on *Aeneid,* VI. 752, wrote that the *Aeneid* told the *gesta populi Romani,* not the story of Aeneas. Vergil was surely right, and Servius may have been right also; both have certainly given the clue which later critics have followed in interpreting the poem. But it is still a poem in which warfare and conquest, the chief activities of the Roman people in their official capacity, are overshadowed by a man, and a man to whom warfare was a hateful business. Only once does Aeneas kill in anger: when he sees the belt of Pallas on Turnus' shoulder in the very last lines of Book XII. That such a hero should be the supreme proponent of Roman patriotism and imperialism, as those who interpret the poem as propaganda imply if they do not actually declare, is to me the most transparent nonsense. Aeneas is made in Vergil's own image; it may well be also, as Hermann Broch conjectured in his magnificent prose poem, *The Death of Virgil*,[6] that Plotia Leria, the woman Donatus (= Suetonius) says was Vergil's mistress, is the model for Dido, clearly the poet's most original contribution to the saga. The brooding pensiveness, the almost languid mysticism, the morbid preoccupation with fate and death and sorrow, are all purely Vergilian, not Roman or imperial. Anchises' famous lines on the mission of Rome ring false and hollow:

> excudent alii spirantia mollius aera—
> credo equidem—vivos ducent de marmore voltus:
> orabunt causas melius, caelique meatus
> describent radio et surgentia sidera dicent:
> tu regere imperio populos Romane memento—
> haec tibi erunt artes—pacique imponere morem,
> parcere subiectis et debellare superbos.
>
> VI. 847-853

We can well believe Vergil as he describes the *Greek* artists who made Rome beautiful, at their work upon reliefs or portrait busts; but that he actually was convinced that any one of another race could give an

---

[6] Translated by Jean Starr Untermeyer (New York: 1945).

oration or plead a law case better than the Romans, with Cicero and Caesar so recently dead, is hard to accept. Astronomy, too, was not a science unknown to the Romans; the poets find their way about in it with great ease if not complete accuracy· That Vergil himself sincerely believed that the sole mission of Rome was to rule peoples, to beat down the proud and to spare the subject, is not borne out by his own passionate interests in philosophy, folklore, history, and agriculture. Cicero had a wider view of Roman civilization than this; Vergil, with a more profound mind than Cicero's, must surely have known that conquests and military control were not enough for Rome.

It is not the warlike ability of Aeneas, although he fights competently enough when pressed, that Vergil chooses to emphasize; indeed, as far as strategy and planning are concerned, Aeneas is a poor soldier. He allows his ships to be set on fire, his men to be surrounded in Latium while he seeks Etruscan allies. His son, without any warning from Aeneas as to how he should conduct himself in a foreign land, kills Silvia's pet deer and fights with the men of Tyrrhus in Book VII, thus making war inevitable just when Latinus has yielded. There is more than one reason why readers do not look upon Aeneas as a proper martial hero.

The fact is evident: Aeneas has been created by a poet to whom the imperial mission of Rome was second in importance to the meaning of existence itself. The clue is given by Vergil:

> Happy is he who has understood natural causes
> And cast underfoot all fear and inexorable fate,
> And the rumble of greedy Acheron. Fortunate he
> Who knows the gods of the country, Pan and Silvanus
> The old man, and the sister-nymphs. The fasces which people
> Give to the magistrates, purple robes of kings,
> Do not awe him; nor discord that stirs faithless brothers to fight;
> Nor the Dacian descending the Danube, in league with its ice;
> Nor the Roman Republic nor kingdoms that soon will perish;
>
> *Georgics,* II. 490-498
> translated by L. R. Lind

Donatus tells us that Vergil decided in his fifty-second year to sail to Greece and Asia, there within three years to make a final revision of the *Aeneid,* and then to devote the rest of his life to philosophy alone. The man who was already a failure as a philosopher at the time he wrote *Catalepton,* V, one of his earliest poems, who wistfully turned to poetry when he discovered he had not the "heat in the heart's blood" (*Georgics,* II. 484) which philosophy demanded—this man was only by an effort of the will a Roman propagandist or imperialist. The splendor of the Empire impressed him, of course; how should it not impress a shy and learned genius who had little acquaintance with political life, a recluse who preferred life in the country to Rome, an abnormally sensitive poet to whom the rattle of arms was intolerable? But hear him again as he plays the philosopher he longed to be:

> He does not pity the poor man nor envy the rich.
> The fruit on the bough, what the fields in their willingness bear,
> He plucks when he wishes, nor gazes on ironclad laws,
> Nor a forum gone mad, nor the archives of public affairs.
> Other men thresh with their oars the black shallows of ocean
> And rush for their weapons, cross palace thresholds of kings;
> This one attacks a city and its wretched gods
> In order to drink from a cup that is studded with gems
> And to sleep upon Tyrian purple; another has hidden
> His wealth and then crouches upon the gold he digs up.
> This man is bewildered by public speakers; that man
> Is carried away, open-mouthed, by the cheers of the plebs
> And patricians sent echoing over the benches again.
> They rejoice in the blood of their brothers which they have spilled
> And exchange their sweet thresholds and homes for exile, to seek
> A fatherland stretching beneath another sun.
>
>   *Georgics*, II. 499-512
>   translated by L. R. Lind

For Vergil the mission of Rome was something more congenial with the description the elder Pliny gave of it than with the proud military conquest of which Vergil wrote in *Aeneid*, VI:

> . . . a land which is at once the nursling and the mother of all other lands, chosen by the providence of the gods to make heaven itself more glorious, to unite scattered empires, to make manners gentle, to draw together in converse by community of language the jarring and uncouth tongues of so many nations, to give mankind civilization, and in a word to become throughout the world the single fatherland of all races.
>
>   Pliny, III, v. 39
>   translated by H. Rackham[7]

Vergil could not look back from a hundred years of the Empire, from the cultured vantage point of the Silver Age; he could only set down

[7] Loeb Classical Library, II (Cambridge, Mass.: Harvard University Press, 1942), pp. 31, 33.

what appeared to be the official program that was needed, now that Augustus had won and victory had to justify itself to a frightened people. *Parcere subiectis et debellare superbos:* a hopeful wish, at least, in which he may have had little confidence at the time; the assurance of a settled and civilized life for other men not so fortunately situated as himself must, with a century of violent revolution and civil war behind him, have seemed remote indeed.

For Vergil as well as for us today the meaning of the *Aeneid* lies not so much in the grandeur of the Roman Empire as in the process by which it was achieved, in the conception of the inner tragedy of human life which is revealed to the hero of the poem rather than in its external events. Aeneas upon a background of war and conquest, the entire sweep of Roman history down to Augustus, is man himself at his best, fighting for a civilized way of life against his own weakness and that of his companions and against the ignorance of his enemies. There is about Aeneas something of the seer who contemplates existence in search of its meaning. At Carthage, before the frieze depicting the Trojan War, he bursts forth with perhaps the most famous and enigmatic line in the *Aeneid: Sunt lacrimae rerum et mentem mortalia tangunt* (I. 462).

We feel that his thoughts well up from the deepest sources of spiritual meditation. The line is for me much more a key to the personality of Aeneas than any other line in the book. One of the finest interpretations, by James Henry,[8] reconciles a generalizing explanation with a specific reference to the immediate situation. Whether or not *rerum* is a predicate, possessive, or objective genitive, the line must mean something of this sort: there are tears (people weep) for (human) affairs (or events), and mortal things (fortunes) touch (stir) the mind (or heart). In spite of the ambiguity such a translation reveals, there is a surprising measure of agreement among English translators as to the essential meaning, which Henry conveyed thus: "Tears are universal (rerum), belong to the constitution of nature, and the evils of mortality (mortalia) move the human heart."[9] The French translator in the Budé edition says more simply: 'Il y a des larmes pour l'infortune et les choses humaines touchent les coeurs."[10] The line is a summing up of Aeneas' tragic sense of life;

[8] *Aeneidea, or Critical, Exegetical, and Aesthetical Remarks on the Aeneid,* with a personal collation of all the first class mss., upwards of one hundred second class mss., and all the principal editions by James Henry (London: 1873).

[9] *Aeneidea,* I, p. 705.

[10] Virgile, *Enéide, Libres I-VI,* texte établi par Henri Goelzer et traduit par André Bellessort, Collection des Universités de France publiée sous le patronage de l'Association Guillaume Budé (Paris: 1925), p. 23.

his adventures and experiences in Italy could only deepen that sense—
which was also Vergil's.

II

The translation of Vergil's *Aeneid* into English and Scots[11] forms
one of the most brilliant chapters in the history of English literature. It
begins with William Caxton's translation ("Eneydos"), printed in 1490,
of a French prose romance based on the *Aeneid*, first published at Lyons
in 1483. Gavin Douglas, bishop of Dunkeld, next translated the *Aeneid*
in 1553 into Scots couplets in a version hugely admired by Ezra Pound
and still a significant document in its effect upon the activity as translators of the new Scots poets who have brought about a minor cultural
renaissance in Scotland. The version of Books II and IV of the *Aeneid*
(1557) by Henry Howard, earl of Surrey, is the vehicle by which blank
verse was introduced to English poetry. Drawing both upon contemporary
Italian translations of Vergil and upon Gavin Douglas' Scots *Aeneid*,
Surrey created a terse and dignified heroic style which was to become a
guide to Spenser and to assist in the formation of a general poetic style
in English. Of Thomas Phaer's *Aeneid* (Books I-VII, 1558; I-IX, 1562,
completed by Twyne in 1573), done in one of the oldest meters in English, the vigorous fourteener, one can now say that it is a valiant attempt
and certainly not the least attractive of versions. Richard Stanyhurst's
translation of Books I-IV (1582-1583) "into English heroical verse"
is a fantastic creation which can scarcely be read today without laughter;
but in spite of its ridiculous colloquialisms, its amazing and picturesque
mixture of bombast and common sense, it was a serious experiment in
quantitative English verse such as was never attempted before or since
at such great length. Here is Dido moving to the temple while Aeneas
gazes at the Trojan frieze in Carthage:

> Whilst prince Aeneas theese picturs woonderus heeded,
> And eeche pane throghly with stedfast phisnomye marcked,
> Too churche Queene Dido, thee pearle of bewtye, repayred:
> Of liuely yoonchers with a galland coompanye garded.
>   I. 494-497

---

[11] The first translation made in the British Isles is the Old Irish "Im-
theachta Aeniasa," made before 1400 and printed in 1907 by David Nutt (London), in the Irish Texts Society Series, 6.

After Stanyhurst, the story of Vergil's translation becomes less color-ful although no less active. Other translators in even greater numbers tackled the job: Sir Richard Fanshawe, John Dryden, Christopher Cranch, Charles Bowen, John Keats (whose schoolboy version in prose is lost), William Morris, John Conington, J. Jackson, James Rhoades, C. J. Billson, J. W. Mackail, Theodore Williams, and others have turned the *Aeneid* into verse or prose of great variety. Fanshawe translated into ornate Spenserian stanzas, quite un-Vergilian in their effect, Dryden into heroic couplets of much sprightliness but also much padding· William Morris used rapid fourteener couplets and Sir Charles Bowen graceful dactylic hexameter couplets.

Of nineteenth-century verse translations, those of the last two trans-lators are probably the most readable now, not too archaic and stilted in language nor too bare and prosy to be endured. Bowen's version bears favorable comparison with another in dactylic hexameters, that of H. H. Ballard (2nd ed., 1911). For the first time in a translation of Vergil, Ballard attempted to make a good case for the English hexameter by using a number of syllables (not, of course, quantitative equivalents of the Latin words) equal to the syllables in each foot of the Latin verse, avoiding all mention of dactyls and spondees. His preface gave careful directions for reading his translation, at one time much read in schools. His analogy with musical notation was misleading, since music still preserves quantity as well as stress, while English verse (including his translation) has lost almost all sense of quantity and relies largely upon stress-accent, however ingeniously one may theorize about long and short English syllables. His lines show a high percentage of three-syllabled feet, perhaps more than Vergil employed; the articles "a" and "the" often serve as the second syllable in a foot of two syllables, producing a rather flat effect, while his first feet in the line are frequently iambs, not trisyllables—again an un-Vergilian practice.

Current translations of the *Aeneid* into verse include those by Rolfe Humphries[12] and C. Day Lewis.[13] Humphries writes a blank verse which is unconventional, easy, colloquial, in a tempo that is rapid and flowing. There are, of course, passages of energetic action in the poem to which such a style lends itself admirably; but it is not adequate to convey the essential dignity and pathos, the tender sadness, of most of the *Aeneid*. This does not mean that Vergil is stuffy. But he does not use words which could properly be understood to mean *what the hell, sort of accidentally on purpose, lay off the threats, bossing the job, telegraphs it, burnt up*

[12] *The Aeneid of Virgil, a verse translation* (New York: 1951).
[13] *The Aeneid of Virgil, translated by C. Day Lewis* (New York: 1952).

(meaning *vexed*), and *stalling*. It is perhaps impossible to maintain the full quality of tone which is peculiarly Vergilian in any translation; but such phrases certainly cannot achieve that tone.

C. Day Lewis uses a hexameter line of an uneven number of syllables ranging from twelve to seventeen but with six usually discernible stresses· This line has been devised in order to avoid the smooth monotony of the conventional hexameter as read in Longfellow's *Evangeline;* but in avoiding singsong regularity, a certain rough confusion of rhythm and an awkwardness of stress arise. The last two feet of the line generally lack the ripple of the more traditional English hexameter based on the dactyl plus trochee or spondee which normally close the Latin hexameter. Thus the flow of the line as felt in the consistently more regular last half of the original line, picking up tempo like a wave about to crash upon the beach, is checked in Day Lewis' version. The remedy for monotony is often clumsiness, although the general effect is not unpleasing. Finally, since his translation was made for broadcasting over the British radio, it can be read aloud more successfully than it can be read silently. In other words, it is a translation for the ear, not the eye, a distinct rarity in an eye-minded age.

The purposes of my translation are modest. I wish to avoid a language which, although modern, is also often un-Vergilian. I do not omit anything of importance or hastily condense details: whatever Vergil thought important enough to set down is not for the translator to delete. The verse form used in this translation varies from a long, loose line packed with words (but with only five beats of blank verse) to a short, spare pentameter that fits the mood and tempo of the particular passage where it is used. Vergil himself has determined when I should shift from one to the other of these varieties of verse; it is a modulation to which blank verse has lent itself increasingly since Milton's time and is the only practical equivalent in English for the classical Latin hexameter, at least as Vergil uses it. It is a fact borne out by much experiment in verse translation that the hexameter is not actually adaptable to English; its rhythm becomes intolerably clumsy and monotonous, even as original English poetry, and, in fact, often looks suspiciously loaded with plain padding. The *Aeneid* is more full of rapid action, continuous and almost unrelieved, with fewer transitional passages of description or reflection, than almost any other epic, despite a strong, specifically Roman, tendency toward rhetoric in the generally short speeches. For translating such a poem an English blank verse which can be shortened or lengthened where necessary in syllable count is the best meter I have found.

No translator of Vergil can escape the frequent problems posed by

repeated words such as *arma* (which I usually translate *ı*
acer, or the difficulty, for example, of fitting the word *reco*
English line as the equivalent of *agnovit*. I have used Walter Janell's
Teubner text[14] as a basis for the translation and have followed the com-
mentaries of Conington[15] and T. E. Page[16] (the latter's handy school text
from which I have borrowed a few phrases). There are certain expres-
sions in the *Aeneid* which, inevitably, can be translated with only one set
of words and in a fixed word order by any translator; I make no apology
for them even when they sound a trifle flat. With Vergil as with Homer,
what was once known as "elegance" of language is not an appropriate
term. His language is almost always simple, hard, brief, and suited to his
undeviating purpose: the account of the struggles which Aeneas had to
undertake in order to found Rome· In fact, one of the reasons why readers
still like the poem is its breathless speed, catching one up in that whirlwind Vergil uses so often as a simile.

I wish to thank Smith Palmer Bovie, general editor of the Indiana
University Greek and Latin Classics, for his very helpful suggestions
toward removing some infelicities from the translation. With his own
exquisite taste in these matters, as demonstrated by his verse translations
of Vergil's *Georgics*[17] and the *Satires* and *Epistles* of Horace,[18] he has
saved me from some awkward phrases. I am also grateful to Mr. Robert
Fitzgerald for a few remarks on my introduction. Professor George E.
Duckworth's article, "Recent Work on Vergil, 1940-1956,"[19] has been
invaluable in helping me bring both the short bibliography and the notes
up to date with the imposing mass of excellent recent scholarship on
Vergil.

I wish to emphasize that the notes to this translation—the first, so
far as I know, that have been provided by any translator since the Bohn
Library Series in the Victorian age—are intended for the Latinless

[14] *P. Vergili Maronis Opera post Ribbeckium tertium recognovit Gualterius
Ianell,* editio maior iterum recognita (Leipzig: B. G. Teubner, 1930).

[15] *P. Vergili Maronis Opera. The Works of Virgil with a Commentary by
John Conington,* in George Long, ed., Biblioteca Classica, 4th ed., Vol. II (London: 1884); 3rd ed., Vol. III (London: 1883).

[16] *The Aeneid of Virgil, edited with introduction and notes,* 2 vols. (London: 1894); reprinted (New York: St. Martin's Press, 1960).

[17] *Virgil, The Georgics, a new translation* (Chicago, Ill.: University of
Chicago Press, 1956).

[18] *Satires and Epistles of Horace, a new translation* (Chicago, Ill.: University of Chicago Press, 1959).

[19] *The Classical World,* 51 (1957-58).

reader, not for the Latin scholar, in order to clear the way toward understanding among those who are experts neither in Latin nor in Vergil. A short account of the life and works of Vergil precedes the brief bibliography and the notes. A map of Aeneas' wanderings and a glossary of names complete the book.

L. R. LIND

Department of Classics and Classical Archaeology
The University of Kansas
Lawrence, Kansas
December, 1961

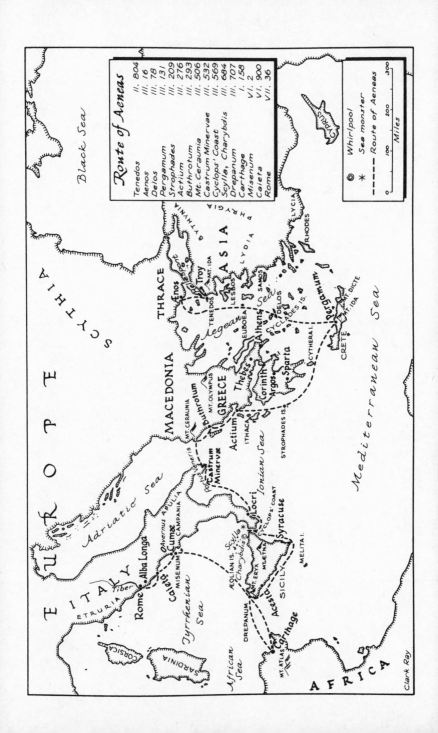

VERGIL'S *AENEID*

Line references in parentheses, in the running heads and throughout the book; refer to the Latin text in the B. G. Teubner edition.

BOOK ONE

The Storm and Carthage

I sing of arms and the man who first from Troy's shores,
Fate's fugitive, came to Italy and Lavinium's
Coast, a man much tossed on land and sea
By the gods' force, through Juno's mindful fury;
He suffered greatly in war until he could found
A city and bring his gods to Latium, whence
The Latins would spring, the Alban fathers, and Rome
With its lofty walls.
           Muse, tell me the reasons why
A wounded power divine, a queen of the gods
In anger compelled him to go through so many dangers,   10
A man outstanding for loyalty, and to struggle
So long? Can celestial spirits harbor such wrath?
     There was an ancient city—some Tyrian settlers
Held it—named Carthage, far away from the Tiber's
Mouth, and from Italy, rich in resources, most fierce
In war, which Juno is said to have favored above
All cities, above even Samos. Here she planned
A center for all the nations, if fate should allow.
She had set her heart for a long time now on this.
But she had heard that a race of Trojan blood   20
Would one day overturn those Tyrian towers;
From this race would rise a folk to rule proudly in war
And widely, and to destroy Libya: so spoke the Fates.
Thus Juno, afraid, remembering the ancient war,
The first that she fought at Troy for her precious Greeks
—Not yet had the cause of her anger, her keen chagrin
Fallen away from her heart; there remained in her soul,
Deep-set, the judgment of Paris, the insult he gave
Her beauty scorned, that hateful race, the honors

Of Ganymede kidnapped. Enraged, she had driven the Trojans   30
Left alive by the Greeks, and the cruel Achilles, across
The entire ocean, had driven them far from the coast
Of Latium. They had wandered for many years,
Pursued by the Fates across every sea. So great
Was the task to found the race and the city of Rome.

     With Sicily scarcely lost sight of, upon the deep
They gave sails to the wind and gaily thrust the bronze prow
Through the salt foam. Then Juno, nursing her endless
Hurt in her breast, gave voice to these words, to herself:
"Am I to be conquered, to give up my plans in defeat,   40
Nor keep off the Trojan king from Italy?
I suppose it's the Fates that forbid. Could Athena burn up
The fleet of the Argives and drown them deep in the sea
Because of the madness and crime of Ajax alone?
She hurled Jove's rapid fire out of the clouds,
Scattered their ships and upturned the ocean with winds,
And transfixed him half-dead with flames that pierced through his chest,
Snatched him up in a whirlwind and stuck him upon a sharp cliff.
Look! I, who walk as a queen of the gods, who am sister
And wife to Jove, wage war for so many years   50
With one people alone. And who is it worships my power
Any longer? What suppliant honors my altar with gifts?"
     Inflamed, and turning such thoughts about in her mind,
She came to the country of clouds, distended with furious
Winds, to Aeolia. Here in a measureless cave
King Aeolus governs the struggling winds, the loud storms,
With his will and controls them in chains and a prison house.
Angry, they loudly protest against their confinement,
The hill that lies over them. He sits on a high citadel,
Holding his scepter; he soothes them and tempers their wrath.   60
If he did not, they'd carry the seas and the lands and the sky
Away with them all and sweep them through upper air.
But the Almighty Father has hidden them in a dark cave
(Afraid of revolt) and heaped the high hills over them
And given a king who knows how to loosen the reins
Or pull them back tight, in unerring agreement with Jove.
Then Juno addressed him in words that a beggar might use:
     "Aeolus, the father of gods and of men has given
You power to calm the waters and raise up the waves.

The Tyrrhenian race which I hate sails over the sea,   70
Bringing Troy and its conquered gods into Italy.
Drive hard with your winds and sink their ships in the waves,
Or scatter them wide, hurl their bodies into the deep.
I have seven nymphs, every one of them beautiful. You
Shall have the most beautiful, Deiopea her name.
I shall join you in stable marriage and call her your own
To live with forever, a wife whom you richly deserve.
She will make you the father of beautiful children."
                                                    But he
Spoke in turn: "It is yours to demand what favor you wish;
O queen, it is mine to obey your orders, for you   80
Have won for me whatever power I hold from Jove.
You gave me the chance to sit down at banquet with gods
And made me the ruler of clouds and of tempests."
                                                    This said,
He struck the butt-end of his trident against the hillside.

The winds, as though they had formed a long battle-line,
Where exit was given, rush forth and whirl over the lands.
They settle upon the sea and from its far depths
The South Wind, the East Wind stir all of it up. The South West,
Abounding in squalls, rolls vast breakers up onto the beach.
There follow the shouting of men and the creaking of ropes.   90
Sudden clouds snatch the sky and the daylight from Trojan eyes.
Black night broods over the sea, the poles thunder out,
The firmament glitters with lightning, bolt upon bolt,
And everything threatens the sailors with instant death.
Straight off, Aeneas' legs are shaken with chills;
He groans and stretches both hands up toward the stars
And speaks: "O you who were three and four times blessed,
Who were lucky to fall at Troy beneath the high walls
Where your parents could see you! And you, Diomedes, the bravest
Of Greeks, why couldn't that right hand of yours have taken   100
My life, so that I could have died upon Ilium's field,
Where fierce Hector lies beneath the sword of Achilles,
Where huge Sarpedon was slain, where so many shields
Of men, and their helmets, and their brave bodies were rolled
In the waters of Simois river, gone under its waves?"
Even as he spoke the shrieking North Wind shattered
The sail with its storm, raised up the waves to the stars.

The oars were broken, the prow swung round and yawed
Broadside to the billows. A steep-climbing mountain of water
Follows. The sailors hang on the crest of a wave.   110
The crest gapes open and shows them the land at the bottom
Where whirlpools rage in the sand. Three ships the South
Wind twisted out of their course on to hidden rocks,
Those rocks the Italians call the Altars; they lie
In the midst of the surge, cruel ridge rising out of the sea.
Three ships the East Wind drove from the open sea
Into the shoals and shallows, frightful to look at,
And dragged them across the bottom and choked them with sand.
One ship that carried the Lycians and faithful Orontes,
Before Aeneas' eyes, a towering column   120
Struck on the stern; the captain, hurled from the deck,
Fell head over heels: look, the water three times whirled
The ship around in that spot and swallowed her up.
Only a few men show in the swirling surf,
Swimming. Their weapons, the timbers, and all their Trojan
Treasure are lost in the waves.
                          Now the sturdy ship
Of Ilioneus, brave Achates', and the one
That carried Abas and aged Aletes, the storm
Overcomes: all the seams in their sides are broken apart,
The enemy water breaks in and the cracks yawn open.   130
Meanwhile Neptune had discovered the storm let loose,
The sea set roaring loudly in wild confusion
And up from the bottom the stagnant refuse flung
By the violent waters, and thrusting out his head
He looked around calmly across the tops of the waves.

On the wide waters he saw Aeneas' fleet
Scattered, the Trojans beset by the heavens' downfall
And by the swells. The anger and trickery
Of Juno were not concealed from him, her brother.
He calls the Southeast Wind to him and the West,   140
And says: "Do you trust so much in your family line
That you dare without my permission to mingle the sky
With the earth, you winds, and raise such mountains of water?
Whom I—but it's better to set the wild waves at rest.
You will pay later on for your deeds in a different way.

Take to your heels and tell this to your king:
The rule of the sea and the savage trident was given
Not to him but to me by lot. He holds the cruel rocks,
Your home, Southeast Wind; let Aeolus play the proud king
In that wide palace, and rule the closed prison of winds."   150

So he spoke, and swifter than speech he soothed swollen waves,
Put to flight gathered clouds and brought back the sun again.
Cymothoe, Triton lend shoulders to pry off the ships
From a sharp ledge. And Neptune himself lifts them up
With his trident, lays bare wide shoals, and tempers the sea:
Then rolls on swift chariot wheels through the crest of the waves.
As often when civil dissension has stirred a great crowd
And the ignoble herd grows ugly, its spirit roiled up,
And now stones and torches go flying, while rage supplies arms,
If by chance they lay eyes on a man of solid repute   160
And prestige, they fall silent and stand with their ears pricked up
Like dogs: he governs their anger and softens their wrath
With his words—so all the sea's tumult is laid to rest,
And Neptune, borne over the water beneath open sky,
Guides his horses, flies on, flicks the reins in his hurrying car.

     The weary Trojans hasten to seek the nearest
Shore in their course and turn to the Libyan coast,
To a secluded cove, where an island offers a port
With flanks on which every wave from the deep is shattered
And into whose depths the waters are drawn and cloven.   170
On this side and that two huge cliffs threaten the sky
With towering peaks; the sea lies quiet beneath.
A back-drop of shining trees hangs over the view
Where dark-green woods lean forth with their shaggy shade.
On the brow of the pendent cliffs a cave can be seen,
Sweet water within it and seats cut from living rock,
The home of the nymphs. Here no hawser need hold the battered
Ships or the tooth of an anchor bind them at rest.
Aeneas comes here with seven ships of the fleet.
The Trojans, eager for land, disembark on the sand   180
And lay themselves dripping with salt along the shore.
Achates first struck a spark of fire from flint
And caught the flame in a cradle of leaves and laid

Dry tinder around to feed it. The sailors break out
Grain wet with water, utensils for milling. Dog-tired,
They prepare to roast it and grind it up in the mill.

Aeneas meanwhile had climbed a nearby cliff
And gazed out widely across the entire sea
To look for Antheus, tossed by the wind, and the Phrygian
Biremes, or Capys, or Caicus' shield high on the stern.   *190*
No ship lay in sight, but three stags he saw as they wandered
On shore, a whole herd behind them, a single long line
Of deer strung out that went feeding through the valley.
He halted there, took up his bow and swift arrows,
The weapons that faithful Achates carried for him.
He shot first the leaders who lifted their antlers high
On their heads like tree-branches. Next, he scattered the herd
And drove them pell-mell to the leafy woods with his missiles,
Nor did he leave off until he had dropped to the ground
Seven great bodies and equalled dead stags with his ships.   *200*
Then he goes to the harbor; the stags are divided for all.
Next, the wine which good Acestes, that hero, had loaded in casks
And given the Trojans departing from Sicily's shore,
Aeneas divides, and he soothes their sorrowing hearts:
"O comrades (for we have known evils like this before),
You have suffered worse things: god will give an end even to these.
You braved Scylla's wrath and the cliffs loud-sounding within;
You have seen the rocks of the Cyclops; call back your courage
And banish sad fear: perhaps you will one day be glad
To remember these dangers. Through changes and chance,   *210*
          through many
Perilous choices we sail on to Italy, where
The Fates show us peaceful homes; there the kingdom of Troy
Shall arise once more (it is right that it should).
                                        Be hard
And preserve yourselves for the good times that are to come."
        So he spoke, grown sick with enormous cares. In his face
He simulates hope, but thrusts sorrow deep back in his heart.

They ready themselves for the prey and for future meals,
Strip backs from ribs and lay the stags' entrails bare.
Some cut up the pieces and stick them on trembling spits,
Others set up kettles on shore and bring wood to the flames.   *220*

With food they call back their strength and, stretched on the grass,
They fill themselves full of old wine and fat venison too.
When, hunger appeased with this banquet, they cleaned up their plates,
They sought for lost comrades by way of long talk about them,
Between hope and fear, unready to think them alive
Or dead, either one, and no more to hear when they're called.
Faithful Aeneas especially laments the cruel fate
Now of keen Orontes, Amycus now, and the fate
Of Lycus, of Gyas the brave, and Cloanthus as well.

Now came the end, when Jupiter from the air's summit   230
Looked down on the sail-flying sea and the lands beneath,
And the shores and peoples spread widely; at heaven's peak
He stopped and gazed hard at Libya's royal domain.
And while he pondered his cares again in his mind,
Venus so sad, her bright eyes welling over with tears,
Spoke up: "O ruler of life for men and for gods,
In eternal command, who have cowed us with lightning bolts,
What could my Aeneas commit against you, what deed
Have the Trojans done, that the whole world is closed to them
Who have suffered so much, because they seek Italy?   240
You promised that as years rolled by the Romans should come,
As leaders of men from the line of Teucer; you promised
They should hold the lands and the sea in an absolute sway—
What opinion has changed you, father? At least I had found
Consolation for Troy's destruction, her grisly ruins,
By thinking good fortune could balance her sorrowful fate.
But now that same *misfortune* follows men harried by crises.
What end, great king, shall you put to their sorrows? Antenor
Could slip through the midst of the Greeks, through Illyrian gulfs,
Through Liburnian realms, and win to the source of the Po,   250
Where through its nine mouths with a huge uproar that great river
Runs headlong down from the hills to flood the broad plain.
Here nevertheless he founded the city of Padua,
The home of the Teucrians, gave a name to the people, hung up
The weapons of Troy; here, his ashes at rest, he lies buried.
But we, your children, who you have agreed shall win heaven,
With our fleet destroyed—O hard to speak!—are betrayed
By the anger of *one*, thrust afar from Italian shores.
This the reward of our loyalty, thus you give power!"

    Looking gently at her, the creator of gods and of men,   260

With the smile on his face that quiets the storms of heaven,
Kissed his daughter and spoke to her: "Do not fear, Cytherea;
The fate of your people remains unchanged. You will see
The city and promised walls of Lavinium rise.
You will bear great-hearted Aeneas aloft to the stars
Of heaven; and no opinion has changed my mind.
I shall speak, since this worry continues to bite at your heart,
I shall bring out the secrets of fate to the light of day.

He shall fight a great war in Italy, fierce peoples he'll crush;
He shall settle his men and walls, establish his customs,   270
Until a third summer shall see him ruling in Latium,
And a third winter pass, with Rutulians conquered at last.
But the boy Ascanius, who bears also the name of Iulus
—For he was Ilus while Troy's kingdom still stood—
Shall fulfill the rule of Aeneas in thirty long years.
He shall move from Lavinium, rule in Alba Longa,
Strong in its power. Here for three hundred years
Shall rule Hector's race until the priestess and queen,
Ilia, pregnant by Mars, shall give birth to twins.
Then Romulus, gay in the tawny skin of his nurse,   280
The she-wolf, will take over power, found Martian walls,
And shall call the Romans by his very own name.
For these I shall set no limits of time or possessions;
I have given them endless power. Implacable Juno,
Who wearies the sea and the lands and the sky with dread,
Shall change her plans for the better and nourish with me
The Romans, those lords of earth, the race of the toga.
Such is my will. There shall come with the gliding years
A time when the house of Assaracus shall enslave Phthia
And famous Mycenae, and rule over conquered Greeks.   290
A Trojan Caesar shall spring from a noble source
To bound his rule with Ocean, his fame with the stars,
Iulius, a name descended from great Iulus.
One day in your peace you shall welcome him into heaven,
Loaded with Orient spoils; vows shall be made to him.
Then the bitter years shall grow mellow, war's fury laid by;
Hoary Faith and Vesta, Quirinus with his brother Remus,
Shall establish laws. The gates of fierce War shall be closed,
Chained tightly with iron. And godless Furor shall sit

Inside on his frightful weapons, hands bound with a hundred   300
Brass knots behind him, and roar with his bloody mouth."
        Jove speaks, and sends Maia's son Mercury down from above,
That the new land of Carthage shall open its citadel wide
To welcome the Trojans, so Dido who knows not their fate
Shall not bar them her borders. He flies through the limitless air
On swift oarage of wings and descends on the shores of Libya.
He does what he's bid, the Phoenicians cease to be warlike
(For it is god's will), and first of them all their queen
Receives with benevolent spirit and kindly mind
The Trojans.
            But loyal Aeneas, careworn through the night,   310
When the first light of nourishing dawn is given, decided
To go out and explore the new land, the shores he has reached,
Find out whether men or wild beasts hold the wastes which he sees,
Then bring back the news to his comrades.
                        He left the fleet hidden
In the curve of the grove beneath the hollow cliff
Cut off by its trees and the hair-raising shadows around.
Achates alone went with him, a spear in each hand,
Whose broad steel he brandished. Aeneas' mother appeared
In the midst of a wood, her face like a virgin's, and wearing
Girl's dress and equipment of Sparta, or like those which Thracian   320
Harpalyce has when she outruns horses or Hebrus,
The river himself, so swift in his flight.
                        From her shoulder
There hung in her fashion a huntress' bow. She had loosened
Her hair to the winds. Her knees were bare and her flowing
Tunic was caught in a knot. She was first to speak:
        "Hold there, young men. Have you seen by chance any sister
Of mine wandering here, her quiver bound on her, and covered
With a spotted lynx hide, or loudly shouting and tracking
A wild boar's spoor?" Venus spoke. Her son replied:
"None of your sisters have I heard or seen,   330
O—how shall I call you, maiden? For in your face
And in your voice I find no trace of mortals—
A goddess surely: Apollo's sister? a nymph?
Be gentle with us, lighten our labors for us,
And tell us where we are, beneath what sky
We wander, knowing neither the men nor the region,

— (millinium - golden age myth)

Driven along by winds and giant waves.
Many a victim shall we slay at your altar."
　　　Venus said: "I am not worthy of such an honor.
The Tyrian girls are used to wear a quiver,　　　　　　　340
To bind their legs high up in purple boots.
You see the realm of Carthage; these are Tyrians;
The city is of Agenor; but on the borders
Lie Libyans, people unsubdued in war.
Dido holds power here; she came from Tyre,
Fleeing her brother. Her tale is one of injustice,
Full of details: I'll tell you the most important.
Her husband was Sychaeus, rich in Phoenician
Land; poor woman, she loved him desperately.
Her father gave her to him as a virgin,　　　　　　　350
Joined her with best of omens. But her brother
Pygmalion held the power at Tyre, a rascal
More cruel in sin than any man. A madness
There came between them. Pygmalion killed Sychaeus
Impiously before the altar, blinded
By love of gold, caught him offguard and stabbed him,
Without regard for his sister's love. He hid
The deed a great while, fooled her by devising
Many an empty hope, poor heart-sick lover.
But in her dreams the vision of his spirit　　　　　　　360
Unburied came to the wife, and lifted up
Its pallid face in marvelous manner, showed
The cruel altar, the breast pierced by a sword,
Revealed to the house the dark and wicked deed.
He urged her to take flight, to leave her country,
Laid bare for her an ancient treasure buried
In earth as aid for travel, a forgotten
Hoard of gold and silver. Thus alarmed,
Dido and her companions prepared for flight.
They met, these men who hated the cruel tyrant　　　　　　370
And those who keenly feared him. Ships which happened
To be at hand they seize on, load with treasure.
Greedy Pygmalion's wealth is borne to sea.
A woman was the leader of the deed.
They came to a place where now you see the giant
Walls of new Carthage and its rising fortress.
They bought the land, called Byrsa from their action:

As much as they could cover with one bull's hide.
But who are you? Where do you come from? Where
Do you travel?" Aeneas answered thus her questions,   380
Drawing his voice with sighs from his inmost breast:
"O goddess, if I should tell you all my story
From its beginnings, and you had time to listen
To this long list of troubles, the Evening Star
Would close Olympus' gates and end the day
Before I finished. We came from ancient Troy,
If ever that name has reached your ears, through many
Seas we were borne. A tempest chanced to drive us
On Libyan beaches. I am loyal Aeneas,
Who bear my ravished household gods with me   390
Away from the enemy, on my ships. In heaven
Above they know me. I seek my fatherland
In Italy and a race sprung from great Jove.
With twice ten ships I sailed the Phrygian sea;
My mother, a goddess, was pilot; I followed my fate.
Now scarcely seven survive from the waves and East Wind.
Hungry, unknown, I wander the deserts of Libya,
Driven from Europe and Asia."
                                  Venus allowed
Him to grieve no more, but thus burst into his sorrow:
"Whoever you are, I do not believe you are hated   400
By heavenly powers, as you draw the breath of life;
You who have come to the Tyrian City, go on
To the queen's own doorway. For I report that your comrades
Are safe, your fleet is restored, the winds are reversed.
(Unless my parents have taught me vain prophecies.)
Look at those twelve swans flying gaily in line!
Jove's eagle was chasing them over the reaches of heaven,
In open sky. Now they seem to alight on the ground,
In a row, or to look down on those who have already landed.
As they have come home, to play with their whirring wings   410
And to cluster in heaven and sing out their songs again,
So shall they return, your ships, and your sailors too:
They're in port, or are sailing there under an unfurled canvas.
Go now, and follow the way where your footsteps fall."
        She spoke, and turning to go, the pink flesh of her neck
Shone forth; her ambrosial hair breathed out odor divine.
Her gown flowed down to her feet; and her very walk

Revealed a true goddess. When he saw that she was his mother,
He followed her, moving away, with words such as these:
"Why do you cheat your son so many times,   420
Cruel one, with visions false? Why may we not
Join hand to hand, speak and hear truthful words?"
He grumbled thus, and turned toward the city walls.
But as he walked, Venus fenced him in with mist
And poured a garment of heavy clouds around him
Lest he be seen, lest anyone should reach him,
Or cause him to delay, ask why he came.
She flew aloft to Paphos, glad to revisit
Her favorite resting place, where stood her temple,
A hundred altars warm with Arabian incense   430
And breathing fragrance from garlands of freshest flowers.
        They took their way meanwhile where lay the path.
Soon they climbed the hill that loomed large above,
Just opposite and facing the citadel.
Aeneas looked in wonder at masses of buildings
Where once were huts, he looked at gates and confusion,
At streets; the ardent Tyrians toiled on.
They chose laws, magistrates, a sacred senate.
Some worked at walls and fortress; with their hands
They rolled up stones. Some chose a dwelling site   440
And marked its outline with a plow-drawn furrow.
Here they dredged the port, on that side laid
Foundations for a theater, hewed from the cliffs
Vast columns, soaring beauty for stages to come.
Just as the bees in summer among the fields,
When flowers are new, work hard beneath the sun,
Bringing their young ones out and packing their honey
With its sweet nectar in cells, or grasping their load
From bees arriving, or forming a battle line
To drive off the lazy flock of drones from the hive,   450
Activity boils, and the honey is fragrant with thyme.

"O fortunate ones, whose walls are rising now,"
Says Aeneas, and gazes down at the topmost towers.
He passes among them, wrapped in a cloud—a wonder
To tell. He mingles with them, is discerned by none.
        A grove in the midst of the city, most grateful in shade:

Here first the Phoenicians, tossed by the waves and wind,
Had dug up the magic object which Juno the queen
Had showed them, the head of a spirited horse.

                                         For thus
Would their race be skillful in war and strong to endure,   460
To live through the centuries.
                        Here Sidonian Dido
Had founded a monstrous temple to Juno, a shrine
Rich with its gifts and the goddess' power. Its steps
Rose shining with brass, its beams and threshold firm
With brass, and the wings of its door swung screeching on brass.
Here, first, the sights he saw in the grove soothed his fear;
Here, first, Aeneas dared hope for the safety he sought,
And to trust that the perilous present might better itself.
For while he awaited the queen beneath the great temple,
He looked at its different details; and while he still wondered   470
At the city's good fortune, the skill and the work of its hands,
He found on the frieze the events of the Trojan War
Set out all in order, its battles known over the world,
The Atreidae and Priam, Achilles so savage to both.
He stood and wept. "What place, O Achates," he said,
"What region of earth is not full of our grief?
                             Look at Priam!
Even here are the precious remains of his pitiful praise.
Life's events bring tears, mortal fortunes trouble the heart.
Do not fear. This fame will bring some salvation to you."
So he spoke, and pastured his spirit on empty pictures,   480
Groaned aloud, till his face was bathed all over with tears.
For he saw how both armies were fighting around Troy's wall.
Here fled the Greeks, there pressed on the Trojan youth.
Here crested Achilles, chariot-borne, chased the Phrygians.
Not far away he could see through his tears the white tents
Of Rhesus, which Tydeus' son in the first dream of sleep
Had betrayed and destroyed with cruel and bloody slaughter,
And driven the spirited horses away to his camp
Before they could drink from Xanthus, taste the pastures of Troy.
On one side fled Troilus, his weapons cast aside,   490
That unhappy boy no match for Achilles in fight.
He was dragged by his horses, face upward upon the ground,
Still gripping the reins of his empty car. His neck

And long hair trailed on the soil. His spear reversed
Wrote something in dust.
                    Meanwhile to the temple of Pallas
Unjust, the Trojan women, their hair in disorder,
Were bearing her peplos. In sadness they beat on their breasts.
The goddess, eyes fixed on the ground, turned her face away.
Three times around Troy's walls Achilles had dragged
The lifeless body of Hector, then sold it for gold.   500
Aeneas groaned loudly from deep within his chest
As he saw spoils and chariot, saw the corpse of his friend,
And Priam who stretched out his helpless hands at the sight.
Aeneas himself he saw among Argive chiefs,
The battle array of the East and black Memnon's arms.
Penthesilea raged in the midst of the men as she led
Her Amazon ranks, recognized by their crescent shields,
A golden brassière holding up her projecting breasts:
Warlike woman, a virgin, she dared to join combat with men.
    While these marvels appeared to the eyes of Dardanian Aeneas,   510
While astonished he stood with his gaze on this single view,
Most beautiful Dido the queen advanced to the temple,
Flanked by a vast crowd of Carthaginian youths.
Just as on the banks of Eurotas or ridges of Cynthus
Diana deploys her chorus, whom Oreads follow,
A thousand on this side and that, as she carries her quiver
On shoulder, and walks, a goddess distinct among all:
Joy seizes the silent heart of Latona, her mother—
Such was Dido; as such she bore herself gladly among
Them, urging the labor they gave for a kingdom to come.   520
At the gates of the goddess, the inner shell of the temple,
Fenced with soldiers, she sat on a throne set fast in the ground.
She gave laws and decrees and assigned to her subjects each task,
Dividing each justly or casting a lot to decide.
Then Aeneas suddenly saw them approach through the crowd,
Antheus, Sergestus, and brave Cloanthus himself,
And other Trojans whom the black storm had scattered
And driven apart to other shores. He was stunned,
Both Achates and he, with joy and with fear at once.
They yearned in wild eagerness to clasp their right hands,   530
But uncertainty troubled them.
                    Clothed in a hollow cloud,
They shrank back and hid, they watched to find out how they fared,

On what shore they had left their fleet and why they had come.
Picked men from every boat went forward to beg
Dido's mercy; they made for the temple and set up a shout.
When, inside, permission to speak was given to them,
Ilioneus the eldest began, with a tranquil heart:
"O queen, to whom Jupiter gave the power to build
A new city, to curb proud peoples, in justice to rule,
We miserable Trojans, borne over all seas by the winds,   540
Pray to you: spare our ships from unspeakable fire,
Be kind to our steadfast race, take us under your wing.
We did not come here to kill Libyan families
Or to carry away to the shore any plunder we steal:
No such arrogant force swells the spirits of those who are beaten.
There's a place which the Greeks call Western Land by name,
An ancient land, strong in arms and in fertile soil.
The Oenotrians tilled it; now later ages report
It is called Italia, from a folk-leader's name.
Here lay our course,   550
When suddenly cloudy Orion rose up with his waves,
Drove us on to blind reefs, overwhelmed us with raging storms,
And scattered us, salt sea our master, on hidden rocks.
A few of us swam to this region upon your shores.
What kind of men, what barbarous customs are these,
Allowed in your country? They drove us away from your beach.
They shook weapons at us and forbade us to set foot on land.
If in scorn you look down on us humans and our mortal strength,
Remember: the gods overlook neither right nor wrong.
Our king was Aeneas; no one was more just than he,   560
Greater in loyalty or greater in war and in arms.
If the Fates still preserve him, if still he subsists upon air
In this life, nor lies hidden among the cruel shadows of death,
We shall have no fear; nor should you regret to take lead
In a courteous rivalry. We are not friendless. We too
Have cities in Sicily, lands, great Acestes the Trojan.
Permit us to haul up our ships which the winds have damaged,
To hew out new beams from your trees and to strip new oars,
And if on to Italy we may sail, our king
And comrades saved, to Latium and Italy   570
We shall gladly go; but if our safety is lost,
And you, great Teucrian father, Africa's water
Has swallowed, and there is no hope left in Iulus,

At least we have Sicily's straits and its settlements:
Then let us seek Acestes, from whom we came."
This Ilioneus; all the Trojan men roared out
Approval with one loud cry.
     Next briefly Dido with downward look replied:
"Do not be fearful, Trojans, do not be anxious.
My difficult position and new power   580
Have made me do such things to guard my boundary.
Who does not know Aeneas' folk or Troy,
Their warlike courage, the havoc of that war?
Phoenicians do not have such stupid minds,
Nor does the Sun yoke horse so far from Tyre.
Whether you sail to Western Land and Saturn's
Fields or the land of Eryx and King Acestes,
I'll send you on with help and escort, safely.
But if you wish to share my power with me,
This city is yours; draw up your ships on shore.   590
Trojan or Tyrian, I shall play no favorites.
I wish your king, Aeneas himself, were here,
Driven up by the same South Wind that drove you here.
I shall send men to the shore to look for him
In Libya's farthest corner, if anywhere
He wanders cast up in any woods or town."
     Their courage pricked up at these words, both brave Achates
And Father Aeneas had long been eager to burst
Out of their cloud. First Achates questioned Aeneas:
"Goddess-born, what plan now rises in your mind?   600
You see all is safe, the fleet and our friends restored.
One ship is gone; we saw it sink ourselves
In the waves; all else agrees with your mother's words."
He had scarcely spoken when swiftly the cloud around him
Divided and purged itself into thin air.
Aeneas stood there and shone in the light of day,
Like a god in face and shoulders; his mother herself
Breathed beauty upon his hair, and the glow of youth,
Bright charm upon his eyes, as an artist's hand
Gives glory to ivory, or when a marble gem   610
Or silver is chased with bands of yellow gold.
He spoke to the queen and, to the surprise of all,
He said: "I am here, that Aeneas whom you seek,
The Trojan, saved from the waves of Africa.

O you who alone have pitied Troy's miserable men,
Survivors from Greeks, from hardships on land and sea,
Poor and exhausted, you offer us city and home.
But we cannot repay you with thanks that can match your aid,
Whoever of us still are scattered throughout the world.
May the gods, if ever their power respects the loyal,   620
If ever their hearts are just and their minds know right,
Give you worthy reward. What happy times have brought,
What parents gave birth to a woman like you?
                                        While rivers
Flow into the gulfs of the sea, while the shadows pass
On the hills, while the Pole feeds the stars of the hollow sky,
So long, and forever, your name and your praise shall last,
Whatever the land that calls me." So he spoke
And went forward to Ilioneus and to Serestus
On right and left, and then brave Gyas, Cloanthus.
    At first Sidonian Dido stood speechless to see   630
A man of such great experience. Then she spoke out:
"What evil fortune pursues you, O goddess-born,
Through so many dangers, what force drives you to cruel shores?
Are you not that Aeneas whom nourishing Venus bore
To Anchises the Dardan, by Phrygian Simois' wave?
But I remember that Teucer came once to Sidon,
An exile from home and seeking new lands to rule
With Belus', my father's, aid. My father was then
Campaigning in Cyprus and gaining a victory there.
From that time to this the tale of your city was known   640
To me, and your name and the names of the Grecian kings.
Though Teucer was hostile, he praised the Trojans and claimed
Descent from the ancient stock of Trojans.
                                    So come
To our houses and homes, young heroes, come in, come in.
I too have been battered by similar hardships; at last
My fortune has wished me to settle upon this land.
No stranger to sorrow, I learn to rescue fate's victims."
So she spoke, and at once led Aeneas beneath her roof,
And at once gave orders to honor the gods in their shrines.
Nor did she forget to send to his comrades on shore   650
Twenty bulls, huge backs of a hundred pigs stiff with hair,
And a hundred lambs as fat as their nursing mothers.
Thus gifts and joy for the day.

The palace within shone with regal luxury,
And servants prepared a banquet in the great hall.
Embroidered coverlets lay on the couches, dyed
Royal purple, all fashioned with skill, and the silver plates
Were embossed in gold that pictured brave deeds of the fathers,
A long, long line of exploits by so many men
Traced out from its origins down through the life of the race.   660
        Aeneas (his fatherly love would not let his heart rest)
Sent Achates the swift-footed on ahead to the ships
To bring word to Ascanius and lead him back to the walls.
All the care of his father resides in Ascanius dear.
He bids him to bring with the boy all the treasure they saved
From Troy's ruins, a long cloak stiff with emblems of gold,
And a veil woven round with yellow acanthus leaves,
The adornments of Argive Helen, which she brought from Greece
When she left for Troy and a marriage forbidden by law,
The wonderful gifts of her mother Leda, and more: 670
The staff that Ilione had carried once,
The eldest of Priam's daughters, a necklace of pearls
Like berries, a crown set with bands of jewels and gold.
In haste to obey, Achates went down to the ships.
        But Venus turned over new plots, new plans in her heart:
How, changed in both face and form, her son Cupid should come
In place of Ascanius sweet, should drive the queen mad
With love and with gifts, weave fire within her bones:
For she feared a treacherous house and the lying Tyrians.
Fierce Juno galled Venus, as night after night came round.   680
So she spoke in words such as these to the winged Love:
"Child, my strength, my great resource, O child, you alone
May scorn the Typhoean thunderbolts of the Sky Father;
In you I take refuge, I beg for your powerful aid.
How your brother Aeneas is buffeted over all shores
Through the hatred of Juno unjust—this is known to you.
And often you too have grieved when you saw my sorrow.
Phoenician Dido holds him, delays him with soft
Entreaties. I fear what Junonian comforts may bring,
For she will not stop now her schemes have reached such a point.   690
So I plan to outstrip her in guile, ring the queen with flame
Which no power can change: she shall fall in love with Aeneas.
Now listen to me while I tell you how this can be done.
The prince is preparing to go to the city of Carthage

At his father's request—that father's greatest concern—
Bearing gifts from the sea left over from flames of Troy.
I shall hide him away, put to sleep, on the heights of Cythera
Or the sacred shrine of Idalium, keep him from knowing
My tricks and prevent him from barring success of the plan.
You shall imitate him for no more than one night; as a boy,   700
Put on another boy's face and assume his features;
So that Dido, most happy, will take you upon her lap
Among the royal tables, amid the free-flowing wine:
But when she embraces you, gives you sweet kisses, you must
Breath into her hidden fire, deceive her with poison."
        Love obeyed the words of his dear creatrix, took off
His wings and rejoiced to walk with Iulus' steps.
Then Venus poured placid repose through Ascanius' limbs,
Nursed him in her bosom and carried him off to the tall
Idalian groves, where soft marjoram wreathed him about   710
With its flowers and cast a sweet shadow on him where he lay.
Now Cupid advanced in obedience to Venus' order
And joyfully brought the royal gifts, with Achates his comrade.
When he came, the queen had arranged herself in the midst
Of rich hangings and sat upon a golden throne.
Now Father Aeneas and now the Trojan young men
Thronged about her, reclined upon their purple covers.
The servants gave water for hands, and baskets of bread;
They brought out the napkins to wipe with, of closely cropped nap.
There were fifty maidservants whose duty it was to prepare   720
The procession of dishes and keep kitchen fires alight.
There were one hundred others, a hundred manservants the same age,
Who loaded the tables with food and set out the cups.
Many Tyrians came through the festive doors, the invited
Guests who were bidden to lie on embroidered beds.
They marvelled at Aeneas' gifts, they marvelled at Iulus,
The flushed god in disguise who spoke his words of pretense,
At the robe and embroidered veil with its yellow acanthus.
That unhappy queen, especially, condemned to destruction,
Was unsated with looking and burned as she looked again.   730
The Phoenician was moved alike by the boy and the gifts.
When he had embraced Aeneas and clung from his neck,
Fulfilling the unbounded love of his fictitious father,
He went to the queen. She clung to him with her eyes,
With all her heart, and sometimes she fondled the boy

In her lap, without knowing how great a god sat there,
Poor woman! But he, remembering Venus his mother,
Began to erase Sychaeus and trouble her mind
With a living love, her passion and heart long numb.
After the first lull in the banquet, the tables were removed,   740
And they set up great wine bowls and crowned the wine.
There was tumult along the hall, and voices rang out.
Bright blazing lamps hung down from the gilded ceiling;
Wax torches let down by ropes conquered night with their flames.
The queen demanded a cup thick with jewels and gold
And filled it with wine, a cup which Belus and all
Of his line had filled often before; a silence was made:
"Jupiter, for you have made hospitality's laws,
They say—may you wish this day to be merry for all
The Tyrians and for those who escaped from Troy,   750
And may our children's children remember this day.
Let Bacchus the giver of joy and Juno the good
Be present, and you, O Tyrians, show your good will."
She spoke and then poured a little wine on the table,
And touched the rim of the cup to the edge of her lips.
Then she passed it to Bitias, challenging him; with a will
He drained it all foaming and soaked his face deep in the gold.
After him came the rest of the nobles.
                              Iopas, long-haired,
Struck his gilded lyre; great Atlas had taught him to play.

He sang of the wandering moon and the sun's hot labors,   760
Whence came men and herds, whence came the rain and the fire,
Arcturus, the rainy Hyades, and the twin Bears,
Why the sun in winter makes haste to dip in the Ocean,
Or what causes there are to hinder the tardy nights.
Both Tyrians, Trojans pursued him with double applause.
And so they extended the evening with various talk;
While unhappy Dido drank long and deep of her love,
Asking much about Priam, much about Hector too:
With what arms the son of Aurora had come to Troy,
What horses were Diomedes', how tall was Achilles.   770
"Come, tell from the start, my guest," she said, "the whole story:
The trap set by Greeks, the Trojan disaster, the way
You wandered; for now it's the seventh summer that brings
You astray upon all the seas and the lands of the earth."

BOOK TWO

The Sack of Troy

They were silent and held their gaze intent upon him.
Then Father Aeneas began from his couch on high:
    "You bid me renew, O queen, an unspeakable sorrow.
How the Greeks wiped out the Trojan state, that lamented
Kingdom, whose wretched defeat I saw myself,
In which I had so great a share; who could tell this tale?
Whether he were a Myrmidon or Dolopian
Or a soldier of hard Ulysses, could he hold back his tears?
And now moist evening falls swiftly down from the sky,
And the setting stars persuade us to sleep.
                                            But if   10
Your wish is so eager to learn our story, though briefly,
To hear of Troy's ultimate sorrow, in spite of the fact
That my spirit recoils from memory and shrinks from its pain,
I'll begin.
        The Danaan leaders, broken in war
And repelled by the Fates through so many gliding years,
Built a horse like a mountain, with Pallas' magic art,
Weaving its ribs from timbers sawn out of pine.
They pretended that this was a gift to bring end to the war;
They put out this rumor. In secret, men picked by the lot
They shut up in the horse's body, the cavern within;   20
They filled its huge hollow with soldiers armed to the teeth.
        Tenedos lay in view, an island well noted in fame,
Rich in resources while Priam's kingdom remained—
But now nothing more than a bay, a bad haven for ships.
To this island they went and hid on the empty shore.
We thought they had gone, had lifted their sails for Mycenae,
And thus the long travail of Troy was over at last.
We opened our gates; it was joy to see the Greek camp,

The land round about the shore, left barren of men.
Here the band of Dolopians, there fierce Achilles, pitched tents.   30
Here lay their fleet; there, the line where they used to fight.
Some marvelled at unwed Minerva's disastrous gift
And the size of the horse; Thymoetes was first to say
We should take it inside our walls, to our citadel.
(Perhaps speaking in treason; or Troy's fate was now set that way.)
But Capys, and those whose thoughts were more balanced, said 'No.'
They ordered this snare of the Greeks, their suspected gift,
To be thrown to the sea, or burned by flames underneath,
Or to bore through its vitals and test the hollows within.
The crowd, undecided, was drawn to contrary desires.   40
        First there before all, with a long retinue behind him,
Excited Laocoon ran down from the citadel's peak,
And, from afar:
        'O poor citizens, what madness so great
Is this? You believe the enemy gone? You suppose
Any gifts from the Greeks lack guile? Don't you know Ulysses?
Either Greeks are concealed within this piece of wood,
Or it's a machine that was fashioned against our walls,
To look into our houses and come down onto the city,
Or some trick lies hidden within; do not trust in the horse.
Whatever it is, I fear the Greeks even with gifts.'   50
So he spoke, and with all his strength he whirled a great spear
Into the beast's side, the curved hollow compact in its structure.
It stuck there, trembling; the empty caverns within
Re-echoed, the matrix gave back the sound in a groan.
If the Fates of the gods, if our minds, had not been unlucky,
He would have defiled the Greek hiding places with steel,
And Troy would be standing, you, Priam's citadel, too.
        Look, in the meanwhile a young man, his hands tied behind,
Trojan shepherds came dragging with outcry intense to the king.
He had freely presented himself, and he had arranged   60
Their meeting, to topple Troy, open it up to the Greeks.
Bold-hearted he was and ready for death or deception.
The young men of Troy rushed out on all sides to see,
They stood round the captive, each eager to mock him the first.
Note now Grecian treachery; and from one man's guilty deed,
Learn to know all of them.
        For as he stood troubled and helpless in midst of their view,
He cast round a glance at the Phrygian ranks of war:

'Ah, what land,' he cried, 'What waters can shelter me now?
Or what now remains for me, miserable wretch that I am?   70
There is no place for me among Greeks, and the Trojans
Demand in their rage my punishment and my blood!'
This wail changed our minds, all our hostility ceased.
We urged him to speak, to tell us of whom he was born,
What he might bring us, or prove to us why we should trust him.
His fear laid aside at last, he spoke these words:
'I swear, king, that everything I shall say is the truth.
I do not deny I'm a Greek first of all, nor if Fortune
Has made Sinon wretched, she's not made him liar and fraud.
Perhaps some account in men's talk has come to your ears   80
Of Belus' descendant, Palamedes, his glory and fame,
He whom the Greeks by betrayal condemned, although innocent;
Because he forbade the war, they sent him to death.
They mourn him now, shut out from the light of day.
My poor father, in the first years of my youth,
Sent me with him to fight, as his friend and relation.
While Palamedes remained unharmed in royal power
And held his prestige at the council board of the kings,
I bore some name and some dignity as well.
After the envy of crafty Ulysses had thrust   90
Palamedes out of this world—what I say is well known—
Dashed down, I led my life in shadow and grief,
In angry though private lament at my friend's foul fate.
In my folly I talked, and if it were ever my luck
To return as a victor to Argos, my father's home,
I swore to revenge him: I stirred bitter hate with my words.
Hence the first tremor of evil, hence always Ulysses
Frightened me with new threats, scattered falsehoods about me
Among the soldiers and sought allies for his scheme.
Nor did he rest until, making Calchas his agent—   100
But why do I vainly recount such unpleasant details?
Or why do I wait, if you lump all the Greeks into one?
Sufficient to know I am Greek: now kill me at last:
The Ithacan wishes it; the Atreidae will pay well for this.'
      Then indeed we were eager to question him, hear the man out,
Unacquainted with Grecian cunning, with evil so great.
He trembled, went on, and spoke in an actor's pretense:
'Often the Greeks have wished to take flight from Troy
And leave it behind, so weary they were of long war.

And would they had fled! Bad weather upon the sea   *110*
Prevented; the South Wind brought terror before they could sail.
Especially then, when the horse made of maple beams
Stood in place, the clouds from the entire ether rang out.
We sent Eurypylus to question the oracle's shrine
Of sacred Apollo; he brought back grim words from the place:
"You soothed the wild winds with the blood of a murdered girl,
When first you came, O Greeks, to the Trojan shore.
You must win your return with blood, with the life of a—Greek!"
This voice in the ears of the crowd benumbed their souls;
Chill tremors ran throughout their inmost bones: *120*
For whom is fate ordained, whom seeks Apollo?
Ulysses here dragged Calchas into their midst,
That seer, with a huge tumult; he asked the question:
"Which way now nods the power of the gods?"
Now many people told my fortune, said
I was the butt of this cruel trick; they watched
What was to come and kept their coward's peace.
For twice five days the prophet did not speak,
Inside his tent, refusing to betray
Some man to death with any word of his.   *130*
Scarcely even then, egged on by loud Ulysses,
He broke his silence—this was planned—and doomed me.
All yelled approval; the fate each feared was his
They saw fall to one poor man's single lot.
Now came the day unspeakable for me;
The rites prepared, the salted grain, the fillets
Around my head: I broke the bonds, escaped,
I must confess. I skulked that night in reeds
Beside a muddy lake, until they sailed,
If they should sail. I had no hope to see   *140*
My land again, my sons, and my dear father.
Perhaps the Greeks will punish them for my
Escape; for what I did they'll pay with death.
By the high gods, the powers who know the truth,
By any faith unbroken still by men,
I beg you, pity me who suffer so,
Take pity on a soul that has been wronged.'
    We gave him life for his tears, yes, pitied him.
Priam first gave orders to unbind
His tight ropes, take off handcuffs; he spoke kind words: *150*

'Whoever you are, forget the Greeks completely;
You're one of us now: speak frankly to my questions.
Why did they build the huge structure of the horse?
Whose plan and why? For worship or for war?'
He spoke. Then Sinon, skilled in Greek deceits,
Raised up his hands, now free of bonds, toward heaven:
      'Eternal stars, I swear by your pure power,
And by this altar, and these ghastly swords
Which I escaped, the fillets which I wore
As victim: it is right that I should break   *160*
Ties of allegiance forced on me by Greeks,
Right to hate them, reveal what they would hide.
I am not bound by fatherland or laws.
Only abide by what you promise, keep
The faith of Troy preserved, if I speak truth,
If I reward you, who have saved my life.'
      'All Greek hope and trust since the war began
Stood firm in Pallas' aid. But since the impious
Diomedes, and Ulysses, schemer
Of evil, killed the guards on the citadel   *170*
To steal her fatal image from her temple,
And dared with bloody hands to touch her fillets,
From that time on their hopes flowed back and fell,
Their force was broken, the goddess was estranged.
Athena gave them unmistakable signs.
They had scarcely set her image in the camp
When flames burst forth from her great staring eyes,
A salty sweat streamed from her limbs, three times
She darted from her base, strange to relate,
Bearing a shield and quivering lance in hand.   *180*
Straightway Calchas prophesied the Greeks
Should flee across the waves: they could not take
Troy with their weapons, unless first they sought
Omens at Argos, brought that divine power back
Which they had once borne over seas in their curving ships.
And now they have sailed off to their Mycenae
For arms and gods and comrades: unexpected,
The sea traversed, they will appear: so Calchas
Explained the omens. At his urging they
Set up this effigy in place of Pallas'   *190*
Image, to make amends for godhead injured,

Atone for sacrilege. He made them build it
Of immense size with girded timbers, skyward,
Not to be drawn through gates or over walls,
Thus not to guard your folk in ancient faith.
For if your hands had damaged the gift of Pallas
Then great destruction—would it had seized on Calchas!—
Would come to Priam's realm and to the Phrygians.
But if your hands should bring it into the city,
Then Asia might attack the walls of Pelops: 200
This destiny would come to your descendants.'
With such deceits and wicked art of Sinon,
By tricks and tears, the captive made us believe him,
We whom no Achilles of Larissa nor Diomedes
Nor ten years nor a thousand ships had conquered.

  Then something more for wretches to shudder at
Was thrust on us, disturbed our thoughtless minds.
Laocoon, by lot the priest of Neptune,
Was solemnly slaying a huge bull at the altar,
When, look! from Tenedos over the quiet water—   210
I bristle with fear to recall—in massive coilings,
Twin snakes crawled over the sea straight to the land.
Their chests erect among the billows, their bloody
Manes rose above the waves; their hind parts skimmed
The deep, they arched their backs into great spirals.
The sea foam roared behind them. Now they landed,
Their burning eyes suffused with blood and fire.
With flickering tongues they licked their hissing mouths.
We fled, all pale to see. In steady progress
They went for Laocoon; and first the little   220
Bodies of his two sons each serpent gathered
Within its coils, and bit and ate their limbs.
Next, when he tried to help and brought his weapons,
They seized the prophet, bound him in huge twinings.
Now twice round the middle, twice round the neck they held him:
Their heads and necks still towered high above him.
His hands tried hard to wrench apart their knots;
His fillets fouled with slaver and black venom,
He sent up shouts of horror to the stars,
Such as the roars, when from an altar lunges   230
A wounded bull and shakes an ill-aimed ax-head
Out of his neck. Up to the topmost temple

The twin snakes fled, to the shrine of savage Pallas,
And hid beneath her feet and her round shield.
Then a new terror slipped into each trembling heart.
They said Laocoon paid for his crime,
Who with his blade had struck the sacred oak
And left his damned spear twisted in its side.
'Lead in the image, pray to the goddess' power,'
They all shout out.   240

We cut through walls and open the city's defenses.
All gird themselves for work, lay down the rollers
Beneath the horse's feet, throw ropes around its
Neck. The fatal engine scales our walls,
Pregnant with soldiers. Boys and unwed maidens
Stand round, sing sacred songs, while each is eager
To touch the rope. Up, up it goes and, baleful,
Slides down to rest in the middle of the city.
O fatherland, O Ilium, home of gods,
And walls of Dardanus so famed in war!   250
Four times it stumbled on the gate's threshold,
Four times its womb gave forth the sound of arms.
We pressed on, mindless, blind, and mad; we placed
The calamitous monster on the citadel.
Once more Cassandra uttered the fate to come,
Which by Apollo's will was never believed.
Poor fools, we crowned the altars of our gods
That day, our last, with garlands through the city.
        The heavens changed meanwhile, Night rose from Ocean,
Cast darkness on earth and sky and Grecian traps.   260
The Trojans were quiet, stretched out beside their walls.
Sleep clasped their tired limbs. And now the Greek
Army came back from Tenedos with ranked ships,
Beneath the silent friendliness of the moon.
They sought the well-known shore. Then Agamemnon's
Ship sent up a signal light astern.
Sinon, protected by gods' adverse fate,
Stealthily loosed the Greeks from their piney womb.
The opened horse released them to the air;
Gladly they issued from its hollow oak: 270
The leaders Thessandrus, Sthenelus, frightful Ulysses
Slid down the hanging rope, Acamas, Thoas,

Achilles' son, Machaon, the foremost,
And Menelaus, Epeus, who made the trap.
They entered the city buried in sleep and wine·
They killed the guards and gathered all their men
Through opened gates, joined forces as they planned.
        It was that time when first a tranquil sleep,
Most sweet, divine, creeps down on weary men.
In dream I saw grief-stricken Hector stand   280
Before me while he wept unceasing tears,
Dragged by the chariot as he was, and black
With bloody dust, his swollen feet pierced through
By thongs, ah me, how changed he was from that
Hector who came back clad in Achilles' armor
Or him who set the Danaan ships on fire!
His beard was filthy, his hair caked with dried blood;
He bore those many wounds he suffered round
Troy's walls. It seemed that I in tears myself
Was first to speak, to force the sad words out: 290
        'O light of Dardania, most faithful hope of Troy,
What kept you away so long? Out of what country
Have you we wait for come? How weary now,
After so many deaths, such shifting fortunes
Of men and city, do we look on you?
What has so foully marred your cloudless face?
Or why these wounds I see?' He did not speak.
He paid no heed to my vain questioning,
But, groaning deeply from within his breast:
'Run, goddess-born!' he said, 'escape these flames: 300
The enemy holds the walls; Troy-towers fall.
Priam and Priam's land have done their best.
If Troy could be defended, my right hand
Would have defended her. Now she entrusts
Her holy rites and statues to your care.
Take them, the comrades of your fate, seek walls
For them where they may rest, your wanderings over.'
He spoke, and in his hands he carried out
Strong Vesta with her fillets, her ageless fire,
From the deep mystic recess of her shrine.   310
        The walls now echoed everywhere with grief,
And more and more, although my father's home
Stood back, withdrawn, protected by its trees.

The battle sounds grew keen, their horror grew.
They woke me, and I climbed onto the roof
To stand with ears pricked up,
                              As when a flame
By South Wind madly driven falls on the wheat,
Or some swift torrent down a mountain channel
Smashes the fields and good crops, work of oxen,
And drags the trees headlong, while from his crag   320
A shepherd hears it in bewildered awe.
Then the real truth, the Greek tricks were revealed.
Already fire had ruined the ample house
Of Deiphobus, and now Ucalegon,
His neighbor, burned. The broad strait of Sigeum
Gave back the glow. The cries of men, the screech
Of trumpets rose; madly I seized my weapons,
Without a planned attack; my spirits raged
To gather a fighter's group and race up to
The citadel with comrades. Furious anger   330
Drove me headlong, and all I thought was this:
To die in battle is the way to glory.
Look! Panthus, slipped away from Achaean missiles,
Panthus, the son of Othrys, priest of Apollo,
Dragged sacred articles of the defeated god
And by the hand, his grandson, to my door
In his wild flight. I shouted to him: 'Panthus!
Which is the place where we must take our stand?'
Scarcely had I spoken when he groaned and said:
'That last of days, that hour we cannot dodge,   340
Has come to Troy. Trojans we were, and Troy
Has been, and Troy's great glory. Jupiter
Fiercely transfers the gods to Argos now.
The Greeks are masters in a ruined city.
Their horse stands high amid our walls and pours
Out armored men, and jeering Sinon stirs
The flames; he triumphs. Others, massed in thousands,
Stand at the open gates, as many men
As ever came to Troy from great Mycenae.
Some block the narrow streets with spear-points levelled;   350
Their naked sword-blades glitter along the columns,
Ready to kill; the sentries at the gateway
Try to fight back; theirs is a blind resistance.'

These words from Panthus with their god-sent power
Drive me to flames and battle, where savage Fury
Roars and the sound is carried up to heaven.
Ripheus and Epytus, strong at fighting, gather
Themselves by me in the moonlight; Dymas too,
And Hypanis, and young Coroebus, son of
Mygdon. It happened that he came to Troy   360
A few days earlier, madly in love with Cassandra,
To bring assistance as a son-in-law
To Priam and the ill-fated Phrygians.
He had not paid attention to the warnings
Of his mad sweetheart.
When I saw them standing shoulder to shoulder
Ready for battle, I began to speak:
'Young fellows, who in vain have the bravest hearts,
If you are eager to follow one who dares
The utmost—for you see where fortune has us: 370
The gods all gone, their shrines and altars empty,
The gods in whom our power lay; you rescue
A ruined city—let us face death by rushing
Into the midst of arms. One sole salvation
The conquered have: to hope for no salvation.'
And so I added madness to their courage.
Like plundering wolves in misty darkness running,
Driven by restless hunger to prowl blindly,
Their cubs abandoned, waiting with thirsty jaws,
So we went racing under the enemy's weapons   380
Through certain death into the city's center.
Black night threw round about us her hollow cloud.
Who could relate the slaughter of that night,
Tell of its dead, or equal tears with anguish?
The ancient city, ruler for many years,
Had fallen; in its streets, among its houses
Lay quiet corpses, and on the temple door-steps.
Not only the Trojans paid penalties of blood:
Often man's courage returned to vanquished hearts,
And Greeks in their triumph fell. Cruel everywhere   390
The struggle, and fear, and the frequent face of death.
     First of the Greeks, a large band at his heels,
Came Androgeos, who thought we were his friends.
All unaware he called us in comrade-speech:

'More speed, my men! What makes you lag behind?
Others are looting through the ruins of Troy.
Have you arrived just now from our tall ships?'
He spoke, but in that breath—our silence showed
His error—he sensed the enemy around him.
He checked his voice, shrank back, and stood stock still,   400
Just as some man among the prickly bushes
Steps on a hidden snake, recoils in fear
To see its swelling anger and blue-black head;
So Androgeos shivered, and stumbled back.
We charged and cut them off beneath our weapons,
Ignorant of the terrain and seized with fear.
Fortune breathed favor upon our first encounter.
Coroebus here, his spirits lifted up
At our success, cried: 'Comrades, let us go
Where fortune with her right hand points the way   410
To freedom: let us change our shields and armor
For Greek equipment. Who will ask us whether
This is a trick or courage? The Greeks will give us
Weapons.' He fitted on the crested helmet
Of Androgeos, his shield with famed device,
And strapped an Argive sword against his side.
Ripheus, Dymas, all the exulting young men
Did as Coroebus, fitted on fresh spoils.
We swept among the Greeks beneath a godly
Power who was not ours, and many a skirmish   420
We fought that dark night, sent many Greeks to Orcus.
The others ran to shore and ships for safety;
And some, turned frightened cowards, clambered back
Into the giant horse's familiar belly.
     Ah, it is never good to put your trust
In gods who have become unwilling toward you.
Look! Priam's virgin daughter, her hair all scattered,
Cassandra, from Minerva's shrine and temple
Was dragged before us, her eyes raised vainly skyward,
Her burning eyes: her tender hands were bound.   430
Coroebus in his rage could not endure this
And rushed to die upon the passing column.
We followed, we attacked, all in close order.
Here first the missiles of our side rained on us
From the high temple's peak, a frightful slaughter

In error, since we wore Greek crests and armor.
The Greeks then, roaring, angry at her rescue,
Attacked us from all sides, Ajax the fiercest,
The twin Atreidae, the army of Dolopians,
As when a storm bursts and the winds in conflict   440
Clash, both West and South, and East rejoicing
In his dawn-horses; forests stand a-screaming
And foamy Nereus rages with his trident,
Stirring the waters upward from the sea floor.
Those whom we had driven back through night's dim shadow
By stratagem, and scattered over the city,
Appeared too; first they recognized our shields
And deceiving weapons and our foreign accents.
Their numbers overwhelmed us, and first Coroebus
Fell by Peneleus' hands at the warlike goddess'   450
Altar; Ripheus fell, most just of Trojans,
Most righteous: yet the gods thought otherwise.
Hypanis, Dymas perished, stabbed by their comrades.
Your holy loyalty did not protect you,
Panthus, from falling, nor Apollo's fillets.
The ashes of Troy, the flames that took my loved ones,
Bore witness as you fell that I avoided
Neither the Greek attacks nor weapons; if the
Fates had willed it, I should have fallen too.
Then we were torn apart. Iphitus with me,   460
And Pelias—one too old, the other wounded
And slowed by Ulysses—went to Priam's palace,
Summoned by shouts. Here fighting was the fiercest,
As though no one fought elsewhere, none was dying
In all the city. We saw unceasing battle,
Greeks rushing to the palace and its threshold
Beset by their locked shields. The scaling ladders
Clung to its walls, and at its very door-posts
They climbed the rungs. Shields on their left arms guarded
The men from missiles; their right hands grasped the gables.   470
The Trojans in defense tore tiles, pried towers
From roof tops—with these weapons they endeavor
To ward off death: they see the end is coming.
They roll down gilded beams, the high-hung glory
Of their ancestors. Some with naked sword blade
Guard the last gates, hold these in close-ranked units.

Our spirits were strong to save the royal dwelling,
To help and to encourage the defeated.
    There was a secret doorway to the palace,
An entrance known to few, that linked its courtyards,   480
Where often while Troy's empire stood, poor woman,
Andromache would walk without her servants
To visit her husband's parents, dragging little
Astyanax by the hand to his grandfather.
I climbed up to the ridgepole on the roof-top,
Where the poor Trojans threw down harmless missiles.
Here was a tower built flush with the outer wall
That sprang up starward from the palace roof;
From it all Troy, the Greek camp, the familiar
Ships could be seen. We set to work with sword blades   490
Where ends of floor-beams offered yielding joints.
We tore the tower from its high base and shoved it
Suddenly over; its crash drew down to ruin
Greek fighters in long lines. But others followed.
They did not cease to hurl stones, any sort of
Flying objects meanwhile.
    Before the entrance hall, within the gateway,
Roared Pyrrhus, shining in bronze glint of weapons,
Just as a snake which, swollen with noxious grasses,
The winter covered, comes up to daylight, now   .   500
Sloughing its skin, in shining youth anew,
And rolls its coiling back, its breast raised upward
Straight to the sun, its three-forked tongue a-flicker.
Beside him stood huge Periphas and the driver
Of Achilles' horses, Automedon the armor-bearer,
And all the men from Scyros. They went forward,
Threw firebrands upon the palace roof.
Pyrrhus, in front, took up a two-edged broad ax
And smashed the strong door, wrenched the plated doorposts
Away from hinges, hacked planks, cut a hole   510
Through solid oak and made a great-mouthed window.
The house within appeared, wide courtyards opened
Before us, the king's own rooms, and of his forebears:
These sacred halls saw armed men on their threshold.
    A confused groaning and a piteous tumult:
From room to room we heard the howls of women.
Their cries rose up to strike the golden stars.

Hysteric mothers wandered through huge chambers,
Embraced the doorposts, clung to them and kissed them.
Pyrrhus rushed on, courageous like his father   520
Achilles; no bars nor guards could hold him off.
The door gave way before repeated ramming,
The doorposts torn from hinges fell before us.
A way was forced; the Greeks broke through and slaughtered
The guards in front, their army filled the palace.
With far less fury a foaming river sweeps
Through broken banks and smashes in its wild whirlpool
The bars thrown up. Across sown crops it rages
At crested flood and over all the fields,
Dragging both stock and stables. It was I   530
Who saw the son of Achilles, crazy with carnage,
The twin Atreidae at the door. I saw
Hecuba and her hundred daughters, Priam
Fouling in his own blood the very altars
Which he had hallowed once with sacred fire.
Those fifty wedding-rooms, such hope of offspring,
Their pillars gilt with foreign gold and proud
With spoils, lay ruined. Greeks held what was not burned.
        Perhaps you ask how Priam met his fate.
When he saw Troy had fallen, his palace gates   540
Wrenched from their site, the enemy within
His family's home, old as he was he drew
Over trembling shoulders the armor he had not worn
For years, strapped on a useless sword, went out
To die among the crowding enemy.
There in the midmost courtyard, open to heaven,
Stood a huge altar near an old laurel tree,
Bending above and shading the household gods.
Hecuba and her children sat vainly round it
Like huddled doves swept headlong in a tempest,   550
Their arms about the statues of the gods.
When she saw Priam in a young man's armor
Hecuba cried: 'What awful thought compelled you
To strap these weapons on? Where are you rushing?
Husband, the moment calls for no such aid
Nor such defenders, not even if my Hector
Were here. Come this way. The altar will protect us,
Or we shall die together.' So she spoke

And drew the old man down and made a place
For him beside her at the altar's edge. 560
    Look! Fled away from Pyrrhus and his slaughter,
Polites, Priam's son, through foe and missiles
Came running down long porticoes and empty
Hallways, wounded. Pyrrhus followed him
With levelled spear. He almost grasped and stabbed him.
At last before his parents' very eyes
Polites fell, poured out his life and blood.
Here Priam, although in the midst of death,
Could not restrain his words or check his anger:
'If there is pity in heaven to take regard 570
For such a crime, may those who dwell there give
You proper thanks and just reward! You made
Me watch my son's death and befouled a father's
Sight with murder. The great Achilles, whom
You falsely claim as parent, did not treat
Priam like this. He blushed to violate
A suppliant's right, gave back the bloodless corpse
Of Hector, and restored me to my kingdom.'
The old man spoke and weakly threw his spear.
It struck the ringing bronze and then hung down 580
From the shield's central boss. Pyrrhus replied:
'You shall go down and carry to my father
This message: tell him of my grisly deeds,
How low I have fallen. Now you die.' So speaking,
He dragged the trembling king to the very altar,
Slipping through his son's blood, then twisted a left hand
In his long hair; next, with the right he drew
A sword and thrust it to the utmost hilt
Into his side. Such was the fate of Priam,
This his allotted end, to see Troy burned, 590
Its citadel fallen, who once ruled in proud Asia
So many lands and peoples. Upon the shore
His mighty torso lies, the head hacked off
From shoulders: it is a corpse without a name.
    Then first wild horror took its stand around me.
I stiffened with fear. The sight of my dear father
Now filled my mind, and as I saw the king,
His age-fellow, breathe out his life from that
Cruel wound, I thought of my wife Creusa deserted,

My home destroyed, the fate of small Iulus.   600
I looked back, counted the soldiers still around me.
They were all gone, had flung their weary bodies
Down to the earth or leaped into the flames.
        And now I was left alone, when on the threshold
Of Vesta's temple, keeping her silent corner
In hiding, I saw Helen: the fires revealed her,
As I looked everywhere, to my wandering eyes.
She feared alike the bitter Trojans, angry
Because Troy fell; Greek punishment; her husband's
Anger: a Fury baleful to Troy and Greece.   610
She hid herself, sat hated at the altar.
My spirit flamed, and rage came over me
To avenge my falling country and exact
Accursed punishment from her accursed.
'So, shall she all unharmed look upon Sparta,
Her home Mycenae, shall she go a queen
In victory, look upon her house and children,
Her husband and her parents, with an escort
Of Trojans and of Phrygians enslaved?
Shall Priam die by the steel, Troy burn in fire,   620
The Trojan shore sweat blood so many times?
Not so. Although one cannot win a name
By punishing women, this victory has praise:
I shall be hailed for wiping out dishonor,
For giving just deserts; my heart will triumph,
Filled with avenging flame, when I have sated
The ashes of my lost ones.' So I boasted.
Madness bore me along,
                                When before my eyes
My mother appeared more clearly than ever before;
Radiant there through the night in her godhead revealed,   630
With that beauty and height she displays to the gods themselves,
She caught my right hand and held me. With rosy mouth
She spoke: 'My son, what sorrow is this so great
That stirs you to boundless anger? Why do you rage?
Why has the love you bear me gone out of your heart?
Why will you not first take care how you leave him behind,
Anchises your father, age-broken? And where is your wife
Creusa? Your son Ascanius? Greek battle lines
Surround them. If I had not given them my protection,

The enemy sword or the flames would have taken their lives.   640
Do not blame the hated beauty of Helen, nor Paris:
The merciless gods, the gods, are the ones who have toppled
The power of Troy and levelled it with the earth.
Now look! I shall snatch away all the mist that dulls
Your mortal vision and wraps you moistly in night.
You must not fear my commands or refuse my advice.
Here, where you see those tumbled masses of rock
Torn from rock, those billows of mingled dust and smoke,
Neptune is prying the walls from their very foundations
With his trident, reducing the entire city to ruin.   650
There stands most fierce Juno, commanding the Scaean gates.
In her fury she calls her allies, the Greeks, from their ships.
She is wearing a sword.
Look! there on the citadel's peak sits Tritonian Pallas.
She shines in her storm cloud and shakes her Gorgonian shield.
Jupiter Father gives spirit and vigor renewed
To the Greeks; he rallies the gods against Trojan arms.
Run away, my son, and put an end to your torture.
I shall be with you everywhere, bring you home safe to your father.'
She spoke; then she hid in the thickening shadows of night.   660
Frightful faces of gods unfriendly to Troy appeared,
Great powers of heaven.
        Then truly all Ilium seemed to settle in flames,
And Neptune's Troy turn upside down to its depths,
Like an ancient ash that stands high on the mountains
Cut by the steel, as farmers take turns at the task
To topple it under their twin-edged axes until
It threatens to fall, the shivering leaves at the tip
Nodding downward, and, conquered at last by continual wounds,
The tree groans, is torn from the ridge, carries ruin before it.   670
I went down, led by a goddess, I escaped through the flames
And enemy. Weapons gave place, and the flames receded.
        And when I had come to the door of my father's house,
My homestead, that father whom I had hoped I could carry
First of all to the mountains, he whom I sought first of all,
Declared he could not go on living, now Troy was cut down,
Or suffer exile. 'O you who are young in your blood,'
He said, 'and whose muscles stand firm in their early power,
Hurry on and escape.
If the gods above had wished me to keep on living   680

They would have preserved my home. Enough and more
Than enough to have seen Troy taken, to see it in ruins.
Thus, thus, bid goodbye to me where I lie, and escape!
I shall take my own life; my foe shall feel pity for me
And search for the spoils: the lack of a tomb I can bear.
I have long been hated by gods, and useless in years
I remain, since the Father of Gods and the King of Men
Breathed on me the wind of his lightning and struck me with fire.'
        Speaking such words he stood fixed and determined before us.
We on our part shed tears, and my wife Creusa,   690
Ascanius, all of his family, implored him, as father,
Not to destroy all nor to rush upon urgent fate.
He refused and stuck at his post with the same resolution.
I rushed for my weapons; most wretched, I hoped for death,
Since what sort of plan or what kind of fortune remained?
'Did you think, O my father, that I could desert you here,
And did such a blasphemous word fall from your mouth?
If it pleases the gods to leave nothing from so great a city,
And if you intend to add to the ruins of Troy
Both yourself and your family, the door to your death stands open.   700
Pyrrhus will soon be here, soaked with the blood
Of Priam: he slaughtered the son before the eyes
Of the father, then killed the father in front of the altar.
Was it for this, my mother, you snatched me from weapons and fire,
To see the enemy here in the midst of my home,
And Ascanius, father, Creusa together, all butchered
In each other's blood? Come, soldiers, bring me my arms!
The last dawn calls to the vanquished. Give me to the Greeks,
Let me see battle renewed, for never shall we
Who stand here today meet death without being avenged!'   710
        So I bound on my sword, inserted a shield on my left arm
And adjusted it. I was rushing out of the house
When there on the threshold my wife threw her arms round my feet
And clung to me, held out little Iulus to his father:
'If you go out to be killed, take us with you, whatever
May happen. But if you have found there is hope in the arms
You take up, then defend this home first of all.
To whom shall little Iulus be left, and to whom
Your father, and I who once was called your wife?'
        Shouting such words, she filled the whole house with her   720
    clamor,

When a sudden portent arose that was wondrous to tell.
For there between his parents' hands and their faces
From the tip of Iulus' cap a slender light
Poured forth, soft flame quite harmless to the touch,
That licked his hair and fed around his temples.
We tried in our fear to shake out the burning hair
And quench the holy fire with streams of water.
But Father Anchises lifted his eyes to the stars
In his joy and stretched out his palms to heaven and spoke:
'Almighty Jupiter, if you are swayed by prayers,   730
Look down on us—only this—and if we deserve it
Because of our faith, give us help, and confirm these omens.'
    The old man had scarcely spoken when suddenly thunder
Crashed on the left, a star fell out of the sky
And fled with its dazzling torch through the darkness of night.
We saw it slip over the top of our house and light up
The roads as it vanished, still shining, in woods on Mount Ida.
It dragged a long furrow of brilliance and scattered the smell
Of smoking sulphur widely about. My father,
Convinced at this sight, arose and worshipped the star   740
As he spoke to the gods: 'Now there is no more delay.
I'll follow wherever you lead. O ancestral gods,
Save my home and my grandson! This is your fortunate sign.
Troy stands by your power. My son, I shall come with you.'
He had spoken, and now a brisker fire was roaring
Among the great walls, heat waves rolled the flames more closely.
'Then come, my dear father, let them place you upon my back.
I shall carry you on my shoulders: your weight is not heavy.
Wherever our chance may fall, one common danger,
One safety shall be our own. Let little Iulus   750
Walk beside me, my wife keep her distance a long way behind.
You servants, pay heed in your minds to the words I say:
Where you go out of Troy are a mound and an ancient temple
Of Ceres deserted and, nearby, an aged cypress
Preserved by the faith of our fathers for many years.
We shall meet at this place but reach it by different roads.
You, father, take up our household gods and their symbols;
I cannot touch them, just come from such war and fresh slaughter,
Until I shall wash my pollution away in a living
Stream of water!'   760
So speaking I bent my neck and on wide shoulders

I laid a tawny lion's skin for garment
And then took up my load. Little Iulus
Entwined his fingers in my right hand and followed
His father with steps not equal, my wife behind us.
We walked through shadows.
                              Now all the breezes frightened,
Each sound disturbed me, fearful alike for comrade
And burden, I whom, shortly before, the weapons
Aimed at me or the squads of hostile Greeks
Had not excited. Now I approached the gate   770
And seemed to have reached my goal, when suddenly
The sound of feet was heard. My father, peering
Through gloom, exclaimed: 'My son, run off, they're coming!
I see the gleam of shields, the flash of bronze.'
Some hostile power here in my confusion
Deprived me of reason, for I had left the streets
I knew and lost my way: was it evil fate
That snatched my wife from me? Did she stop running?
Did she too lose her way? Sink down and fall?
I do not know. I had not looked at her   780
Nor noted her absence, nor even thought of her
Before we reached the mound and the temple of Ceres.
Here when at last all gathered, she alone
Was missing, lost to comrades, son, and husband.
Which god or man did I not madly accuse,
Or what more cruel had I seen in the ruined city?
I turned Ascanius, father, the Trojan house-gods
Over to others, hidden in a curving valley.
I sought the city, I strapped on shining armor,
Ready for risks again, to go through all   790
Troy, to expose my self once more to peril.
I came to the walls, the shaded gateway threshold
Whence we had fled, retraced the steps I'd made.
Fear met me everywhere, the very silence
Struck me with terror. I came back to my home
Upon the chance, the chance she might be there.
The Greeks had filled it and now held all the house.
There winds rolled greedy flames to the very roof top,
Fire rose over it, blasts raged up on high.
I moved on, Priam's palace and citadel   800

I saw again. In empty colonnades
Guards chosen, Phoenix and the fierce Ulysses,
Kept watch with Juno's aid over piles of plunder.
Here everywhere the Trojan treasure, looted
From burned-out temples, tables of the gods,
Wine bowls of solid gold and captured garments
Were heaped. Here children and frightened mothers stood
In a long line nearby.
But yet I dared to shout among the shadows
And fill the streets with clamor for Creusa;   810
In vain again, again, I cried for her,
Sadly. When I had searched through house and city,
Mad, without end, Creusa's shade, her unhappy
Ghost stood before me, an image larger than life.
Stock-still, my hair stood stiff, my tongue stuck fast.
Then thus she spoke; her words assuaged my fear:
'What help is there to break down with insane sorrow,
Sweet husband? These things do not happen without
The power of gods. It was not right to take
Creusa companion with you, Jove forbids it.   820
Long exile, and vast seas to plow, before you
Reach Western Land, where Lydian Tiber flows
Gently among rich meadows of strong men.
There Italian rule and wealth, a royal wife
Will be your share: weep not for loved Creusa.
I shall not see proud homes of Myrmidons
Or Dolopes, or slave for Grecian mothers,
Dardanian I and Venus' daughter-in-law.
But Cybele will hold me on these shores.
And now goodbye, and love our son for me.'   830
When she had said this, though I wept and wished
To say much more, she left me, vanished in air.
Three times I tried to throw my arms around her,
Three times in vain, the image fled my grasp
Like fickle winds, but most like a fleeting dream.
         Night ended, thus I saw at last my comrades
Once more and, wondering, found their numbers grown
By new arrivals, mothers and their men,
Youth grouped for exile, a crowd that stirred my pity.
Prepared in heart and gear, from everywhere   840

They came, to sail wherever I might wish.
And now the morning star rose over Ida's
Top ridge and led the day. The Greeks were holding
The threshold of the gates: no hope of rescue.
I yielded, lifted my father, and sought the mountains."

BOOK THREE

Across the Mediterranean

"After the gods decided to overthrow
The power of Asia and the race of Priam,
All undeserved, proud Ilium had fallen,
And all Neptunian Troy smoked on the ground;
By gods' decree we were scattered into exile
And forced to find a land where no men lived.
We built a fleet beneath Antandros-town
Where rise the mountain heights of Phrygian Ida.
Uncertain where the fates might bear us, where
We might find rest, we gathered our men together.   10
The summer had scarcely begun when Father Anchises
Ordered our fated sailing. Tearfully,
I left my country's shores, its harbor, the fields
Where Troy had been: an exile on the deep
With comrades, son, god-images small and great.

  The land of Mars far-off with its wide fields
—The Thracians till them—ruled by fierce Lycurgus,
Long since, had made guest-friends with Troy, allied
Her families while Troy's fortune held. I sailed
To this place, on its curved shore built the walls   20
That rise first in a city—fate was hostile—
And named it Aeneadae from my name.

  A sacrifice to Venus I was making,
To mother, and to other gods, auspicious
Toward my task just begun, and to that god
Supreme among sky-dwellers and their king,
A shining bull I slew upon the shore.
By chance there stood nearby a mound of earth
Upon whose top a cornel-thicket grew
And myrtle bristling dense with thorny spikes.   30

45

I climbed the mound and tried to pick some plants
Whose fronds might make a covering for my altar,
And saw a marvel frightening to relate.
For that first bush I pulled from broken roots
Dripped gouts of black blood, staining the earth with gore.
Cold horror shook my legs, my blood went cold.
Seeking the hidden cause, I tried again
To pluck another bush, as it resisted.
And once again black blood flowed from its bark.
Greatly disturbed, I prayed to the country nymphs   40
And Father Mars, who guards the Getic Land,
That they might turn the evil sight to good.
I pulled a third bush, with a greater effort,
And braced my knees in struggle on the sand.
Then—shall I speak or not?—a piteous moaning
I heard from the mound, and a voice came up to my ears:
'Why do you rend poor me, Aeneas? Spare
One who is buried, keep your pure hand from sin.
I am Trojan, no foreigner; blood drips from this plant.
Run from this cruel land, from the greedy shore.   50
For I am Polydorus. I was transfixed
By an iron crop of missiles, and sharp spears
Grew over me.'
        Weighed down by fear, uncertain,
Stock-still, my hair stood stiff, my tongue stuck fast.
        Unhappy Priam once in secret sent
This Polydorus with a great weight of gold
To live with the king of Thrace, when he lost faith
In Trojan arms and saw the city ringed
By siege. That king, when Trojan power was broken
And fortune withdrew, went over to Agamemnon   60
The victor's side, breaking all solemn faith:
He killed Polydorus and took the gold by force—
To what ends do you not drive men, cursed hunger for gold?
After the trembling left my bones I told
Picked leaders of my people, and first my father,
About this god-sent sign, asked their opinion.
All of them wished to leave that wicked land
With its polluted hospitality
And sail away. We buried Polydorus
Anew and heaped the earth high on his grave.   70

There rose an altar to his shades, surrounded
By gloomy drapes and one black cypress tree;
And Ilian women, their hair unbound, stood near.
We brought him foaming cups of tepid milk
And bowls of blessed blood; we laid his soul
To rest within its grave and cried farewell.

    When we could trust the sea and the winds provided
Calm water, when the gentle South Wind sighed
And called us to the deep, my comrades crowded
Down to the beach and launched our fleet of ships.   80
We sailed from harbor, land and cities vanished.
A sacred island lies in the midst of ocean,
Dear to Aegean Neptune and the Nereids' mother.
The loyal Archer God had tied it down
From drifting round the beaches and the shores
To lofty Myconos and Gyaros,
And gave it, motionless, to be inhabited
And to despise the winds. I sailed to it.
This very placid port received us weary
But safe. We landed, worshipped Apollo's city.   90
King Anius, both king and priest of Apollo,
His temples bound with fillets and sacred laurel,
Ran up and recognized his old friend Anchises.
We joined right hands in friendship and entered his house.

    In the temple built of ancient stone I prayed:
'Thymbraean, give us our proper home, give walls
To tired men and offspring, a city abiding.
Preserve another citadel for Troy,
Spared from the Greeks and merciless Achilles.
Whom shall we follow? Where do you bid us go?   100
Where found our home? Give us your augury,
O father, and slip down into our souls.'
Scarcely had I spoken when all things seemed to tremble,
Apollo's threshold and laurel, the entire hill
Moved, the tripod roared from the opened shrine.
Bent over, we fell to earth, and we heard a voice:
'Long-suffering Dardanians, the land which first
Bore you from parent-stock will take you back
With joyful breast. Seek out your ancient mother.
This house of Aeneas will dominate all shores,   110
His children's children and those to be born from them.'

Thus Phoebus: huge joy rose from mixed tumult,
And all inquired where those walls might be
Toward which he called us wanderers to return.
Then Father, mulling over ancient stories,
Said, 'Hear me, nobles, and learn to know your hopes.
Crete, island of great Jove, lies amid the sea;
There stands Mount Ida and the cradle of our race.
The Cretans have one hundred cities, large,
With very fertile lands. It was from there,   120
If I remember rightly, that Teucer sailed,
The father of our race, to Trojan shores
And chose a place for kingship. Ilium,
The Pergamean fort, had not yet risen.
The people lived in valleys. There came from Crete
Cult-mother Cybele and all her crew
Of Corybants, bronze-clashing in the groves
Of Ida, and her worship's reverent silence,
And lions yoked to pull her chariot.
Come then, let's follow where the gods command,   130
Placate the winds, and seek the Gnosian realms.
They lie not distant; Jupiter will aid us.
The third dawn hence will place us on Cretan shores.'
He spoke, and made due offerings at the altar,
A bull to Neptune, a bull to you, Apollo,
A black sheep to Storm, a white to joyous Zephyr.
      Then Rumor flew that Idomeneus,
Leader of Crete, was driven from paternal
Shores, had left the land of Crete deserted,
Its houses empty. We sailed from Delos' harbor   140
And sped across the sea, past Naxos' ridges,
Where Bacchants play, and green Donusa Island,
Olearon, snowy Paros, Cyclades
Scattered across the water; we tacked our way
Through inlets where the tide washed many shores.
The shouting sailors competed at their tasks;
They urged each other: 'Crete! and our ancestors!'
A wind arose to blow us on our stern.
At last we glided to the ancient shores
Where dwell the Curetes. Then eagerly   150
I laid the walls of a city we had longed for.
I called it Pergamea, and my people

Were happy with this name. I urged them to
Love their hearths and raise a citadel
To guard their houses. Now almost all our ships
Were drawn upon dry shore. Our young men busy
With marriage and new fields, I spent my time
In giving laws and assigning homes. Then swiftly
A frightful plague from a poisoned tract of sky
Rotted out limbs and trees: a year of death.   160
My people lost cherished lives or dragged their sickly
Bodies about. The Dog Star burned the sterile
Fields, the grass dried up, the feeble crops
Denied us livelihood. Once more my father
Urged us to sail again to Delos and Phoebus,
To ask the oracle how our distress
Might end, and whence it might order us to find
Assistance for our trouble, and where to sail.
        It was night. Sleep held the animals of earth:
The sacred images of our Trojan gods   170
Which I had carried from Troy, from the midst of fires,
I saw before my eyes as I lay sleeping,
Clearly, in brilliant glow, where the full moon's light
Streamed through windows set into the walls.
Thus then they spoke; their words removed my fears:
'That oracle Apollo would have given
If you had sailed to Delos, here he sings it.
Look! he sends us willingly to your room.
We followed you and your arms when Troy was burned,
With you we sailed across the swollen sea.   180
And we shall raise your grandsons to the stars,
Give power to your city. Prepare great walls
For your great gods: shirk not long toil of flight.
You must change dwellings. Delian Apollo
Did not select this shore for you nor order
Your settlement in Crete.
                    There is a place—
The Greeks named it Hesperia, Western Land—
Ancient, powerful in arms and fertile soil.
Oenotrians tilled it. Report says their descendants
Have called it Italy from a folk-leader's name.   190
This is our proper home; here Dardanus
Was born, and Father Iasius, source of Trojans.

Rise up and gladly tell your aged parent
He must not doubt us; let him seek Corythus
And lands of Italy. Great Jupiter
Forbids you to remain in Mount Dicte's fields.'
Astounded at such a sight and the voice of gods
—This was no dream, I saw their faces before me,
Their hair enshrouded, their very countenances,
While cold sweat dripped from my entire body—   200
I jumped up from my bed and raised my hands
Palm-upward to the sky in prayer, I poured
Libation of unmixed wine upon the hearth.
Pleased to have done them honor, I told Anchises,
Explaining each detail as it had happened.
He recognized his twin lines of descent,
Ambiguous ancestry, for he had been
Deceived anew about these ancient places.
He said: 'My son, chief bearer of Troy's fortune,
Only Cassandra foretold such fate for me.   210
I now recall her prophecies: she cried,
"Hesperia! Italian realms for you!"
But who'd believe the Teucrians would come
To western shores? And who believed her then?
Warned by Apollo, let us yield and follow
A truer course!" He spoke: we cheered, obeyed him.
We sailed away and left behind some comrades.
In hollow hull we raced across the ocean.
        After we reached the high seas and no land
Remained in sight but only sky and sea,   220
Then overhead a black cloud burst upon me,
Bringing the night and storm and ruffled waves.
The winds beat up the ocean, raised great surges,
And we were scattered on the boiling water.
Clouds wrapped up daylight, and the rainy night
Snatched heaven from us, lightning doubled its flashes
Through clouds torn open. We were driven off
Our course and wandered blindly on the billows.
Our helmsman Palinurus said he could not
Distinguish night from day in heaven, recall   230
His route in mid-sea. Three days we were derelicts,
Three pitchblack nights without the shining stars.
At last the fourth day came, the first to open

The distant mountains to our sight and rolling
Smoke. Our sails fell, oars we seized, and quickly
We swept blue water into twisted foam.
Saved from the waves, the shore that first received me
Was of those islands the Greeks call Strophades
In the wide Ionian sea; these dread Celaeno
And other Harpies cherish, since Phineus' house   240
Was closed to them, and they in fear abandoned
The tables where they fed before. No monster
More shocking, no pest or embodied wrath of gods
More fierce than they arose from Stygian waters.
They have the face of virgins; from their bellies
Flows out the foulest discharge, and their hands
Are talon-like, their features always pallid
With hunger.
We entered the port where we were driven: look!
We saw fine cattle scattered in the fields,   250
And flocks of goats unguarded as they pastured.
We rushed on them with weapons and invited
The gods and Jove himself to share our plunder.
Then on the curving shore we set up couches
And dined upon the best of solemn banquets.
But in one sudden horrifying rush,
The Harpies swooped upon us from the mountains,
Their wings a-clatter, snatched our banquet, dirtied
Our food with filthy touch. Their cries were awful,
Their stench disgusting.
              Back into the inlet,   260
Beneath the hollow cliff closed round with trees
And hair-raising shadows, we drew our banquet tables
And lit our altar fires afresh.
              Once more,
From a different point of heaven where they had hidden,
The noisy taloned crew flapped round our food
And fouled it with their mouths. I told my comrades
To take up arms and fight these dreadful people.
No sooner said than done: they placed their swords
Concealed among the grass and hid their shields.
Then when they swooped and shrieked along the curving   270
Beach, Misenus from his high vantage place
Blew on a hollow trumpet. My men charged

To fight strange battles and befoul their blades
On these repulsive creatures of the sea.
But neither back nor feathers of the birds
Received our blows or wounds; in rapid flight
They rose to heaven, leaving our food half-eaten,
And dirty claw-prints.
                          One alone, Celaeno,
A gloomy prophet, perched on a soaring cliff
And broke into speech: 'Now is it war you offer   280
In payment for our cattle slain, our bullocks
Slaughtered, you offspring of Laomedon?
Do you bring war to drive us harmless Harpies
Out of our father's land? Hear what I say
And fix my words within your souls, predictions
Apollo heard from the Almighty Father
And told to me, the greatest of the Furies.
You sail to Italy with winds called to your aid.
You shall reach Italy, be allowed to enter its ports.
But you cannot circle with walls the city Fate gives you,   290
Until, requiting your assaults upon us,
A frightful hunger forces you to gnaw
And to devour the very tables you use!'
She spoke, and flew aloft into the woods.
My comrades' blood chilled stiff with sudden fear.
Their spirits fell; no longer with our weapons
They urged me to seek peace, but with prayers and vows,
Whether they were mere dread foul birds or goddesses.
And Father Anchises with palms outstretched from the shore
Called on the great powers and told us what honors to pay them: 300
 Gods, fend off these threats! Gods, turn aside such a fate!
And peacefully save good men.' Then he ordered the ropes
To be thrown from shore, the sheets uncoiled and eased off.
The South Winds stretched our sails; we fled through the foaming
Waves where the breeze and our helmsman called out the course.
Now in the midmost flood appeared wooded Zacynthos,
Dulichium, Same, Neritos steep with its rocks.
We fled from the cliffs of Ithaca, realm of Laertes,
Cursing the land that bore the savage Ulysses.
Soon there loomed up to view the cloud-covered summit   310
Of Mount Leucata, Apollo's temple, feared
By sailors. We made for it wearily, came to its small city.

The anchors were thrown from the prow, the ships stood on shore.
At last we had gained an unhoped-for foothold on land,
Where we washed off defilement, made prayers and burnt offerings
   to Jove,
And held Trojan games in a throng on Actium's shore.
My naked companions, their bodies slippery with oil,
Took their sport in events they had followed from ancient times,
Happy to have escaped from so many cities
Of Greece and contrived to flee from the midst of their foes.   320
Meanwhile the sun in its course rolled round a great year
And glacial winter made bitter the waves with its winds.
On some door-posts I fixed up a shield with its hollow bronze
That great Abas had worn, and I marked my deed with a verse:
'AENEAS DEDICATES THESE ARMS TAKEN FROM VICTORIOUS GREEKS.'
Then I ordered them all to leave port and to sit at the thwarts.
My comrades in rivalry struck at the sea, swept its water.
       Quickly we lost from view the towering heights
Of Phaeacia, followed the coast of Epirus, and entered
The port of Chaonia, came to the high-placed city,   330
Buthrotum. Here we heard an incredible story:
Priam's son Helenus ruled among these Greek cities,
Held the power of Pyrrhus the Aeacid, also his wife
Andromache, married once more to a man of her race.
Bewildered, I burned with a wonderful longing to speak
To the man and to learn how such things could have ever occurred.
Leaving my fleet on the shore, I walked up from the harbor,
When by chance I met Andromache making sacrifice
And setting out sacred food, sad gifts for Hector,
In a grove near the city beside a stream named Simois   340
(After the real one), calling upon his ghost
And pouring wine on his ashes in front of his tomb,
Empty of all but green turf, where as cause for her tears
She had set up twin altars.
                       When she saw me coming and round me
The Trojan weapons, quite out of her wits at the sight,
She stiffened to see such portents; the warmth left her bones;
She tottered and for a long time she could scarcely speak:
'Is the face I see real, do you bring me true message, O goddess-
Born, do you live, or if your life's light has faded,
Where is Hector?' She spoke, and poured out her tears and filled   350
All the place with her wailing. While deep hysteria gripped her,

I could barely fling in a few words, yet I babbled an answer:
'I am truly alive, though I live among all kinds of danger;
Do not doubt; you see rightly.
But what peril has seized you, cast down from so stately a marriage,
Or is it some brighter lot that comes back to you?
Hector's Andromache, are you still wife to Pyrrhus?'
She looked down and away, then spoke in a lowered voice:
'O happy alone before others, that daughter of Priam
Who was ordered to death beneath the high walls of Troy   360
Near her enemy's tomb, who suffered no slavery by lot
Nor touched as a captive the bed where her conqueror lay.
When my fatherland burned I was carried on diverse waters,
Bore children in bondage, endured the proud scorn of Achilles'
Young son, who then married Hermione, daughter of Leda,
And transferred me to Helenus, servant in keeping of servant.
But Orestes, pursued by the Furies because of his murders,
Inflamed with great love for the girl whom that Pyrrhus had stolen,
Seized him unaware by his ancestral altars and killed him.
When Pyrrhus was dead, his part of the kingdom reverted   370
To Helenus, who gave their name to Chaonian fields
And to all of Chaonia itself, from Chaon near Troy.
He added this fort to the ridge, and this Ilian citadel.
But what winds brought you here, what fates gave you access to land,
Or which of the gods drove you, ignorant, onto our shores?
Where's the boy Ascanius, alive and breathing air,
Whom you had at Troy . . . ?
Does he miss his mother, the lost, does he show any promise
That his father Aeneas, his uncle Hector, have stirred
In his heart an ancient courage, the soul of a man?'   380
As she poured out such words and wept, sobbing deeply, in vain,
The hero Helenus, son of Priam, came down
From the walls with many companions and recognized us,
Led us on in his joy to the gateway, mingled words with his tears.
I walked forward and saw 'little Troy' and its citadel
Copied after the large one, a dry river bed named Xanthus,
And the threshold of gates called Scaean which I embraced.
My Trojans enjoyed this friendly city with me.
The king took them into wide-spreading colonnades;
In the midst of the hall they dined upon golden plates   390
And made libations of wine from the cups in their hands.
Now day after day the breezes called to our sails;

The canvas was filled with a swelling South Wind. I addressed
The priest Helenus and spoke as follows: 'O Troy-born
Seer of the gods, who knows the power of Phoebus,
His tripods, his laurel of Claros, the stars, and the tongues
Of birds, and the omens that rise from their swift-borne flight,
Come, tell me—for revelation divine has spoken
Of prosperous fate for my voyage, and all the gods
With their signs have guided me onward to Italy,   400
To try unknown lands: the single disheartening token
Was given by Harpy Celaeno, who sang disaster
And prophesied gloomy anger and ominous hunger.
What perils shall I first avoid? And what shall I follow
So that I may conquer such hardships and agony?'
Here Helenus, first having slaughtered some bullocks as usual,
Prayed for peace from the gods. Then from his holy brow
He loosened the fillets and, gripped by great power, he led me
To the threshold of Phoebus and uttered inspiring words:
'Goddess-born—it is clear that you sail under highest protection,   410
As the king of the gods decides lot and fate and life's changes,
And sets all in order—I shall speak few words out of many,
So that you may safely traverse the sea and take shelter
In Italy's harbor; for the Fates prevent Helenus
From knowing more; Juno forbids him to prophesy.
To begin, that Italy you think lies near you now,
In your ignorance ready to sail to its neighboring ports,
Lies far in the distance; a path that is not a path
Divides you by stretches of land from the land that you seek.
You must first lean on oars in Sicilian waters, your ships   420
Must sail the salt water of Italy, pass by the lake
Of the underworld and the island of Aeaean Circe
Before you can build your city upon a safe soil.
I shall give you a sign: keep it hidden within your mind.
When you in your sadness shall find near the rush of a lonely
Stream a huge sow lying under the oaks on the bank
With a litter of thirty just farrowed, all white like their mother,
Round her teats, that place shall be the site of your city,
Sure respite from labors. Do not shudder at eating your tables:
Fate will find a way and Apollo will come when he's summoned.   430
But the lands that lie near and this shoreline of Italy,
The closest of regions washed by the tide of our sea,
You must fly from: its cities are peopled by hostile Greeks.

Here Locrians of Narycium founded their walls;
Lyctian Idomeneus occupied Sallentine fields.
Here is little Petelia, built by the Meliboean
Leader Philoctetes, based firm on its circling wall.
But when you've passed by them and anchored across the sea,
You shall set up an altar on shore and fulfill all your vows.
You shall cover your head with a cowl of purple cloth,   440
Lest amid sacred fires in honor of gods some unfriendly
Sight shall appear and trouble the omens of heaven.
Keep this manner of sacrifice; let your companions preserve it;
May your austere descendants abide by this sacred rite.
Now when you depart, the wind will push you to the shore
Of Sicily, the straits of Pelorus shall open to you.
Then steer for the land to port and the waters to portside,
Shun the shore and the waves far to starboard.
                                   These places, they say,
Were shaken by earthquake and torn into mighty ruins—
So much can antiquity shift with the passing of time—   450
And the sea burst between where the lands lay unbroken before.
The strength of the sea cut Italy off from Sicily;
The lands and the cities on shore were washed by a narrow
Strait: on the right Scylla blocks you, and on the left
Lies Charybdis, who three times each day from the whirlpool's depth
Sucks up a great flood and three times into the air
Spews it forth, while the waves of her gulping lash even the stars.
Scylla hides in a cavern; she thrusts out her mouths at the sea
And drags ships on rocks. The upper half of her is human,
She has the fine breasts of a girl above her waistline;   460
A monstrous whale below, she joins dolphin tails
To the bellies of wolves. You should double around Pachynus
In a roundabout way that will slow your approach. This is better
Than to look upon hideous Scylla there in her vast cavern
Even once or to hear the rocks ring with the barks of her blue
Sea-hounds. Furthermore, if Helenus has any foresight,
If a seer can be trusted, if Apollo gives truth to his soul,
Goddess-born, I repeat and repeat this word above all:
I admonish you once and for all: bow in worship to Juno's
Great power, adore her and pray to that potent mistress,   470
Overcome her with gifts so that, victor at last, you shall voyage
To Italy's border and leave Sicily behind you.
When you have come thither and reached the city of Cumae

With its underworld lakes and the whispering woods of Avernus,
You shall see a mad prophetess sitting deep in a cave
Who sings out one's fate and writes symbols and names upon leaves.
Whatever the prophecies she has inscribed upon leaves,
She sorts them in order and keeps them locked up in her cave.
They remain in their place and never fall out of their order,
Unless a slight breeze turns the door of the cave on its hinge   480
And the door shakes the delicate leaves; the prophetess never
Takes care to recover her songs and reduce them to order
As they fly through the hollow rock. Those who question the Sibyl
Go away without answers and hate the place where she lives.
Although you may think the delay too costly to linger,
And although your men murmur, call you loudly to sail your course
When a favoring wind fills the canvas, you cannot refuse
To visit the prophetess, beg for her prophecy too:
Let her sing incantations and willingly open her mouth.
She will speak of Italian people, of wars still to come,   490
And where, in what way, you may grapple with hardship or dodge it,
And when she is worshipped she'll give you a favorable route.
These are the warnings my voice is permitted to give you.
Come, hurry, and carry great Troy to the sky through your deeds!'
        After the prophet had spoken these friendly words,
He ordered gifts heavy with gold and carved ivory also
To be carried into our ships and laid down in the holds,
Huge treasure of silver and cauldrons that came from Dodona,
A breast-plate of linked chain mail triple-twilled in the weaving,
And a conical helmet all splendid with long waving crest—   500
The arms of Achilles' son as gifts for my father.
He added horses and guides,
Supplied us with oarsmen, equipped my companions with arms.
        In the meanwhile Anchises ordered our fleet to be fitted
With sails, to make no delay for a favoring breeze.
The priest of Apollo addressed him with greatest respect:
'Anchises, judged worthy of marriage with Venus the proud,
By the care of the gods twice rescued from Pergamum's ruins,
Look! the land of Ausonia before you! Seize on it with sails!
Yet you must pass by the eastern shore on this side;   510
That side far away is the one which Apollo throws open.
Go onward,' he said, 'O happy because your son
Is loyal to you. But why do I speak and delay
By my words the South Winds rising to carry you on?'

Then Andromache, sad as the moment of parting arrived,
Brought (no less) a garment embroidered with golden thread
For Ascanius, a Phrygian cloak that was equally rich
In the fruits of the loom; she loaded them on him and said:
'Take these, the tokens my hands have created for you,
My boy; let them speak of Andromache's enduring love,   520
Of Hector's wife: take the last gifts you will have from your kin,
O you who survive as the sole image of my son
Astyanax! You have his eyes, his hands, and his mouth!
And if he had lived he would be just as old as you are.'
I replied as I left her, the tears springing into my eyes:
'Live happily, you whose fortune has ended its course;
We are summoned from fate to fate, one after the other.
You have won your rest, you need furrow the sea no more,
Nor seek those Ausonian fields that keep always retreating.
You look upon Troy and the image of River Xanthus   530
Which your hands, as I hope, have made for times better than these,
Out of danger at last from attacks of the hostile Greeks.
If ever I enter the Tiber and the fields near it
And gaze upon walls god has promised my people, I shall
In the future make sister cities of yours and of mine,
Joined close to Epirus, its neighboring peoples, unite
Western land to eastern, of one fate and one founder, Dardanus;
We shall be one Troy; and let our posterity guard it!'
     We sailed out to sea past the nearby Headland of Thunder,
Those mountains whence passage to Italy is the most brief.   540
The sun set meanwhile, and the mountains were shrouded in darkness.
We landed and stretched on the longed-for breast of the earth
Near the sea, after drawing our lots at the oars; scattered out
On the dry beach, we rested our bodies; sleep stiffened our weary
Limbs; night, driven on by the hours, had not reached its midpoint
When alert Palinurus rose up from his bed to discover
Which winds blew; he listened, he noted the stars as they fell
Through the silent heavens, Arcturus, the Hyades
All rainy, the twin Bears, Orion girt round with his gold.
And after he saw that all things were at rest in the sky,   550
He gave a clear call from the stern; we broke up our camp
And moved on as we spread to the wind the wings of our sails.
Now Aurora grew pink since the stars had been put to flight,
When we saw from afar the dim hills and the low-lying shape
Of Italy. 'Italy!' shouted Achates the first,

And 'Italy!' shouted his comrades in noisy delight.
Then Father Anchises put wreaths round a great bowl of wine
And filled it unmixed and prayed to the gods above,
Standing high on the stern:
'You gods who rule over the sea and the land and the storms,   560
Bring a favoring wind for our voyage and blow us along!'
The breezes we hoped for rose quickly, the port was revealed
Even nearer, Minerva's temple showed up on the heights.
We gathered the sails and twisted the prows toward the shore.
The harbor was curved like a bow by the beat of the East Wind;
Hidden rock-shoals foamed over with the salt sea spray.
The harbor lay snug; towering cliffs sent down arms from twin walls.
The temple stood back from the shore. The first omen I saw
Were four horses who browsed in a pasture, as white as the snow.
And Father Anchises spoke: 'O strange land, you bring war.   570
These horses are armed for war, this herd threatens war.
Yet often such creatures are trained to draw chariots too
And to travel in harness without any baulking; there is
Hope for peace,' he said. We prayed to the holy powers
Of arms-clashing Pallas, the first to welcome my men,
And we veiled heads with Phrygian mantles before the altar.
We followed the urging of Helenus, his solemn request,
And to Juno the Argive we sacrificed as he desired.
No delay: when our prayers had been uttered, in immediate sequence
We swung out the yard-arms and sails to catch every breeze,   580
And we left the homes of the Greek-born, the fields we mistrusted.
Next we spied the bay of Tarentum, where Hercules anchored
(If one can believe it); Lacinian Juno's temple
Arises across from it; here stood Caulonia's fortress
And shipwrecking Scylaceum. Then far off from the sea
Trinacrian Aetna arose, and we heard the loud beat
Of the ocean a-smash on the rocks and the booming of breakers
On shore; the shoals spurted up, the tide twisted on sand.
And Father Anchises: 'I'm sure that all this is Charybdis.
Helenus told us of cliffs and of frightening rocks.   590
Get away, my men; keep together and bend to your oars.
They did as they were commanded, and first Palinurus
Pulled the screeching prow to the waters upon portside.
Then all of our company followed with oars and sail.
We were tossed to the sky on a curving mountain of water,
And next we descended the maelstrom, down, down into Hades.

Three times the cliffs roared out among hollow rocks,
Three times we saw foam dashed upward and dripping stars.
The wind left us, and the sun too. We were weary.
Adrift from our course, we coasted the Cyclopes' shore.   600
     The harbor itself was huge and sheltered from winds;
But close by it Aetna roars with frightful eruptions.
She sometimes throws out a black cloud to the upper sky,
Smoking, a whirlwind of pitch and incandescent ash.
She lifts up her balls of flame and licks at the stars.
Sometimes she belches forth crags torn out of her entrails,
And melted stone that she gathers and hurls into air
With a roar that boils up from the inmost depths of her base.
They say that the body of Enceladus, half-burned
By lightning, lies under her mass, and huge Aetna above him   610
Breathes out flames from her bursting furnace.
                                        Each time that he turns,
His tired body makes all Sicily quake; the sky
Is veiled with her smoke. All night we hid in the woods
Enduring mysterious noises whose source was unseen.
For the stars gave no fire, no light in the upper sky
Round the pole; in the murky heaven was nothing but clouds,
And the darkest night held the moon in a stormy mist.
     Now the morning arose with dawn's gleam in the distant East,
When suddenly out of the woods came forth the strange shape
Of a man spent with hunger and pitiful to our sight;   620
He extended his hands to us, pleading, near the shore.
We looked at him, heavy with dirt, a long tangled beard,
His rags held together by thorns; for the rest, he was Greek
And sent long ago against Troy with his country's troops.
When he saw that our dress was Dardanian, our weapons Trojan,
He was frightened and stood for a moment stock-still on the spot,
Then slowly came forward, next hurried headlong to the shore
And beset us with prayer and with weeping:
                                        'I swear by the stars,
By the gods in heaven, the shining air of our life,
Take me with you, O Teucrians, to whatever lands you go.   630
This will be enough. I know I was with the Greek fleet,
I admit I attacked the Trojan Penates in war.
For this, if my crime is so terrible in your sight,
Then scatter me piecemeal on ocean, plunge me in the deep.
If I die, it will please me to perish at human hands.'

As he spoke he grasped our knees and grovelled on earth,
Clinging to us. We asked him to tell who he was,
Of what family, and how fortune had treated him ill.
Father Anchises himself without any delay
Gave the young man his hand, reassured him by this friendly   640
    gesture.
At length, having laid aside fear, the stranger replied:
'I come from Ithaca, a comrade of ill-fated Ulysses,
I am called Achaemenides; Adamastus, my father, was poor
When I left him for Troy (and I wish I had never departed!).
Here my comrades forgot me while, frantic, they fled from the threshold
Of the Cyclops' cruel cavern. His home drips with gore from revolting
Banquets of men; it is huge, it is dark on the inside.
He's a giant so tall that his head strikes the stars (gods protect us
From such a foul pest!), he's repulsive to look at, to speak to.
He dines upon black blood and entrails of miserable men.   650
I saw him myself when he seized two of my companions
Within his huge hand as he lay on his back in the cave,
And smashed them on rock, then wallowed in gore he had spilled
On the threshold. I saw him devour their bodies all dripping
With dark blood; their warm limbs quivered beneath his teeth.
Yet not without vengeance: Ulysses rebelled at such horrors
And in that great danger lived up to the fame he had won.
For once Cyclops was sated with dining, lulled with wine
He laid head on breast and sprawled over the cave in his hugeness,
Belching up blood in his sleep and the morsels of food   660
All mingled with gory wine. We prayed to the powers,
Drew lots for our turn, and sprang upon him together
And bored out his eye with a long sharpened piece of wood—
That enormous eye, lurking so lonely beneath his wild forehead,
Like an Argolic shield or the shining torch of Lord Phoebus;
And at last we avenged in our joy the shades of our comrades.
But run, wretched men, run away and throw off the hawser
From shore,
For as many, as big as Polyphemus in his hollow cave
When he closes his sheep and presses the milk from their udders, 670
Are one hundred others like him who live on this shore,
Unspeakable Cyclopes wandering on the high mountains.
For the third time the horns of the moon are filling with light
While I drag out my life in the woods where the wild beasts roam
And look at the terrible Cyclopes from a high rock

And tremble to hear their voices, the tread of their feet.
The boughs give a meager living of berries and stony
Cornel cherries; I pasture on grass torn up by its roots.
Always watching the scene, this fleet was the first that I saw
Coming this way. I trusted you, whatever might happen.   680
It's enough to have fled from that horrible people. Destroy
This soul of mine with whatever ruin you wish.'
    Scarcely had he spoken when over the top of the mountain
We saw him a-move in all of his bulk through the flocks,
Polyphemus the shepherd, making his way to the beach,
A horrible monster, ungainly, huge, lacking his sight.
He steadied his steps with the trunk of a pine in his hand;
The wool-bearing sheep gathered round him, his only delight
And a solace of woe.
    After he came down to water and touched the deep waves,   690
He washed out the gore that flowed from his gouged-out eye,
Grinding his teeth in a roar, and walked out in the sea
To his waistline; not yet did the waves wet his lofty sides.
We took the stranger on board, hurried off in retreat,
(He had earned his escape), and quietly cut the rope.
We bent to the oars and, in rivalry, swept down the surface.
He heard us and twisted his steps toward the sound of our boat,
Without the power to grasp us in his right hand,
Nor able to follow by wading through Ionian waves.
He sent up a great clamor that shook all the sea and the waves   700
And frightened the inland of Italy; Aetna roared out
Through her curving caverns. The Cyclopes people rushed out
To the port from the woods and high mountains; they filled the beach.
We saw them stand helpless and glaring, the brothers of Aetna,
Lifting heads to the sky in horrible council, as when
On the top of a mountain the towering oaks or cone-bearing
Cypresses stand in Jove's deep grove or Diana's.
Sharp terror drove us headlong to shake out the sheet ropes
And stretch out our sails to the following winds in whatever
Direction. The urgings of Helenus on the contrary   710
Forbade us to sail between Scylla, Charybdis—a passage
Where on either side lay a narrow division from death.
We resolved to sail back. Look! the North Wind sent from the narrow
Headland of Pelorus arose; we were blown past the harbor
Of Pantagia with its live rock, the bay of Megara,
And low-lying Thapsus. Achaemenides, the comrade

Of ill-fated Ulysses, informed us about these shores
By which he had wandered before.
                                        There's an island lies
In front of Sicania's bay, Plemyrium the wavy:
The ancients had named it Ortygia. They tell how Alpheus,   720
A river of Elis, had forced his way under the ocean,
And now with your spring, Arethusa, has mingled his waters.
Obeying Anchises' command we worshipped the powers
That rule there, then sailed beyond Helorus' rich low-lands,
Hence skirting the projecting rocks and deep reefs of Pachynus.
Camarina loomed up, which the Fates said should never be moved,
And the plains of Gela, and Gela, called after its river
So dangerous. Acragas, lofty with walls widespread,
Showed up afar off, once breeder of high-hearted horses;
And I left you, palmy Selinus, when wind-thrust was given,   730
And skirted Lilybaean shoals, with their harsh hidden rocks.
Then the harbor of Drepanum, shores of my sorrow, received me.
Here, driven by so many storms over ocean, I lost
Anchises my father, the solace of every misfortune
And care. Here you left me, all weary with travel, behind you,
O father the best! snatched in vain from so many perils.
The seer Helenus, when he warned me of horrible dangers,
Did not speak of this grief; Celaeno the foul had not told me.
This was my last blow, this the goal of my long adventure.
I had set out from here when god drove me upon your shores."   740
    Thus Father Aeneas alone, with all eyes fixed upon him,
Recounted the fates of the gods and explained his voyage.
At length he fell silent and rested, his tale at an end.

BOOK FOUR

Dido and Aeneas

But Queen Dido long since had been nourishing deep in her veins
The wound of a love that gnawed her with hidden fire.
There recurred to her mind his great courage, the equally great
Nobility of his descent; his face and his words
Remained fixed in her breast; her concern gave no rest to her limbs.
The light of the following day was traversing the earth
While Aurora dispelled the moist shadows from out of the sky,
When, distracted, she spoke to her sister of like heart and mind:
"Anna sister, how sleeplessness frightens and worries me now!
What a stranger is this who has come as a guest to our home!   10
How he carries himself, how brave in heart and with weapons!
He is god-born: at least I believe it; my faith is not empty.
Fear shows a low character. How he was tossed by the Fates!
What wearisome wars he described! If I had not decided
Most firmly to marry no more since my first love deceived me
By dying, if I were not weary of torches and bed
As a bride, I could yield to a sinful love for this man.
I will confess, Anna, since poor Sychaeus has died
At the hands of my brother, his blood spattered there in our house,
This one man alone has shaken my senses and stricken   20
My wavering heart. I note traces of an old flame.
But I should prefer that the earth gape open and swallow
Me first or the Father All-powerful kill me with lightning,
Drive me to pale shadows of Erebus and deepest night
Before I should violate honor or break my vows.
He took love away from me, he who first joined me to him:
Let him keep it with him and preserve it within the tomb!"
So she spoke, and the stream of her tears wet her robe at the top.
       Anna said: "O sister dearer than life to me,
Must you waste your youth in loneliness and in sorrow,   30

Nor have knowledge of love's delights nor of sweet children?
Do you think that dead ashes or spirits take heed of your grief?
Granted no suitor of Libya nor, earlier, of Tyre,
Could tempt you from mourning, Iarbas the scorned or the other
Chiefs whom rich Africa cherishes with its triumphs—
Will you struggle against a love which is pleasing to you?
Have you not remembered among whose fields you dwell?
Here the Gaetulan cities, a folk unsurpassed in war,
And unbridled Numidians hem you, and perilous Syrtis;
On that side a region of desert and far-raging Barcaeans.   40
What shall I say of wars rising out of Tyre,
The threats of your brother?
Under favorable auspices, I believe, and a kindly Juno,
The Ilian keels have held their course, blown by the wind.
What a city will rise, what a kingdom, my sister—you see it,
With a husband like him! To what heights Punic glory will rise
With Teucrian comrades! Please beg the indulgence of heaven,
Make acceptable sacrifice, entertain him, keep weaving
A mesh that will hold him, while winter and stormy Orion
Rage over the sea and his ships are shattered, the weather   50
Unsuitable."
       Thus she inflamed Dido's heart with love,
Gave her hope, dispelled her shame, and resolved her doubts.
First they entered the shrine and sought the favor of heaven,
They properly sacrificed sheep well-selected to Ceres
Law-giver, to Phoebus, and also to Father Lyaeus,
To Juno before all, who preserves the ties of a marriage.
Most beautiful Dido, a winebowl held in her right hand,
Poured wine between the horns of a glistening white cow
Or walked to the reeking altars before the gods' statues
And made the day memorable with gift after gift from the flocks,   60
Gazing into their quivering entrails for signs from the gods.
Ah, ignorant minds of soothsayers! What vows can avail
For one who is mad, what altars? A gentle flame burned
Meanwhile in her marrow, a live wound lay hid in her breast.
Unhappy Dido aflame wandered over the city
In anguish, as when a deer has been struck by an arrow
Which a shepherd has shot at her while she was unaware
In the forests of Crete and, unknowing, has left the swift missile
Within her; she wanders in flight through the woods and glens
Of Dicte; the death-giving arrow clings deep in her side.   70

Now she led Aeneas among the walls of the city
And showed him Sidonian strength and Carthage arising.
She began to speak, then paused with the words half-spoken.
At the end of the day she was eager for banquets again,
Again half-mad to listen to Trojan adventures;
She implored him and hung on his words as he spoke once more.
When the guests had departed and the moon's light had faded, the stars
As they fell counselled sleep. She alone, left behind in the hall,
Lay disconsolate on his couch. She heard him and saw him,
Though absent; entranced by the image of his father,   80
She held Ascanius tight in her lap to assuage her
Inexpressible love. Her towers, begun, ceased to rise,
Her armed youth to parade, the harbor remained half-built,
The fortifications as well; work hung interrupted,
The great frowning walls and the cranes as high as the sky.
          When Juno (the dear wife of Jove) perceived Dido held
By love's tender affliction, not restraining her love to preserve
Her honor, the daughter of Saturn spoke these words to Venus:
"You and your boy are certainly winning great honor
And praise; what a power so fine and noteworthy is yours   90
To betray a lone woman with tricks—and you two of the gods!
I have noticed your fear of our walls and the mistrust you hold
For the houses of towering Carthage. How far will you go?
What is the use now of carrying strife to such lengths?
Shouldn't we rather make peace and the pledge of marriage?
You have that which you sought with all effort. Dido the lover
Is burning with passion, she has drawn it deep into her bones.
We should govern this people in common, with equal power.
Let Dido serve a Phrygian husband and give up
Her Tyrian people to your right hand as a dowry."   100
          Then Venus replied, for she sensed that Juno was speaking
Deceitfully only to turn the Italian power
Toward Libyan shores: "Who would be so mad to refuse
Such a pact or prefer to struggle at war with you?
If only good fortune may favor the deed you describe.
I cannot interpret the Fates, whether Jupiter wishes
One city made up of Tyrians and men from Troy
Or approves such race-mixture, the joining of federal bonds.
You're his wife; it is right for you to discover his thoughts.
Come, I will follow." Then Juno the queenly replied: 110
"This shall be my task. But now what our procedure should be

I'll explain in a few words: listen. Aeneas and Dido,
Poor woman, are going out hunting tomorrow at dawn,
When the Sun at his rising spreads rays over forest and earth.
While their beaters are ringing the glens with men and with nets
In their haste, I shall cover the two in a cloud mixed with hail
From above, and shatter the sky all around them with thunder.
Their companions will flee and be shrouded in darkness of night.
The Trojan leader and Dido will come to the same
Cave. I'll be there, and if I can be sure of your sanction,   *120*
I shall join them in marriage securely, proclaim it abroad.
This shall be their bridal." Then Venus of Cytherea
Nodded approval and laughed at the scheme Juno made.
　　　Meanwhile Aurora arising had left the Ocean.
Picked youths at her radiant appearance went out of the gates.
They brought wide-meshed nets and smaller path-nets and the hunting
Spears with broad blade; Massylian horsemen ran
And sturdy keen-scented hounds. The first of these waited
For Dido delaying upon the threshold; her charger
Stood pawing, resplendent in purple and gold, and quite fiercely   *130*
Champed at the bit. At last she walked out and they started,
A thickly pressed crowd. She was dressed in a Tyrian garment,
Its hem embroidered with pictures; her quiver was golden,
Her hair was bound up with gold, and gold was the breast-pin
That fastened her purple gown.
　　　　　　　　　There came up the Trojans
And happy Iulus; Aeneas, more handsome than any,
Had joined the company now as one of their comrades.
Just like Apollo when he departs from the winter
Of Lycia and flowing Xanthus, and visits his mother's
Island of Delos and starts up again there its chorus   *140*
Of dancers, and Cretan followers and Dryopeans
And tattooed Agathyrsi mingle and shout round the altars,
When Apollo himself walks along the ridges of Cynthus
And presses a wreath of soft laurel upon his blown hair,
And a crown made of gold, and his weapons ring on his shoulders—
No less briskly than he, Aeneas came on and his beauty
Shone out of his face as well.
　　　　　　　　　When they came to the lofty
Mountains and pathless tracts, look, some wild goats were driven
Down from a peak of stone; in another direction
A herd of deer scudded by huddled closely together   *150*

Through the open fields and in dusty line from the mountains.
But Ascanius, boy that he was, in the heart of the valley
Rejoiced in his mettlesome horse, first outstripping these,
Then those, at a headlong run, and he hoped to see
Among such spiritless game as this a foaming
Boar or a tawny lion descending the mountain.
  Meanwhile the sky was shaken in wild confusion;
There followed a storm with mingled rain and hail.
The Tyrian comrades and the Trojan youth,
The Dardanian grandson of Venus, ran through the fields   *160*
In fear, seeking shelter; the streams rushed down from the mountains.
The Trojan leader and Dido came to the same cave.
Primeval Earth and bride-escorting Juno
Gave signal; lightnings flashed in the upper sky,
Aware of this union; nymphs wailed from a mountain peak.
That day was the first cause of death, the first of evil.
Dido was moved by gossip or appearance
No longer, kept her love no longer secret.
She called it marriage, concealed her shame with words.
  Straightway flew Rumor through the Libyan cities,   *170*
Rumor, than which no evil flies more swiftly.
She flourishes as she flies, gains strength by mere motion.
Small at first and in fear, she soon rises to heaven,
Walks upon land and hides her head in the clouds.
Mother Earth, as the story goes, gave birth
To Rumor last of all, provoked to anger
Against the gods, a sister to Coroebus
And Enceladus, swift in feet and wings.
A frightful monster, huge, upon whose body
The feathers match in number watchful eyes   *180*
(A wondrous thing to say!) and match her tongues
And mouths and ears—she pricks them up to hear.
She flies at night through sky and land in shadow,
Shrieking, nor shuts her eyes in gentle sleep.
By day she sits on guard at peaks of roof tops
Or lofty towers and terrifies great cities.
She clings as hard to false and wicked news
As she is ready to distribute truth.
She filled the folk with gossip of various kinds,
Enjoying herself, blabbed fact and fiction too: *190*
That Aeneas, born of Trojan stock, had come,

That Dido had deigned to join herself to him,
How winter-long they dallied in soft indulgence,
Forgetful of kingdoms, seized by their low passion.
These words the foul goddess spread on the mouths of men.
Then straight to King Iarbas she twisted in her course
And spoke to him, burned his soul, heaped up his anger.

    This man was born of a Garamantian nymph
Whom Jupiter Ammon raped; he had erected
A hundred huge temples to Jove through his wide borders,   *200*
A hundred altars with holy fire kept burning
And priests to watch them always; the ground was heavy
With gore from slaughtered flocks, the thresholds garnished
With varied garlands. He was driven frantic,
Incensed with bitter rumor. Before the altar,
Among the gods' great powers he prayed to Jove
And raised his hands palm-upward as he spoke:
"All-powerful Jove, to whom the Moorish people,
Who feast on couches of embroidered cloth,
Now pour the wine of honor, do you see this?   *210*
Or do you, Father, when you hurl the lightning
Frighten us all in vain? Do those fires hidden
In clouds cause us to shudder, and the thunder
Is merely empty murmur? The woman who wandered
Among our borders, founded a modest city
By purchase, to whom we gave a beach to harrow
Under conditions of tenure, has rejected
My offer of marriage, has taken Aeneas as master
Into her realm. And Paris now, followed
By half-men, with a Phrygian bonnet tied   *220*
Beneath his chin, upon his perfumed tresses,
Masters his prey. I bring my offerings
Into your temple and cherish your name in vain."

    Speaking such words, Iarbas clung to the altar.
Jupiter heard him and turned his eyes to the walls
Of Dido's city, to lovers who had forgotten
Their better repute: then to Mercury gave these orders:
"Go, son, call the western winds and glide down on your wings
To the Dardan leader, who lingers in Tyrian Carthage
And pays no attention to cities given by Fates.   *230*
Speak to him, carry my words through the quickening air:
Not for such a sluggard did his beautiful mother make promise

Or twice save his life from the weapons of Greeks, but to be
The man who should rule an Italy pregnant with empire,
Noisy with warfare, beget from the lofty line
Of Teucer a race, and submit all the world to law.
If no glory from exploits like these can stir him to action
Nor move him to labor for praise in his own behalf,
Does a father begrudge to Ascanius Italy's towers?
What are his plans? His hopes among hostile people,   240
Ignoring Ausonian progeny, fields of Lavinium?
Let him sail! This is all I shall say, my message to him."
        He had spoken. Mercury prepared to obey this command
From on high. First he bound winged sandals of gold on his feet;
These carry him far over water or land like the wind.
Then he grasped his staff; with this he calls souls up from Orcus,
Pale things, and sends others down to sad Tartarus,
And gives sleep or takes it and closes men's eyes in death.
Using this staff he outstrips winds and flies through the clouds.
He discerns in his flight the peak and the towering sides   250
Of rugged Atlas, who shores up the sky with his summit,
Whose pine-bearing head is thickly wrapped round with black clouds
And beaten by wind and rain; snow covers his shoulders,
Streams hurry down the old man's chin, and his beard
Is shaggy and stiff with ice. Here Mercury first
Took a stand, poised on balanced wings; then he swooped toward
        the waves
Like a bird which flies round the shore and the fishy cliffs
Or low on the waters nearby. Thus the grandson of Atlas,
Cyllenian Mercury, flew between land and sky
And split the winds to Libya's sandy shore.   260
As soon as with winged feet he touched the suburbs,
He saw Aeneas laying foundations for
The citadel, building new homes. And his sword was studded
With tawny jasper, his cloak gleamed with Tyrian purple
As it fell from his shoulders, a gift that rich Dido had made him,
Weaving thin gold in the web. Straightway he assailed him:
"Are you laying tall Carthage's base, for a woman's sake
Are you building a beautiful city, forgetting your own
Kingdom and destiny? The ruler of gods,
Who turns heaven and earth with his power, has sent me to you   270
From bright Olympus, and bids me convey his commands
On the swift breeze: What are you building? With what hope

Do you wear away leisure hours in Libyan country?
If no glory from exploits like these can stir you to action
Nor move you to labor for praise in your own behalf,
Consider your growing Ascanius, the hope of your heir
Iulus, for whom the kingdom of Italy
And the Roman land are destined." So Mercury spoke,
Then departed from mortal view in the midst of his words
And vanished away from all eyes into thin air.   280
    But Aeneas, aghast at the sight, was struck dumb with fear;
His hair stood on end with horror, his voice stuck in his throat.
He burned to take flight and depart from this land of love,
Bewildered by such a great warning command of the gods.
Ah, what should he do? And how could he circumvent Dido,
Infatuate queen, with his tongue? What new preamble utter?
Now to this side his swift mind darted, divided,
Next swept to the opposite course and ranged over the field.
In his doubt this procedure seemed wiser than any other:
He called Mnestheus, Sergestus, he called upon brave Serestus,   290
And told them to ready in quiet the fleet and the crew
On the shore, to take arms, and dissemble the change in their plans.
He meanwhile, when goodhearted Dido was still without warning,
Not expecting such love to be ruined, would try to approach her
When the moment was ripest for speaking and the way clear ahead.
All joyfully followed his orders and carried them out.
    But the queen had foreseen his deceit (who can fool a lover?),
Had sensed first of all what would happen, mistrusting her present
State of affairs. Cursed Rumor came while she fretted,
To tell her the fleet was preparing, the route had been planned.   300
Helpless, she raged in her heart and ran through the whole city
Like a Bacchant disturbed as the Bacchic utensils are shaken,
When the god's name is called at triennial orgies and nightly
Mount Cithaeron shouts to her. Thus she accosted Aeneas:
    "Did you hope to deceive me, you treacherous man, and dissemble
Such a dastardly deed and depart without even a word?
Does not our love or the faith we pledged detain you?
Nor the thought that Dido will cruelly die if you leave?
Do you build a fleet in the winter and hasten to sail,
Cruel man, in the midst of the howling northern winds?   310
If you were not seeking an alien land and homes
Unknown and if ancient Troy still stood, would you
Have sailed even there through the wavy deep in your ships?

Are you running from me? By these tears and your right hand, by
(Since I have left nothing besides for me now in my grief),
Our union, our marriage attempted, if I have deserved
Any kindness from you, if ever I made you happy,
Take pity on me and my tottering house, and if any
Space is still left for my prayers, throw aside this plan.
On account of you the Libyan tribes and the nomad   320
Tyrants hate me, the Tyrians are hostile; because of
You my honor is dead and my earlier fame,
By which alone I was rising to heaven. To whom
Do you leave me, half-dead, my Guest, since that is the only
Name that remains from what was to be Husband? But why
Do I linger? Until my brother Pygmalion crushes
My walls or Iarbas the Gaetulan takes me as slave?
If at least I had borne you a child before you took flight,
If some little Aeneas should play in my halls, who could look
Like you, I should not feel trapped and deserted as well."   330
        She had spoken. He held his eyes fixed firmly on Jove's
Stern commands and struggled to hide the pain in his heart.
At last he spoke briefly: "My queen, I shall never deny
You are perfectly right when you list all the favors you've done me.
I shall never be loth to remember Elissa, as long as
My memory holds, while my breath still governs these limbs.
I shall speak to the point. I did not hope to conceal
My departure by shabby deceit (do not think that) nor ever
Pretended to be your husband or entered such bonds.
If the Fates should allow me to lead my life at my will,   340
And it were my own to settle my cares as I wished,
I should cherish Troy city and first the remnants of my loved ones.
If Priam's tall roofs remained, I should have restored
Troy's citadel after the conquest. But Grynean Apollo
Has ordered me to great Italy, to seize it according
To his Lycian prophecy: this is my love, this my country.
If Carthaginian towers, the sight of a Libyan
City detains you here, why do you resent
Our Teucrian wish to settle Ausonian lands?
It is right for us also to seek kingdoms far away.   350
The troubled vision of Father Anchises affronts me
As often as night covers earth with its misty shadows,
As often as fiery stars rise up in the sky,
To warn me in dreams; my boy Ascanius also

I think of, the injury I may do his dear self
In defrauding him of those lands that are his by fate,
Of Hesperian rule. Now Jove's messenger sent by the god
(I swear by my head and yours) brings through the swift air
Jove's order. I saw the god himself in the light
As he entered the walls, and I drank in his voice with my ears.　360
Cease to trouble me and yourself with your complaints.
Not by my will do I go to Italy."
　　　While he spoke she had kept from looking him in the face
Though her wandering eyes had examined him up and down
In silence; at last she burst into anger and said:
"No goddess gave birth to you, no Dardanian father
Begot you, unfaithful, but Caucasus rough with its rocks;
Hyrcanian tigers presented their teats to your mouth.
For why should I cloak my feelings or wait for worse wrongs?
Has he wailed as I wept? Or cast me a single glance?　　370
Has he yielded to tears or pitied me, who am his lover?
I am at a loss what to say. Now, now neither Juno
The highest nor Jupiter Father can look upon me
With impartial eyes. Faith is nowhere preserved. I received him
Cast up upon shore and destitute, crazed as I was,
And gave him a share in my kingdom, restored his fleet,
And brought back his comrades from death. I am borne by the Furies,
I burn! Now Augur Apollo, now Lycian lots,
Now the messenger god is sent from Jupiter, bringing
His dreadful commands on the air. This task the divine ones　380
Assume, evidently; this is the task that disturbs them!
I do not hold you, I do not disprove your words.
Go, seek Italy, find your kingdom with the winds
And over the waves. But I hope, if the powers are just,
You will drink up your punishment there in the midst of the rocks;
You will often call 'Dido!' From afar off I shall follow
With flames of the Furies; when cold death has taken away
The soul from your body, a shadow I'll be in all places.
You'll pay, you scoundrel, for this. I shall hear as you suffer.
The news of your pain shall come to me where the dead lie."　390
She broke off these words in the middle and hurried away,
Poor soul, and concealed herself, leaving him nervous with dread
And the wish to say much. She fainted. Slaves lifted her up,
Brought her back to her marble boudoir and put her to bed.
　　　But loyal Aeneas, although he desired to soothe

Her sorrow and drive it away with consoling words,
Groaning deeply and shaken in soul by the great love he bore her,
None the less obeyed the gods' orders and went to his fleet.
Then the Teucrians bent to their task and they launched their ships,
Tall all along the beach. The keels coated with tar   400
Were afloat; they brought barely stripped oars with leaves clinging to
    them
And beams rough-hewn from the woods in the zeal of their flight.
You could see them departing and streaming out of the city,
Like ants when they plunder a huge heap of grain and remember
The winter and store it at home. In a long black line
They move out to the fields, they carry their loot through a narrow
Path in the grass. Some push large kernels of grain,
Their shoulders braced hard. Some bring up the rear of the line
And punish the laggards. The whole path seethes with their toil.

Dido, what did you feel when you saw such a scene,   410
What sighs did you utter when widely upon the shore
You saw from the citadel's peak all the men a-stirring,
The sea-surface loud with their clamor before your eyes?
O shameless love, to what lengths do you drive human hearts!
Love forced her once more to tears, once more to entreaty,
And to humble her pride as a suppliant to her passion,
Lest she should leave something untried and thus die in vain.
    "Anna, you see them hasten around the shore;
They gather from everywhere; canvas now calls to the breeze.
The joyful sailors hang garlands upon the sterns.   420
If I was able to foresee so great a sorrow,
My sister, I can endure it. Do only this much
For miserable me. That faithless man was fond
Of you alone, he entrusted his secret thoughts
To you; you knew the time and place to approach him.
Go, sister, and humbly speak to that proud enemy.
I never conspired with Greeks at Aulis to ruin
The Trojan people, I sent no fleet against Troy
Nor dug up the ashes or spirit of Father Anchises.
Why should his harsh ears refuse to listen to me?   430
Where does he rush? Let him give the last gift to his wretched
Lover, let him wait for an easy flight and good winds.
I no longer beg for that marriage which he betrayed,
Nor wish him to give up that beautiful Latium of his

Or relinquish his realm. I wish for an idle season,
A breathing-space from the madness of his departure,
Until my fortune can teach me to grieve in defeat.
I beg for this final indulgence (O pity me, sister!),
And when he gives it, I'll pay him with interest by dying."
    So she prayed, and her grief-stricken sister carried her words   440
And her tears to Aeneas again and again. But he was
Unmoved by either nor yielded to hear her voice.
The Fates blocked his way, heaven sealed his ears, willing to listen.
As when a strong oak with its ancient timber is shaken
By north winds blowing now here on some Alpine height,
Now there, as they try to uproot it, a creaking ensues,
And its towering branches are smashed to the earth when the trunk
Is shattered; it clings to the cliffs and, as far as its peak
Ascends to heaven, its roots go as far into earth,
Thus the hero was buffeted by her constant appeals,   450
Suffered agony in his great heart; but his mind was unchanged.
Vain tears rolled down Anna's cheeks.
                      Then unhappy Dido
In fear of the Fates sought death; she was weary of looking
Upon the vault of the sky. So she hastened her plan
To leave the light of the day. As she offered her gifts
On the altar where incense was burning, she saw the libation
Turn black and the poured wine turn into loathsome blood.
She spoke of this vision to no one, not even her sister.
Besides, there was in her house a chapel of marble
Where she worshipped with singular faith the ghost of her husband,   460
Its walls hung with snowy white fleeces and bright green boughs.
From this chapel it seemed that she heard him calling to her
When night with its shadows possessed the earth; and a lonely
Owl would often complain in funereal song
From the rooftops, projecting its voice in a long lament.
Furthermore, many sayings of earlier prophets dismayed her
With terrible warning. Wild Aeneas himself in her dreams
Would drive her toward madness; yet always she seemed left alone
To walk a long road uncompanioned, to search for the Tyrians
In a land deserted. As Pentheus once saw the long lines   470
Of the Furies advancing, when two suns appeared in the sky
And Thebes was made double; or Orestes, pursued on the stage
When he flies from his mother who brandishes torches at him
And black snakes in her hands, while avenging Furies crouch down

On the threshold, so conquered by agony, seized by the Furies,
She decided to die and chose both the time and the place
In secret. With calm of hope on her face she concealed
Her plan and spoke to her sorrowing sister: "I've found
A way that will bring him to me or release me from love.
Congratulate me! At the ends of Ocean and near   480
The setting sun lies Ethiopia, farthest from us,
Where great Atlas twists on his shoulder the axis of heaven
Ablaze with its stars.
In this place a priestess of the Massylian race
Has been shown me; she keeps the temple of Hesperides
And feeds its dragon, takes care of the sacred branches
On the tree. She scatters moist honey and sleep-giving poppy.
She says she can free one's mind from care with her charms,
Whichever she wishes, but can give harsh cares to another,
Or stop the water in rivers and turn the stars back,   490
And bring up the ghosts of the night. You will see the earth
Roar under her feet and the ash trees descend from the mountains.
Dear sister, I swear by the gods and by your sweet life
That unwillingly I undertake these magical arts.
Build me an open-air pyre within our house
And place on it the armor he left hanging upon the walls
Of my bedroom, the garments he wore, and the bridal bed
Where I perished. I choose to destroy each memory
Of that unspeakable man. So the priestess advises."
She spoke and fell silent; swift pallor seized on her face.   500
Nor did Anna believe that her sister was cloaking her death
With new rites, that her mind was possessed by such madness, nor fear
That worse things might happen than even at Sychaeus' death.
Therefore she carried out orders.
        Thus the queen built her open-air pyre in the heart of the palace,
Erected of pine and huge oak split up into logs.
She hung garlands round, decorated this place with the wreaths
Of death. On the pyre she placed his clothes and the sword
He had left behind, his image upon the couch,
Not ignorant of the future. The altars stood round her.   510
The priestess, her hair flowing, invoked three hundred gods,
Erebus and Chaos and triformed Hecate, three
Faces of virgin Diana. She sprinkled some water
Supposed to be from Avernus. She gathered fresh herbs
Cut down with bronze sickles by moonlight and swelling with milk

Of black poison, and with them a love-charm ripped from the brow
Of a foal just a-borning and torn away from its mother
Before she could bite it off.
Dido beside the altar raised up her pure hands
With meal in them, one foot unsandalled, her garment unloosed,   520
And, soon to die, she swore to the gods and the stars
Which knew her fate. Then she prayed to whatever power
Is just and remembers those lovers whose pact is unequal.

    It was night. Men's weary bodies enjoyed soothing sleep
On the earth. The woods and violent seas were quiet
While constellations whirled through the midnight sky.
Every field was at rest, the herds, and the gay-feathered birds,
All the creatures that live on clear lakes or in country briars
Lay still in the silent night and were smoothing their cares
Away, and their minds had forgotten the troubles of life.   530
But the mind and the heart of unhappy Dido were not
Surrendered to sleep; her eyes and her breast received
No rest. Her cares were redoubled and, rising again,
Her love was raging, her anger flowed like the tides.
Thus still she insisted and pondered these things in her heart:
"Oh, what shall I do? Shall I suffer once more the cruel jibes
Of my former suitors, and beg for a nomad marriage
With husbands I have so often disdained before?
Shall I sail with the Trojan fleet, obey their last orders?
Were they truly pleased with the help and relief I gave them,   540
And are they grateful, do they remember my kindness?
Who, if I wished, would accept me upon his proud ship,
Unwelcome? O lost, are you stupid and do not know
Even yet the treachery of Laomedon's race?
What then? Should I go alone with these joyful sailors,
Or take my whole Tyrian retinue with me and lead
Those men whom so recently I snatched away from Tyre
To sea again, bid them hoist sail to the winds once more?
There is nothing to do but die, as you well deserve,
And remove your sorrow with steel. It was you, my sister,   550
Who gave way to my tears and thrust me into these evils,
A prey to the enemy. I was not permitted to live
Free from a marriage, without reproach, like a beast
Untouched by despair. I have not kept faith with you,
Sychaeus!" She burst her breast with laments like these.

    Aeneas, high on the stern, now determined to go,

Was enjoying his rest, his affairs all duly in order.
A phantom resembling the god appeared in his dreams,
In all things like Mercury, in voice and complexion and hair
Golden-yellow, with limbs that had the beauty of youth.   560
And it seemed to warn him: "Born of a goddess, can you
Prolong your slumber beneath such a hazard as this
Nor see what dangers surround you, mad that you are,
Nor hear the favoring breeze of the West Winds blow?
That woman is planning deceit and a dreadful crime.
Ready to die as she is, the tide of her anger
Flows back and forth. Won't you fly headlong while you can?
You will see the ocean covered with ships, and the savage
Torches will shine, the shore flame up with her fires
If Aurora shall find you lingering in these lands.   570
Come, shout 'heia!' to the sailors! Break off your delay.
A woman is always inconstant and changeable." So
Having spoken, Mercury blended with darkness of night.

        Then Aeneas in fear at the swift apparition sprang up
From his sleep and began to chivy his men:
                                        "Look alive!
All hands to the oars on the double, sit down at your thwarts!
Unfurl those sails and be quick. A god from high heaven
Is pricking us on into flight, to cut twisted ropes.
See, he does it again! We follow you, holy one
Of the gods, whoever you are, we obey your order   580
And greet you once more. Be present and help us, we pray;
O graciously bring us the stars that we need in the sky."
He spoke and from its sheath drew his shining sword
And struck the hawser with its naked blade.
One passion seized upon all; they hurried and ran,
They deserted the shore, the sea lay covered with ships.
At the oars they beat up the foam and swept the blue water.
        And now Aurora, leaving the saffron bed
Of Tithonus, scattered her first faint light upon earth.
The queen as she saw from her summit the day grow bright   590
And the fleet moving forward, its sails in an even row,
And sensed that the shore was empty, no oar in the port,
Then struck at her beautiful breast three times and four,
And cut off her golden hair. "By Jupiter! He
Will go," she said, "and deride my kingdom, a mere
Adventurer! Let them send arms, let my soldiers march
From the entire city, let others pursue him in ships!

Go, carry flames quickly, give weapons, bear down on the oars!
What am I saying? Where am I? What madness moves
My mind? Poor Dido, do impious deeds now touch you?   600
Why did you not think of them then when you offered him power?
This is the right-hand pledge of a man they say
Has carried his household gods with him, this is the man
Who bore on his shoulders a parent far gone in age!
Why did I not scatter his mangled corpse on the waves
And slaughter his comrades and place the boy Ascanius
As main dish for a banquet upon his father's table?
The result of the fight was doubtful? It might have been.
Yet whom had I to fear, on the brink of death?
I might have flung torches into their camp, I might   610
Have filled their holds with fire and destroyed both son
And father, with all their race, and myself besides.
O sun, who light up with your flames all the works of earth,
And Juno, the cause and the witness of all my sorrow,
You who are howled at as Hecate by midnight
At crossroads, and you avenging Furies and gods
Of dying Elissa, receive these offerings, turn
Your power against those men who deserve your wrath
And hear my request. If that unspeakable man
Must come to port and touch the land and if   620
The Fates of Jove demand it, and this is the goal
Firm-fixed; then, harassed by people audacious in war,
Exiled from his lands and torn away from Iulus'
Embrace, let him beg for help and see his kin dying
Unworthily, nor when he has made a shameful
Peace, let him enjoy his reign or the light
Of life: let him fall untimely and lie unburied
In the midst of the sand. I pray for this, I pour
This last word forth with my blood. Then, O Tyrians,
Exercise hate toward his race and posterity   630
And give this reward to my ashes. Let there be no
Love, no treaty between his people and ours.
Let some avenger arise from these bones of mine
To harry the Dardan settlers with fire and sword
Now or in future, whenever they grow to strength.
Let shore be opposed to shore, our waves against theirs,
Our arms against theirs; let them and their offspring fight."
       She spoke and turned her attention in every direction,
Seeking to break away as soon as she could

From the hated light. Then briefly she spoke to Barce,   640
The nurse of Sychaeus (for black ashes hid her own
Nurse in her natal earth): "Dear nurse, fetch my sister.
Tell her to hurry and sprinkle her body with river
Water, bring beasts and appointed atonement gifts.
Thus let her come, and bind your own brows with a holy
Fillet. The rites to Stygian Jove I have duly
Prepared. I shall complete them and thus put an end
To my troubles, commit to the flames the pyre which holds
The life of the Trojan." So she spoke, and the nurse
Quickened her aged step in eagerness. Dido,   650
A-tremble, insane with the monstrous plan she was making,
Turned round her blood-shot eyes while her quivering cheeks
Were flecked with red spots amidst the pallor of death
To come. She burst through the door of the inner house
And, raging, ascended the pyre, unsheathed the sword
Of Aeneas, a gift never meant for such use as this.
There, while she looked at the Ilian garments, the bed
So familiar to her, she delayed for a time in tears
And in thought; then she lay on the bed and spoke these last words:
"Sweet garments, sweet while Fates and the god allowed,   660
Receive this soul and set me free from my sorrow.
I have lived my life and accomplished that course which my fortune
Once gave. Now my great spirit will go under earth.
I founded a noble city, I saw my walls.
I avenged my husband and punished the brother who was
My enemy. Happy, alas, too happy, if only
The keels of Dardania had never touched on my shores!"
She spoke, and she kissed the bed: "I shall die unavenged,
But I *shall* die," she said; "it is good to go under the shadows
In this way, this! Let the cruel Trojan drink up   670
With his eyes this fire from the deep, and let him take with him
The ominous sight of my death."
                                        She spoke. As she was speaking
Her companions saw her hands sprinkled with foaming blood
From the sword thrust. A cry rose up to the palace roof.
Rumor raced madly throughout the stricken city.
The roofs rang out with lament, with sobs, and with women's
Wailing, the upper sky resounded with shrieks,
Not otherwise than if all Carthage were falling
Under a hostile invasion, or ancient Tyre,

The furious flames sent billowing over the rooftops   680
Of men and of gods. Her sister heard. She was frightened.
Trembling, half-dead, she ran while she scratched her cheeks
And beat on her chest, through the crowd and called out the name
Of her who was dying: "So this was it, sister? You tried to
Deceive me? This pyre, these fires and altars were readied
For this? You forsake me: of what shall I first complain?
Did you not scorn your sister, your comrade, in dying?
Would you had called me with you to share the same fate!
The same moment, the same swift steel, would have killed us both.
With these hands I even helped build your pyre, I called   690
On ancestral gods, yet when you lay down to die
I was cruelly absent! You have destroyed yourself,
My sister, and me, and your people, the Tyrian nobles,
Your city. Come, show me your wounds! I shall wash them in water
And if any breath still lingers I'll gather it up
In my mouth." So speaking, she climbed to the top of the steps
And pressed her half-dead sister close to her breast;
Sobbing, she tried to dry up the black blood with her dress.
Dido attempted to lift her eyes heavy with death;
The wound in her breast where the sword stood fixed gave a gurgle.   700
Three times she raised herself up and leaned on her elbow;
Each time she rolled back on the couch while her eyes roamed upward.
She looked for the light in the sky and groaned when she found it.
    Then Juno all-powerful, pitying Dido's deep anguish,
Her difficult death, sent Iris down from Olympus
To loosen her struggling soul from her clinging limbs.
Because she was dying a death undeserved and unnatural,
Poor pitiful woman, untimely, burned by sudden madness,
Not yet had Proserpina cut the gold lock from her head
Nor doomed her to Stygian Orcus. So Iris arose   710
Shining like dew on her saffron wings through the sky
And, trailing a thousand bright colors across the sun,
She flew down and stood by her head: "This offering to Pluto
I bear by command, and I sever you from this body."
She spoke and with right hand cut off the lock; all Dido's warmth
Fell away at once and her life withdrew to the winds.

BOOK FIVE

The Funeral Games for Anchises

Meanwhile Aeneas held his course far out
Upon the sea, unwavering, and plowed
Black billows under the North Wind. Looking back,
He saw the walls of poor Elissa, glowing
With flames. He could not guess how such a fire
Was set alight. Her great love's poignant sorrow
And bitterness, how a woman acts in madness,
Were known to Teucrian hearts: these brought forebodings.
After they reached the high seas and no land
Remained in sight but only sea and sky,   10
Then overhead a black cloud burst upon him,
Bringing the night and storm and ruffled waves.
From the high stern the helmsman Palinurus:
"Whew! why such clouds around the height of heaven?
What do you bring us, Father Neptune?" Speaking
Like this, he ordered us to make all snug and bend
Upon strong oars and set the sails aslant
To meet the wind, and spoke again as follows:
"Greathearted Aeneas, not if Jove gave his promise,
In such foul weather would I hope to reach   20
Italy. The winds have turned athwart
Our course and grumble from a blackened West.
Air thickens into clouds. We strain to move
But make no progress. Since fortune is the stronger,
Let's sail wherever she calls us. The friendly shore
Of your half-brother Eryx, Sicilian ports,
Lie not far distant, I believe, if only
I still recall the way to steer by stars
I watched before." Then loyal Aeneas answered:
"I too have seen for some time what the winds   30

82

Demand, seen you try vainly to make headway.
Turn where you wish. Is any land more welcome
Where I should like to beach my tired ships
Than that which holds for me Dardan Acestes
And Father Anchises' bones within its earth?"
When he had spoken, they made for port; a favoring
West wind swelled out their sails. The fleet was carried
Through a swift wake and finally the joyful
Crew tacked toward sands which they had seen before.

    In wonder, afar upon a mountain peak,   40
Acestes saw the friendly ships approach.
Rough-clad in Libyan bearskin, clutching spears.
His Trojan mother bore him to Crinisus,
The river god. Remembering his parents,
He wished them well on their return, and delighted,
Shared what his fields afforded, and comforted them
In weariness, with gestures of his friendship.

    Next morning when bright day had put the stars
To flight with rising Dawn, Aeneas called
His comrades in a group along the shore   50
And from a mound of earth addressed them: "Sons
Of Dardanus the great, men sprung from noble
Blood of the gods, the circle of the year
Has now swung full with its completed months
Since that time when we laid the bones and relics
Of my god-like father in earth and dedicated
His altar. Now that day, unless I err,
Is here which shall be always full of sorrow
And full of pride: for so the gods have willed.
If I were exiled in the shallow sea   60
Of northern Africa or caught upon
The sea of Argolis or in Mycenae,
I should no less fulfill these yearly vows
And solemn ceremonies in due order,
Heaping his altar with these offerings.
Now we too stand beside his bones and ashes
(By no means, so I think, without the will
And power of gods); we are blown to friendly ports.
Come, stir yourselves, and let us pay him joyful
Honor; let us ask him for winds. May he   70
Wish that each year the rites be completed in temples

Established for him in the city I found. Acestes,
True Trojan, gives two head of cattle for each of your ships.
Now invite the ancestral Penates to dine and those
Gods whom Acestes bows down to. Moreover, if Dawn
On the ninth day is lucky for mortals and covers the earth
With its rays, I shall set up for Trojans a race in swift ships,
A foot-race, a javelin-throw, light arrow contest, a match
For the man who dares slip the rough boxing glove on his hand.
Let everyone enter and strive for well-merited prizes.   80
Keep silence religiously, circle your temples with wreaths."

    So speaking, he covered his temples with myrtle, held sacred
To Venus his mother. Helymus did this, Acestes
More ripe in his years did so, and Ascanius too.
The rest of the young men followed. Aeneas went off
From the council with many a thousand and came to the mound
In the midst of a great throng of comrades. Here, making libation,
He poured, as is custom, two bowls of pure wine on the ground,
Two bowls of fresh milk, and two full of sacred blood.
He scattered bright flowers around and then uttered these words: 90
"Hail, holy parent, we greet you once more, those ashes
I rescued in vain, the spirit and shade of my father!
I was not allowed to seek out with you the borders
Of Italy, fate-given fields, or Ausonian Tiber,
Wherever it is." He had spoken, when out of the lowest
Recess of the shrine a huge slippery snake dragged itself
In seven great folds, seven coils, and embraced the tomb,
Then gently crept over the altar. Its back was blue-spotted;
The light from its scales glittered golden, as rainbows on clouds
Throw a thousand bright colors across the light of the sun.   100
Aeneas was stunned at the sight. In a long trailing movement,
It wound among bowls and smooth cups and tasted the liquids,
Then harmlessly glided again to the base of the mound,
Leaving the altar it fed on. Aeneas, more eager
Than ever, renewed the rites just begun for his father,
Uncertain to think whether it was the spirit that tended
That place or his father's attendant. He slaughtered, as proper,
Two sheep and two pigs, the same number of black-backed oxen,
And poured out the wine from the bowl and summoned the soul
Of Anchises the great and his spirit freed from Acheron.   110
His comrades, contented, brought gifts, whatever they had.
They loaded the altar and slaughtered the bullocks. In line

They set up their kettles, while some, stretched out on the grass,
Placed live coals beneath their spits and roasted the entrails.

  The day they awaited arrived. On the dawn of the ninth,
The horses of Phaethon carried them clear-lighted weather.
The fame and the name of Acestes had brought in the neighbors.
With a rollicking throng they filled up the beaches to see
The men of Aeneas; but part of them came to compete.
First, the prizes were placed in the middle before their eyes: *120*
Green crowns, sacred tripods, the palms which the victors would win;
Arms, clothing dyed purple, a great weight of silver and gold.
From the mound in the center a horn gave its sign to begin.
First event: four heavy-oared ships chosen out of the fleet,
All equally matched. Mnestheus with a lively crew
Commanded the Shark. He was soon to be an Italian
Mnestheus, from whom came the Memmii. Gyas was captain
Of the giant Chimaera, a ship like a city in size;
Dardanian youths in three rows with three banks of oars ·
Drove her forward. Sergestus, from whom came the clan of Sergius, *130*
Set sail on the Centaur; Cloanthus, from whom you Roman
Cluentii sprang, commanded the dark-blue Scylla.

  Far out on the sea, beyond the foaming shores,
Lies a rock, sometimes hidden, that's pounded by swelling tides
When winds from the Northwest cover the stars of winter.
In still weather it rises above the unruffled waves,
A haven for sea birds who love its flat top in the sun.
Here Father Aeneas set up a green goal made of leafy
Oak branches and made it a rallying point for the crews,
Where they should swing round and retrace the long course they *140*
  had made.
Each captain drew lots for his place and stood up in the stern,
Resplendent in clothing made bright with both purple and gold.
The rest of the young men were covered with poplar branches;
The oil they had rubbed on their naked shoulders was gleaming.
They sat at the thwarts, they poised their arms on the oars,
Every muscle was strained: they awaited the signal, all anxious,
Each throbbing heart drained of blood, consumed by desire
For praise. Then the trumpet blew clearly and everyone jumped
From his place without lagging. Their roar rose high in the sky.
The waters they struck when they drew back their arms turned *150*
  to foam.
As one they plowed the furrows; the whole sea yawned,

Was wrenched apart by oars and trident prows.
Not so headlong do two-horsed chariots race
Across the field nor spring from their barrier;
Not so do drivers shake the rippling reins
Of teams urged on, hang forward with their whips.
The grove resounded with spectators' cries,
The roar of those who cheered their favorites.
The beach rolled back the noise like a sounding board;
The hills around sent echo bounding back.   *160*
First Gyas raced before the others, slipped
Into the waves ahead amidst the shouting
And tumult; then Cloanthus followed him,
The better man with oars, but his pine ship
Was slow and heavy. After these there came
The Shark and Centaur side by side, attempting
To catch the leader. Now the Shark was gaining,
Now the huge Centaur had the edge. Together
At last their prows were joined and plowed salt shallows
With their long keels. And now they neared the rock   *170*
And were about to reach the goal, when Gyas,
Ahead at midpoint of the course and victor,
Cried to Menoetes, helmsman of the ship:
"Where are you going, so much off to starboard?
Steer this way, hug the shore, and graze the rocks
To port without the oars! Let others hold to
The deep!" He spoke, but fearing hidden boulders
Menoetes swung his prow toward open sea.
Then Gyas called again: "Where are you going,
Wide of the course, Menoetes? Make for the rocks!"   *180*
He looked behind and saw Cloanthus gaining
Upon his stern and keeping to the inside.
He scraped between Gyas' ship and the roaring crags
To port and suddenly passed him. Then he abandoned
The goal and rowed beyond it through quiet water.
Now monstrous anger burned the young man's bones,
His cheeks were wet with tears. Without a thought
For self-control, the safety of his comrades,
He pushed the slow Menoetes from the steep
Stern of the ship headlong into the sea,   *190*
Then took the helm himself, spurred on his men,
And turned her toward the rock. Menoetes, dripping

In his soaked garments, a man no longer young,
Came to the surface and swam until he reached
The rock and sat upon it. The Teucrians laughed
At him as he sank and rose and spouted out
The salt sea water from his choking lungs.
Here joyful hope blazed up for those behind,
Sergestus and Mnestheus, to beat the lagging
Gyas. Sergestus took the place in front   200
And neared the rock. He led by not quite all
A keel's length. At his side the Shark pressed onward.
Mnestheus, who strode in the gangway among them, exhorted
His comrades: "Now, now, rise up on your oars, companions
Of Hector, my friends whom I picked from Troy at its final
Collapse, now show us the strength and spirit you showed me
Among the Gaetulan shallows, Ionia's ocean,
And the ravenous waves of Malea. I do not desire
To be the first nor do I seek to win,
Although, oh—they will be the victors, Neptune,   210
To whom you have given that favor. Yet I am ashamed
To come in the last. At least do better than this
And keep off disgrace." They swung to the oars with tremendous
Strokes; the brazen stern was shaken beneath them.
The sea-surface sped from below. Their panting breath
Shivered their limbs and dry mouths, their sweat flowed in rivers.
Luck brought the wished-for honor to Mnestheus' crew.
For while Sergestus in fury turned prow toward the rocks
And entered the narrow dangerous space on the inside,
He grounded his ship unhappily on jutting crags,   220
Struck hard on them and smashed his oars on their peaks
Till the rammed prow hung in the air. The sailors rose
And shouted loudly about the delay, then seized
Their iron-shod pikes and boathooks with sharp points
And picked up the broken oars from the swirling sea.
But happily Mnestheus, more agile because of success,
With swift play of oars and sails set full for the wind
Made straight for the quiet sea and reached open ocean.
As a dove, when suddenly startled out of a cave
Where she lives with dear nestlings in hollows of pumice stone, 230
Flies over the fields and flutters her wings in fright
Against her shelter: soon, fallen through quiet air,
She glides on the watery way without moving swift wings;

So Mnestheus and the Shark cut water along the home stretch,
So the dash of their movement alone sent them flying ahead
To leave Sergestus struggling on the high rock
Amid the brief shallows, calling in vain for help
And trying to row with his shattered oars. Then Gyas
And his huge Chimaera came on but they fell behind,
Despoiled of their pilot. Alone at the end of the race,   240
Cloanthus remained. Mnestheus tried to overtake him
With all of his strength. Then clamor redoubled. The sailors
Urged on the pursuer, the sky resounded with shouts.
The men of Cloanthus, angered to think that they might
Not hold their advantage, were eager to barter their lives
For glory. Success nourished those who pursued: they succeeded
Because they thought they could win. Perhaps prow and prow
The race might have ended if Cloanthus had not stretched his hands
To the ocean and prayed and called upon gods with a vow:
"Gods, rulers of ocean, whose sea-surface now I skim,   250
I shall offer you gladly a shining white bull on this shore,
Held by my vow at the altar; its entrails I'll throw
To the salt sea waves, and gleaming wine I shall pour."
He spoke, and the chorus of Nereids under the sea,
The chorus of Phorcus, and the virgin Panopea heard him,
And Father Portunus pushed him on with his large hand.
More swift than a bird or an arrow, the ship fled to land
And stowed itself in the deep port. The son of Anchises
Called his men together as usual, in the loud voice
Of a herald declared Cloanthus the winner, and veiled   260
His brows with green laurel and gave to the crew of each ship
Their choice of the prizes: three bullocks with wine and a heavy
Talent of silver to carry away. To the captains
He gave special honors: a golden cloak to the victor,
Where a wealth of deep Meliboean purple ran round
In a double meander. Upon it was woven the royal
Boy Ganymede on leafy Ida a-chasing the deer
With his javelins, and shown as he panted. The eagle of Jove
Armor-bearer snatched him up within its hooked claws.
His aged attendants raised palms to the stars in vain;   270
The barking of savage watch dogs rose in the air.
To the second-place winner Aeneas presented a breastplate
Of smoothly-joined links and a three-ply weave of gold,
Which he himself had taken from dead Demoleos

Beside rapid Simois there under lofty Troy.
He gave it, a gift for a hero, a glorious protection.
His two retainers, Phegeus and Sagaris, could scarcely
Bear its great weight on their straining shoulders. But Demoleos
Had worn it once when he chased the retreating Trojans.
Third gifts he made, twin cauldrons cast from bronze,   280
Two bowls of silver rough with raised designs.
      Now all had gifts, and proud of wealth they'd won
They moved with scarlet ribbons round their heads,
When scarcely struggling free by extreme skill
From that fierce rock, oars lost and one tier lacking,
Sergestus brought his ship in without honor,
A butt of laughter.
                  As often when a snake
Is caught upon a bank beside the road,
Crushed by some slanting wheel of bronze or stricken
By stone some traveller has hurled, half-living,   290
It tries for vain escape and twists long coils,
Still vicious, bright-eyed, hissing as it lifts
Its head high, limp and helpless with the wound,
It struggles on, writhes back upon itself:
With such an oarage the ship moved tardily;
She spread her unfurled sails and came to harbor.
Aeneas gave Sergestus what he'd promised,
Relieved because the ship was safe, its sailors
Rescued: his prize a Cretan slave-girl, skillful
At handcrafts of Minerva, Pholoe   300
Her name; she suckled twins, both baby boys.
      This race concluded, loyal Aeneas hurried
Into a grassy field which curving hills
Encircled, crowned with woods, and with its valley
Providing nature's amphitheater.
There the hero, with many thousands gathered,
Sat down upon a platform in the center.
Here he invited those who wished to race
And stirred their souls with prizes. Everywhere
The Teucrians mixed with Sicanians crowded round,   310
First Nisus and Euryalus.
Euryalus, handsome in the bloom of youth,
Nisus, his loyal lover; then there followed
Diores, sprung from royal blood of Priam,

Salius the Acarnanian, and Patron,
Arcadian, his family from Tegea.
Then two Sicilians, Helymus, Panopes,
Used to the woods, comrades of old Acestes,
And many more whose fame is now obscure.
Aeneas then spoke thus among them all: 320
"Receive my words and gladly pay attention.
No one of these will leave without a prize.
Two Cretan arrows shining with smooth iron
I'll give, a double-ax inlaid with silver;
These are rewards for all. First three to finish
Shall have their heads adorned with pale green olive.
The winner shall have a horse with ornaments;
The second an Amazon quiver full of arrows
From Thrace, a baldric bright with gold around it
And buckled with a polished gem. The third man   330
Shall leave contented with this Argive helmet."
When he had said this, at a sudden signal
The runners from their places started forth
And scattered like a cloud, eyes fixed on goal.
Before them all by far ran Nisus, flashing
And swifter than the wings of wind or lightning;
Next to him but at a long interval
Salius followed; then with a space between
Came Euryalus, third.
Helymus followed him, and at his heels   340
Flew Diores, his shoulder thrusting forward
So closely that if they had raced a longer
Distance he would have crossed the finish line
A winner, or have tied.
                    Now in the home stretch
Came the weary runners, when Nisus, unlucky,
Slipped on a bit of ground where bulls were slaughtered
And their spilled blood had soaked the grass around.
Here the young victor as he reached the spot,
Already triumphing, staggered and fell
Face down in filthy slime and sacred gore.   350
Yet not forgetful of Euryalus,
His love, he rose from the slippery ground and blocked
Salius: he in turn rolled over on the
Hard-packed sand. Euryalus flashed ahead

To win first place, thanks to his friend, as if flying
Amidst applause. Helymus came in second
And Diores third. Then Salius filled the arena
Of spectators, the row of fathers watching,
With a huge shout, demanding that the honor
Unfairly snatched from him should be returned.   360
Favor protected Euryalus, and his seemly
Tears, the manhood shown in his fine body.
Diores helped by loud insistence: he
Who came in last would have no prize at all
If the first honors were returned to Salius.
Then Father Aeneas said: "Boys, all the prizes
Are yours to keep, and no one changes order.
Permit me to express my deep regret
For our innocent friend's bad luck." He spoke and gave
To Salius the huge hide of a Gaetulan lion,   370
Heavy with hair and with its gilded claws.
Here Nisus said: "If so great are the prizes
Won by the losers, and you're sorry for
The ones who tumbled, what gift do I deserve?
I would have won first prize and praise if fortune
Had not been cruel to me, as she was to Salius."
And as he spoke he showed his face, all dirty,
And his unsightly legs wet with the mire.
The best of fathers smiled at him and ordered
A shield be given him, made by the art   380
Of Didymaon, stolen by the Greeks
From Neptune's sacred temple doorpost; this he
Gave to the fine young man, a fine gift too.
        Now when the race was done, the gifts were given:
"If anyone has courage and the heart
Within his breast to try, let him come forward
And lift his arms with boxing gloves tied on them."
He spoke and showed twin prizes for the fight:
For winner, a bull enwreathed with gold and ribbons;
A sword and shining helmet for the loser   390
As consolation. No delay: then Dares,
A man of massive strength, arose, came forward
Amid a mighty shouting. He alone had
Been accustomed to contend with Paris
Beside the very tomb where lay great Hector.

He struck Butes the champion, huge of body,
Who claimed Bebrycian Amycus as ancestor,
And stretched him lifeless on the tawny sand.
Such was Dares, who lifted high his head
For the first match and showed his brawny shoulders,   400
Thrust out his arms alternately and beat
The air with shadow-boxing.
                                        Now he needed
A challenger. No man from such a crowd
Dared meet him or put on the boxing gloves.
So, thinking all had withdrawn from the contest,
He swaggered up to Aeneas and without
Demur grasped with his left hand the bull's horn
And spoke: "If no one, goddess-born, now dares
To trust himself to fight me, where's the end
Of this delay? How long should I wait here?   410
Tell me to take the prize." The Trojans all
Shouted approval, said he should take the prize.
        Now grave Acestes scolded his neighbor Entellus
Who lay upon a bed of fresh green grass:
"Entellus, once the bravest of our heroes
(But vainly), will you let the prize be taken
So meekly from your grasp without a fight?
Where now is Eryx, that god vainly called
Our boxing teacher? Where your fame that spread
Through all of Sicily, those spoils of yours   420
That hung within your house?" Entellus replied:
"My love of praise and glory does not yield
To fear; it is the slowness of old age
That chills my blood and my worn body's power.
If I had that which once I had, in which
This braggart trusts, if I had now that youth
He still has, I would fight without a prize,
A handsome bull; I would not wait for gifts."
He spoke and threw into their midst the heavy
Twin boxing gloves which expert Eryx used   430
To bind upon his arms with their rough leather
When he went out to fight. Their minds were stunned
To see those seven huge oxhides stiff with strips
Of lead and iron sewn upon their surface.
Dares himself above all was bewildered

And hung back in refusal while great-hearted
Aeneas tested their weight and endless thongs
This way and that. The elder fighter spoke:
"Ah, what if you had seen these gloves, the arms
Of Hercules himself, and on this shore   440
His fearful fight? It was your brother Eryx
Who wore these gloves (you see them smeared with blood
And bits of brains). With these he faced the doughty
Grandson of Alceus; I used to wear them too
While richer blood gave strength, while jealous age
Had not yet scattered grey upon both temples.
But if the Trojan Dares rejects these weapons,
And loyal Aeneas approves, and so does Acestes,
Let us be equal fighters. I'll take off
The hides of Eryx (do not be afraid),   450
And you, take off the Trojan boxing gloves."
So speaking, he removed his double cloak
And stripped his mighty limbs and bones and arms
To stand immense among them on the sand.
Anchises' son then brought out matching gloves
And fitted equal weapons on their fists.
Each stood on tiptoe suddenly and stretched
His arms up fearlessly to upper air.
They drew their heads, held high, far back from blows,
And glove to glove they sparred to start the fight.   460
Dares was better at foot work and trusted his youth;
Entellus was strong in his limbs and weight, but slow
In the trembling knees, with labored breath that shook
His tremendous members. They struck deadly blows at each other
In vain and pounded their rib-cages, chests, till they rang.
Often their fists went wandering round ears and temples;
Their jaws kept clattering under harsh punishment.
Heavy Entellus stood still in the same spot, straining,
Escaping the blows by alertly shifting his body.
Dares, like one who attacks a high-placed city   470
With siege-machines or camps round a mountain fortress,
Tried this, now that approach, used all his tricks
Skillfully, yet in a vain assault. Entellus
Feinted his right, high up, but Dares saw it
Coming above and dodged with swift-moving body.
Entellus wasted his strength on the air, lost balance,

And heavily struck the earth with his heavy frame,
As sometimes a hollow pine tree on Erymanthus
Or great Ida comes down when its roots are torn from the soil.
The Teucrians, the Sicilian young men, sprang up   480
In their eagerness, shouting arose to heaven, and first
Acestes ran up and anxiously lifted his friend
And age-fellow from the ground. But the hero, not frightened
Nor slowed by his fall, went more eagerly back to the fight.
His anger gave strength, and shame set fire to force.
His conscious courage drove Dares headlong across
The entire plain, now pummelling with his right hand,
Now with his left. No rest, no pause: as clouds
Heavy with hail rattle down upon rooftops, Entellus
With right after left battered Dares and spun him around.   490
Then Father Aeneas no longer allowed the fierce winner
To rage in cruel spirit; he put an end to the fight
And saved weary Dares; he spoke to him soothing words:
"Unhappy man, what great madness has seized your mind?
Don't you see strength has shifted, the gods change their sides and oppose?
Yield to the god." He gave the command to stop.
The faithful companions of Dares dragged him along,
His knees buckling under him, his head drooping to either side
As he spat out blood clots and teeth mingled with the blood.
They led him down to the ships and, when called, they returned   500
To receive the sword and the helmet; they relinquished the prize
And the bull to Entellus. The victor, exulting in heart,
And proud with his bull, said, "Goddess-born and you Teucrians,
Acknowledge the force I had when my body was young,
And the death from which you have called back Dares and saved him."
He spoke, took a stand in front of the bull nearby,
His prize for the fight, and poising his gloves, drew back;
Then he swung down his right in the middle between the horns
From above and, crushing the bone, dashed out its brains
And stretched it, trembling and lifeless, upon the earth.   510
Above it, he poured out words like these from his breast:
"This better soul instead of the death of Dares
I offer you, Eryx. Here, victor, I lay down my gloves
And my boxing career."
                Aeneas, immediately calling
For men to join in an archery match, offered prizes
And with his large hand set up a mast from Serestus'

Ship. He suspended a swift dove tied to the mast
By a cord passed around its body at which they might shoot.
The men came together, the helmet of bronze took the lot
That was to be cast. The first bowman was Hippocoon,   520
The son of Hyrtacus, who came forth amid favoring clamor.
Mnestheus, who won the boat race, came next, a Mnestheus
Crowned with green olive; the third, Eurytion, your brother,
O most famous Pandarus, who once broke the truce when Minerva
Gave orders and first shot an arrow amongst the Greeks.
The last lot remained in the helmet—the lot of Acestes,
Who dared with his hand to try the sport of young men.
Then each bent his curving bow with all of his strength;
They took out their arrows from quivers, and first through the sky
The arrow of Hyrtacus cut the swift breezes and twanged   530
Its bowstring: it reached and sank into the tree-like mast.
The mast shook, the frightened bird on it fluttered its wings,
And everything rang with a huge applause. Then sharp Mnestheus
Stood up with drawn bow, aimed upward, and sighted with eyes
And arrow together. The poor man did not succeed
In hitting the bird; but he cut the linen cord
That bound it to hang by its leg from the lofty mast.
The bird flew away on the south wind into black clouds.
Then holding his arrow long against the drawn bow,
Eurytion prayed to his brother and aimed at the dove,   540
Now beating its wings with delight in the open sky
Beneath a black cloud: he shot and pierced the bird.
Dying, it fell and left its life in the stars
While it brought back to earth the arrow fixed in its body.
The prize now lost, Acestes remained alone.
He nevertheless shot an arrow into the air
Just to show his skill, old man, with the twanging bow.
Here to their eyes was suddenly shown a sign
(A later event was to prove its great augury true,
Though the terrified seers sang out their omens too late).   550
For, flying among the bright clouds, the arrow flamed up,
Defining its path with fire, and then growing dim,
Was consumed on the winds, as often the falling stars
Pass over the heavens and leave their trail behind.
Sicilians, Teucrians stood in astonishment, prayed
To the gods, nor did greatest Aeneas deny it an omen
But embraced the joyful Acestes, weighed him down with gifts,

And spoke: "Take them, father; the great king of Olympus has wished
By such signs that you should draw a particular prize:
You shall have this gift of the aged Anchises himself,   560
A bowl engraved with figures, which Thracian Cisseus
Gave to my father in memory and pledge of his love."
So speaking he bound his temples with fresh-growing laurel
And called Acestes first victor before them all.
Nor did good Eurytion envy the honor preferred,
Although he alone had knocked down the bird from the sky.
The next to win gifts was the man who had cut the cord;
The last was he who had struck the mast with his arrow.

    But before the match had been finished, Father Aeneas
Called Epytides, the guard and comrade of young   570
Iulus, to him and spoke to his faithful ear:
"Go tell Ascanius, if now his squadron of boys
Is prepared and the ranks of their horses already lined up,
To lead on his bands for his grandfather, show himself in arms."
Aeneas himself gave orders that all the people
Who filled the space around him should fall back and leave
The fields in the oval arena free for the game.
The boys advanced in an even alignment before
The eyes of their fathers, they shone upon bridled horses;
The young men of Troy and of Sicily marvelled and cheered them. 580
All of them wore by custom trim wreaths on their hair;
They carried two spears of cornel-wood tipped with iron.
Some wore a light quiver on shoulder; a flexible chain
Of twisted gold circled each neck at the top of their chests.
Three bands of horsemen there were, and each had three leaders
Who rode back and forth. Twice six boys followed each leader,
Shining in a line divided among twelve troop-leaders.
One troop of happy young men was led by little Priam,
Named after his grandfather, your noble son, Polites,
Destined to increase the Italians with his descendants.   590
He rode a piebald Thracian horse with white spots
Who lifted on high his white pasterns and his white forehead.
The second troop had as its leader a small boy named Atys,
From whom were to come the Latin Atians, a boy
Beloved by the boy Iulus; the last and most handsome
Of all was Iulus, who rode a Sidonian charger
Which beautiful Dido had given in memory and pledge
Of her love. The remaining young men were carried on horses

Sicilian-bred, provided by the elder Acestes.

  They nervously took their applause; the Dardanian folk   600
Rejoiced as they gazed, and discerned in those youthful faces
A family resemblance to ancestors long since gone.
When they had paraded past all, including relations,
Epytides shouted from far off his loud command
To the horses prepared for the signal, and then cracked his whip.
They wheeled in their equal divisions to right and to left.
By drawing their groups off they parted the columns, three leaders
Now on each side; at a signal converted their pattern
And charged with their spears at the ready; then countermarching,
Confronted each other with rank facing rank across space,   610
Intersecting their circling movements with new evolutions.
They stirred up pretense of armed combat, now turned in retreat,
Now levelled their spear-points for battle, then made peace again.
As once, it is told, the Labyrinth in high-mountained Crete
Had a pathway sent weaving between interlacing walls
With no openings, thousands of passages built in a maze
Where unsolvable error would not allow a return
But baffled the man who sought for clues he might follow,
In just such a course the Teucrian boys wove their movements,
Mock-flight and mock-battle, like dolphins detected at play   620
As they swim through the waves of Carpathian and Libyan oceans.
While he was encircling Alba Longa with walls,
This manner of riding, this contest, Ascanius first
Revived and taught the old Latins to celebrate,
Just as, when a boy, he had done with the Trojan youths.
The Albans then taught their own boys, and Rome at her greatest
Took over the sport and preserved it in ancestral honor.
To this day the boy's game is called "Troy" and their marching "Trojan."

Thus far with the games in honor of blameless Anchises.

  Here fickle Fortune first changed her faith—for the worse.   630
While the solemn rites at the tomb were paid by these games,
Saturnian Juno sent Iris down from the sky
To the Trojan fleet, and blew her a wind on the way.
She was busy with plots, her old sorrow was not yet assuaged.
Iris hastened to fly through the thousand colors
That make up the rainbow, and no one saw as she flew.
She looked down at the crowd and, traversing the shore, she saw

The haven deserted, the ships left unguarded behind.
But far off, apart in a lonely spot on the beach,
The Trojan women were weeping for dead Anchises,   640
And all of them looked at the ocean depths as they wept.
"Alas for the weary, that so much water to cross,
So much sea-bottom remains," was their single cry.
Disgusted with ocean travel, they prayed for a city.
So Iris into their midst flung herself, an expert
At mischief, and, laying her goddess-appearance aside,
Became Beroe, the old wife of Tmarian Doryclus,
Who once had a family, a famous name, and sons;
In this disguise she joined the Dardanian mothers:
"O pitiful women, whom hands of the Greeks did not drag   650
From the war to your death beneath your ancestral walls!
O unhappy people, for what fate does Fortune preserve you?
The seventh summer now ends since the sack of Troy,
Since we have been carried through seas and all lands, and so many
Rocks we have grazed and sailed under so many stars,
While we sought for an Italy fleeing us over the ocean,
While we were tossed on the waves. This land belongs to our brother
Eryx, our host is Acestes; and who will prevent us
From building our walls and giving our people a city?
O fatherland, household gods snatched in vain from the foe,   660
Shall Troy be said to have no walls any longer?
Shall I never see Hector's rivers, the Xanthus and Simois?
Why don't you go down with me, burn those unlucky ships?
I dreamed in my sleep that Cassandra's ghost had appeared
To give me a burning torch: 'Look here for your Troy,
Here is your home,' she said. It is time to act.
We must not delay with portents so great. See the four
Altars to Neptune! The god himself gives us torches
And courage." She spoke and herself was the first to snatch up
The ravening flame, shake it high in her right hand, and throw.   670
The minds of the women were stirred, their hearts were bewildered.
Then one of the crowd, the eldest, named Pyrgo, royal nurse
To so many sons of Priam, said: "This is not Beroe,
No woman of Rhoeteum, mothers, nor wife of Doryclus.
Look at the signs of her beauty divine, her bright eyes!
What spirit, what face, what a sound in her voice, how she walks!
I left Beroe a short while ago, ill, protesting
That she should alone miss the games and Anchises' honors."
These words she spoke.

But the mothers at first were uncertain; they spitefully looked   680
At the ships, torn between their wretched love for the land
Where they were and a kingdom that called them with voice of the Fates,
When the goddess arose through the sky upon balanced wings
And in flight cut a mighty arc underneath the clouds.
Then, astonished at such a sign and driven by madness,
They shouted, seized fire from hearths in adjoining houses.
Some plundered the altars and threw together both branches
With leafage and torches. Vulcan, the god of the fire,
Raged without bridle through thwarts, oars, and painted pine-sterns.
Eumelus brought the news of the burning ships   690
To Anchises' tomb, to the wedge-like tiers of spectators.
They looked back to see the ashes fly up in black clouds.
First Ascanius, just as he led the cavalry troops
In his joy, now in eagerness raced to the excited camp.
His breathless attendants were unable to hold him back.
"What new madness is this? Where now, where are you aiming,
You miserable citizens? No enemy, no hostile camp
Of the Argives it is that you're burning! You're burning your hopes!
Look, I am your own Ascanius." Then he threw down
At their feet the helmet, now empty, he wore when he urged   700
His boys in sham-battle. Aeneas rushed up at the moment
With the Trojans. The women fled hither and there on the shore
In their fear and sought refuge in woods or in hollow rocks.
They were ashamed of their deed, of the light; once again
Themselves, they recognized friends, and Juno was stricken
Out of their breasts. But the flames and the fire did not
Reduce their indomitable force. Beneath the damp oak
The caulking still burned as the slow smoke gushed and the smouldering
Heat ate the hulls, and destruction came down on all timbers.
Useless the strength of the heroes, the water they poured.   710
Then loyal Aeneas tore the gown from his shoulders and prayed
To the gods for their aid as he raised his palms in the air:
"All-powerful Jupiter, if you do not yet hate the Trojans
To the last man, if your ancient mercy still spares us,
Grant now that the fleet may be saved from the flames, O father,
And snatch from destruction our slender possessions, or else,
If I must receive it, bring death by your lightning bolt
On what is now left to us, dash me down with your right hand."
He had scarcely spoken when a black storm of unusual
Fury poured down its torrent; the heights and the plains   720
Shook with its thunder. From out of the entire sky

The murky rain, deepest black beneath heavy south winds,
Filled the boats, the half-burned timbers were soaked until
The fire was quenched, and all except four ships were saved.
     But Father Aeneas, struck down by this bitter disaster,
Turned here, now there the grievous cares of his breast,
His mind undecided whether, forgetting the fates,
He should settle in Sicily or make for Italian shores.
Then elder Nautes, the one man Tritonian Pallas
Had taught her great art and made him distinguished in it   730
(For through it he prophesied that which the gods' huge anger
Portended or whatever sequence the fates demanded
For coming events), consoled Aeneas with this:
"Goddess-born, let us go whither Fates draw, and draw us again;
Whatever shall happen, misfortune is conquered by patience.
There is Dardanian Acestes, sprung from the gods.
Take him as ally in your planning; he will not refuse you.
Turn over to him the survivors of ships that are lost
And those who are sick of your great adventure, of sharing
Your fortunes, the old men, the mothers weary of water,   740
Weak, fearful of danger, and let them have walls in this land.
They shall call their city Acesta, when Acestes allows it."
Then, stirred by this speech from his elderly friend, Aeneas'
Mind was divided among all his various cares.
And black night on high in her chariot held to the Pole.
The image of Father Anchises was seen to descend
From the sky and to speak in sudden words such as these:
"My son, one more dear than my life, when life still remained
To me, my son now harassed by Ilian fates,
I come here at Jove's command, who drove off the fire   750
From the ships and showed pity at last from the lofty sky.
Obey the wisest advice which the elderly Nautes
Now gives; lead picked youths, bravest of hearts, to Italy.
In Latium you must fight off a people both hard and rough
In their way of life. But first you must go to the home
Of Dis, down below, and then meet me in deepest Avernus.
For godless Tartarus, abode of the sorrowing shades,
Does not hold me; I dwell in Elysium and share the mild councils
Of those who are just. The chaste Sibyl will lead you there
When you in your sacrifice shed much blood of black cattle.   760
Then you will learn about all of your race and the walls
Which will be given you: now farewell; misty night

Turns back in her midmost course, and the savage East Wind
Has loosed upon me the panting breath of his horses."
He spoke and fled off like thin smoke into the air.
Aeneas cried: "Where do you rush, where hasten headlong?
Whom do you fly from? Who bars you from my embrace?"
As he spoke he stirred up the ashes and slumbering fire;
In suppliant fashion he worshipped with sacred meal
And abundant incense the Lares of Pergamum at   770
The shrine of the grey-haired Vesta.
                              At once he called to him
His comrades, but first Acestes, and told him the orders
Of Jove and the warning his dear father gave, the decision
His own mind had reached. There was no delay at the planning
Nor did Acestes refuse to obey. They transferred the
Mothers and others of like mind from the rolls, and those spirits
Who stood in no need of great praise. They renewed rowers' benches,
Restoring the timbers half-burned in the flames, and then fitted
Their ships with oars and with ropes for a crew small in numbers
But lively with courage for war. In the meanwhile, Aeneas   780
Had marked out the city by plowing and cast lots for their houses.
He ordered this place to be called Ilium and these environs
Troy. Trojan Acestes rejoiced in his realm and proclaimed
A court and gave laws to the fathers when they were assembled.
Then was founded a shrine to Idalian Venus on Mount Eryx,
Close up to the stars; a priest for Anchises was added
To tend his tomb and a sacred grove spreading widely.

     Now for nine days all the people feasted, paid honors
At altars; when placid winds had calmed the sea-surface,
The South Wind rose steadily, calling them back to the deep.   790
A great wailing rose along the curving beach.
Embracing each other, they lingered a night and a day.
Now even the mothers, and those men to whom once the sea
Had appeared so unpleasant, a name they could scarcely bear,
Wished to go and endure all the labor of sailing again.
Good Aeneas consoled these people with friendly words,
And, weeping, commended them to his relation Acestes.
Then he ordered three calves and a lamb to be slaughtered to Eryx
And to the Tempests, to cast off the hawsers in order.
He wound round his head some leaves clipped from the olive,   800
Stood high on the prow with a bowl in his hand, threw the entrails
Into the salt sea waves and poured glistening wine.

A favoring wind blew up at the stern as they sailed.
The comrades in rivalry struck at the sea, swept its water.
But Venus meanwhile, disturbed by her cares, spoke to Neptune
And poured such complaints as these from her inmost heart:
"The deep wrath of Juno, her unassuaged sorrow, compel me,
O Neptune, to stoop to all kinds of beseeching before you;
For neither long days nor any loyalty shown her
Can soften her, nor Jove's command nor the Fates subdue her.   810
It is not enough that by her foul hatred she swallows
The Phrygian city from out of the midst of its people
And brings ruin on all of them; she pursues what is left,
Both ashes and bones of the city destroyed: let her tell us,
If she knows, what may be the cause of such wrath. You are witness
What sudden great storm she loosed over me in Libyan waters
Just recently; she mixed all ocean with sky, though she vainly
Relied on the tempests of Aeolus; such was her boldness
In your very kingdom.
Look! she has even egged on Trojan mothers to crime   820
And shamefully burned our ships, and when they were lost,
Forced us to leave our allies in an unknown land.
For the rest, I pray that you give us fair sailing, allow us
To reach the Laurentian Tiber, if what I ask was given
By former agreement, if those walls were granted by Fates."
Then Saturnian Neptune, the master of ocean, replied:
"It is quite right, Cytherea, for you to entrust
Yourself to my kingdom, for you once arose from the sea.
I have deserved your trust also; I often repressed
The mighty madness and fury of water and sky.   830
Not less upon earth (I call Xanthus, Simois to witness)
Is my care for Aeneas, your son. When Achilles was driving
The Trojan lines, weary of battle, against their own walls
And gave many thousands to death, and the groaning rivers
Were filled with the dead, and Xanthus could not discover
A way to the sea, then I snatched Aeneas from combat
With the brave son of Peleus, unequal in strength and the aid
Of the gods, though I wished to root up from their very foundations
The walls of a perjured Troy that were built by my hands.
My mind is unchanged now within me; dispel your fear.   840
He will enter in safety that port of Avernus you hope for.
There will be one man you will seek in the whirlpool of ocean,
Only one loss: one man shall be given for many."

With these words he soothed the heart of the goddess to gladness.
Then Father Neptune yoked up with a collar of gold
His fierce horses and placed the bits in their foaming mouths
And allowed all the reins to flow loosely under his hands.
In his sea-blue chariot he flew lightly over the surface;
The waves settled down, the swollen plain was made smoother
Beneath his thundering wheels; the clouds fled from vast heaven.   850
Then various forms of companions appeared, great sea monsters,
The elder chorus of Glaucon, Ino's son Palaemon,
Swift Tritons and all the army of Phorcus; the nymph Thetis
Came on his left, and Melite and virgin Panopea,
Nisaee, Spio, Thalia, and Cymodoce.
Then sweet joys by turn tried the tense mind of Father Aeneas.
He ordered the masts to be lifted, sails stretched on the yardarms.
All ships worked the sheets together, now loosened the left,
And together the right sail, then twisted the yards back and forth.
The winds blew each ship. And first before all, Palinurus   860
Was guiding the close-sailing line, while the others as ordered
Moved after him. Now misty night had almost touched her goal
In the middle of heaven (the sailors, stretched out on hard benches,
Had loosened their limbs in repose beneath the oars),
When soft Sleep glided down from the stars of the topmost sky,
Dispelled the dark air and scattered the shadows in search
Of you, Palinurus, and brought you sad dreams, undeserving.
The god settled down on the lofty stern in the likeness
Of Phorbas and poured out these utterances from his mouth:
"Son of Iasius, Palinurus, the sea-surface itself   870
Is bearing the fleet; the winds blow evenly; time
Is given for rest. Lay your head down and steal from their labor
Your eyes that are weary. I'll take over the helm in your place."
Scarcely raising his eyes Palinurus replied: "Do you ask me
To forget the face of the quiet sea and the waves,
To trust this treacherous monster? Shall I trust Aeneas
To winds that deceive, when I have been tricked on so many
A voyage by skies that were clear?" He spoke and clutched tightly
The rudder, and never released it, his eyes on the stars.
Look! the god took a branch that was dripping with Lethaean dew   880
And a power for sleep the Styx river gave; then he shook it
On the temples of Palinurus, although he resisted,
And brought slumber upon his eyes as they swam.
                                        He had scarcely

Relaxed his limbs in an unthought-of rest when above him
The Sleep-god bent down and threw him over the side
Into shining water, still holding the tiller and part of
The stern itself. He fell headlong, calling in vain
To his comrades again and again. Then the god flew off
Into thin air, soaring lightly. The fleet sailed on,
No less safe than before, without fear, under Neptune's promise.   890
And now they approached the cliffs of the Sirens, once frightful
And strewn with the white bones of sailors. Just then there resounded
The smashing of waves on harsh rocks from a great way off,
And Father Aeneas discovered his helmsman was missing,
The boat sailing aimlessly. He guided her through the dark water,
Groaning, soul-stricken at what had become of his friend:
"O Palinurus, who trusted too much in clear sky and ocean,
You shall lie unburied somewhere on an unknown shore."

BOOK SIX

The Underworld

He wept as he spoke and commanded his fleet to sail.
At last he glided to shore at Euboean Cumae.
They turned the prows from the sea toward the beach and then
The anchor secured the ships with tenacious teeth.
The sterns curved along the shore like a garment's fringe.
An ardent band of young men darted down
The Hesperian shore; some sought the seeds of flame
Hidden in veins of flint, some scoured the dense
Haunts of wild beasts or showed others the streams they had found.
But loyal Aeneas went up to the heights where Apollo   10
Presides, and, farther away, to the retreat of the Sibyl,
That dreadful witch, in her monstrous cave, whom the Delian
Prophet has breathed on with mind and spirit and opened
The future to her. Now they entered the grove of Diana,
The cross-roads goddess, her golden temple.
                                        The story
Has it that Daedalus, fleeing the kingdom of Minos,
Had dared to entrust himself upon swift-moving wings
In heaven, had travelled an unaccustomed route
To the chilly North, and at last he stood lightly upon
The Chalcidian citadel. Restored to earth, he bequeathed   20
His oarage of wings to you, Phoebus, and built a huge temple.
The death of Androgeos was carved on one door; then the Athenians
Ordered to pay the penalty each seven years
Of the lives of their children; the vase stands with the lots drawn.
On the opposite door the Cnossian land risen up
From the sea made the picture complete. Here the cruel love
Of the bull, the secret mating of Pasiphaë,
Their revolting offspring, the two-formed child Minotaur,
Was carven, memorial of unnatural lust.

Here too was that house so laboriously built, the wandering   30
Error no man could solve; but Daedalus, full
Of compassion for that great love of Ariadne, revealed them,
The snares and the windings, guided the stumbling steps
Of Theseus by paying out thread. You also would have
Had your great share in a work so great if his sorrow,
Icarus, could have permitted him. Two times
He tried to sketch out in gold the mishap you suffered,
And twice did his father's hands fall down at the task.

They would have examined everything with their eyes
If Achates, sent on ahead, had not then arrived   40
With Deiphobe, daughter of Glaucus, the priestess of Phoebus,
And Hecate too, who spoke these words to the king:
"There is no need, no time, to be looking at pictures;
Now kill seven bulls untouched by the yoke and the same
Number of chosen sheep as our custom demands."
So she spoke to Aeneas (the men did not lag at the rites
They were ordered to pay); then the priestess summoned the Trojans
Into the lofty temple.
                        The huge side of Euboean
Rock was hewn out as a cave, where a hundred broad paths
Led on and a hundred doors whence as many voices,   50
The Sibyl's responses, roared forth. They had reached the threshold
When the virgin cried out: "It is time to beseech the Fates.
Look! the god, the god!" As she spoke, there before the entrance
Her face and her color grew different, the hair on her head
Fell uncombed; her breast with sighs and her heart with rage
Were swollen, she seemed much greater than mortal in size
And sound, since the breath of power was loosed upon her
By the god who stood closer to her: "Do you fail to hasten
Your vows and your prayers, Aeneas the Trojan?" she said.
"The doors of this mighty house will not open for you   60
Before." She spoke and fell silent. A tremor of chill
Ran through the hard bones of the Trojans; the king from the depths
Of his breast poured out prayers:
                                  "O Phoebus, who pitied the heavy
Sorrows of Troy, who directed the weapons of Paris
Into Achilles' body, with you as my leader
I entered so many oceans and lands that lay near them,
The home of the Massyli hidden away, and the plowlands

That border the Syrtes. Now, fleeing, at last we have reached
The boundaries of Italy. May the bad fortune of Troy
Follow me thus far, no farther. O all gods and goddesses,   70
It is right you should spare the people of Pergamum now,
You gods by whom Ilium and the soaring glory
Of Troy have been hampered. And you, most holy priestess,
Knowing the future, allow me (I ask for a kingdom
Not unallotted by Fates) to settle the Teucrians
In Latium, my wandering divinities, the harassed powers
Of Troy. I shall build a temple of solid marble
To Phoebus and Hecate, declare the days of a festival
Named after Phoebus. Great shrines shall await you also
In my domain. I shall place there your lots and hidden   80
Fates spoken to my people and consecrate
Men who are chosen to serve you, O fostering one.
Do not entrust your songs to the leaves lest the rapid
Winds make them whirling playthings, I beg you to sing
The prophecies yourself." He made an end of his speaking.
    But the priestess, not yet enduring Phoebus' huge frenzy,
Raged in her cave and tried to drive out of her breast
The great god. All the more did he weary her madly raving
Mouth, subdue her wild heart, and mold her with pressure.
A hundred wide doors stood open now in her household   90
Of their own accord, and the cries of the priestess were carried
Abroad on the air:
                "O you who have finished at last
The great dangers of ocean (worse dangers await you on land),
The Trojans shall come to Lavinium's kingdom (put this care
Out of your heart), but they shall wish they had not.
Wars, frightful wars I see, and the Tiber foaming
With blood. The Simois, Xanthus, the Dorian camp
Shall be yours again. Now another Achilles is born
In Latium, he too a goddess' son. Nor shall Juno,
The Teucrian foe, be absent when you as a suppliant   100
In desperate need ask aid of so many Italian
Tribes, and of so many cities. The cause of such evil
Again for the Trojans is a foreign wife and again
A bride from abroad.
Yet, do not yield to misfortune, but press on more boldly
Than your fortune allows you. The first road to safety will open
From a Greek city, where you would least expect it."

With such words the Sibyl of Cumae from out of her sanctum,
Sang frightful mysteries and roared back in her cave,
Involving the truth with obscurity. So did Apollo   110
Shake reins upon her until she raved, and twist goads
Under her breast. As soon as her fury abated,
Her raving grew still, then Aeneas the hero began:
"O virgin, no new or unthought-of likeness of sorrow
Rises up to assail me, for I have foreseen it and pondered
Them all in my mind. One thing I beg of you: since
The gate of the king of darkness is said to be here
And the shadowy swamp that is Acheron's overflow,
Let me go to the sight of my dear father, his presence;
May you show me the way and open the sacred doors.   120
I snatched him from flames and a thousand pursuing weapons;
I carried him out of the enemies' midst on my shoulders.
My companion upon the way over all of the oceans,
He bore with me all the threats of both water and sky,
Though unwell and exhausted beyond the lot of old age.
Nonetheless, he gave orders that I, as a suppliant, seek
Your threshold and prayed that I should—take pity, I beg,
On a son and his father, O fostering one; you are able
To do everything, and not vainly did Hecate make you
Her mistress in groves of Avernus. If Orpheus could   130
Go down to the ghost of his wife with the aid of his Thracian
Lyre with harpstrings of song, if Pollux could rescue
His brother by dying for him and could go and come back
So often the same road—why should I mention great Theseus
Or Hercules? I too am sprung from the greatest Jove."
        He prayed in such words and clung with his hands to the altar,
When the priestess began to speak: "O child of the gods' blood,
Trojan son of Anchises, the descent to Avernus is easy
(For the gate of black Dis stands open by day and by night),
But to recall your steps and to reach upper air,   140
This is the task, this the labor. Few, born of the gods,
Whom Jove, who is just, has loved or their excellent virtue
Has raised to the heavens, have done it. Woods stand in the middle
Between this temple and Dis, and Cocytus the river
Winds round with black waters. If you are so anxious to see it,
Have such a desire to cross twice the Stygian lake,
To look twice on darkest Tartarus, if it is pleasing
For you to indulge in mad labor, then listen to me:

First you must do this. A golden bough there is hidden
Upon a dark tree thick with leaves and tough twigs and branches.   150
It is said to be sacred to Infernal Juno; the whole grove
Covers it up in the shade of an obscure valley.
But you cannot go down to the hidden parts of the earth
Before you have plucked this golden-leafed bough from the tree.
Lovely Proserpina orders this gift to be brought her.
Another as golden appears when the first bough is torn
Away, and its stem leafs out with the same kind of metal.
Then search for it well with your eyes, and when once you have found it,
Pluck it off with your hand, for willingly, easily too,
It will come if the Fates are calling you; otherwise,   160
No force can detach it or any tough blade shear it off.
Moreover, your friend lies dead (ah, you do not know it!)
And defiles all the fleet with his lack of a burial while
You visit my oracle, linger upon my threshold.
Give him his proper resting place in a tomb.
Lead forth black cattle; let these be your first atonement.
Thus after all you will look upon Stygian groves
And a kingdom untrodden by live men." She spoke, then grew silent.
          Aeneas, his eyes cast down in a mournful face,
Stepped forward and left the cave, turning over in mind   170
These obscure events. There went with him faithful Achates,
His comrade, who walked under similar heavy cares.
Then between them they plaited the threads of a varied discussion
As to which man the prophetess meant, or whose body to bury.
But they saw, as they came, Misenus upon the dry shore,
Cut off by a death undeserved, he the son of Aeolus,
Than whom no one else was more skilled to inspire the soldiers
With trumpet of brass and to kindle their courage with song.
He was the companion of Hector the great and went with him
To battle, outstanding with spear and the trumpet of war.   180
When victor Achilles slew Hector, Misenus the bravest
Of heroes, had joined Dardanian Aeneas and followed
No less a commander. But once, while he blew his horn,
A hollow conch shell, on the waters (the madman!) and called
The gods to a contest of song, jealous Triton had caught
Misenus and drowned him among foaming ocean and rocks,
If the story is worth our belief.
                    All the men cried out
In a great lamentation, especially loyal Aeneas.

Then they followed the Sibyl's orders without any delay
And wept as they built up an altar, a pyre with boughs   *190*
Which they tried to raise high as the heavens. They went to the ancient
Forest, the deep retreat of the beasts, and felled
Pine trees; the holm-oak rang with the blows of an ax.
Ash-beams and oaks fit for cutting were riven by wedges.
They rolled huge ash trees down from the mountain sides.
Aeneas was first at such labors; he cheered on his men
As he swung an ax too like the others. But these thoughts he turned
About in his sad heart; he looked at the wide woods and prayed:
"If now that gold bough would reveal itself on the tree
In such a vast grove, since all you have told us is true   *200*
About Misenus, O prophetess! Only too true!"
He had scarcely spoken when twin doves came flying by chance
Down from the sky in front of his face and alighted
Upon the green turf. The great hero recognized
The birds of his mother and joyfully sent up this prayer:
"Become our leaders, if there is a way, and direct us
Through the groves with your flight to where the costly bough darkens
        the rich earth.
And, goddess my mother, be with me in difficult fortunes."
So he spoke and slowed pace to observe what the signs might bring,
And where the birds moved. They fed, as they flew, at intervals,   *210*
Not advancing beyond the sight of the men who followed.
Then, when they had reached the ill-smelling jaws of Avernus,
They lightly rose up and gliding through glistening air
They settled on favorite perches in the twin-natured tree
Where the glitter of gold flashed distinctly along the branches.
As the mistletoe blossoms each year in the winter's cold
And produces new leaves in the woods, which the tree does not have,
Surrounding smooth trunks with its growth of a yellowish-white,
Such was the sight of the golden leafage upon
The dark holm-oak, the thin plate of metal that rattled   *220*
In the soft breeze. Aeneas immediately seized it
And broke it away in his eagerness, though it resisted,
And carried it into the house of the prophetess Sibyl.
        Meanwhile on the shore the Teucrians mourned for Misenus
And gave to his unresponding ashes the last
Honor. They built a huge pyre of heavy pitch pine
And oak cut in pieces. They wove dark leaves at its sides
And placed funereal cypress in front, and above

They adorned the pyre with shining weapons. Then some
Made fires for boiling water a-ripple in kettles;   230
They washed Misenus' cold body and rubbed it with oil.
A wailing went up. Then they laid the corpse they lamented
On its bier, and threw over it purple garments, the usual
Coverings. Others came up to the enormous death-couch
Performing sad service, and, in our ancestral manner,
With faces averted, applied the torch underneath.
They burned gifts of incense heaped up, food, olive oil poured
From its bowls.

        Afterward, when the ashes had fallen and flame
Grown quiet, they poured wine on what remained and the thirsty
Embers; then Corynaeus collected the bones   240
In an urn of bronze. He purified his comrades
By carrying pure water three times around them and sprinkling
A delicate dew from a branch of auspicious olive.
He spoke the last words. But loyal Aeneas laid down
Upon the huge mass of the tomb the dead man's equipment,
His oar and his trumpet. He lies beneath a high mountain
Called Misenus now from him. It preserves his name
Forever.

        This done, Aeneas quickly obeyed Sibyl's orders.
There was a deep cave that yawned with enormous chasm,
Rocky but sheltered by its black lake and the shadows   250
Of forest around. No bird could fly over it safely,
So deadly the breath it poured from its night-black jaws
To the vault of the sky. The Greeks called the place Aornos,
Or "Birdless". The priestess first stationed here four black bullocks
And poured wine upon their foreheads. Between their horns
She cut off the bristles and laid them in sacred fire,
First fruits of her worship. She called upon Hecate, mighty
In heaven, and Erebus. Others slashed the bulls' throats
And collected their warm blood in bowls. Aeneas himself
Dispatched with a sword a black lamb to the mother of Furies,   260
Black Night, and to her great sister, Earth, and to you,
Proserpina, sacrificed a cow that was barren.
Then he began the nocturnal rites to Jove Stygian
And laid on the flames the entire bodies of bulls,
Pouring fat oil on the entrails that hissed as they burned.
Look! at the first light of the sun when it rose in the sky,
The earth underfoot began to rumble, the forest

Ridges to move, dogs seemed to howl through the darkness
While the goddess approached. "Far off, stay far off, unholy
Men!" cried the prophetess. "Leave this entire grove!   270
You, Aeneas, move forward and draw your sword from its sheath.
Now you need courage, now strong heart."
                                        This was all she said
In her frenzy. She entered her open cave; he came after
And equalled his steps, unafraid, with those of his leader.
        Gods who rule over spirits, O voiceless shades,
Chaos and Phlegethon, broad regions of silent night,
Let it be proper for me to tell what I've heard
And by your power reveal the secrets deep hidden
In earth and sunken in gloom of the lower world.
They walked unseen in the lonely night, through shadows,   280
Through Hades' empty house and through his realm
Of nothingness, as when the moon shines faintly
With fitful, malignant light. The road led onward
Through woods where Jove had hidden the sky in darkness
And black night drawn day's color away from things.
There on the very threshold and in the jaws
Of Hell crouch Sorrow and avenging Cares.
There dwell pale Illnesses, and sad old Age,
And Fear, and Hunger that counsels evil, and squalid
Poverty, frightful forms to see, Destruction,   290
Pain, and Sleep, Death's brother, the sinful joys
Of Lust, and deadly War on the threshold's edge,
The Furies' steel-cold bedroom, insane Discord,
Weaving her snaky hair with bloody ribbons.
There in the center a huge and shady elm
Spreads out its aged arms in branches; here
False dreams, they say, reside and cling beneath
All of its leaves, and many shapes beside
Of strange wild beasts: the Centaurs in their stalls,
Two-formed Scyllas, hundredfold Briareus,   300
The beast of Lerna, hissing and horrible,
Chimaera armed with flames, the Gorgons, Harpies,
The shadow-shape of Geryon, with three bodies.
Shaking in sudden fear, Aeneas snatched his
Sword and turned its edge toward their approach,
And, if his wiser comrade had not warned him
That they were tenuous incorporeal spirits

Flitting in hollow semblances of forms,
He would have rushed and with vain steel slashed shadows.
   From here the way led down to Acheron's banks.   310
A murky whirlpool there boils mud and belches
All of its mass into Cocytus' river.
A frightful boatman guards these flowing waters,
Charon, filthy and squalid, whose white hair,
Unkempt, abundant, covers his chin. His eyes
Stare wide with flame. His dirty cloak hangs down
By a knot from his shoulders. He steers his craft with a pole
And runs up its sail and ferries dead bodies across
In a dark-blue skiff. His old age is green and sturdy.

Here, toward the banks the entire crowd kept rushing,   320
Mothers and husbands and heroes great-hearted but dead,
Boys, unmarried girls, and children placed on their pyres
In front of their parents' eyes, as many as when
The leaves in the woods fall down with autumn's first frost,
Or as many as birds who gather on land from deep ocean
When winter has driven them over the water to regions
Where the sun shines. They stood and begged to be first,
Extending their arms in desire of the farther shore.
But the grim ferry man chose now these, now those,
And drove all the rest far back along the beach.   330
Aeneas (he wondered at seeing the noisy crowd)
Said: "Tell me, O virgin, what does this hubbub mean
On the river bank? What do these spirits wish?
Why are some left behind, while others are rowed
Across the dark water?" The old priestess briefly replied:
"Son of Anchises, undoubted child of the gods,
You see the deep pools of Cocytus, the Stygian marsh,
By whose power the gods are afraid to foreswear and deceive.
All this poor crowd you see lies still unburied;
That is the ferryman, Charon; the people he carries   340
Across have been buried. They are not given to him
Or to these gloomy banks with their roaring waters
Until their bones have been laid to rest in graves.
They wander a hundred years and they fly about
These shores; at last accepted, they revisit
The pools they long for." Anchises' son stood still
Deep in his thoughts and pitying their sad lot.

For he saw them before him, sad, without death's honor,
Leucaspis and Orontes, admiral
Of the Lycian fleet, who sailed from Troy together   350
Across the windy water. The South Wind drowned them,
Crushing both ship and men beneath the waves.
    Look! Palinurus the helmsman was passing along,
Who recently fell from the stern and was drowned in the waves
On the Libyan voyage while he was watching the stars.
When at last Aeneas could recognize his sad figure
Among the deep shadows, he spoke to him first: "Palinurus,
Which god snatched you from us and drowned you in open sea?
Come tell me, for he who was never before deceitful,
Apollo, deluded my spirit with this one reply: 360
He said you would come to Italy safe from the sea.
Is this the faith that he promised?" Palinurus replied:
"Apollo's oracle did not deceive you, Aeneas,
Nor did a god drown me in ocean; for while I was steering
The ship I had charge of, I happened to wrench off the tiller
And carried it with me overboard. I swear
By bitter seawater I had no fear for myself
But only that you, deprived of the rudder, your helmsman
Knocked out, would go under, so great were the rising waves.
For three winter nights the South Wind carried me on,   370
Beaten by waves across the wide water until
Upon the fourth dawn I could barely see Italy from
The top of a huge wave. I gradually swam to the land.
Already in safety I grasped with hooked fingers at jagged
Projections of rock, when cruel men attacked me with swords,
Weighed down by wet clothing; they thought I had wealth on
    my person.
Now the waves hold me, the winds roll me round on the beach.
I beg you by heaven's delightful glow and its air,
And by your father, by the increasing hope of Iulus,
Save me from these evils, unconquered one; or cast only   380
A handful of earth over me (for you can), and seek out
The harbor of Velia; or if there be any way
Which the goddess, your mother, has shown you (since not without
    power
Of gods do you now prepare to pass over such rivers
And the Stygian swamp), give a miserable man your right hand,
Take me with you over the waves and allow me at least,

Dead as I am, to rest in a quiet place."
When he had spoken these words the prophetess said:
"Where did you find, Palinurus, such a dreadful desire?
Shall you, unburied, look upon Stygian waters,   390
The terrible river of Furies, unbidden approach
Its banks? Cease hoping by prayer to deflect gods' fates.
But take my words and remember; they'll soothe your sad lot.
For neighbors abroad far and wide in the cities, impelled
By portents from heaven shall make their peace with your bones
And heap up a mound, hold funeral rites beside it.
The place shall forever possess the name: Palinurus."
His cares were removed by these words, his sorrow a little
Dispelled from his sad heart. The name of the land gave him joy.
      They took up their journey again and came close to the river.   400
Now the boatman, although at a distance, had seen them approach
As he looked from the Stygian waves, when they turned their steps
Through the silent grove. He spoke to them first and reproved them:
"Whoever you are who come armed to my river, speak up
And tell why you come. Halt there! Don't budge from the spot!
This is the place of Shadows, of Dreams, and of Night
Full of sleep. It is sinful to carry live bodies across
In my Stygian boat. I did not rejoice when I ferried
Hercules over the lake nor Theseus or Pirithous,
Although they were born of the gods and had never been conquered.   410
Hercules tried to tie up the watchdog of Hades
And drag him off trembling from the very throne of the king;
The last two attempted to kidnap the mistress of Dis
From her bedroom." The Amphrysian prophetess spoke in reply:
"There are no such ambushes on foot here: do not be disturbed.
These arms have no force. Let the huge watchdog bark in his cave
And frighten pale shadows forever, let chaste Proserpina
Remain in her uncle's abode. Aeneas the Trojan,
Outstanding in loyalty and in the use of his weapons,
Goes down through Erebus' deepest gloom to his father.   420
If the image of such great loyalty does not affect you,
Then note well this branch." (She produced it from under her robe.)
There abated the swelling anger in Charon's heart
And he said no more but admired the worshipful gift
Of the fatal bough, seen once more after long interval.
Then turning his blue boat toward them, he steered for the shore
And drove off the other souls sitting upon their long benches;

He lowered the gangway, received huge Aeneas on board.
The sewn-leather skiff groaned under his weight; through its cracks
It shipped much swamp water. At last safely over the river   430
He landed both seeress and hero in the dark weeds and foul slime.

    From three throats huge Cerberus filled this realm with his barking,
Savagely crouched in his cave. The prophetess saw
His neck bristle up with serpents. She threw him a cake
To bring sleep, made of honey and meal that was mingled with drugs.
Rabid with hunger, he opened three throats and swallowed
The offering, then loosened huge backs as he stretched on the floor
Of the entire cave. Its guardian unconscious, Aeneas
Raced to the entrance, escaped from the banks of the water
That permits no return.

                At once they heard sounds of loud wailing,   440
The souls of small children crying upon the threshold,
Whom a dark day had snatched from their mother's breast and bereft
Of the lot of sweet life and plunged them in bitter death.
Beside them were those condemned to die on false charges,
Their places assigned through judges appointed by lot.
Minos presides at the vote-urn; he calls the assembly
Of dead souls and reviews their lives and the crimes they are
    charged with.
The next places were held by sad folk who had killed themselves,
Though guiltless; they hated the light of day, so they threw
Their lives away. How they wished that in upper air   450
They might now endure both poverty and its harsh labors!
Divine law prevents them, the hateful marsh with its gloomy
Water restrains them, and Styx, nine times encircling.
    Not far away appeared the Mourning Fields—
For so they are called—extending in every direction.
Here those whom harsh love destroyed with its cruel sorrow
Are concealed by secret paths, and a thicket of myrtle
Covers them: care does not leave them although they are dead.
Here he saw Phaedra and Procris and sad Eriphyle,
Pointing at wounds her cruel son had inflicted,   460
And Evadne and Pasiphaë; here Laodamia
Walked as their comrade, and Caeneus, once a young woman,
Then a man, but by Fate changed back to her earlier form.
Among them Phoenician Dido, with her fresh wound,
Went wandering in a great wood. When the Trojan hero
Stood at her side and recognized her in the shadows,

As one at the first of the month either sees or imagines
He sees the moon through the clouds, he wept and spoke to her
In sweet love: "Unhappy Dido, was the report
That came to me true, that you had taken the last step   470
And died by the sword? And was I the cause of your death?
I swear by the stars, by the gods, by the faith there may be
In the depths of the earth, that I left your shores, queen, with reluctance.
But the orders of gods which now force me to pass through these
          shadows,
This wasteland of deepest night, compelled and commanded.
I could not believe when I left I should bring you such sorrow.
Stand still and do not withdraw yourself from my sight.
Whom do you flee from? This word that I speak is the last
That Fate may allow me." Aeneas attempted to soothe
With these words the anger that blazed from her eyes and her soul,   480
As he burst into tears. She fixed her gaze on the ground.
Her features averted were not more stirred by his speech
Than if they were made of hard flint or Marpessian marble.
Then she flung herself off and fled back to the shadowy grove,
Still hostile, where her first husband Sychaeus replied
To her sorrow with kindness and equalled her love with his own.
Shocked by her tragic misfortune, Aeneas came after
At a distance and wept for her, pitied her as she went on.
          Then he took the course given. They now reached the fields
                    that lay farthest,
Where those who were famous in war held secluded places.   490
Here Tydeus met him, and Parthenopaeus, much talked of
For skill with his weapons, the image of pallid Adrastus,
Many Trojans who fell in the war and were mourned by survivors.
He groaned as he saw them all pass in a long line:
                                        Glaucus,
Medon, Thersilochus, three sons of Antenor, Polyboetes
Consecrated to Ceres, Idaeus still holding his weapons
And chariot. Souls crowded round him on right and on left.
To look at him once did not satisfy them; they were eager
To hold him and linger and learn his reasons for coming.
But as the chiefs of the Greeks and Agamemnon's phalanxes   500
Saw the man and his weapons glittering through the shadows,
They shook with great fear; some fled, as once they had fled
To their ships, and some lifted up a thin little sound.
This attempt at a battle cry mocked their wide-open mouths.

Here he saw Deiphobus, Priam's son, with his body
All torn, his face cruelly mangled, and both of his hands,
His ears slashed off from the temples, his nostrils agape
With a hideous wound. As soon as he saw him, crouched backward
And trying to hide his terrible suffering, Aeneas
Spoke to him first in a voice long familiar in friendship: 510
"Deiphobus, mighty in arms, descended from Trojan
Nobility, who chose to punish you cruelly like this?
Who had the power to do it? The word that was brought me
That last night at Troy said you had sunk down on the heaps
Of corpses, weary among the vast slaughter of Greeks.
Then I set up an empty tomb on the Rhoetean shore
For you and called loudly three times to your ghost. Your name
And weapons now mark the spot. But I could not see
You, friend, or departing lay you in ancestral earth."
The son of Priam replied: "You left nothing undone,   520
My friend; you have paid every debt to Deiphobus and
To his ghost. But my fates and the murderous sin of the Spartan
Helen have plunged me in this distress; she has left me
These mementoes. You know our false joy upon that last night;
You must remember it only too well. When the fatal
Horse leaped over the Trojan wall and delivered
Its belly-full of armed men, she danced as if sacred
Rites were afoot and led the women exulting
In Bacchic delight. She lifted a big torch among them
And called to the Greeks from the citadel's summit. At that time   530
I lay in my bedroom, unhappy, worn out with my cares
And heavy with sleep. Sweet, deep was the quiet that held me,
Most like to calm death. Meanwhile, that egregious helpmate
Had moved all the arms from the house; she had even slipped off with
My reliable sword from under my pillow; she summoned
Menelaus inside and opened the doors, no doubt hopeful
To curry great favor with him who had once been her lover
And wipe out the stain of old evils which she had occasioned.
Why delay? They broke into the bedroom. Ulysses, descendant
Of Aeolus, inciter to evil, came as a companion.   540
Gods, pay back the Greeks for such crimes, if with blameless speech
I ask for such vengeance! But tell me, what chance brings you here
Alive? Do you come from wandering over the sea
Or warned by the gods? What misfortune is harassing you
To visit these sad, sunless homes, this land of confusion?"

While they exchanged these words Aurora had traversed
In her rosy chariot the middle of heaven; they might have
Expended in speech all the time that fate had allotted
Had not his companion the Sibyl admonished him briefly:
"Night rushes upon us, Aeneas; we drag out the hours   550
With weeping. Here is the place where the road divides.
The right hand fork leads us under the walls of great Pluto,
Our route to Elysium; the left hand road leads the wicked
To punishment, sends them to impious Tartarus."
Deiphobus said: "Great priestess, do not be angry.
I shall leave, add myself to the shades and fill out their number.
Go, pride of our race; may your fate be better than mine."
This was all that he said, and he turned away as he spoke.
    Aeneas looked about him and suddenly saw
At the foot of a cliff on his left a broad stronghold surrounded   560
By triple walls which a rapid river flowed round
In a torrent of flame, Tartarean Phlegethon,
Rolling its grinding boulders. A huge gate stood near him,
Its columns of solid adamant. No human power
Could destroy them with steel, not even the gods themselves.
A tower of steel rose up in the air: Tisiphone
Sat there in a bloody robe and wakefully guarded
The vestibule night and day. From within there came groans
And the sound of horrible flogging, the shrieking of steel,
Of chains being dragged. Aeneas stood still, terrified   570
At the noise. "What forms of wrong-doing, O virgin, are these
Arising?" The prophetess thus began to reply:
"Famous leader of Teucrians, divine law forbids that the guiltless
Should set foot on the threshold of sinners. But when Hecate gave me
Full charge in the groves of Avernus she led me all over
And explained each punishment. Rhadamanthus of Cnossus
Rules here, and most harshly. He hears the offenses committed,
The facts in each case, whenever a man has attempted
To cheat divine law, postponing his punishment vainly
Until death, but too late.
                    Tisiphone straightway avenges   580
His crime. With a whip in right hand she beats and torments him.
In her left hand she brandishes snakes and calls on the savage
Cohorts of her sisters. At last awful doors are spread open
To screech on their hinges dread-sounding. You see what doorkeeper
Sits in the entrance, what form keeps watch at the threshold?

A hydra much worse, with fifty black horrible yawning
Mouths. Then Tartarus extends sheer downward, twice
As far toward the shadows as the distance to airy Olympus.
Here the ancient race of Earth, offspring of Titans,
Struck by the thunderbolt rolled into uttermost depths.   590
I saw the twin bodies immense of the sons of Aloeus,
Who attacked great heaven and tried to thrust Jove from his kingdom
With their hands. I saw Salmoneus severely punished
For usurping the lightning and thunder of Olympian Jove.
Borne by four horses and shaking a torch in his hand,
He rode among people of Greece through the center of Elis
And its city in triumph, demanding his honors divine.
A madman, to simulate thunder and inimitable lightning
With chariot bronze and the horn-footed gallop of horses!
The Almighty Father twirl-twisted his weapon through dense   600
     clouds;
He did not use torches or smoky pitch-pine, but he drove him
Headlong in a monstrous whirl.
                         I could also see Tityos,
An offspring of all-bearing Earth; over nine complete acres
His body lay stretched. A large vulture with hooked beak kept plucking
Away at his undying liver and entrails prolific
Of punishment, ripping them, dwelling beneath his high chest.
No respite is given these tissues to grow back again.
Why mention the Lapiths, Ixion, and Pirithous,
Above whom the black rock now, now is about to fall
(Or so it appears)? The golden supports of the couches   610
Spread out for high banquet, the food that is set out before them
In regal array, the eldest of Furies who crouches
Beside them and restrains their hands from touching the tables,
As she shakes a torch and roars at them, deep in her throat?
Here are those who hated their brothers while they were alive;
Or struck at a parent; or cheated a client bound to them;
Or, having found wealth, bowed selfishly over it, shared none
With relatives (these formed a very large group); or those murdered
Because of adultery; those who fought unrighteous battles
Nor feared to deceive their masters: all these were imprisoned,   620
Awaiting their punishment. Do not inquire what this was
Nor what was the form of misfortune that swallowed them up.
Some roll a huge stone, some hang spread out on a wheel.
Unhappy sits Theseus, and there he will sit forever.

Phlegyas, most wretched of all, bawls out through the darkness,
Advising all men and invoking himself as a witness:
"Learn justice when warned and do not despise the gods."
Here a man had sold his country for gold and imposed
A powerful master on her, fixed laws for a price,
Then annulled them. That man had invaded his daughter's bedroom 630
For incestuous marriage. All had dared to do frightful wrong
And attained what they dared. Not if I had one hundred tongues
And one hundred mouths and a voice of iron could I
Recount all the forms of their crimes or run over their names."

When she had thus spoken, the elderly priestess of Phoebus
Said: "Come, on your way, and complete the task undertaken.
Let us make haste. I see the walls of the Cyclopes
Forged in their furnace, and gates in the archway before us,
Where we are instructed to lay down our gifts." She had spoken.
They walked side by side through the shadowy way and then hurried 640
Across the midspace and approached the doors. Here Aeneas
Went inside and sprinkled his body with fresh running water
And placed the bough upright upon the threshold before him.

When this had been done, their duty complete toward the goddess,
They came to the region of joy and the pleasant green spaces,
Abode of the blessed, and the groves of the fortunate souls.
Here a more generous air clothed the fields with a dazzling
Light; they knew their own sun and their own stars.
Some of them exercised on a grassy playground,
Competing at games and wrestling on yellow sand.   650
Some beat with their feet in a chorus and sang as they danced.
There Orpheus, singer of Thrace, in a flowing robe,
Accompanied them on the seven strings of his lyre,
Striking them now with his fingers, now with ivory pick.
Here was the ancient race of Teucer, most handsome
Descendants and great-hearted heroes born in happier times,
Ilus, Assaracus, Dardanus, founder of Troy.
From a distance he marvelled to see their arms and chariots,
Empty of men; their spears stood fixed in the ground;
Their horses, released, pastured here and there through the field.   660
For the pleasure they took in chariots, arms, while alive,
Their interest in caring for glossy horses, remain
When their bodies are laid in the earth.
                                    He looked at the others
To right and to left on the grass as they feasted and sang

A joyful paean in chorus, there in the fragrant
Laurel grove where the great river Eridanus rolls
Through the woods to the upper world.
                              Here was a band
Of men who had suffered wounds while fighting for country;
Some who were priests and chaste while their life remained,
And others loyal seers who spoke things worthy of Phoebus,   670
Some creative in arts which enrich man's life,
And others whose merit had made men remember them.
All of them wore a white fillet around their temples.
They thronged about as the Sibyl spoke to them thus,
To Musaeus above all, for that most populous crowd
Looked up as he towered above with his head and shoulders:
"Say, happy souls, and you, the best of all poets,
What region, what place holds Anchises? We came for his sake
And crossed the great rivers of Erebus." To this request
The hero gave, briefly, response: "There is no fixed home   680
For anyone. We inhabit the darkling groves
And lie on the cushion-like banks and the meadows refreshed
By streams. But you, if that is the wish in your hearts,
Climb up on this ridge, and I'll set you an easy path."
He spoke and moved on and showed them the shining fields
Down below. They descended here from the highest summits.
     But Father Anchises, deep in a blooming valley,
Examined quite closely those souls which would rise to the light,
Reviewing by chance the number of all his descendants,
The grandsons so dear, their fates and fortunes and deeds,   690
Their characters too. When he saw Aeneas approaching
Toward him through the grass, he stretched eager hands toward his son,
His cheeks bathed with tears, and managed to utter this word:
"You have come at last, that loyalty which I knew
Has conquered your difficult course. Do I really see
Your face, son of mine? Do I hear and reply to your words?
So I felt in my heart that I should, and I reckoned the hours
Before you could come: anxiety did not deceive me.
What lands and wide seas you have travelled to reach me, my son,
And beset by what dangers! How I feared that the powers of Libya 700
Might injure you!" Aeneas spoke: "It was your sad image
Appearing again and again that brought me, my father,
To this threshold. My ships lie anchored off Tyrrhenian shores.
Give me your right hand, father, and do not retreat from

My embrace." So speaking he bathed his cheeks in tears.
Three times he tried to throw arms round his father's neck;
Three times that image escaped the vain grasp of his hands
As if it were soft breeze, or most like a fleeting dream.
　　　Meanwhile Aeneas saw in a nook of the valley
A secluded grove and rustling thickets in timber,   710
And the river of Lethe that flowed past homes that were peaceful.
Races and peoples unnumbered were flitting around it,
Just as the bees in meadows when summer is peaceful
Alight upon various flowers and swarm round white lilies
And fill the whole field with their murmur.
　　　　　　　　　　　　　　Aeneas was startled
To see them so suddenly, and he inquired the reasons,
Not knowing what rivers these were or what men filled the stream banks
With such a great throng. Then Father Anchises gave answer:
"They are souls who are fated to live in a second body.
They are drinking the waters of Lethe that make them forget   720
And free them from care. I have long been eager to tell you
Who each of them is and describe each of my descendants.
We shall thus find more pleasure together when Italy's won."
"Must I suppose, O father, that some of these souls
Will ascend to the light and return to their slow-moving bodies?
What a dreadful desire to live in the light have these wretches!"
"I shall certainly tell you, my son, nor prolong your suspense,"
Said Anchises, revealing each detail in proper succession.
　　　"To begin with, the sky and the lands and the watery plains,
The luminous globe of the moon, the Titanian sun   730
And the stars, a spirit within them nourishes.
　　　　　　　　　　　　　　　　Mind
Gives life to the mass, infused through the members of each,
And mingles throughout the great body. Thence comes the creation
Of men and of beasts and of birds and the monsters which ocean
Bears under its shining water. Their vigor is fiery,
Divine is the seed of their being as long as they are
Not hindered by harmful, slow bodies or limbs that are earthly
And members death-bound. Their bodies give rise to their dread,
Desire and grief and joy; shut up in their shadows
And windowless prison they cannot catch sight of the air.   740
Yet even when life has deserted the last light above,
Not all of their evil departs from miserable men,
Nor all bodily ill; for these grow (as they must) with deep roots,

Are ingrained a long time in a marvelous way. They are punished
Therefore and pay penalties for their old sins. Some are offered,
Hung up, to the winds, and others beneath a whirlpool
Have the crimes that infect them washed out, or burned out with fire.
Each of us suffers the lot of death that was fated;
Then we are sent through wide Elysium; few
Of us hold happy fields until a long daytime is ended   750
And time's circle complete removes the corruption grown ingrained,
Leaving ethereal sense unpolluted and fiery.
When one thousand years have rolled by, god will call all those souls
To the river of Lethe in a long line so that they may
Without memory rise to the vault of the upper world
And begin to desire return to bodies." Anchises
Had spoken. He drew his son and with him the Sibyl
Into the midst of the murmuring crowd, took his place
On a mound where he could survey them all in a long line
Before him and recognize faces of those who came: 760
    "Come, I shall tell of the glory to come for Dardanian
Offspring, descendants unborn of Italian race,
Illustrious souls who shall bear our name; I shall show
What your fate shall be. That young man who leans on a spear
Without blade, who holds the nearest place to the light,
Is the first to rise up to the air with a blood that is mingled
Of Trojan and Italian, Silvius, an Alban name,
Your posthumous son; your wife Lavinia shall
Bear him to you in your late old age. In the woods
She shall rear him as king and father of kings, whence our race   770
Shall rule over Alba Longa. Next to him is Procas,
The glory of Trojan stock, and Capys and Numitor,
And Aeneas Silvius, who will revive your name,
Outstanding alike in loyalty and in the use
Of weapons, if ever he shall succeed to the rule
Of Alba. What young men they are! Look, what strength they display!
How they wear on their brows the civic crown with its shadow!
They shall build on the hills Nomentum and Gabii,
Fidenae the city, Collatia's citadel, build
Pometii, fortress of Inuus, Bola, and Cora,   780
All places now nameless, but then they shall have these names.
Yes, even Romulus, son of Mars, shall join
His grandfather; his mother Ilia shall rear him up
From the blood of Assaracus. Look, how twin crests stand high

On his head, how his father now marks him with honor to be
Of the gods above! Beneath his auspicious omens,
My son, noble Rome shall equal her power with earth,
Her might with Olympus, surround her seven citadels
With a single wall, happy with offspring of men, like the mother
Of Berecyntus borne in her chariot,   790
Wearing her crown with its towers through Phrygian cities,
Happy in sons she has given the gods and embracing
One hundred grandsons, all dwellers in heaven and all
Having houses on high. Now turn your eyes this way to see
This race and your Romans. Here Caesar and all of the clan
Of Iulus will come to the great vault of heaven. This man,
This is he whom again and again you have heard in the promise
Of prophecy, Caesar Augustus, son of a god.
He shall found once again an era of gold in the land
Of Latium, throughout the fields that Saturn once ruled.   800
He shall carry his power beyond Garamantes and Indians
(A land that shall stretch beyond stars and beyond the paths
Of the year and the sun, where sky-bearing Atlas shores up
On his shoulders the axis studded with shining stars).
Against his arrival, the Caspian kingdom, the land
Of Maeotis, already shakes with the holy prophetic
Responses of heaven, the trembling mouths of the seven-
Fold Nile are astir. Not even Alcides traversed
So much of the earth, though he shot the bronze-footed deer,
Made peaceful the groves of Erymanthus and frightened the hydra   810
Of Lerna with his bow; not Bacchus, who drove as a victor
With reins made of vines on the backs of his tigers from Nysa's
High summit. And are we in doubt to extend our manhood
Thus far with our deeds? Or do we fear to place feet
On the soil of Ausonia? Who is that bearing afar
The sign of the olive branch and the equipment of worship?
I know his white beard and his hair. He is Numa the king,
Who will give our new city its laws; he will come from small Cures,
Barren in soil, to great power. Then Tullus will follow
To break up the fatherland's ease and to drive sluggish men   820
Toward their weapons and battlelines long unacquainted with triumphs.
Next to him follows the rather too arrogant Ancus,
Who even now glories too much in the popular favor.
Do you wish to see also the Tarquin kings and proud spirit
Of Brutus avenger, the fasces that he recovered?

He first shall receive the power of consul, the axes
So savage; a father, he shall call his sons to their doom .
For starting new wars—he shall do this in freedom's fair cause.
Unhappy man, however ages that follow may speak
Of these deeds, love of country will conquer and measureless lust   830
For praise. But see also, afar off, the Decii and Drusi,
Torquatus fierce with his ax, and Camillus returning
The standards once lost. But those souls which you see with their
     gleaming
Armor alike are at peace with each other while darkness
Of night presses down on them: ah, what a war they will stir up,
What clashes of battle, what slaughter, when they reach the light
Of life! A father-in-law who descends from the Alpine
Ramparts and from the height of Monoecus, a son-in-
Law who arranges his battle ranks drawn from the East!
Do not, my children, accustom your spirits to warfare   840
So great, nor turn toward the vitals of your fatherland
These strong forces! And you, who are sprung from Olympus, from
     my blood,
Be first in your mercy, throw weapons away from your hands.
That victor shall drive in his chariot to the high Capitol
When Corinth is captured, distinguished for slaughter of Greeks.
This one shall uproot both Argos and Mycenae, the city
Of Agamemnon, kill Perseus, Achilles' descendant,
So mighty in arms, and avenge his forebears and Minerva's
Temples at Troy defiled by the Greeks. Who would leave you,
Great Cato, or Cossus, unmentioned? The Gracchi and their clan,   850
The twin Scipios, two lightning bolts of war, the destruction
Of Africa, or you, Fabricius, rich with a little,
Or Regulus, you, who sowed your furrow with seed?
Where do you eagerly drive me, you Fabian men?
You are that Maximus, he who alone saved our country
By his delaying!
                    Others will fashion the molten
Bronze with more skill (at least I believe this), will carve from
Marble live faces, will plead cases better, and sketch out
The paths of the heavenly bodies with pointers, and forecast
The rising of stars.
                    You, Roman, remember to govern   860
The peoples with power (these arts shall be yours), to establish
The practice of peace, spare the conquered, and beat down the haughty."

Thus Father Anchises, and added these words as they marvelled:
"See how Marcellus, illustrious with the Best Spoils,
Moves forward, a victor who towers above all men.
He shall set Rome in place again after the foreign uprising;
The hoofs of his horses shall trample the Poeni, the Gallic
Rebel; to Father Quirinus he'll offer the captured
Arms for the third time." And here Aeneas addressed him
As he saw a young man, most handsome and shining in armor,   870
Walking beside Marcellus, but with face and eyes
Cast down and unhappy: "Who, father, is that who comes with him?
A son or some other from your long line of descendants?
What a shouting of comrades! What genuine greatness is in him!
But black night envelopes his head with its gloomy shadow."
Then Father Anchises replied, with tears in his eyes:
"O son, do not search into the great sorrow of our
Descendants. The Fates will merely show him the earth
But forbid him to live there further. O gods above,
Rome's stock would appear too powerful if your gifts   880
Should remain among men. What groans shall the Field of Mars
Carry to that great city, what funeral rites
Shall you see, river Tiber, when you flow past his fresh-made
Tomb! No other boy of the Ilian clan shall exalt
His Latin ancestors with such high hopes, in none
Of its offshoots shall Romulus' land take so great a pride.
Alas for his loyalty! Alas for his ancient faith,
His right hand still in war unconquered! None
Unscathed could have brought arms against him, whether
On foot or spurring a foaming horse's flanks.   890
Alas, you piteous boy, if ever you could
Break out against your Fates!
                          You shall be a Marcellus!
Give lilies with full hands; I too shall scatter
Bright flowers, heap gifts of these at least for my
Descendant's soul, perform an empty honor!"

Thus did they wander through that entire land,
In wide and misty fields, reviewed its features.
But when Anchises had led his son about
Among these sights and fired his soul with love
Of fame to come, he told his hero-heir   900

The wars which must be waged and described the peoples
Of Laurentum, Latinus' city, and how he might flee
From each trial, or bear it.
                    There are twin gates of sleep.
One is of horn, they say, where an easy exit
Is given to shades which are true; the other is white
And perfect, of gleaming ivory. Through it the Ghosts
Of the Underworld send false dreams to the light. Anchises,
His words completed, went with his son and the Sibyl
And sent them out through the ivory gate. Aeneas
Made his way to the ships and rejoined his comrades, then sailed   910
Along the straight shore to Caieta's harbor.
                              The anchor
Was thrown from the prow; the ships stood on the beach.

BOOK SEVEN

Italy and War

You also, nurse of Aeneas, gave endless fame
To our shores when you died, Caieta. The honor we pay you
Preserves your name and your bones in Hesperia,
The great Western Land, if there is glory in this.

But loyal Aeneas performed her funeral rites
Duly and heaped up a well-built mound as a tomb.
When the deep ocean was calm, he spread sails and left
The harbor. Winds blew into the night, and a shining
Moon did not keep herself from his course but glowed
With a trembling light on the sea. They skirted the near-   10
By shores of the land of Circe, the opulent daughter
Of Sun, where her inaccessible groves ring out
With her constant song, and odorous burning cedar
Serves as a light in darkness through her proud halls,
While she passes her humming shuttle across the slender
Threads of a web. One heard the angry growl
Of lions straining against their bars and roaring
Late in the night, and bristling boars, and bears
Penned up enraged, the shapes of hulking wolves
Howling, whom that fierce goddess had transformed   20
With potent herbs from human shape to wear
The face and hides of beasts. The sea-god Neptune
Filled sails with favoring winds to keep the loyal
Trojans from undergoing such dread changes
And brought them to port lest they draw near that frightful
Coast, gave them escape past boiling shoals.
Now ocean grew pink with the rays of the sun; from the sky
Saffron Aurora shone forth in her rosy chariot,
While the winds ceased and all their blowing abruptly

Was still. The oars splashed down on a quiet surface.   30
Aeneas, far out on the water, now saw a wide forest
Where Tiber flowed through in a pleasant stream, with swift eddies
Yellow from so much sand carried down to the sea.
Various birds, at home on its banks and the channel,
Soothed the air with their song as they flew in and out of the wood.
He ordered his comrades to turn their prows to the land,
And gladly he entered, to sail up the shadowy river.

Now come, Erato, what kings, what events and times,
What was the condition of ancient Latium when
First this strange army put in to its shores with a fleet   40
I shall tell, and the war's beginning I shall recall.
Goddess, advise me, your bard! I shall speak of terrible
Wars, battlelines, and kings who were driven to death
By their angry pride, the Tyrrhenian band, and Hesperia
All roused up in arms.
                    A greater order of things
Comes to birth for me; I begin a greater task.

Latinus the king, now old, held rule over placid
Cities and fields. His peace was long. We are told
That his father was Faunus, his mother a nymph of Laurentum
Named Marica. Picus was father of Faunus, and he   50
Claimed you as his father, Saturn, the ultimate source
Of his line. The gods had fated Latinus should have
No son, no male issue; his son had died in his youth.
One daughter alone kept house in so great a home,
Now ripe for a man, now old enough to be married.
Many from mighty Latium and all of Ausonia
Had sought her as wife. Most handsome of all was Turnus,
Strong in his lineage of great- and grandfathers. The queen
Hastened with deep affection to win him as son-in-
Law, but the portents of gods with their various terrors   60
Stood in the way.
                    A laurel tree grew in the center
Of the tall palace, its branches sacred, an object
Of awe for many a year. Father Latinus
Himself, they said, had found it there, when first
He based the citadel, had consecrated
The tree to Phoebus. From its name he called

The colonists Laurentians. A heavy swarm of bees
Borne to its summit through the liquid air
Had settled on it, buzzing loudly, clung
With feet to feet—a wondrous thing to tell—   70
And hung from the boughs. At once the prophet said:
"I see a foreign fighter coming, battle-
Lines moving this way from that direction whence
The bees came, dominating the citadel."
And more—while the girl Lavinia stood beside
Her father as he burned chaste torches at
The altar, she seemed—a fearful sight—to burst
On fire with her long tresses, all her costume
Crackled in flames, her royal hair and crown
Lovely with gems; then she was wrapped in yellow   80
Smoke and scattered sparks through all the house.
This frightening, marvelous sight was bruited round.
The prophets sang that she would have a glorious
Fame and fate, but bring great war upon
Her people. The king, made anxious by these omens,
Sought out the oracle of prophetic Faunus,
His father, in the woods beneath the heights
Of Albunea, where the broadest grove
Rings with its sacred fountain and the shadows
Breathe forth foul sulphur vapor. Here the clans   90
Of Italy and all Oenotrian land
Sought answers to their doubts. When the priest had brought
Gifts to this place and in the silent night
Lain down on scattered pelts of slaughtered sheep
In search of rest, he saw the flitting visions
Of many images in wondrous fashion,
Heard various voices, gained comfort from discourse
With gods and spoke to Acheron in the depths
Beneath Avernus. Here Father Latinus,
Seeking response himself, slew properly   100
One hundred woolly sheep and propped his back
Upon their scattered skins and stretched among them.
From the deep grove a sudden voice was heard:
"Seek not alliance for your daughter in
A Latin marriage, O my offspring, trust
In no arranged betrothal. There will come
Sons-in-law from abroad, who with their blood

Shall bear our name to heaven, from whose stock
Descendants shall see all the world beneath
Their feet, where the sun returning looks upon   110
The ocean in both East and West, made subject
To Roman rule." Latinus, when he heard
The words of Father Faunus and his warning
Beneath the soundless night, did not keep silence,
But Rumor flying now both far and wide
Throughout Ausonian cities spread the news,
While Trojan youth moored ships to the grassy shore.
        Aeneas, his chief leaders, handsome Iulus,
Lay down under the branches of a soaring tree.
They started to eat and laid meal-cakes on the grass   120
For food—it was Jove himself who advised them to do this—
And piled country fruits upon these cakes. Having eaten
The fruit, their hunger drove them to chew the thin cakes,
To break in their hands and bite with bold jaws the round edges
Of the fateful broad crusts nor to spare their markings in squares.
"Hello," said Iulus, "We're even eating our tables!"
He made no more jokes. That word, as soon as they heard it,
Brought an end to their troubles. His father grasped at the statement
From his very lips; in awe at its meaning, he stopped him
From speaking again. Then quickly he said: "Hail, the country   130
The Fates have destined for me! Hail, gods of the household,
Faithful to Troy! This home, this land are yours.
For my father Anchises told me such secrets of fate,
I recall, as these: 'When, son, you have sailed to an unknown
Shore, and your food is gone, and hunger shall force you
To eat your tables, then hope for a home; although weary,
Remember to choose a house-site and build up your ramparts.'
This was that hunger, the hunger that would be the last
And put an end to our labors.
Then come, and at first light of sun let us search out, delighted, 140
What places these are, what men, and where is the city
These people defend. Let us scatter in different directions
Away from the harbor. Now lift up your wine bowls to Jove;
Then call on Anchises in prayer, set the wine back on tables."
So he spoke and bound a burgeoning wreath round his temples.
Then he prayed to the local spirit, to Earth, first of the gods,
To the nymphs and to rivers thus far unknown, then to Night,
And to Night's rising stars, to Jove of Mount Ida, the Phrygian

Mother, in series, and to his two parents, to Venus
In heaven, Anchises in Erebus. Then the Almighty Father   150
Thundered clearly three times from high heaven and brandished a cloud
That gleamed with rays of bright gold from the ether above.
The rumor passed swiftly among the lines of the Trojans:
That day had now come when they should build the walls due them.
They hastened to banquet and, cheered by the momentous omen,
They set up the wine bowls and crowned them with tendrils of vine.

    When the following day began to cast light on the lands,
They explored the city, the borders, the shores of this people.
They found that those pools were of Numicus' spring, that this river
Was called the Tiber, and here the brave Latins dwelt.   160

    The son of Anchises then chose one hundred spokesmen
From every rank to go to the worshipful palace,
Each of them veiled with boughs from the olive of Pallas,
To bring the king gifts and to ask his peace toward the Trojans.
They made no delay but hurried as they were ordered,
Borne on with rapid steps. Aeneas marked out
The walls with a shallow ditch and worked at the site.
He built their first home on the shore in the shape of a camp
And encircled it with a rampart and battlements.
Their journey accomplished, the young men sighted the towers   170
And high-rising roofs of the Latins, approaching the walls.
In front of the city both boys and young men in the flower
Of youth exercised their horses and mastered the driving
Of chariots deep in the dust, or bent their strong bows
And hurled tough pikes with their arms, or challenged each other
At racing or boxing, when a messenger rode up on horseback
Bringing the news to the ears of the aged king
That huge men in unknown dress had arrived.
                          The king
Ordered that they be summoned within, and he seated
Himself in the middle upon his ancestral throne.   180
The palace of Laurentine Picus was large and majestic;
It stood at the top of the city on one hundred high columns;
The people were awed by its ancient, nearby forest.
Here kings had received their scepters and taken up fasces,
An omen for good; this temple was also their law court.
Here was the place for their sacred banquets, and here,
When a ram had been sacrificed, the fathers by custom
Sat down at long tables that stretched in unbroken line.

Then too, here stood in the vestibule statues of ancient
Cedar-wood showing the ancestors set up in succession: *190*
Italus, Father Sabinus, the planter of vines,
Who kept his curved sickle as part of his portrait, Saturnus,
The image of two-faced Janus, and other kings
From earliest times. They bore the wounds they had suffered
Defending their country. Upon sacred doorposts hung
Many weapons besides, captured chariots, and curved axes,
Crests from helmets, huge bars brought from gates, both spearheads
          and shields,
And prows torn from ships. The horse-tamer Picus, himself,
With the Quirinal staff of an augur, girt up in short toga,
Sat holding a shield in his left hand. Circe, his wife,   *200*
Enthralled by her love, had touched him with her golden
Wand, then drugged and changed him into a bird
And scattered his wings with colors. In such a temple
Of gods Latinus sat on his father's throne
And summoned the Trojans within. As they moved forward,
He spoke to them first in a placid voice:
                                        "Sons of Dardanus,
Tell me—we are not ignorant of your city
Or race, we have heard how you set your course over the sea—
What is it you seek, what need, what cause brought your ships
To the shore of Ausonia over so many blue shallows?   *210*
Whether because of an error in navigation
Or driven by storms, which many a sailor has suffered
So often on high seas, you entered the banks of the river
And anchored in port, do not flee from the welcome we give you
Nor ignore the Latins, the folk of Saturnus, whose justice
Requires no fetters or laws. They govern themselves
By free will in the way of their ancient god. I remember—
The story has grown somewhat dim with the years—that the elder
Auruncans were accustomed to tell how Dardanus, risen
Among these fields, had travelled to Idaean cities   *220*
Of Phrygia and Thracian Samos, now called Samothracia.
It was thence, from the Tyrrhenian settlement of Corythus,
That he came. Now the golden palace of starry heaven
Receives him upon a throne; he increases the number
Of altars to gods." He had spoken; Ilioneus answered:
          "O king, noble offspring of Faunus, no dark storm has driven
Us here to your lands with its waves, no star has betrayed us,

No coastline deceived. We have all sailed here with a purpose
And with willing hearts, driven out of our realm, once the greatest
The sun ever looked on in journeying from farthest Olympus.　　230
From Jove is the source of our race; the Dardanian young men
Rejoice in their ancestor Jove. Our king, himself risen
From Jove's highest stock, Aeneas the Trojan, has sent us
Here to your threshold. How great was the storm that spread outward
From savage Mycenae through Idaean fields, how driven
By fates both the continents of Europe and Asia clashed
In battle, each man has heard, even he who dwells farthest
Away at earth's end where the river of ocean flows circling,
Or the man who lives far in the zone that is burnt by the sun,
The middle of five zones. After that disaster, borne over　　240
So many vast seas, we begged the gods for a small foothold
For the gods of our folk, and a share that was harmless, air, water
Free for all men. We shall bring no disgrace on your kingdom
Nor shall your repute be slight, nor the favor you gather
From such a great deed die away. You will never regret it,
Nor the Ausonians either, to receive Troy into your bosom.
I swear by the fates of Aeneas and his mighty right arm,
Whether known by good faith or in war and its testing of weapons,
Many peoples and tribes—do not scorn us, we offer these fillets
In free will, with words of entreaty—have sought us as allies　　250
And wished us to join them. But the Fates of the gods have commanded
That we should search out your land. Here Dardanus rose:
Hither Apollo recalls us with portentous orders
To Tyrrhenian Tiber and the sacred springs of Numicus.
Aeneas, moreover, now gives you small gifts from his former
Possessions; he saved them, poor relics from burning Troy.
From this cup of gold his father Anchises poured wine
At the altar. These trappings were Priam's when he gave
Laws to his people by custom, his scepter and sacred
Tiara, his garments, the work of Ilian women."　　260
　　　　Latinus sat still on his throne, looked down, and was silent,
Moving only his eyes intently as Ilioneus spoke.
It was not the embroidered garments of Priam nor the scepter
That filled the king's thoughts but his daughter's wedlock and marriage,
And he pondered old Faunus' prediction within his mind:
This man was that son-in-law whom the Fates prophesied
Was to come from a foreign abode, called to power with equal
Auspices; from him would come those descendants renowned

For their courage, to conquer the entire earth with their strength.
At last he spoke gladly: "May the gods favor our undertaking   270
And their prophecy. You will receive what you hope for, Trojan.
I do not reject your gifts. While Latinus is king,
The bounty of fertile soil or the riches of Troy
Will not fail you. Now let Aeneas himself come forward
If he wants us so much, and is eager to join in guest-friendship,
To be called an ally, nor recoil from our friendly faces.
It shall be for me part of our peace to have touched the right hand
Of your ruler. Now carry my answer back to your king.
I have a daughter whom oracles from our ancestral
Shrine do not permit me to join to a man of our people.   280
Many portents forbid it. They prophesy this lot for Latium:
Sons-in-law from foreign shores shall come to mix blood
With ours and exalt our name to the stars. And I think that
This man is the one that the Fates are demanding. I hope so,
If my mind has a glimpse of the truth." Having spoken these words,
The father chose horses for all—three hundred were standing
Smooth and bright in their lofty stalls—and for each of the Trojans
He ordered a horse to be led out in line, with their trappings
Of purple and embroidered cloth, the wing-footed creatures.
They were covered with gold, and gold collars hung down on their   290
    chests.
They chewed on gold bits with their teeth. To absent Aeneas
He gave a twin team and a chariot. Of heavenly stock,
The horses breathed fire. Their race was of those clever Circe
Had bred for her father as mongrels from a substitute mother.
With such gifts and words from Latinus the men of Aeneas
Swung high on their horses and wheeled to report the peace.

        Look! the fierce wife of Jove was returning from Argos,
The city of Inachus, holding her course through the air.
From aloft in the ether she saw a cheerful Aeneas
And the Dardanian fleet from Pachynus in Sicily.   300
She saw them beginning to build their houses, to trust
In the land, their ships now abandoned. She stood transfixed
With sharp sorrow. Then shaking her head she poured forth these words
From her breast: "Ah, hateful race and fates contrary
To mine, fates of Phrygia, could you men not have died
On Sigean plains, when captured could you not have
Remained as captives? Could Troy when it burned have not

Destroyed you as well? Through battle lines and fire
These men found a way. Am I to believe my power
Lies weary with hatreds, that I am sated at last   310
And grown quiet, when I was the one who dared to pursue them,
Expelled from their land, with my malice, to block their escape
By means of the entire ocean? The force of the sky
And the sea has been exhausted against the Trojans.
What use to me were the Syrtes or Scylla or vast
Charybdis? The Trojans are anchored within the longed-for
Channel of Tiber, safe from the ocean and me.
Mars had the strength to destroy the monstrous race
Of Lapiths, the father of gods himself gave ancient
Calydon over to angry Diana. But what   320
Was the sin of the Lapiths, or why did Calydon merit
Such punishment? Here am I, the great wife of Jove,
Yet unhappy, who left no deed undared, who turned
To every device—I am beaten by Aeneas.
If my godhead cannot prevail, I shall not delay
To call on whatever power there may be. If I
Am unable to bend the high gods, I shall stir up Acheron.
I grant that I shall not be able to bar them from winning
Their Latin domain; his consort Lavinia remains
Steadfastly his by the fates: but this I can manage,   330
To drag out events and to add delay to such massive
Adventures; to cut off the peoples of both the kings.
Her father, her husband may come together by paying
The price of their folk: you, virgin, shall have as your dowry
Both Trojan blood and Rutulian; Bellona, war-goddess,
Shall preside as your matron of wedding; not only Hecuba,
Cisseus' daughter, pregnant with a torch, gave birth
To a nuptial flame. No, Venus herself had such offspring,
Who has borne one more Paris, a deadly firebrand burning
Once more against Troy's newly risen walls."

                                    Having spoken,   340
The frightening goddess went down to the earth. She called up
Allecto the Fury, who brings only grief, from among her
Cruel sister-goddesses, out of the shadows of Hell.
Her pleasure is war with its sadness, both anger and plotting,
And hideous crimes. She is hated by Pluto her father;
Her sisters in Tartarus hate her, the monster. So many

The shapes she turns into, the faces so savage she shows us,
So many black snakes coil all over her! Juno addressed her
And sharpened her malice with words such as these:
                                        "Dark daughter
Of night, accomplish this one special task, that my honor   350
And fame, still unbroken, may not yield place, nor Aeneas
Be able to wheedle Latinus by marriage, or capture
Italy. You can make loving brothers draw arms
On each other, ruin homes with hatred, bring whips and torches
Of death to their roofs. Yours are a thousand names,
A thousand vile arts. Now rack your ingenious brains,
Break up the pact that was settled, sow seeds of war
Through recriminations. Let their young men wish for weapons,
And demand them and seize them at once."
                                        Allecto, infected
With the poison of Gorgons, immediately made for the lofty   360
Home of the Laurentine monarch and Latium. In silence
She sat at Amata's threshold. That lady already
Was burning with feminine anger and cares at the coming
Of Trojans and Turnus's wedding. The Fury flung at her
A snake from her blue-black hair; it crept to Amata's
Bosom and hid in its intimate depths, to reduce her
To madness and make her create a disturbance at home.
Between her garments it slid and across her smooth breasts
And coiled (though she felt no touch) and drove her insane.
With its cunning it breathed a viperous soul into hers .   370
The huge snake became the golden necklace around her
Neck, became part of the ribbons that wound round her head
And twined in her hair, and wandered all over her limbs
With its slippery body. And when the first oozing of poison
Crept under her skin in its moisture, it attacked her senses,
Wove fire into her bones. But before her whole spirit
Took flame in her entire heart she spoke very softly,
In the way that a mother would speak, in her usual manner,
While she shed many tears for her daughter and her Trojan wedding:
"Is Lavinia given to Teucrian exiles for marriage,   380
O father, and have you no pity on her or on yourself,
No pity on me, her mother, whom with the first North Wind
This treacherous robber will leave, when he's kidnapped her daughter,
And taken her over high seas? Did not Paris, the Phrygian
Shepherd, thus steal into Sparta and carry off Helen,

The daughter of Leda, to Troy? What of your holy faith,
What of your ancient concern for your own, and your right hand
So often pledged to Turnus, who is your relation?
If a son-in-law of foreign race is sought for the Latins,
And if this is settled and the orders of Faunus, your parent, 390
Press hard upon you, then I think that each land that is free from
Our rule is a foreign land, and this is the meaning
Of what the gods say. And Turnus, if you are intent on
The search for his origin, had Inachus and Acrisius
For his ancestors. They came from the midst of Mycenae."
When she had spoken these words and found they were vain,
When she saw Latinus was stubborn, and deep in her heart
The maddening serpent's venom had sunk and spread over
Her entire body, then truly the unhappy woman,
Disturbed by gigantic horrors, ran out of control 400
And raged through the wide-sprawling city, as sometimes a top
Spins under the whip of its twisted cord while boys
Keep driving it, bent on their game, round an empty room,
And crowd in a wide ring to watch while the lash propels
It in circles; the wondering band of beardless youth
Hovers above the whirling boxwood and gives
New life to it with new blows: so Amata rushed
As swiftly throughout the city and its fierce people.
Even into the forests she ran, pretending the power
Of Bacchus controlled her, to commit a greater sin 410
Against heaven, a greater madness. She hid her daughter
In leafy mountains, to snatch her from Trojan marriage
And delay its torches. "Euhoe, Bacchus," she shouted,
Calling you worthy alone of the girl; for you
She was seizing the pliant thyrsus, for you she was dancing
In chorus, growing a sacred hair-lock for you.
The news of Amata flew far. Each mother was fired
With madness to seek in like fashion new homes. They deserted
Their old ones and, baring their necks and hair to the winds,
They filled the air with a tremulous howling. Their dresses 420
Were animal-skins, they carried vine-stalks as spears.
In their midst Amata brandished a flaming pine-torch
And chanted a wedding-song for her daughter and Turnus,
Twisting her blood-shot gaze about. Then abruptly
She screamed like a savage: "O Latin mothers, wherever
You are, if unhappy Amata finds favor in faithful

Spirits, if care for the rights of a mother concerns you,
Take the bands from your hair and join these orgies with me."
Thus did Allecto spur onward the queen through the forests
And haunts of wild beasts everywhere with the pricking of Bacchus.   430
      But when she had seen that Amata's first madness was sharpened,
That the plans of Latinus, his entire house, were subverted,
Straightway from this place the gloomy goddess rose upward
Upon her dark wings and was borne by the speed of a South Wind
To the walls of the bold Rutulian leader, the city
Established by Danaë for her Acrisian settlers
(Or so it is said). Our ancestors once called it Ardea.
Its great name abides but not its good fortune. Here Turnus
At midnight in his high halls was enjoying his slumber.
Allecto put off her wild face and the maddening aspect   440
Of her limbs and transformed herself into an old woman,
With unsightly forehead all furrowed with wrinkles, assumed
White hair bound with ribbons, then twined it with olive-spray.
Thus she became old Calybe, the priestess of Juno's
Temple, and offered herself to the young man's sight
As she spoke: "Will you let so many labors be wasted,
Turnus, in vain, and your scepter be transferred to Trojan
Settlers? The king is refusing your marriage, the dowry
Bought with your blood, he is seeking a stranger as heir
To his realm. Go, offer yourself as an object of laughter   450
To thankless dangers. Go, scatter the ranks of Etruscans
And shelter the Latins with peace. All-powerful Juno
Sent me to speak these words while you slept in the peaceful
Silence of night. Come, order your young men to arm them-
Selves in their gladness and move to the gates. Let them burn
The bright-painted boats of the Trojan leaders at anchor
Upon our fine river. The power of heaven commands.
If Latinus the king denies he will keep his word
Nor allows the marriage, let him learn to test Turnus in war."
      Here the young man began in his turn to deride   460
The prophetess: "Word that a fleet has sailed to the Tiber
Has not, as you think, escaped my ears. Don't fashion
Such terrible fears for me. Royal Juno has not
Become unmindful of me.
But old age, rusting your mind, has worn out the truth
In you, O mother, and harassed you with vain cares,
Beguiled the prophetess to false fear among

The wars of kings. It is your duty to guard
The images of the gods and their temples: let men
Wage wars and make peace, for this is their work to do."   470
    Allecto burst into rage as she heard these words.
But a sudden trembling seized on his limbs as he spoke,
And his eyes were fixed in a stare, the Fury hissed
With so many serpents, her form grew to such great size.
Then rolling her flaming eyes, she repulsed him as
He tried to say more, but faltered; she made twin snakes
Rise up from her hair, she cracked her whip, and spoke
From her raving mouth: "So I am one whose mind
Old age has rusted and worn out the truth in me
And beguiled to false fear among the wars of kings!   480
Look what I bring! I come from the dwelling place
Of my dread sisters: wars and destruction I bear
In my hand."
So speaking, she threw a torch at the youth and pierced
His breast with the smoking brand and its murky flame.
Great terror broke off his sleep, while the sweat poured down
From his entire body all over his bones and limbs.
Madly he roared for weapons, for weapons he searched
Both bed and house. Then love of the sword grew wild,
And war's wicked insanity; above all, anger, as when   490
With a vigorous crackle a fire of brush is laid
At the ribs of a bubbling cauldron, and liquids spurt up
With the heat, the boiling water within goes mad
And steam shoots high in a burst of foam while the water
No longer contains itself, but black vapor flies out.
Then, since the peace had been broken, he ordered the chiefs
Of his young men to march on Latinus, to ready their weapons.
For he said they must protect Italy and thrust out the foe
From its borders; that he was a match for both Trojans and Latins.
When he had given these orders and prayed to the gods,   500
The Rutulians cheered on each other to fight; the charm
Of his beauty and youth encouraged one man; another
Was stirred by the thought of his regal forebears; and a third
Was impressed by the glorious deeds of Turnus' right arm.
    While Turnus was filling his men with boldness of spirit
Allecto flew off on her Stygian wings to the Trojans.
Scheming afresh, she spied the place on the shore
Where handsome Iulus was chasing and trapping wild beasts.

Here the girl from Cocytus urged on her dogs to a sudden
Rage and touched their noses with a familiar smell   510
That made them eager to follow a stag: this was
The first cause of evil. It kindled the minds of the farmers
To war.
           There was a stag of remarkable beauty
And wide-branching antlers, which Tyrrhus and his sons had weaned
Away from its mother and reared. Father Tyrrhus had charge of
The herds of the king where they wandered afar in the fields.
The deer was his daughter Silvia's pet; she wove garlands
To place on its horns. She curried and washed the wild creature
In clear-running water. The stag was tame and accustomed
To feed at its master's table, to run in the forest   520
And return to the familiar threshold whatever the hour
Of night. The wild dogs of the hunter Iulus had flushed it
As it happened to float down a stream and to cool its hot body
Upon the green bank. Ascanius, fired with longing
For uncommon praise, aimed an arrow from his curved bow
At the deer. A god was there to steady his right hand.
Loudly the arrow whirred as it pierced the deer's belly
And flanks. The hurt animal fled to its well-known home
And, moaning, crept into the stable, where, streaming with blood,
It filled the whole house with its cries as though it were pleading. 530
First Sister Silvia, striking her palms on her arms,
Called for help and roused the rough farmers. With unforeseen
      promptness
They ran to her aid—for the desperate Fury lay hidden
Among the still woods—some armed with half-burned-out torches
And others with clubs that were heavy with knots, while their anger
Made weapons of whatever came to hand. As it happened,
Tyrrhus was splitting oak logs four ways with wedges
Deep driven. He called the troops, and, heaving with monstrous
Rage, he seized his ax. But the terrible goddess
Had spied out the moment for further harm from her lofty   540
Look-out and flew to the top of the stable and from that
Summit she sang out the shepherd's signal: she blew
A blast out of Tartarus on her curved horn. The deep woodlands
And groves re-echoed and trembled. The lake of Diana
Heard from afar; and Nar River, its stream white with sulphur,
Heard it, and the springs of Velinus; and shuddering
Mothers pressed children close to their breasts. Then swiftly
Men ran when they heard the sound of the frightening horn,

Snatching up weapons from all sides, the unconquered farmers.
The Trojans youth poured out to help Ascanius.   550
From the open camp they came, formed battle lines. No longer
Was this a mere quarrel of rustics, fought with hard cudgels
Or fire-hardened stakes. They settled the issue
With two-edged steel. War's dark harvest bristled
Afar with drawn swords and shimmered with brazen weapons
Struck by the glint of sunshine reflecting its light
Under clouds, as when the waves grow white with the wind
And the sea lifts a little and tosses the waves
Higher and higher until from its very depths
The surge rises up to heaven. Here, first in the line,   560
The young man Almo, eldest of Tyrrhus' sons,
Was killed by a whistling arrow. The wound clung deep
In the throat and silenced his liquid voice and his slender
Life with its blood. Men's bodies lay wide about,
And with them the old Galaesus, one of the justest
Of men, once the richest of all in Ausonian fields.
Five bleating flocks were his, five herds of cattle
Returned to his barns. He plowed with a hundred plows.
He was killed as he stepped to the center to ask for peace.
While through the fields undecided combat was waged,   570
The powerful goddess, her promise fulfilled (since blood
Had been shed in battle and death had occurred in its first clash),
Deserted Hesperia and, borne through the winds of heaven,
As a victor spoke proudly to Juno: "There, discord through sorrow
Of war is created for you. Say whether in friendship
These may come together or join their hands in a treaty.
Since I have sprinkled the Trojans with Ausonian blood,
I shall add this, if your good will remains firm toward me.
I shall carry my rumors into the neighboring cities
And kindle their spirits with insane love of war   580
So that help may come from all sides. I shall scatter arms
Through the fields." Then Juno replied: "There is enough terror
And treachery now; the causes of war are established;
They fight hand to hand. The arms that fortune first gave
Are stained with new blood. Let the outstanding family of Venus
And King Latinus himself rejoice at such union
And celebrate such a marriage. That father, the ruler
Of lofty Olympus, would not wish you to wander more freely
Amid upper air. Leave this place. I shall govern these matters
If the chance of new trouble arises." So spoke Saturn's daughter.   590

Allecto arose on her wings with their hissing snakes;
She made for her home in Cocytus and left the steep sky.

There is a place in mid-Italy at the base of high mountains,
Noble and famous and mentioned on many a shore,
The vale of Ampsanctus. Dark with dense foliage, a slanting
Grove hems it in. In its middle a raging torrent
Resounds among rocks and a twisting whirlpool. A frightful
Cavern appears and the breathing-holes of dread Pluto.
A vast abyss from a fissure of Acheron opens
Its pestilent throat, where the hated Fury was hidden,   600
Relieving the earth and the sky of her presence. However,
Juno now placed her finishing touch on the fighting.
All of the shepherds rushed out of the line to the city
To bring back the bodies of Almo the boy and Galaesus,
With mangled face. They implored the gods and appealed
To Latinus. Turnus was there in the midst of the clamor
And fire of anger against the slaughter; he doubled
Their terror. He said the Trojans had been invited
To share the power, that Phrygian stock had been mingled
With Latin, that he was being thrust out of the palace.   610
Then those whose mothers, bewildered by Bacchus, were dancing
In chorus through pathless groves—for the name of Amata
Carried great weight—gathered round and shouted for battle.
Contrary to omens and fates of the gods, all demanded
Unspeakable war on the spot, through some perverse power.
As zealous rivals they crowd round the house of Latinus.
He, like a motionless rock on the seashore, resisted,
Some rock where the waves from the deep crash with a great thunder,
Holding its place by its weight as the billows bark round it;
The cliffs and foaming crags scream about it; the seaweed,   620
Crushed on its surface, is washed back again. When no power
Is given to quell this blind plan, and affairs go as Juno
Decides with her nod, then Father Latinus calls often
Both on the gods and upon the empty winds:
"We are broken, alas, by the Fates, we are borne by the tempest!
You will pay for this sacrilege with your own blood, you poor wretches.
A terrible punishment waits for you, Turnus; you'll pray to
The gods, but too late. I have earned my rest and my quiet,
But just as I enter the port I am robbed of a peaceful
Burial." Saying no more, he barred himself up in   630
The palace, relinquished the reins of his government.

In Hesperian Latium a custom obtained, which thenceforward
The Alban cities held sacred, and now Rome, the greatest
Power in the world, observes it whenever she moves toward
New battles, brings tearful war to the Getae or Arabs
Or to the Hyrcanians or pushes on to the Indians,
Or follows Aurora to seek back the standards from Parthia.
There are twin gates of War—for that is the name which they give them—
Sacred in worshipful fear of Mars, the fierce war-god.
One hundred bronze bars, the eternal resistance of iron,　　640
Close the door, nor does Janus, its guard, step away from the threshold.
When the elders' decision for war is entirely certain,
The consul himself in his Quirinal robe and the cincture
Of Gabii opens the screeching doors, calls for battle.
Then the rest of the young men take up the cry, and the bronze horns
Breathe out their hoarse-voiced approval of what he has done.

By this custom Latinus was bidden to declare war on Aeneas
And to open the sinister gates. He recoiled from their touch,
From this repulsive task; he hid in dark shadows.
Then the queen of the gods slipped down from the sky. With her　　650
　　own hand
She pushed the delaying doors. As the hinges swung outward,
She broke the iron-bound doorposts of War. Ausonia,
Silent before and unstirred, now burned with excitement.
Some prepared to walk out to the fields, some rode about fiercely
Through dust on tall horses, and all of them shouted for arms.
Some polished their shields and spears till they shone with thick pig-grease
And sharpened their axes on whetstones. It pleased them to shoulder
The standards and hear the horns blowing. As many as five
Great cities set up their anvils to hammer out weapons,
Atina the strong, proud Tibur, Crustumeri, Ardea,　　660
And towered Antemnae. They hollowed out helmets, bent willows
As frames for their shields. Some forged bronze breastplates or shining
Greaves from tough silver. Their pride in the plow-share and sickle,
All love for the plow gave way to this. They remolded
Their fathers' swords in the furnace. The trumpets now sounded;
The watchword, the signal of war, passed along. Here one snatched up
His helmet from home; there one forced his trembling horses
To the chariot and put on his shield and his triple-gold mail coat,
And strapped on his faithful sword.
　　　　　　　　　　　Now, goddesses, open
Wide Helicon's heights and stir me to sing which the kings were　　670
Who urged on their men to war, which troops each led

To fill up the fields with their ranks, what men the rich country
Of Italy nourished those days, what weapons it brandished.
For you have the memory, goddesses; you can recall them:
To us the scarce audible whisper of their fame has drifted.

    First entrant to war from Tyrrhenian shores was the bitter
Mezzentius, scorner of gods, and his men. At his side
Went Lausus, his son, than whom no one was more handsome
Except Laurentian Turnus. A tamer of horses
And conqueror of wild beasts, he led from Agylla   680
One thousand men, but in vain; a son who was worthy,
Who might have been happier under his father's command
If only Mezzentius had treated him as a father should.

    After these handsome Aventinus, the son of
Handsome Hercules, showed off his prize-winning chariot
And horses upon the grass. He carried his father's
Device on his shield: one hundred snakes and a hydra
Surrounded by serpents. His mother was Rhea, the priestess,
Who bore him in secret upon the shores of light
In a wood on the Aventine hill, a woman who mingled   690
In love with a god, after Hercules, victor from Tiryns,
Had killed the monster Geryon and come to Laurentine
Fields and watered his cattle from Spain in Etruscan
Streams. Aventinus' men carried pikes in their hands
And terrible sword-sticks. They fought with a smooth-pointed sword
And Sabellian lance. He twisted the hide of a lion,
Huge, shaggy with terrible mane and studded with white teeth,
Drawn over his head; and thus he walked up to the palace,
Bristling, his shoulders clad in Hercules' mantle.

    Then twin brothers left the walls of Tibur,   700
Named for their brother Tiburtus; they were Argive youths,
Catillus and eager Coras. They rushed to the front line
Among the dense missiles, like two centaurs born from the clouds,
Who come down on the run from a high mountain top as they leave
Homole and snowy Othrys. Great forests give way
To their passage and underbrush yields with a thundering clatter.

    Nor was Caeculus, Praeneste's founder, absent,
Born among country cattle to be a king
And discovered beside the fireplace (each age
Thus far believed he was the son of Vulcan).   710
He led a gathering from farm and field,
Men who lived at high Praeneste, who
Tilled Gabii's land and Juno's near the cool

Anio river and the Hernican rocks
Dripping with streamlets, men whom Anagnia
The rich gave life to, or the river Amasenus.
Not all of them had arms or shields or chariots
To rattle; the largest share of them had slings
And shot of leaden grey; some brandished spears,
One in each hand, and wore brown caps of skin   720
From wolves upon their heads. They trod with bare
Left foot; the right was shod in boot of rawhide.

    Messapus, tamer of horses, Neptune's offspring,
Whom by gods' law no steel or fire could kill,
Called men to arms, to draw the sword again,
In tribes long quiet and unused to war.
Some formed Fescennine battle lines, some Aequian
And Faliscan; some dwelt upon the heights
Of Mount Soracte, or on Flavinian farms,
Mount Ciminus with its lakes, Capena's groves.   730
They marched to even rhythms and they sang
To praise their king, as sometimes snow-white swans
Among the shining clouds come back from feeding
And utter sonorous song from their long throats.
The river echoes and the Asian marsh
Resounds afar.
No one would think so long a marching line
Was made of bronze-clad ranks, but that an air-borne
Cloud of rough-voiced birds was crowding toward
The beaches from the whirlpools of the sea.   740

    Look! Clausus, of old Sabine blood, himself
Like some great army, led a long marching line.
From him the Claudian tribe and clan descend
Through Latium, after Rome shared power with Sabines.
A huge contingent came from Amiterna,
Old Quirites, a band from Eretum
And olive-bearing Mutusca; those who dwell
At Nomentum, the fields of Rosea
Near Lake Velinus, those who occupy
The cliffs of shuddery Tetrica and Mount   750
Severus and Casperia, Foruli,
The river of Himella, those who drink
The Tiber and Fabaris, those whom chill
Nursia sent, the groups from Hortina,
The Latin people, the region Allia

(Unlucky name!) cuts through, as many as
The waves that roll on Libya's level sea
When in its wintry surge Orion hides
His savage face, or dense as heads of wheat
Warmed by fresh sun upon the plain of Hermus   760
Or yellow fields of Lycia. Shields resounded
And earth was frightened by the thud of feet.

    Here Agamemnon's ally, foe to Troy,
Halaesus, yoked his horses to the car
And drove a thousand warlike clans to Turnus:
Men who chop up with hoes the Massic soil,
Fruitful in grapes, and those Auruncan fathers
Sent from high hills; the men from Cales; those
From Sidicinum's plains, the men who dwell
Along the shallow stream Volturnus; rough   770
Men from Saticula, the Oscan band.
They had smooth javelins fitted with tough thongs;
Bucklers covered their left arms; they used scythes
For fighting hand to hand.
               Nor shall you be
Omitted from my song, Oebalus, whom
Telon begot upon the nymph Sebethis,
The story goes, when he was holding sway
Among the Teleboeae of Capreae,
A man advanced in years. His son was not
Contented with his father's fields; even then   780
He ruled wide lands among Sarrastian folk
Where the river Sarnus irrigates the plains,
The men who hold Rufrae and Batulum,
The farms of Celemna, or those who dwell
Where walls of apple-bearing Abella
Look down, accustomed in the Teuton way
To whirl barbed spears. They wear upon their heads
Bark torn from cork-trees; their bronze targets glitter;
Their bronze swords gleam.
            You, Ufens, mountainous
Nersae sent to battle, known to fame   790
For lucky weapons. Your race, Aequiculi,
Was fitted by much hunting for its rough soil.
Wild men they were; they tilled the ground while armed
And always liked fresh plunder, to live by booty.
    Umbro, the priest, from the Marruvian clan,

Bravest of men, who wore an olive branch
Upon his helmet, was sent by the command
Of King Archippus. He scattered sleep among
The viper race and among hydras, breathing death
By incantation and the skill of hands.   800
He soothed their wrath and healed their stings with art.
Yet he could not dispel the blow he suffered
From a Trojan spear, nor could his incantations
Or herbs sought out on Marsian hills avail him.
Angitia's grove, Fucinus' glassy water,
The liquid lakes mourned you.
        Virbius, offspring of Hippolytus,
Famous and handsome, went to war. His mother
Aricia sent him. He was raised amid
Egeria's grove along the dripping shores   810
Where mild Diana's shrine stands, rich with gifts.
The story runs that when Hippolytus
By his stepmother's craft was killed and suffered
With his own blood the vengeance of his father,
Torn by frightened horses, he arose
To upper air beneath the sky again,
Called back by Paeon's herbs and Diana's love.
Then the Almighty Father, outraged to see
A mortal rise from lower shades to light
Of life again, thrust down to Stygian shades   820
The Phoebus-born discoverer of such art
Of medicine by hurling his thunderbolt.
But generous Trivia hid Hippolytus
In secret haunts and bound him to the nymph
Egeria and her grove. Alone, unknown,
He spent his life in woods of Italy;
Virbius was his name when it was changed.
Hence even now horn-footed horses are
Kept off from Trivia's temple and sacred grove,
Because they overturned both chariot   830
And young man on the beach when they were frightened
By monsters from the sea. His son, however,
Drove horses over the plain and rushed to war
With chariot.
            Turnus himself brandished his weapons
Among the leaders, a man of splendid body,
Taller by a head. His triple-crested

Helmet flaunted a chimera who breathed
Aetnaean fires from its jaws: the more
Raging and wild with grimmer flames, the more
The battle quickened with the blood men shed.   840
Io with raised horns marked his bright shield,
Now thick with bristles, now a heifer—this
A mighty subject drawn in gold—and Argus,
The guardian of the virgin, Father Inachus
Pouring his stream from an urn carved in relief.
There followed a cloud of infantry; beshielded
Ranks filled all the fields, Greek youths, Auruncan
Bands, Rutulians, old Sicanians,
Sacranian lines, colored shields from Labicum,
Those who farmed your wooded pastures, Tiber,   850
The sacred shore of Numicus, and those
Who sink the plow upon Rutulian hills,
The ridge of Circeii, where Anxur's god,
Jupiter, presides, where Feronia's happy
In her green grove, where Satura's black marsh
Spreads out and chilly Ufens seeks a way
Along the valley and is merged with ocean.
        With these Camilla came. Of Volscian stock,
She led her troops of horsemen bright with bronze,
A warrior woman. Not for her the distaff   860
Or woman's hands accustomed to wool-baskets
Of Minerva; she was a girl to suffer
Harsh battles and outstrip the winds at running.
She could have flown above the stalks of wheat
Nor harmed their tender ears, or moved suspended
Above the middle of the swelling waves,
Dry-shod. A crowd of mothers, all the young men
Came pouring out to marvel, as she passed,
From house and field, to gape in wonderment,
To see the regal purple of the robe   870
That graced her shining shoulders and the brooch
Of gold that bound her hair, and how she carried
Her Lycian quiver and a shepherd's staff
Of myrtle; at its tip a spear-blade rose.

BOOK EIGHT

Rome and Evander

As Turnus lifted war's standard from the height
Of Laurentum's citadel, and horns blared out
Their raucous song; as he urged on the lively
Horses and clashed his weapons, at once the minds
Of all were stirred, all Latium surged with tumult,
The wild young men grew wilder. The leaders first,
Messapus and Ufens and Mezzentius,
Despiser of the gods, collected troops
From everywhere, brought farmers from wide fields.
Venulus was sent to the city of great Diomedes   10
To ask for aid, to say the Trojans had
Set foot in Latium, Aeneas and his fleet
Had brought their vanquished household gods, that fate
Demanded he proclaim himself a king,
That many tribes were rallying to the Trojan,
His name was spreading far abroad in Latium.
What he might build on these beginnings, if
Fortune should follow him, the outcome he
Might wish for the fight, appeared to Diomedes
More clearly than to the kings Latinus or Turnus.   20
      Thus the events in Latium. The hero-son
Of Laomedon, seeing all, was buffetted
Upon a great tide of cares; now here, how there
He divided his agile mind among different thoughts,
Turning it this way and that, traversing all
The problem's possibilities, as when
A trembling light on water in a bronze
Vessel, reflected from the sun or from
The shining moon, flits widely everywhere

And now is lifted to the air and strikes   30
The panelled ceiling.
            It was night. Through all
The lands the tired animals, the tribes
Of winged things, of herds, were gripped by heavy
Sleep, when Father Aeneas on the river
Bank, beneath the chilly height of heaven,
Disturbed in heart by grim war, sank to sleep
And gave his limbs belated rest. The local
God Tiberinus from his lovely stream
Appeared to him, an old man rising up
Among the poplar leaves: a slender veil   40
Of grey-green linen covered him, and shady
Reeds his hair. He spoke, to take away
Aeneas' cares:
            "O you, sprung from the race
Of gods, who bring Troy's city back to us
And save eternal Pergamum, for you
Laurentine soil and Latin fields have waited.
Here is your changeless home, your household gods
Abiding—do not shrink, do not be frightened
By threats of war: the swelling wrath of heaven
Has now subsided fully.   50
And lest this seem the figment of a dream,
Upon the shore beneath oak trees shall lie
A huge sow who has farrowed thirty pigs.
White, she lies on the ground; the young that suck
Her teats are white. Your city shall stand here,
A certain rest from labors. Thirty years
From now Ascanius shall found famous Alba.
I sing events by no means doubtful. Now
In which way you may carry out the task
That lies at hand, I shall explain, and briefly.   60
The Arcadians, a people sprung from Pallas,
Who followed King Evander and his standards,
Chose place upon these shores and built a city
Among the hills, Pallanteum from the name
Of their forefather Pallas. These wage war
Continuously with the Latin folk.
Make them your allies, join them to your camp
By treaty. I shall guide you from my banks

With a straight current so that you may row
Upstream against the water. Come, arise,   70
O goddess-born, and when the early stars
Are setting, offer ritual words to Juno,
Placate her wrath and threats with suppliant vows.
When you are victor you shall honor me.
I am the dark-blue Tiber. With full stream
I press these banks and cut through fertile fields,
The stream most favored by the gods. From here
My great home rises, head of lofty cities."
    He spoke, and then the river god concealed
Himself in the deep stream-bed, diving down.   80
Night left Aeneas, and his sleep. He rose
And gazed upon the sunlight in the East,
Then raised cupped hands with water from the river
And spoke these words to heaven:
                        "Nymphs, Laurentine
Nymphs, from whom the rivers spring, and, Tiber
Father, with your holy stream, receive
Aeneas, guard him at long last from danger.
Whatever pool or fountain holds you or
Whatever land you flow through, loveliest
Of those who look with pity on my fortunes,   90
You shall be always honored by my gifts,
Horned river, ruler of the western waters.
Be with me and display your force more firmly."
He spoke and picked two biremes from the fleet,
Fitted them with their oars and armed his comrades.
    Look! suddenly a sight most wonderful!
A white sow, with her litter white as she,
Gleamed upon the green bank; she had lain
Down in the forest. Aeneas offered her,
Bringing the sacred gear, to you, great Juno,   100
And with her brood he placed her at your altar.
Tiber smoothed his swollen stream that night,
Long as it was, and made his ripples silent
Like those upon a still pool or a placid
Swamp, so still the oars found no resistance.
They went their way more swiftly, cheering loudly.
The greased pine hulls slipped through the shallows. Waves
Wondered, the woods too wondered at the shields

Far-shining of men seldom seen, at painted
Keels drifting by. They wore the day and night   *110*
Away with rowing, rounded the long bends,
Were hidden by various trees and cut through green
Forests upon the peaceful river-surface.
The fiery sun at midday rose to heaven
Before they saw, far off, the walls and fortress
And houses here and there. Now Roman power
Has lifted them to heaven; but Evander
At that time had a small domain. They turned
The prows toward land and swiftly approached the city.
       By chance that day the Arcadian king was bearing   *120*
A solemn honor to Amphitryon's son,
To Hercules and to the other gods
In a large grove that stood before the city.
Pallas his son was with him, all the first
Young men, the Senate, men of small estate;
They offered incense, warm blood smoked on the altars.
Then as they saw the tall boats gliding past
The shady grove, the men in silence bending
Upon their oars, the sudden sight brought terror
And all rose up, the tables left behind.   *130*
Bold Pallas said they must not break the rites
And flew before them with his weapon drawn.
He shouted from a distance on a mound:
"Young men, what reason forced you to come here
On unknown ways? Where do you go?" he cried.
"What race, what home is yours? Do you bring peace
Or war?" Father Aeneas from the lofty stern
Spoke thus, an olive branch of peace in hand:
"You see the Trojan-born and weapons hostile
To Latins, who repelled us exiles with   *140*
An insolent attack. We seek Evander.
Carry this word and say that chosen leaders
Of Dardania have arrived and seek
An armed alliance." Pallas was struck with silence
To hear so great a name. "Land here," he said,
"Whoever you are, and speak to my father. Come in
As a guest to our house." He grasped and drew him close,
Embraced him and clung to his right hand. As they walked,
They entered the grove and left the stream behind.

Then Aeneas addressed the king with these friendly words: *150*
"Best of the Greek-born, Fortune wished me to speak
In entreaty to you and to offer these branches adorned
With a woolen fillet. I did not fear you, indeed,
Because you were leader of Greeks, an Arcadian,
And related by blood to the stock of the two Atreidae.
My courage, the holy oracles of the gods,
And our kinsmen fathers, your fame spread over the earth,
Have joined me to you and driven me, yielding to fate.
Dardanus, father of Troy and its founder, born
Of Electra, the daughter of Atlas, the Greeks declare,   *160*
Sailed to the Teucrians; Atlas, that greatest of men,
Who bears heaven's orb on his shoulder, fathered Electra.
Your family's father is Mercury, whom shining Maia
Conceived and bore on the chilly height of Cyllene.
But Atlas, if we are to put any trust in tradition,
Was father of Maia, that Atlas who holds up the stars.
Thus the stocks of our family split from the same blood-source.
Dependent on facts such as these I sent you no message,
I made you no overtures carefully planned in deceit.
I presented myself to you, offered my life; I came   *170*
As a suppliant to your threshold. That Daunian race
That drove you in cruel war drives us. If they banish
Us from this land they believe they will conquer completely
All of this western soil, send it under the yoke,
And control the seas that wash it on North and South.
Receive, and give me, a pledge: our spirits are brave
For war; we have courage and youth that is tested in action."
Aeneas had spoken. While he was speaking Evander
Had looked at his face and his eyes for a long time,
Examined him from head to feet. Then he briefly replied :   *180*
"How gladly I welcome and recognize you, the bravest
Of Teucrians, how I remember the words of your father,
The voice and the face of Anchises the great! I remember
How Priam, Laomedon's son, came to Salamis, visiting
The realm of his sister Hesione, then came to the chilly
Land of Arcadia. Youth in first flower was clothing
My cheeks with a beard. I gaped at the Teucrian leaders,
At Laomedon's son; but Anchises walked taller than any.
My heart in young eagerness yearned to engage his attention,
To grasp his right hand. I came forward and zealously led him   *190*

Under Pheneus' walls. He gave me when he was departing
His unusual quiver, his Lycian arrows, a chlamys
Embroidered with gold, and two golden bits which my Pallas
Has now. Thus the pledge which you seek has been made by that treaty
With Priam. Tomorrow at dawn I shall send willing helpers
With goods to assist you. Meanwhile, since you come in all friendship,
Be pleased to take part in these annual rites; our religion
Allows no postponement. Consider yourselves our companions
And sit at the tables." When this had been said, King Evander
Gave orders that both food and drink be replenished. He seated   200
The men on the grass. To Aeneas he gave special welcome
Upon a low bed covered with lion-skin; he invited
Him up to the maple-wood throne. Then young men, selected
For service, the priest of the altar, all eagerly carried
Roast meat from the bulls and piled bread in baskets, those gifts which
Ceres gives laboring mankind, and poured wine of Bacchus.
Aeneas at once and the Trojan young men made a banquet
From an entire side of beef and the ritual entrails.
      When hunger was satisfied, their love of eating abated,
Then spoke King Evander: "No vain superstition enforces,   210
No ignorance of ancient gods, these rites or this banquet
We eat by our custom, or this altar to such a high power.
Trojan guest, we are men who were saved from terrible dangers,
And thus we perform and renew these merited honors.
First look at this cliff, overhanging with stones, where that mountain
Lair now stands deserted among scattered masses, leaving
A huge ruin of rock on its trail. Here was the cavern,
Deep in extensive retreat, where the cruel face of Cacus,
Half-man and half-beast, kept out all approach of the sunlight.
The soil at its edge dripped always with blood of fresh slaughter;   220
Upon its proud doors were fixed human skulls, pale and rotten.
To this monster Vulcan was parent. He belched out his father's
Black fire as he lumbered along with his gigantic carcass.
Time at last brought to us in our need some assistance
With a god's arrival. For Hercules, greatest avenger,
Proud of the slaughter and spoils of three-headed Geryon,
Came driving great bulls as a victor; his cattle were holding
The valley and stream. But the mad brain of Cacus the robber,
Lest he leave any crime or deceit undared, unattempted,
Singled out four beautiful bulls from the herd and as many   230
Heifers of outstanding form. To wipe out any traces

Of sharp-pressing hoofs he pulled them by tail to the cavern
And covered the signs of his plunder within the dark rock.
To anyone searching, no evidence led to the cave.
In the meanwhile when Hercules readied his herd to move onward,
Well-fed from their grazing, the cattle lowed at their departure
And filled all the grove with complaints and the hills with their clamor.
One cow in the deep cave returned an answering bellow
And cheated the hopes of Cacus that she was well hidden.
Now Hercules' rage and his sorrow flamed up with black venom.   240
He snatched arms, his club made of oak-wood heavy with knots,
And ran up the steep-sided mountain that rose high above him.
Then for the first time we saw terror shine in the eyes
Of Cacus. He fled from the spot, more swift than the East Wind.
He ran for his cave, and fear added wings to his feet.
He shut himself up and dropped a huge rock, having broken
The chains that suspended it, fashioned by his father's skill,
Thus blocking the doorposts by placing the rock square between them.
Look! the Tirynthian, mad in his anger, arrived,
Scanning all access and glaring this way and that,   250
Grinding his teeth. Three times in a transport of fury
He paced the whole Aventine hill, tried the stony threshold
Three times in vain; three times he sat down in the valley,
Tired. There was a sharp rock with the stone cut sheer round it
That rose on the ridge of the cave, a vision most lofty
And a home that was fit for the nests of fierce birds of prey.
This hung on the left of the ridge slanting down to the river.
Hercules pushed at the rock from the right side and wrenched it
Off from its roots. He suddenly shook it. Great ether
Resounded, the banks sprang apart, and the river ran backward   260
In terror. The vast cave of Cacus appeared from its cover,
His palace was seen, and the shadowy cavern lay open.
It was as if earth by some force had yawned upward completely
To disclose the regions below and the realm of the pallid,
Detested by gods, and the monstrous abyss seen from somewhere
Above it, the ghosts set a-tremble by light that now entered.
So Hercules, having caught Cacus in glow unexpected,
Trapped in his hollow rock, roaring more loudly than ever,
Shot missiles at him and called every arm into service,
Attacked him with tree-branches, huge blocks of stone. But now   270
    Cacus—
There remained no escape from his danger—sent forth from his jaws

Thick smoke—a marvel to tell—and filled all his palace
With blinding darkness that snatched any vision from eyes.
He rolled up the smoke-bearing night, fire mingled with darkness,
There in his cave. But Hercules' heart could not bear it.
He jumped down headlong through the fire just where the smoke gathered
Most densely in waves as its black cloud boiled through the cave.
     Here he seized Cacus, still belching out flame in the darkness,
Yet vainly. He tied him in knots and squeezed out his eyes
Till they bulged, and he choked him until his throat was dry   280
Of all blood. Then at once the doors of the dark cave flew open.
The black home within was revealed, and the stolen cattle,
The plunder he swore was not his was laid bare to the heavens.
Hercules hauled out his shapeless hulk by the feet.
Those who stood by could not satisfy their deep desire
To look at those terrible eyes, that face, and the hairy
Chest with its half-beastly bristles, the jaw whence the fire
Had faded. From that time to this Hercules is honored.
A happy posterity, and the first founder, Potitius,
The house of Pinarius, guards of the temple, observe   290
Hercules' day. In this grove he established this altar,
Which shall always by us be called Greatest and greatest shall be.
So come forward, young men, to honor such glorious deeds:
Encircle your hair with leaves, take a cup in your right hand.
Call on the gods whom we share and pour wine with a will."
He spoke, while with bi-colored poplar, Hercules' shade-tree,
He veiled his hair as it hung intertwined with the leaves,
The holy cup in his right hand. Soon all of the others
Poured wine in their gladness at table and prayed to the gods.
     Meanwhile the Evening approached as Olympus sloped   300
          downward
And now the priests, with Potitius first, came walking,
Bound round in their custom with skins, and they carried torches.
They fell to the feasting again and brought pleasing gifts
For the second course; they loaded the altars with heaping
Platters of food. Then Salian priests sang songs
Round the burning altars, their brows twined with poplar branches.
On this side the chorus of youths, on that side the old men
Sang praises of Hercules and of his deeds, how he strangled
And crushed the twin snakes, his stepmother Juno's first monsters.
How he shattered fine cities in war, Troy, Oechalia;   310
How he bore a thousand harsh labors by fates of an unjust

Juno for King Eurystheus: "You, the unconquered,
Killed with your hands those cloud-born centaurs, the twin-shaped
Hylaeus and Pholus; you slaughtered the Cretan monster
And under Nemea's cliff its huge lion. The Stygian
Lake trembled to see you, the gate-guard of Orcus reclining
On half-eaten bones in his bloody cave. No face frightened
You, not even Typhoeus, his weapons held high. Lerna's serpent,
A hubbub of heads, assailed you nor found you unready.
Hail, true descendant of Jove, splendor added to godhead,   320
Approach with a favoring step both your worship and us."
Such deeds did they praise in their hymns. Next, they wound up the series
Of exploits with Cacus' cave and himself, breathing fire.
The entire grove rang out with the riot; hills echoed.
    Then, all of their services done, they returned to the city.
The king, weighed down with his years, walked beside Aeneas,
Holding his son by the hand, and he lightened their journey
With various remarks. Aeneas, wondering, looked round him.
His quick eyes saw all; in delight with the place, he inquired,
And heard, about each of the things men of old had left there.   330
Then spoke Evander the king, who founded Rome's fortress:
"These groves the indigenous Fauns and the Nymphs used to dwell in,
And a race of men sprung from trunks of hard oak who had neither
Culture nor custom nor knew how to yoke bulls nor gather
Their food nor to store it when gathered. They nourished themselves
With fruit from the boughs, with prey from rough hunting.
                                                        First from lofty
Olympus came Saturn, who fled from Jove's weapons, an exile
Deprived of his realm. He collected these indocile people
Dispersed through high mountains, he gave them laws and decided
To call their land Latium because he lay hidden in safety   340
Within it. Those years were golden when he was king.
He ruled over people in peace till a tarnished age,
One gradually worse, came on, and a madness for war
And a love of possessions. Then a band from Ausonia, clans
From Sicania, came. Saturnian land often changed
Its name. Then came kings, and rough Tiber with his
Huge body. Afterward we Italians gave
The river his name. Old Albula lost its true title.
Omnipotent fortune and ineluctable fate
Placed me in this land, an exile from home who sailed   350
The uttermost edge of ocean. The dreadful commands

Of my mother, the nymph Carmentis, compelled me, the will
Of the god Apollo." He scarcely had spoken these words
When, walking along, he showed the Carmental shrine
And the gate of that name, as the Romans call it, the first
Honor the nymph received, the prophetic priestess
Who chanted the future greatness of the descendants
Of Aeneas, the future fame of Pallanteum.
Evander displayed the wide grove which brave Romulus
Set aside for asylum, the Lupercal under its chill   360
Cliff, so named in Arcadian fashion from Pan
The Lycaean. He showed him the sacred wood Argiletum,
Called the place to witness and told him how Argus, his guest,
Met his death. From here he led Aeneas until
They reached the abode of Tarpeia and Capitoline heights
Now golden, but then all shaggy with wilderness-brambles.
Already at that time religious awe of the spot
Kept alarming the shivering farmers, already they trembled
At wood and at rock. "This grove, this hill with its leafy
Top is the home of a god: who he is I know not.   370
The Arcadians think they have seen great Jove himself
Shaking the deep-black aegis in his right hand
And driving the rain-clouds along. In addition, you see
Two cities in ruin, mere remnants, reminders of the
Men of old time. Janus-father founded this fortress,
And Saturn that one. Janiculum this one was called,
And Saturnia that." With such words, they came to the house
Of the poor Evander and saw the cattle abroad
In the Roman Forum, lowing amid the Carinae
Quarter, so rich today. When they came to the palace,   380
Evander said: "The victor Alcides walked over this threshold,
This palace received him. Endure as my guest to despise
Riches and make yourself worthy of godhood. Do not
Disdain my poor household." He spoke and led huge Aeneas
Beneath his small roof, laid him on a bed of strewn leaves
And the skin of a Libyan bear.

                              Night swept down and encircled
The earth with its dusky wings. But Venus, a mother
Distracted at heart with good cause at the threats of Laurentum,
And moved by harsh tumult, spoke to Vulcan her husband in his
Golden bedroom and breathed on him heavenly love with her words: 390
"While the Greek kings were ravaging Troy, which was destined to fall,

And her fortress was ready to sink beneath enemy fire,
I asked for no help to my wretched ones, asked for no weapons
Wrought by your skill and expense, dearest husband of mine.
I did not wish you to work without object although
I owed a great deal to the children of Priam and wept
Often at Aeneas' harsh toil. Now by order of Jove
He has landed on Rutulian shores. Thus I come as a suppliant
To beg of your godhead for arms, a mother for her son.
The daughter of Nereus, Thetis, and Aurora, the wife   400
Of Tithonus, could sway you with tears. See how peoples assemble,
How cities with gates closed are sharpening swords against me
And against my own folk." The goddess had spoken. With snowy
Arms she embraced him softly on this side and that
As he resisted. But suddenly love for her flamed as it used to,
The warmth he well knew sank deep in his marrow and ran through
His tottering bones, not otherwise than when the fiery
Lightning breaks out with its sparkling glow amidst thunder
And runs through the clouds. His wife sensed the change in his feeling,
Delighted with plots and aware of her beauty. Her husband,   410
Enchained by a love that would last for eternity, answered:
"Why do you look for your reasons afar, do you trust me
No more, goddess? If your concern had been as it now is,
It would have been right for me then to give arms to the Trojans.
No father all-powerful, no Fates forbade Troy to flourish
Or Priam to live for another ten years. And now, if you
Are ready to fight and your mind is made up, cease by begging
To doubt your own strength. Whatever I can I shall promise,
My skill to make weapons of iron and melted electrum,
Whatever my fires and bellows produce." Having spoken,   420
He gave her the clinging embrace she desired and, lying
Upon her soft breasts, he sought placid sleep from her body.
When the first quiet of night from its midmost course
Had passed and driven off sleep, when the housewife arises
To earn a bare living by spinning, without much help
From Minerva, and fans the fire that rests in the ashes,
Adding the night to her labor and urging her servants
To their long tasks by the hearth-light, so that she can manage
To keep her home chaste and to raise her husband's small children;
Not different from her nor lazier at that hour,   430
The Mighty-With-Fire arose from his soft bed to work at
His forge. Near the coast of Sicily and Aeolian Lipare

An island ascends, steep-up with its steaming rocks,
Under which are the cave and the grottoes of Aetna made hollow
By the Cyclopes' smithy, loud with strong strokes on the anvils;
Their grunting and groaning resound through the echoing chamber,
And iron bars hiss in the furnace where fire is roaring.
Here is the home of Vulcan; the land is Volcania.
Here then the Mighty-With-Fire descended from heaven.
The Cyclopes worked over iron within their vast cavern,   440
Brontes, Steropes, Pyragmon, his legs and arms naked.
They held in their hands a shapeless mass, partly finished.
A thunderbolt such as the Father throws down in great numbers
From heaven to earth, but part of it still was imperfect.
They had added three rays of the twisting hail, three of rainy
Cloud, three of ruddy fire and the flying South Wind.
Now they mingled the frightening thunders, the sound and the dread
And the anger that rise from pursuing flames. In another
Place they were hurrying work on a chariot for Mars
With swift-rolling wheels with which he stirs cities and people,   450
And a horrific aegis, the weapon of angry Minerva,
They burnished in rivalry with serpent-scales of gold
And the Gorgon herself on the breast of the goddess with twined snakes:
Her eyes kept on rolling around though her neck had been severed.
"Take all of this off," he said, "Remove what you've started,
Aetnaean Cyclopes, and turn your attention to this:
We have weapons to make for a man of keen courage. Now hurry,
Use all of your strength and swift hands and your masterly skill."
No more did he speak. All as one they fell quickly to labor,
Dividing the work. Both bronze and gold flowed in rivers.   460
Wound-making iron grew liquid within a vast furnace.
They made a huge shield, one shield against all Latin weapons,
Seven layers upon layers held fast. Some worked at the bellows,
With air in and out; others thrust hissing bronze in a dip-tank.
The cavern resounded from anvils in place. Their great power
Of arm lifted hammers; they turned massive metal with tongs.

While the Lemnian father made haste with this work on Aeolian
Shores, the nourishing daylight was waking Evander
From his humble home, to the morning sound of the birds
Under his eaves. The old man rose, slipped a tunic   470
Over his legs and laced on Etruscan sandals.
Then he slung to his side and his shoulder a Tegean sword

And twisted the hide of a panther about him; it hung
From his left arm. Twin watchdogs descended the high stairs before him
And kept steady pace with the footsteps of their master.
This hero set out for the quarters reserved to Aeneas,
Mindful of their conversation and what he had promised.
No less early than he, Aeneas was astir in the morning.
Evander's son Pallas came with him; Achates moved forward,
Aeneas' companion. When met, they shook hands and sat down   480
In the midst of the palace. At last they could talk at their pleasure.
First the king said:
"You are the greatest of Teucrian leaders; while you are
Alive I shall never admit that Troy's fortunes and kingdom
Have perished. Compared with a name so great, our power
To aid in a war is little. On this side the Tuscan
River, on that the Rutulians hem us in.
Their weapons clash round our walls. But for you I am ready
To marshal great peoples and camps that are rich with their kingdoms,
Salvation which fate unexpected presents. You were brought here   490
By Fates that demanded you. Not far away stands the city
Of Agylla, based on its ancient rock, where the people
Of Lydia, famous in war, had settled among the
Etruscan mountains. It flourished for many years.
Then a king named Mezzentius gripped it with pride and with power
Of savage arms. Why should I recall the revolting
Slaughter he made, or the beastly deeds of this tyrant?
May the gods punish him and his children with similar suffering!
For he joined living bodies to dead ones, bound hand to hand
And face to face as a kind of torture, destroying   500
His victims with long-drawn-out death in this wretched embrace,
Dripping with gore and decay, till at last his own people,
Weary of such unspeakable horror, took arms
And surrounded the madman's home, cut down his retainers
And hurled torches upon his roof. In the struggle that followed
Mezzentius escaped to Rutulian fields and the armed
Protection of Turnus, his guest-friend. All Etruria
Was roused to just fury and, threatening war, they demanded
The king should be punished. Aeneas, I add to their thousands
You as their leader. They roar; all the length of the shore   510
Their ships lie close-drawn; they order the signal for action.
An aged soothsayer, foretelling the fates, now restrains them:
'O chosen young men of Maeonia, flower and courage

Of earlier men, a just sorrow, a wrath he deserves,
Mezzentius kindles in you. No Italian man
Has the right to command such a people in war. Choose a leader
Apart from your race.' Then the Etruscan army subsided
In their fright at such warning from gods in a camp on this plain.
Tarchon himself sent his envoys to me with the scepter
And crown of his kingdom; he turned these insignia over   520
So that I might come to his camp and assume the Tyrrhenian
Rule. An old age worn down by my years is too slow
And too cold to take up this command; my strength has grown feeble
For bravery now. I should urge my son to take over
Instead if he were not a mixed breed held loyal to this country
By descent from a Sabine mother. But you are a man
To whose stock and years the Fates have been kind, whom the spirits
Above are demanding. March on, bravest leader of Trojans
And of the Italians. I shall send Pallas to join you,
My hope and my solace, with you as his teacher to master   530
The hardship and labor of war, to look up to you, model
His youth by your deeds. Two hundred Arcadian horsemen,
Picked strength of our young men, I give you. And Pallas shall give
You a similar number in his name." He scarcely had spoken,
While Aeneas, the son of Anchises, and faithful Achates
Both stood looking downward, sad-hearted, and thought of their troubles,
When Venus gave sign from a cloudless sky.

                                        For the lightning
Came shivering down from the ether to startle them. Thunder
Rang out of a sudden, creation itself seemed to topple,
As an Etruscan horn blared clangor abroad through the heavens.   540
They looked up. The huge crash resounded again and again:
They saw weapons glowing bright red through the clouds in a clear
Part of the sky; these rattled as if they were struck.
The others stood still in bewilderment, but the Trojan hero
Recognized the loud noise and the promise of his divine mother.
Then he spoke: "Friend and host, do not ask what misfortune these
          portents
May bring us. Olympus is calling me. My goddess-mother
Foretold she would send me this sign if the war should break out,
And that she would bring weapons made by Vulcan to aid me,
Through heaven's air.   550
Ah, what a miserable slaughter awaits the Laurentians,

What revenge you shall give me, Turnus, how many the shields
Of men, and their helmets, and their brave bodies shall roll
In your waves, Tiber father. Let them seek battle and break
Their treaty." When he had said this, he rose from his throne
And stirred first the sleeping fires on Hercules' altar,
Then joyfully came to the hearth-god of yesterday
And the little house-spirits.

                       Evander, together with those
Young men of the Trojans, slaughtered some sheep they had chosen
According to custom. Aeneas then walked to the ships   560
And rejoined his companions. Out of their number he picked
Men of outstanding courage to follow his lead
In war. The remainder were carried downstream by the lazy
Help of the river, with news to Ascanius from
Aeneas about his affairs. Now horses were given
To those Teucrians bound for Tyrrhenian fields. They led out
For Aeneas a mount well-selected, threw over its back
The skin of a tawny lion with bright gilded claws.
Suddenly Rumor went winging throughout the small city
To say that swift horsemen approached the Tyrrhenian king's   570
Palace: the mothers redoubled their prayers in fear.
Their fear was as great as their danger; the image of Mars
Appeared ever larger. Then Father Evander seized hold
Of his son's right hand in departure, incessantly wept,
And spoke to him thus: "If Jupiter might bring me back
The years that are gone and make me as once I was,
When under the wall of Praeneste I crushed their first line
And burned heaps of shields in my victory and sent their king,
Herulus, down into Tartarus with this right hand—
Herulus, to whom his mother Feronia gave   580
Three lives at his birth—a frightening tale—three sets
Of weapons to handle, three times to be laid low in death;
Yet this right hand took all of his lives and his weapons
Away: if I were like that, my son, I should never
Be torn from your arms, nor would Mezzentius ever
Have heaped me, his neighbor, with insults or slain with his sword
So many a corpse, have widowed the city of so
Many a citizen. But you, O gods, and you greatest
Chief of the gods, I ask you, Jupiter, pity
A king of Arcadia, hear the prayers of a father.   590

If your power divine, if the Fates shall preserve my Pallas
And I see him alive and shall meet him again, I pray for
My life; I shall suffer whatever distress may be mine.
But if you, O Fortune, now threaten unspeakable downfall,
Now, now may you break off my cruel life, while my sorrows
Are doubtful, while hope in the future is dim, while I hold you,
My dear boy, my only, my late joy, here close in my arms,
Before any worse news can wound me." Thus prayed this father
At parting; his servants brought him to his house in collapse.

And now through the open gates the cavalry galloped,   600
Aeneas among the first, and faithful Achates,
Then other Trojan nobles, and Pallas himself
In the midst of the line, his cloak and his weapons noteworthy
For their varied designs.
                          As when Lucifer, wet with sea water,
Whom Venus delights in above all other bright stars,
Lifts up his holy face and dispels the night-shadows,
Frightened mothers stand on the walls and seek out with their eyes
The dust cloud where troops in glittering bronze stand in line.
The armed men press on through thickets, by shortest of roads.
A roaring arises, the battle-line forms. Horses' hoofs   610
With four-footed thud strike the crumbling field.
                                        There's a huge
Cool wood near the river of Caere, held sacred afar
In the faith of our fathers. Hollow hills surround it, a grove
Dark with pines. Story tells that the ancient Pelasgians, who
Were the first long ago to hold the region of Latium,
Devoted it to Silvanus, the god of the fields
And flocks, and assigned him the wood and a feast day as well.
Not far from here Tarchon and the Tyrrhenians held
Safe position in camp, and from a high hill all their gathering
Now could be seen as it stretched far away through the plains.   620
Here Father Aeneas and the young men he chose for the war
Came, weary with travel, to care for their mounts and themselves.

But Venus, bright goddess, came down from the heavenly clouds,
Bearing gifts, and she saw her son in a lonely valley
Beyond the cool river. She suddenly came and spoke to him:
"Look at the gifts I promised, prepared by my husband's
Skill! Do not hesitate now to challenge bold Turnus
In battle, or the proud Laurentians, my son." Her speech ended,
She embraced him and placed the shining armor beneath

An oak tree before him. Delighted with such a great honor   630
And with her gifts, he could not be satisfied, gazing
At each of them over and over. He turned in his hands
The helmet with terrible crests flashing flame, the fate-bringing
Sword, the huge breast-plate stiff with bronze, blood-colored,
And shining afar like a cloud with the sun's light upon it;
Then the greaves, smooth with gold and electrum, the spear, and the
     art-work
Embossed on the shield, indescribable.
                                        The Mighty-With-Fire,
Well-knowing the prophecies and the events still to come,
Had depicted upon it Italian history, triumphs
Of Romans, the people that were to descend from Ascanius,   640
The wars they would fight, each in order. His pictures included
The she-wolf, her litter, crouched there in the green cave of Mars,
The twin boys at play without fear round her udders and sucking
Her teats as she bent her smooth neck to caress them and lick their
Bodies. Near them he had added the image of Rome,
And the Sabine women raped with such violence from
The throng that had gathered to watch the great games in the circus,
Where a sudden new battle arose between Romulus' men
And the stern folk from Cures who followed old Tatius. Thereafter,
The struggle decided, their kings faced each other in front of   650
The altar of Jupiter Armed, with a bowl in their hands,
And concluded a pact by means of a sacrificed sow.
Not far off Mettus was torn apart by two chariots
Driven in opposite ways—O Alban, you should have
Stood by your word!—and Tullus was dragging the entrails
Of the liar through woodlands and spattering brambles with blood.
Porsenna elsewhere was commanding that Tarquin the exile
Be restored and was laying a massive siege against Rome.
Aeneas' descendants were rushing toward death for their freedom.
You could see him (Porsenna) again as he angrily threatened   660
Because Cocles dared to cut down the bridge, and Cloelia
Had broken her bonds and was swimming the river.
                                                   The guardian
Of Tarpeia's citadel stood at the top of the shield,
Manlius holding the heights of the Capitoline Hill,
Where the palace of Romulus bristled with thatch fresh at ridge pole.
Here among golden columns there fluttered a silver
Goose which gave warning the Gauls were upon the threshold;

They had crept through the bushes and were almost within the stronghold,
Protected by shadows, the gift of a gloom-filled night.
Golden their hair and golden their garments; their striped cloaks   670
Were gleaming; their milk-white necks were encircled with gold.
Each man held two glittering Alpine spears in his hand.
Long shields protected their bodies.

                Here, Salian priests
Leaping in air, and the naked Luperci were wrought
In the bronze, and there were the wool-crowned caps, the twelve shields
That fell from heaven. Chaste mothers in cushioned chariots
Escorted the sacred objects throughout the city.
At a distance were added the tall gates of Dis and the region
Of Tartarus, atonement for crime. You, Catiline, hung
From a threatening cliff and shuddered to see Furies' faces.   680
The righteous were separate: Cato was giving them laws.
Between these there lay the image of swollen Ocean
Done in gold, its blue water foaming with white-capped waves,
And around it the bright silver dolphins were sweeping the surface
And cutting the swell with their tails.

                      In the middle a bronze-clad
Fleet at the battle of Actium.

                  You could have discerned
All Leucate aboil with ranked ships, the waves shining in gold.
Here was Caesar Augustus, who led the Italian navy,
With the Senate, the People, the Little Gods and the Great,
Standing high on the stern; twin flames flashing out at his temples,   690
On his head shone the star of his father.

                    At one side Agrippa
With the help of the winds and the gods led his towering squadron,
The proud ensign of war, the beaked naval crown, on his temples.
Here Antony sailed with barbarian forces and varied
Arms, the victor from lands of morning, the Red Sea
Shore, bringing with him the strength of Egypt, the East,
And farthest Bactria; his Egyptian wife—
O sinful!—came following. All rushed together. The sea
Was everywhere shattered to foam by the oars drawn back
And trident prows. They made for deep water.

                      You might   700
Believe that the Cyclades Islands had been torn up
To float in the sea, or high mountains had clashed on mountains,
So great was the mass of men on the turreted decks.
Flaming tow scattered by hand went flying with steel

Of arrow heads. Neptune's fields grew red with fresh slaughter.
The queen in the middle with her ancestral sistrum
Marshalled her fleet; not yet did she see twin asps
At her back. Dog-barker Anubis and the monsters of all
Kinds of gods held their weapons against Neptune and Venus,
Against Minerva. Mars raged in the middle of battle,   710
Embossed in steel, and fierce Furies out of the heavens;
And Discord, striding in tattered robes, rejoiced.
Bellona came after her, swinging a bloody whip.
Apollo of Actium, viewing the scene, bent his bow
From above. Each Egyptian, every Indian, all
The Arabs and all the Sabaeans turned tail in fear.
The queen herself could be seen, having called on the winds,
To set sail as she loosed the slackening ropes more and more.
The Mighty-With-Fire had pictured her, pale at the death
Which was coming, amid the slaughter as she sailed through the waves   720
Rolled up from the West-North-West. Before her the Nile,
Grief-stricken in that huge body, spread open his robe
And called her with all of his garments to rest on his blue
Bosom, the vanquished to hide in his secret streams.
But Caesar, borne through Rome's walls in a triple triumph,
Was making a deathless vow to Italian gods:
He would build three hundred great temples throughout the whole city.
The streets were an uproar of laughter and clapping and games.
In all of the temples a chorus of mothers, in all
Sacrifice lay on each altar. Slain bullocks lay sprawled   730
On the earth before each.
            Caesar sat on the snowy white threshold
Of Phoebus to acknowledge gifts from the peoples, to hang them
Upon the proud doorposts. The conquered races went by
In a long procession, as varied in tongue as in dress
And weapons. Here Nomads and ungirdled Africans,
There Leleges, Carians, Gelonians with their arrows
Were pictured by Vulcan. Euphrates now flowed with more humble
Waters. Morini, the farthest of men, and the Rhine
With twin horns, the unconquered Dahae, Araxes angry
Because of his bridge:
            Aeneas wondered at such   740
Strange scenes on the shield of Vulcan, his mother's gift,
And rejoiced in it, ignorant of things to come, lifting upward
Onto his shoulder the fame and the fate of his offspring.

BOOK NINE

Attack on Aeneas' Camp

While these events were occurring in distant parts,
Saturnian Juno sent Iris down from the sky
To bold Turnus. He happened then to be seated within
A grove of the valley sacred to his ancestor
Pilumnus. The rosy-mouthed daughter of Thaumas spoke:
"Turnus, that which no god might have dared to promise
A suppliant, time in its turning has given you, see,
Of its own accord. Aeneas has left the city,
His comrades and fleet, to seek the Palatine scepter
And Evander's house. No, more; he has gone to the farthest   10
Cities of Corythus and to the band of Lydians.
He arms the collected farmers. Why wait? Now's the time
To call for your horses and chariots. Break off all lingering!
Seize with surprise his camp!" She spoke and to heaven
Arose on her balanced wings and as she was flying
Traced a huge rainbow under the clouds. Young Turnus
Recognized her and lifted both hands toward the stars.
He followed her flight with these words: "O Iris, adornment
Of heaven, who sent you down from the clouds to me
And the earth? Whence came this weather, so clear, so sudden?   20
I see the sky part in the middle, the stars go wandering
Round the pole. I follow omens so great, whoever
You are that call me to arms." So he spoke and proceeded
To dip up some water from the pool's surface and pray
Long to the gods and to burden the heavens with vows.
And now all the army went marching through open fields,
Rich in good horseflesh, rich in bright garments and gold.
Messapus led the first line, the young men of Tyrrhus
Brought up the rear, while Turnus took charge of the center,
Brandishing weapons, a full head taller than others,   30

As the deep Ganges surging with seven calm streams,
Or Nile with its opulent flood when it flows from the fields
And sinks back to its channel.
                     The Teucrians suddenly see
A cloud of black dust rolling up and shadows invading
The fields. First Caicus from the vanguard cried out:
"What rounded mass of darkness rolls this way?
Quickly, bring me my sword! Take weapons and climb
The walls! The enemy comes, heia!" The Trojans
With a great shout took cover and stationed their men
At gates and on walls; for when he departed, Aeneas,   40
The best man at arms, had advised them if crisis of fortune
Should arise, not to venture in battle nor dare to begin
Attack in the field but to keep themselves safely in camp,
Behind its earth-walls. And therefore, although they were angry,
Ashamed not to fight, they obeyed and shut up the gates
And awaited the enemy, armed in their hollow towers.
Turnus flew on ahead of the slow-moving column
With twenty picked horsemen and suddenly came to the city
On a white-spotted Thracian horse; he wore a gold helmet
Decked with a crimson crest: "Which one of you young men   50
Shall attack with me? Look!" He flung a spear into air
To start off the battle and, tall in the saddle, rode out.
His comrades took up the clamor from him and followed
With frightening noise. They wondered to see the slack courage
Of the Teucrians, shunning fair combat, not hurling their weapons
Against men but clinging to camp. He rode wildly about
And sought through the pathless environs an approach to the walls,
Like a wolf that is lurking on watch outside a full sheep pen
To howl at the holes in the fence and to weather the wind
And the rain at deep midnight, while safely crouched under their   60
    mothers
The lambs bleat; but, cruel and implacably angry, he rages
Against what he cannot devour, and the madness to eat them,
Long checked, makes him weary, his jaws dry of blood that he longs for.
Not otherwise Turnus, gazing at walls and the camp,
Burned with anger; its pain warmed his hard bones and made him
Think how to dislodge the Trojans, bring them out in the open.
He struck at the fleet, moored and hidden on one side of the camp,
Fenced in by earth-works and by the waves of the river.
He called on his cheering comrades for fire and fiercely

Grasped a pine torch. They fell to; his presence inspired them all   70
And as one man they caught up black firebrands, showered them round.
The pitch-pine glared smokily, Vulcan threw up to the stars
Ash mixed with flame.
                    What god turned this furious fire
Away from the Trojans, O Muse? Who drove from the fleet
Such flames? Speak out: the basis for faith in the deed
Is ancient, its fame everlasting.
                    At that time when first
Aeneas on Phrygian Ida was forming a fleet
And preparing to sail the deep sea, the Berecyntian goddess,
The mother of gods, spoke as follows to great Jupiter:
"Grant your dear mother's request, my son, lord of Olympus.   80
A pine wood was mine, which I loved for many years,
A grove on the citadel's height where men carried their offerings,
Shadowy with black pines and maple timbers.
Gladly I gave these to Dardanus' young descendant
In need of a fleet. Now, anxious with fear, I am worried.
Dispel my dread and give me, your parent, the power
To keep them unscathed in their course and to conquer the wind-storm.
Let it be their good fortune they grew up on my mountains."
Her son then replied, he who guides the stars in the heavens:
"O mother, where do you summon the Fates or what do you   90
Ask for these ships? Should keels made with human hands
Have an immortal right? Should Aeneas securely
Pass through uncertain perils? To which god was ever
Granted such power? No! When they have served their purpose,
At anchor in Italian ports, that is, those which survive
The waves and carry the Trojan leader to fields
Of Laurentum, I shall deprive of their mortal shape
And turn them into sea-goddesses such as Doto,
The daughter of Nereus, and Galatea who cleave
The foaming sea with their breasts." He spoke and in nodding   100
Proclaimed that his words had been ratified at Styx-waters,
The stream of his brother, by banks where black pitch flowed in
        whirlpools:
And with his nodding he caused all Olympus to tremble.

The promised day had arrived and the time which the Parcae
Had set was completed, when Turnus' plan caused the Mother
To drive his torches away from the sacred ships.

Here first the new light was seen and a large cloud scudding
With Mount Ida's dancers across the sky from the East.
Then a terrible voice broke through the air and resounded
Among battle lines of both the Rutulians and Trojans: 110
"Do not rush to defend my ships, Trojans, or to arm your bands.
The power to burn up the sea will be given to Turnus
Before he can burn the sacred pines. Sail on,
With hawser unloosed; go, goddesses of the sea.
Your mother commands you."
                              Immediately each of the sterns
Broke its rope from the banks and plunged the beak into water
Like a dolphin that dives to the depths—a marvelous portent!—
And from them there rose the figures of girls, just as many
As the ships with bronze prows that were previously moored at the shore,
To float on the sea.
                      The Rutulian courage was baffled,   120
Messapus himself was frightened, his horses disturbed.
The rough-roaring Tiber delayed, drew its foot back from the ocean.
But confidence did not depart from bold-hearted Turnus;
Beyond that, he cheered them with words; beyond that, he ranted:
"These portents threaten the Trojans; Jupiter has taken
Away the help they were used to. No weapons or fire
Await the Rutulians. No Trojan hope of escaping
Over the pathless sea: half the world is denied them.
The land is in our hands, so many thousands
Of people in Italy now bear arms; the pronouncements   130
Of fate do not frighten me, although the Phrygians
Boast of the gods' responses. To Venus and Fates
Enough has been given, since Trojans set foot on the fertile
Fields of Ausonia. My Fates stand opposed to theirs,
To root out with my sword this damned race which has stolen my bride.
This sorrow came not to the Atreidae alone, and Mycenae
Not alone was allowed to take arms. The Trojans may say
That to perish once was enough. It should have sufficed
For them to sin once before, in their hatred of women,
Almost all. Their trust in the wall between us, the hindrance   140
Made by this ditch, brief check to destruction, gives
Them courage. Yet did they not see the walls of Troy,
Constructed by Neptune's hands, sink down in flames?
But among you, chosen ones, who is ready to cut with his sword
That wall and with me invade their trembling camp?

I need not the arms of Vulcan nor a thousand ships
Against the Teucrians. Let all the Etruscans at once
Become their allies. They need not fear the shadows,
The pointless theft of the statue of Pallas (her guardians
Slain on the citadel height), nor that we shall be hidden   150
Within the horse-belly. I have decided by daylight
To circle their walls with fire. I shall show them they deal with
No Greeks, no Pelasgian youths, whom Hector once held off
Until the tenth year.
                    But now, since the better part
Of the day has passed, spend that which remains in the care,
After work well done, of your bodies: and rest content
That a battle awaits you."
                        Meanwhile Messapus is charged with
The task of detailing a guard on the gates and to ring
The walls with watch-fires. Fourteen selected Rutulians
Patrol the walls with a hundred soldiers for each,   160
Young men whose crests were shining with purple and gold.
They scattered, took turns at guard, or lay stretched on the grass,
Drinking their wine and emptying bronze mixing-bowls.
Their fires burned brightly, the guards spent a sleepless night
In gambling.
The Trojans above the valley looked down upon this
And held the heights under arms, while with anxious care
They tested the gates and linked their bridges and towers,
Carrying weapons. Mnestheus and alert Serestus
Gave orders. Aeneas the father had put them in charge,   170
Should a crisis arise, to command and direct affairs.
The entire group, lots drawn for the perilous stations,
Was on duty, each taking his turn where the detail placed him.
        Nisus stood guard at the gate, most keen with his weapons,
Hyrtacus' son, whom Ida, the huntress-mountain,
Had sent as Aeneas' comrade, alert with his light
Arrows and javelin. With him came Euryalus;
None among the men of Aeneas
Was more handsome a wearer of armor; his face was a boy's
In its early and unshaved youth. Their love was united,   180
They rushed into battle together. They held at the moment
Joint guard at the gate. Nisus asked Euryalus:
"Do gods give this eagerness to our hearts, or does each
Man make a god of what is his own fierce desire?
For some time my mind has been stirring within me to fight

Or to rush upon some great venture; it does not rest easy
In placid content. You see how the Rutuli trust
In their strong position? Their campfire lights are few,
They are stretched out in sleep and wine. All around them is silence.
Hear what I'm planning, the thought which springs up in my mind: *190*
All the people, the fathers, demand that Aeneas be summoned
And men should be sent to bring back a trustworthy report.
If they promise you what I ask—the fame of the deed
Is enough for me—I think I could find a path
Under that hill to the rampart walls of Pallanteum."
Euryalus, stunned, and stricken with great love of praise,
Spoke thus to his ardent friend: "Are you trying to leave me
Out of this daring plan? Shall I send you alone
Into such danger? My father Opheltes, a fighter
Accustomed to war, did not train me this way while the terror   *200*
Of Argos was raging and Troy was in travail of death.
Not thus did I fight by your side and follow great-hearted
Aeneas and ultimate fate. My spirit despises
The light of existence; I know how to barter my life
For this honor you seek: and it is cheap at the price."
Nisus replied: "I had no such fear about you.
This would be blasphemous. No; but I wish great Jupiter
Might return me in triumph to you—or whoever it is
That looks on this life with impartial gaze. Yet if any
Mischance, any god should sweep me to my destruction   *210*
As you see often happens in danger so great as this,
I should wish you to live after me, for your youth is more worthy
Of life. Let there be someone to rescue my body
From battle, or ransom it, dead, and lay it in earth.
But if Fortune forbids this, as she is accustomed to do,
Let him carry out funeral rites at my empty tomb.
May I bring no such sorrow upon your mother, the only
One of so many mothers who dared to come
With her boy, and to leave the walled city of great Acestes
Without any pangs." Euryalus answered: "You're weaving   *220*
A tissue of reasons together in vain. My decision
Is unchanged, does not yield. Let us hurry," He stirred up the watchmen.
They followed and each took his turn. Euryalus, leaving
His station, accompanied Nisus. They sought Prince Ascanius.
     All other live creatures on earth were relaxed in sleep,
Their cares and their labors forgotten, their hearts at rest.
The leaders, first men of the Teucrians, picked men in their prime,

Were discussing in council high matters concerning their rule,
What to do, whom to send to Aeneas. They leaned on long spears,
Held their shields in the midst of the camp and the field.
                                                    Then Nisus   230
And Euryalus eagerly asked to be heard on a subject
Of urgent importance, well worth their delay. First Iulus
Received them impatiently and ordered Nisus to speak out.
Then the son of Hyrtacus said: "Comrades of Aeneas,
Listen with open minds and do not judge
Our actions by our years. The Rutuli
Are silent, sunk in sleep and wine. We have
Spied out a spot for ambush where two roads
Meet at a gate outside, near to the sea.
The fires are out there; black smoke ascends to the stars.   240
If you will permit us to test our luck and find
Aeneas and the walls of Pallanteum,
You'll see us soon returning with our spoils
And with great slaughter done. The road will not
Escape us: we have scouted the city limits
In frequent hunting trips through shady valleys
And know the river channel thoroughly."
Here grave Aletes, ripe in years and mind,
Replied: "Gods of our fathers, in whose care
Troy lies forever, you do not yet prepare   250
To blot the Teucrians out completely since
You bring us young men with such heart and courage
Of certainty." He spoke and grasped their shoulders,
Then their right hands, and flooded his face with tears:
"What fit reward for men who win such praise
Can I devise for you? The gods and your own way
Of living will do that most handsomely,
And first of all. The rest our loyal Aeneas
Will give you, and Ascanius, still untouched
By age, forever mindful of such merit."   260
"Yes, so I swear," broke in Ascanius,
"To you, sole means of bringing back my father,
By the great gods, Assaracus' guiding spirit,
By white-haired Vesta's shrine, whatever fortune
And hope I have, I trust, Nisus, to you.
Call back my father, make me see him. I
Shall not be sad when he is saved. I'll give you

Two perfect cups of silver, rough with figures
Set in relief (my father took them when
He conquered Arisba), twin tripods, two great talents   270
Of gold, an ancient mixing-bowl which Dido
Of Sidon gave. If I shall be victor in Italy
And wield its scepter, give out the loot by lot—
You have seen the horse that Turnus rides, all golden
In armor? That horse I shall withhold from sharing,
His shield and his crimson-crested helmet too:
They shall be yours as prizes from this moment.
In addition my father shall give you twelve hand-picked matrons
And as many male captives, each of them with his weapons,
Plus the land King Latinus owns.
                                          Euryalus, you   280
Are not much older than I am; I receive you in honor
And embrace you, my comrade, with all my heart, whatever
May happen. I shall not seek glorious deeds without you.
Whether it's war or peace I am waging, my greatest
Faith in both word and action shall rest in you."
Euryalus answered: "No day shall prove me unequal
To such deeds of daring, if only my Fates are propitious
And not adverse. But beside all the gifts you have given
I beg one more: my mother is of the old line
Of Priam; the Ilian land did not keep her, poor creature,   290
From coming with me, nor the city of King Acestes.
Now I shall leave her; she knows not how great my danger,
Whatever it is, may be. I shall leave without saying
Farewell: night and your right hand bear witness I cannot
Endure her tears. But I beg you to comfort her,
And protect her when she is left helpless. Allow me to take
This hope in your aid. I shall meet more bravely each danger."
        The Dardanian men were stricken to tears in their sorrow,
And more than all, handsome Iulus. The image of love
He held for his father flashed over his spirit. He uttered   300
These words:
"Be assured your success will be worthy of your great adventure.
Your mother shall be as my mother and only Creusa,
Her name, will be lacking. The gratitude that she deserves
Is great for giving you birth. Whatever the fate
Which companions your deed, I swear by this head, as my father
Was accustomed to swear by it, what I have promised to give you,

Safe and returned, that same shall belong to your mother
And to her descendants." He spoke thus in tears and took off
From his shoulder the golden sword which Lycaon of Cnossus   310
Had made with accomplished art, and the ivory scabbard
Well fitted to hold it. Mnestheus gave Nisus the skin
Of a bristling lion; faithful Aletes exchanged
His helmet for Nisus'. Thus armed, they set out at once.
The band of the chiefs, both young and old, prayed for them
As they stood at the gates and watched the two going forward.
And handsome Iulus, revealing beyond his years
A spirit responsible as a grown man's, gave them many
A message to take to his father. But winds out of heaven
Blew them away and gave them, unheard, to the clouds.   320
      They set out and climbed over the ditches, through shadow of night,
Toward the enemy camp, to bring death to many a man
Before they should die. They saw men's bodies sprawled over
The grass, in a stupor of wine, and their chariots uptilted
On the beach, with the drivers lying among reins and wheels
With their weapons and wine cups around them. First Nisus spoke:
"Euryalus, now our right arms must be daring; this foray
Demands it. The road lies ahead. Watch and warn from afar
If an enemy band should surprise us with rear attack.
I shall kill those I find here and make a broad path for you."   330
So speaking, he checked his voice and advanced, sword in hand,
Against proud Rhamnes, who chanced to be lying asleep,
Breathing deeply upon thick carpets piled high. He was chieftain
And augur most favored by Turnus the chief. But he could not
Dispel his destruction with augury. Then Nisus struck down
Three servants of Remus sprawled heedless among their weapons,
His armor-bearer, his charioteer, whom he found
Near his horses, and cut off their nodding heads with a sword.
Then he took off their master's head and left his trunk there
Still gurgling blood. Wet with black gore, the earth   340
And the bedding dripped. He killed Lamyrus and Lamus,
And the young man Serranus, so handsome, who most of the night
Had been gambling and lay overcome by the wine god's power:
Happy if he had been playing the whole of that night
And kept it up into the day!
                    Nisus was like a
Lion unfed who rages through pens full of sheep,
Driven on by mad hunger, and rends them and drags them away,

The soft flock dumb with fear, his bloody mouth roaring.
No less was Euryalus' slaughter. In ravenous fury
He fell upon many a nameless and humble soldier   350
Who lay in his path, Fadus, Herbesus, and Rhoetus,
Abaris, unconscious. Rhoetus was awake and saw all
But hid in his fear behind a large mixing-bowl.
When he rose to confront him, Nisus buried his sword
Deep in his breast and drew it back with the blood
Gushing in death. He poured out his life with red vomit,
And mixed with his blood as he died was the wine he had drunk.
Euryalus pressed on in stealth. Now he turned to Messapus'
Comrades. He saw their camp fires dwindling and horses
Properly tethered and grazing, when Nisus spoke briefly—   360
For he sensed they were carried too far in their bloodthirsty slaughter:
"Let's stop; the dangerous daylight is coming. Our vengeance
Has drunk its fill; we have made a road through the enemy."
They left behind many a weapon whose mountings were solid
Silver, and fine bowls, and carpets. Euryalus plundered
The trappings of Rhamnes, his gold-studded sword belt—the gifts which
Caedicus the rich man sent to Remulus of Tibur
As symbols of friendship in absence; when Remulus died
He gave them to his grandson; when he too had perished,
The Rutulians gained them in battle fought during a war—   370
And fitted them on to his brave shoulders in vain.
Then he put on Messapus' helmet, ornate with its crest,
A perfect fit. They left the camp and set out for safety.
        Meanwhile the horsemen sent out from the Latin city,
While the rest of the army remained drawn up in the fields,
Were riding and bringing replies from the Latins to Turnus
The king; they were three hundred shields, with Volcens their leader.
And now they were nearing the camp, coming under its wall,
When they saw from a distance these two men bearing to leftward.
The helmet Euryalus wore in dim shadow of nightfall   380
Reflected the moon and betrayed him to his opponents.
They sighted him well. Volcens shouted out from the column:
"Stand, men! What's your purpose here? Why are you armed and where
        headed?"
They made no reply but hastened their flight to the forest,
Confiding in darkness. The horsemen pushed on to a road-block
At a crossing they knew and set guards at each path to surround them.
The woods bristled widely with black ilex-trees and dark thickets,

Filled everywhere with dense brambles. The pathway led faintly
Across hidden trails. The shadow of tree boughs, the heavy
Burden of loot slowed Euryalus, fear made him lose   390
His way. Nisus ran off and now, without thought, he had fled from
The enemy and from the place which was later called Alban
From Alba, but then used by King Latinus for cattle,
When he stopped and looked back in vain for the friend who was
        missing.
"Unlucky Euryalus, where have I left you? Which way
Shall I follow, retrace all the tangle of paths through the baffling
Forest?" He noted and traced at the same time his footprints
And wandered through silent brush. He heard horses, heard noises,
The signals of those who came after. Then shortly their clamor
Reached his ears and he saw Euryalus, whom the whole party   400
Had caught, overmastered by that tricky ground and the darkness
And the sudden unnerving tumult; though he struggled most stoutly,
They dragged him away.
                    What to do, what power, what weapons
Could he use and thus rescue the young man or die in the midmost
Of enemies, hasten by wounds to a noble death?
He looked at the moon on high and drew back his forearm
To twist the javelin more swiftly and prayed in a loud voice:
"You, goddess, be present, assist in my danger, O glory
Of stars and the guardian of groves, daughter of Latona,
If ever my father Hyrtacus brought gifts to your altars   410
For me, if at all I increased them with spoil from my hunting,
And hung them within your temple's dome, from its gables,
Allow me to scatter this band, guide my shafts through the air."
He spoke, and with all of his body astretch threw his spear.
Whirling, it cut through night shadows and stuck in the back
Of Sulmo, then broke, having pierced his heart with its shattered
Wood. He rolled down, spewing forth a hot stream from his breast,
While his sides heaved with spasmodic gasps and his body grew chill.
They gazed in different directions about them. Encouraged,
Nisus then levelled a spear at the top of his ear.   420
As they trembled, it whistled, struck Tagus through both his temples,
And warm with his blood clung there in his transfixed brain.
Fierce Volcens went wild; the man who had thrown it he could not
See anywhere, nor which way to hurl himself madly:
"But you meanwhile," he said, "will pay for both
With your hot blood," and, pulling out his sword,

He rushed upon Euryalus. Completely
Unnerved to madness, Nisus could no longer
Conceal himself in darkness or bear such sorrow:
"On me, on me, who did it, turn your swords!   430
Rutulians, all the crime is mine. This boy
Dared nothing, nor was able to, I swear
By heaven and the stars that know these deeds,
He only loved too well a luckless friend."
Such words he spoke, but, driven with force, the sword
Passed through Euryalus' ribs and burst his shining breast.
He rolled down in death and over
His lovely limbs flowed blood and on his shoulder
His head fell back as when a crimson flower
Cut by the plow falls limp and dies, or when   440
Poppies with weary stems bend down their blossoms,
Heavy, perhaps, with rain. Nisus rushed
Alone amidst them all, attacking Volcens
And only Volcens. All circled round about him,
The enemy on this side and on that
Rushed at him. Yet he carried on and whirled
His flashing sword until he plunged it into
The shouting face of the Rutulian leader
And took away that life. Then on his lifeless
Friend he fell, run through, in peaceful death.   450
        Fortunate both, if my poems shall have any power;
No day shall ever remove your memory from Time
So long as the house of Aeneas, immovable stone
Of the Capitol, shall be dwelt in, a Roman father
Continue to wield there a general's command over men.
        The Rutulian victors, regaining booty and spoils,
Bore back to their camp in tears the lifeless Volcens.
No less was the sorrow in camp when they found the bloodless
Rhamnes, and all their chiefs slain in one great ambush,
Serranus and Numa too. Great was the thronging   460
Around their bodies and round the wounded, the soil
Wet with the recent slaughter where rivers of blood
Ran foaming. They recognized spoils, among them the shining
Helmet of Messapus, trappings won with great sweat.
        Already Aurora, leaving the saffron bed
Of Tithonus, was scattering light once more on land.
Now when the sun shone down and all things were revealed

In its glow, first Turnus aroused his men to arms,
Then armed himself. Each leader harried his own
Bronze-clad ranks into battle and sharpened their anger   470
With many a varied rumor. They thrust upward the heads
Of Euryalus and Nisus on spears and followed them, shouting—
A sight full of sorrow.
        Tough men of Aeneas along the left-hand wall
Arranged their line—for the right was hemmed by the river—
And held the huge trenches, stood sadly in lofty towers,
Stirred to their depths by the faces fixed upon spears,
Known all too well to sad comrades, though dripping with black gore.
        Meanwhile the winged messenger Fama was rushing
Throughout the shuddering city; she slipped to the ears   480
Of Euryalus' mother. The heat left her wretched bones
At once. Her distaff was struck from her hands, the skein
Of wool unwound. She rushed out, all distraught,
Tearing her hair in agony, screaming as only
A woman can scream; she ran to the walls in her madness,
Where the vanguard was marching, heedless of men, of the danger
Of missiles, and filled the heavens with her despair:
"Can this I see be you, the late and last
Resource of my old age? How could you leave me alone,
Euryalus, cruel boy? And I, your wretched mother,   490
Could not speak to you before you died
Upon a mission of so great a danger.
Ah, in an unknown land you lie, the prey
Of Latin dogs and birds. Your mother could not
Follow your corpse to burial, close your eyes
In death or wash the wounds upon your body,
Cover you with the robe which day and night
I hastily wove for you, consoling the sorrow
Of an old woman with its web and woof.
Where shall I follow you now? What earth shall hold   500
Your mangled limbs, your corpse? Are these remains
What you have brought me? Is it for this I followed
Over the land and sea? Turn all your spears
On me, if you have pity! Rutulians, kill
Me first, or you, great father of the gods,
Thrust down this head to Tartarus with your bolt,
Since otherwise I cannot end the cruelty
Of life." Their hearts were stricken with her weeping.

A moan of sadness rose from all, their strength   510
Fell slack and weak for battle. Iulus, deeply
Grieving, and Ilioneus, urged Idaeus
And Actor to take her in their arms and place her
Beneath a roof. Her grief gave fuel to sorrow.
    But from afar the brazen horn resounded,
Tuneful, terrible; clamor followed, bellowed
Back. The Volscians ran up on the double,
Their shields arranged in tortoise-form, preparing
To fill the trenches and tear down the rampart.
Part of them tried for an entrance, to climb the walls   520
On ladders, where stood a thin line and the rampart crown
Was not so thick with men. The Teucrians hurled
All kinds of missiles at them and pushed them down
With hard pike-poles; they had been trained to guard
Their walls by war continuous. They rolled rocks
Of murderous weight, trying to burst the covered
Line. But firm beneath its dense testudo
Those men bore everything that was hurled at them.
Yet not for long. Where huge troop forces gathered,
The Trojans tore and rolled a mass of rock   530
Immense and mountainous crashing through the shields,
Shattering both Rutulians and their armor.
The bold Rutulians did not wish to struggle
Further with blind destruction, but they tried
To drive the enemy back from the wall with missiles.
On the other side,
Mezzentius, frightful to behold, was shaking
An Etruscan pine tree that sent out smoke and fire.
But Messapus, tamer of horses, son of Neptune,
Broke down the wall and called for scaling ladders.   540

    O you, Calliope, breathe grace upon
The singer, and you, Muses, tell what slaughter,
What deaths were wrought by Turnus' sword, which man
Each fighter sent to Orcus, and unroll
With me the lengthy tale of this great war:
For you recall and you can tell the story.

There was a tower that overlooked vast space,
In a strategic spot, with high traverses.

All the Italians tried to storm it, using
All of their forces, rivaling each other.   550
The Trojans in defense threw stones and, crowded
Together, hurled javelins through the open portholes.
Turnus, their chief, tossed fire-darts and stuck them
To the tower's side where, driven by the wind,
They caught the beams and burned into the pillars.
Inside the tower rose panic and vain desire
To run from death. Men huddled where the fire
Had not yet seized the flooring, till the tower
Collapsed beneath their weight and all the sky
Roared with the rising crash. Half-dead, they came   560
Down to the earth, the great mass sliding with them,
Stuck with their own spears, and their chests were pierced
By hardwood fragments. Barely did Helenor
And Lycus scramble free. Helenor was
The elder, whom a slave Licymnian bore
A bastard to the Lydian king and sent
To Troy with forbidden weapons, lightly armed
With naked sword and undistinguished shield,
Still white. When he discovered where he was
Among the men of Turnus, thousands of them,   570
And on this side and that the Latin ranks,
As when a wild beast ringed round in close circle
By hunters rushes madly on their weapons,
Knowing that she must die, and in her leap
Impales herself upon a hunting spear,
So this young man rushed on his enemies,
Choosing the point where weapons bristled most thickly.
But Lycus, more swift of foot, between opposing
Men and missiles ran for the walls and tried
To reach their cover and grasp his comrades' right hands.   580
Turnus threw his spear at him and chased him;
Insulting, spoke in triumph: "Fool, did you think
You could escape our hands?" And he pulled him back
As he clung, and with him a large part of the wall,
As the eagle, arms-bearer of Jove, in its curved claws carries
A hare or a white-bodied swan; or as when a wolf,
Sacred to Mars, steals from the fold a lamb
That bleats while its ewe-mother seeks for it.
Everywhere clamor was raised. Some invaded the ditches

And filled them with dirt while others threw burning torches   590
Up to the roof tops. Ilioneus crushed
Lucetius with a stone, a huge fragment of mountain,
As he came up and began to burn the gate.
Liger killed Emathion and Asilas killed
Corynaeus; the first was good with the javelin; the latter
Shot a far-flying deceptive arrow. Caeneus
Killed Ortygius; Turnus killed the victor.
Then he killed Itys and Clonius and Dioxippus,
Promolus and Sagaris and Idas, who stood on the top
Of the tower. Next Capys killed Privernus, whom   600
Themillas had blooded with his light spear—a madman
To throw his shield away and touch the wound
With his free hand. The arrow slipped down on its wings
And fixed the hand to his left side, lodged within
And broke off the breath of his soul with a lethal wound.
The son of Arcens stood in his excellent armor,
His embroidered cloak red with its Spanish dye,
Noble of face. Arcens, his father, had sent him,
Raised in a grove of Mars by the river Symaethus,
Where Palicus' altar, fat with slain beasts, grants favor.   610
Mezzentius, spears laid aside, swung the whistling thong
Of his sling three times round his head and split through the middle
Of his enemy's temple with the melted sling-shot and laid
Him out on a stretch of sand.
                              Then first, it is said,
Ascanius aimed a swift arrow in battle, though never
Before had he done more than chase wild animals. Under
His hand fell Numanus the brave. His surname was Remulus.
He had recently married the younger sister of Turnus.
In the front line he had been shouting words worthy to tell,
And some that were not, his chest swollen up with pride   620
At his new position in power. He boasted aloud:
"You twice-captured Phrygians, aren't you ashamed to be caught
Once again under siege and ramparts, to ward off death
With walls? Look at those who are asking a marriage with us
By warfare! What god, what madness has driven you here
To Italy? There are no sons of Atreus here,
No weasel-with-words Ulysses. We carry our young,
A sturdy race from our stock, to the rivers and make them
Tough in the savage ice and water. Our boys

Rise early to hunt, they wear out the woods with their wandering.   630
Their games are horse-breaking and shooting with bows and arrows.
Accustomed to little, our young men are patient in labor
To conquer the soil with their hoes or crush cities in war.
Our whole life is spent with the sword, and we weary the backs
Of our bullocks with butt-end of spear, nor does tardy old age
Weaken our spirits or lessen our vigor of mind.
We press a helmet upon our grey hairs; we are always
Delighted with booty that's fresh and to live by our plunder.
Your gowns are embroidered with saffron and shining with purple.
Sloth is your heart's wish, you love to go dancing, your tunics   640
Have sleeves and your caps have ribbons. O Phrygian women,
To speak truly, not men, rush out on the heights of Mount Dindymus,
Where the double-flute gives out a tune to its devotees.
The kettle-drum calls you, the Berecyntian flute of the Mother
Of Ida; yield arms to he-men and give up your swords."
        Ascanius could not endure such terrible language,
Such boasting and taunts, but turning toward him he aimed
His arrow with horse-gut string and spread his arms wide,
First praying to Jove and naming the gifts he would give him:
"All-powerful Jupiter, nod in assent to my daring   650
Attempt. I shall carry religious gifts to your temples
And place at your altars a shining bullock with gilded
Horns; it shall carry its head as high as its mother's,
Shall butt with its horns already and scatter the sand
With its feet." The Sky-Father heard; from an undisturbed quarter
Of heaven he thundered to leftward. The fate-bringing bowstring
Twanged out at the same time; the arrow drawn back fled with frightful
Screech through the head of Remulus, piercing his hollow
Temples with iron: "There, taunt brave men with your insults!
The twice-captured Phrygians send this response to Rutulians."   660
This was all that Ascanius said. The Teucrians followed,
Shouting with joy as they lifted their souls to the stars.
        Long-haired Apollo was looking by chance from a region
Of upper sky on Ausonian ranks and their city.
He sat on a cloud and spoke thus to the victor Iulus:
"Bless your young valor, my boy: that's the way to reach heaven,
You offspring and father of gods. All the wars yet to come
By fate to the race of Assaracus shall be concluded
In justice and peace. Troy cannot contain you."
                                        As soon as

He said this he sent himself down from the top of the sky,   670
Dividing the breezes, and came to Ascanius.
Then he changed his appearance to that of Butes the ancient—
Arms-bearer once to Anchises the Dardan and faithful
Watchman at his gate, and afterward chosen as comrade
In charge of Ascanius by Father Aeneas—Apollo
Came walking like him in his age, his voice, and complexion,
His white hair and weapons that rang with a savage sound:
And he spoke thus to ardent Iulus: "Let this be enough,
Son of Aeneas, that Numanus lies slain with your missile
While you are unharmed. Great Apollo concedes you this first praise 680
And does not begrudge you a weapon that matches his own.
But in future refrain from the war; you still are a boy."
In mid-word Apollo left mortal observers behind
And vanished from sight at a distance and into thin cloud.
The chiefs of the Dardans had recognized him and his weapons
Divine and had heard his quiver resound in his flight.
Thus obeying the words and the power of Phoebus, they held
The avid Ascanius back from the war. Into battle
They rushed by themselves, exposing their lives to clear danger.
A clamor went up through the entire walls and defenses.   690
Keenly they doubled their bows and twisted their spear-thongs.
The ground was all covered with missiles, their shields and hollow
Helmets rang out as they clashed, and the fighting grew bitter,
As when from the West a rainstorm lashes the earth
At the rainy Kids' rising, or as the great hail which the clouds
Hurl down into shallows of sea when Jupiter bristles
With South Winds, twists up a wet gale and bursts hollows of heaven.
      Pandarus and Bitias, sons of Alcanor, on Ida
Raised by the wood-nymph Iaera in Jupiter's grove,
Young men as tall as the pines on their father's mountain,   700
Threw open the gate which their leader's command had entrusted
To them, and, relying upon their weapons, of their own
Accord they invited the enemy into the walls.
They took up their stand on the inside to left and to right
Of the towers, their swords in hand and helmet-crests shining
Upon their tall heads, like twin oaks that soar into heaven ·
Along flowing rivers, near banks of the Po or the charming
Adige, lifting their unshorn heads to the sky,
And nod with their tops from on high. The Rutuli burst
Through the entrance, seeing it open. Quercens at once,   710

Aquiculus, handsome in armor, and Tmarus, headlong
Of heart, and warrior Haemon, with all of their fighters
Either fled or upon the gate's threshold laid down their lives.
Then anger grew greater within their discordant souls,
And now the massed Trojans were clustered together upon
The same spot and dared to fight hand to hand, to move forward.
    To Turnus the leader who raged at a distance the message
Was brought, while he roused up his men, that fresh slaughter had
    inflamed
The enemy and that their gates were now open. He left
His task and, stirred up by huge anger, he rushed to the Trojan   720
Gate and the brothers so proud. First, with a javelin
He killed Antiphates—first to come forward—the bastard
Son of Sarpedon the great and a Theban mother.
The dart of Italian cornel wood went flying
Through the soft air, sank deep in his stomach, passed upward
Into his chest; the black wound's hollow gave back
A foaming wave, and the steel transfixed in his lung
Grew warm. Then with his right hand he brought down
Merope, Erymas, then Aphidnus, then Bitias, burning of eye
And raging in soul, but not with a javelin, for he   730
Would never have died by the javelin. A catapult dart
Came whistling loudly, twisted and driven like lightning.
No two bulls' hides nor double-scaled breastplate of gold
Could faithfully stand against it. His enormous limbs
Fell to the earth in ruin. The earth gave a groan
And his vast shield thundered above.
                            As sometimes on the beach
At Cumaean Baiae, a mass of cement and rubble
Constructed to form a breakwater falls into the sea,
Draws forward ruin with it and, crushed, lies deep in the shallows:
The sea waters mingle together, the black sand is roiled up;   740
At the sound tall Prochyta trembles and so does the hard
Bed of rock named Inarime, placed by the orders of Jove
Over Typhoeus.
              Here Mars, the power in arms,
Added courage and strength to the Latins and turned sharp goads
Into their breasts, but into the Trojans sent
Flight and black Fear. The Latins flocked from all sides
Since a chance for fighting was given and the God of War
Passed into their spirits. As Pandarus saw his brother,

His body stretched out, and where his fortune now lay,
What evil brought on his doom, he twisted the gate   750
With great force of turned hinges, leaning great shoulders against it,
And left many comrades in harsh conflict, shut out by the walls;
A madman to shut others in by his rescue, including
The king of the Rutuli (he did not see him among
The mass) and to shut him up freely within the city.
At once a new light gleamed out of his eyes like a giant
Tiger's among weak flocks; his frightful arms rattled.
The blood-red crests on his head were set quivering, shining
Lightning flashed from his shield. The men of Aeneas
Recognized his dread face in confusion and saw his huge limbs.   760
Then Pandarus, ungainly, jumped out and, boiling with anger
At his brother's death, cried out: "This is no royal dowry
Of Amata the queen, no midmost Ardea shelters
Turnus with ancestral walls. You look on a hostile
Camp. There is no possible way for you to escape."
With quiet heart Turnus smiled at him, saying: "Begin,
If your soul is courageous, and come to grips with your right
Hand; you shall tell Priam that even here you have found
An Achilles." He spoke. Then Pandarus threw his spear,
A rough shaft of knots and green bark, with all of his strength.   770
The breezes received it; Saturnian Juno deflected
The wound as it came; the spear stuck fast in the gate.
"But you shall not escape this weapon my right hand hurls
With strength. I'm a man who makes wounds when I throw my spear."
He spoke thus, raised the sword high, and full in the middle
Between Pandarus' temples and beardless cheeks divided
His brow in a ghastly wound. Pandarus fell with a crash
As the earth rang out with his clumsy weight.
                                                   He lay
Dying, his limbs collapsed and his armor bloody
With brains. His head in equal parts lolled over   780
On this side and that from each shoulder. The Trojans fled,
Wheeling in shivering fear. Had the victor cared
At once to break down the bars with his hand and admit
His comrades within the gates, that day would have been
The last of the war and the race. But fury and mad
Desire for slaughter drove him in eagerness toward
His adversaries.
He killed Phaleris first, then Gyges, hamstringing the man,

Snatching their spears and stabbing them in the back
As they fled. Juno gave him courage and strength. He added   790
Halys among the dead, and Phegeus, piercing
His shield, then Alcander, Halius, and Noemon,
And Prytanis who stirred the fight on the walls unaware.
Turnus overcame Lynceus, who strained toward him, calling his
          comrades;
On the right from the rampart he thrust his whirling sword,
And his head with its helmet lay at a distance,
Severed by one blow dealt him at close range.
Next he killed Amycus, spoiler of beasts: no other
More skillful at smearing arrows and poisoning steel.
Then Clytius, son of Aeolus, and Cretheus, friend   800
Of the Muses and their companion, a lover of music
Of the lyre and verses fitted to stretched strings, who always
Sang about horses and weapons of men and of battles.
          At length the Teucrian leaders Mnestheus and Serestus
The bold, when they heard of the slaughter among their men,
Rushed up to see their companions in flight, their opponents
Inside the gate. And Mnestheus shouted: "Where are you
Running to? What other walls or fortifications
Have you beyond these? Has one man, O citizens, guarded
On all sides by your own walls made such terrible havoc,   810
Unpunished, throughout the city and sent down to Orcus
So many fine young men? Are you not ashamed, without pity,
For your wretched country, your ancient gods, and for mighty
Aeneas?" With such words he kindled and strengthened their spirits
To make a stand in dense ranks. Then gradually Turnus
Began to retreat from the battle and make for the river
And a terrain cut off by water. The Trojans more keenly
Fell to with great clamor and gathered their band for the fight,
Like a party of hunters surrounding a savage lion,
Their spears at the ready; terrified, bitter, ferocious,   820
The lion gives ground, nor do anger or courage allow him
To turn his back, nor to fight through weapons and men,
Though he wishes to do so. Not otherwise Turnus retreated,
But stubbornly, slowly, and anger flamed up in his heart.
Twice even then he invaded the enemy midst,
Twice he turned back his lines from their flight through the wall.
But the band from the camp came together with haste in one place.
Saturnian Juno did not dare bolster his strength,

For Jupiter sent airy Iris down from the sky
To bring his ungentle orders to sister and wife   830
If Turnus should not retreat from the lofty walls
Of the Trojans. The young man could not resist with his shield
Alone or his right hand, so overwhelmed as he was
By missiles from all sides. His helmet rang with a steady
Rattle around hollow temples, its unimpaired bronze
Was split by the stones, its plumes knocked down from his head.
His shield-boss could not hold out against blows. The Trojans,
Among them the thunderous Mnestheus, redoubled their spears.
Then over the entire body of Turnus the sweat
Streamed down like a river of pitch, and he could not breathe.   840
His weakened panting shattered his tired limbs.
Then, only then, did he leap headlong with his armor
Upon him into the river. Its whirlpool of yellow
Received him and carried him on with its gentle waves
And restored him, rejoicing, to comrades, washed clean of slaughter.

BOOK TEN

Rescue and Battle

Meanwhile the house of Olympus all-powerful stood
Wide open; the father of gods and the king of men
Called a council within his starry dwelling, from where
High up he looked down on all lands and the Dardan camp
And the Latin peoples. The gods sat down in the hall
With doors at both ends. He himself began: "Great sky-
Dwellers, why have you reversed your decision and why
Do you strive with your spirits at variance? I had forbidden
Italy to war upon Teucrians. What discord against
My command has arisen, what fear has persuaded these men   10
And those to seek weapons and challenge the sword? There shall come
A time that is right for war, do not hasten its coming,
When fierce Carthage shall send great destruction upon Rome's fortress,
And the Alps are broken open. Then you shall be free to contend
With your hatreds and seize your plunder. Now cease from your quarrel
And happily settle the pact on which I have decided."
   Jupiter spoke these few words, but Venus the golden
Replied with many: "O father, eternal ruler
Of men and of things—for what other is there we can pray to?—
You see how the Rutuli triumph and glorious Turnus   20
Is driving his horses through Trojans and, swelling with pride,
Rushes on in a fortunate war. No longer do walls
Shelter the Teucrians; inside the gates and the very
Earthworks their enemies mingle in battle and flood
The ditches with blood. Unknowing, Aeneas is absent.
Will you never allow them relief from a siege?
                                             Once again
An enemy threatens the walls of a nascent Troy
And a second army is here, once again from Aetolian
Arpi Diomedes is rising against the Trojans.

I suppose that my wounds are awaiting me; I, your offspring,   30
Am delaying the weapons of mortals. If without approval
From you and against your will the Trojans sought Italy,
Let them pay for their sins and do not assist them; but if
They followed so many responses from gods up above
And ghosts down below, how could anyone now be able
To reverse your commands or found a new fate for them?
Why should I recall the ships burned on the shore of Eryx,
Or the king of the storms and the raging winds let loose
From Aeolia, or Iris sent down from the clouds? Now Juno even
Stirs up the spirits of death—this lot of creation   40
Had remained yet unthrown—and Allecto is suddenly loosed
On the earth and has rioted through the Italian cities.
I am not disturbed about empire; we hoped for it while
Fortune was ours; let those whom you favor prevail.
If there is no region your pitiless wife will allow
To the Trojans, I beg of you, father, by the smoking ruins
Of Troy in destruction, permit him release from the war,
Ascanius unharmed; allow my grandson to survive.
Let Aeneas be tossed, if you will, upon unknown waves;
Let him follow whatever the path that Fortune may give him.   50
Let me protect Ascanius and withdraw him from dreadful
Battle. Amathos is mine, and sheer Paphos and Cythera,
And my home at Idalia. Let him live out his years
Without glory and weapons. Give orders for Carthage to rule
Ausonia with strong dominion; let no hindrance arise
For the Tyrian cities from Italy. What good did it do
That Aeneas escaped war's plague and fled through the middle
Of Argive fires and wore out the perils of many
An ocean and vast tracts of earth while the Trojans were seeking
Latium and Troy's citadel rebuilt? Was it not   60
Better to settle upon the last cinders, the soil
Of our fatherland, Troy? I beg you, give back to the wretched
Trojans their Xanthos and Simois, let them, full-circle,
Retrace their disasters."
                        Then regal Juno was driven
By passionate hatred: "Why do you compel me to break
My deep silence and share with the world my hidden sorrow?
Which man or god ever drove Aeneas to warfare
Or to face King Latinus in enmity? By fate's compulsion
He sought Italy: so be it—urged by Cassandra's ravings.

But I did not urge him to leave his stronghold, or trust   70
His life to the winds, or leave the command of the war
In the hands of a boy, or to trust in his walls, or disturb
The Etruscan allegiance and quiet peoples, did I?
What god was it drove him to trickery, what harsh power
Of ours, where is Juno in all this, or Iris sent down
From the clouds? For the people of Italy it is unworthy
To burn nascent Troy and for Turnus to take a stand
On the soil of his own fatherland, he whose grandfather was
Pilumnus, his mother the goddess Venilia. Why
Do the Trojans attack the Latins with torches that make   80
A black ruin, and press down their yoke on fields not their own,
Or drive off their booty? Why do Trojans choose unasked fathers-
In-law and fiancées abducted from parental bosoms,
Seek peace with a suppliant's hand but stack arms on their ships?
You are able to spirit Aeneas away from the Greeks
And to dupe them with clouds of mere wind instead of the man.
You are able to change his ships into so many nymphs.
Is it wrong on my part to assist the Rutulians a little?
Aeneas knows nothing, is absent; let him stay there, unknowing.
Paphos is yours, and Idalium; yours is sheer Cythera: 90
Why do you stir up rough hearts and a city that's pregnant
With wars? Or have I been trying to overturn
The ebbing power of Phrygia from its foundations?
Was it I who exposed the poor Trojans to ruin by the Greeks?
What reason was there for Europe and Asia to rise
Up in arms and to break their bonds with a thievish abduction?
Was it at my suggestion the Trojan adulterer stormed
The country of Sparta, did I supply weapons or foster
The war through *my* Cupid? That was the right moment of dread
For your partisans. Now you come here with your unjust and tardy   100
Complaints and throw into our faces your baseless objections."
    Juno held forth in these words, and all the sky-dwellers
Roared mingled assent and reproach, like the earliest blast
When a forest is seized by a storm and the muffled murmur
Rolls through it, foretelling to sailors the winds to come.
Then the Father Almighty, whose power is greatest within
All creation, began—as he spoke, his tall palace grew silent,
Earth trembled in depth, sheer ether fell still; then the breezes
Were quiet, and ocean pressed down the tops of its waves:
"Receive to your hearts and fix there these words of mine.   110

Since it has not been permitted to join the Trojans
And Ausonians by treaty, nor is there an end to your discord,
Whatever hope each man pursues, whatever his fortune
Today, be he Trojan, Rutulian, shall make no difference
To me, whether by the Fates of Italians the camp
Of the Trojans lies under siege or by some evil error
Of Troy and misguiding responses; nor do I absolve
The Rutulians: for each man misfortune or fortune arises
From his own beginnings. King Jupiter is the same
For all. Fate will find its way." He made this avowal   120
By the Stygian stream of his brother, by banks full of pitch
And that whirlpool so black; all Olympus shook with his nod.
Here an end to the speaking. Jupiter rose from his golden
Throne, and the sky-dwellers led him across the threshold.
      Meanwhile the Rutuli hastened round all the gates
To slaughter their enemy and ring the walls with flame.
But Aeneas' army was pinned within the stockade
Without hope of flight. The wretches stood on the high towers
In vain, a thin crown of defenders. Among them Asius,
The son of Imbrasus, Thymoetes, son of Hicetaon,   130
The two Assaraci, old Thymbris, and Castor beside him,
In the front line. Sarpedon's two brothers were there,
Clarus and Thaemon, companions from lofty Lycia.
Acmon of Lyrnessus, not less than his father Clytius
Or his brother Mnestheus, a huge man, who with all of his body
Strained to carry a rock that was no small part of a mountain.
These men strove to fight with their javelins, those men with rocks;
Some shot fire-arrows, some fitted plain arrows to bow-string.
There in their midst, the most proper disquiet of Venus,
Look, the Dardan boy with his shapely head bare, was shining   140
Like a jewel that divides tawny gold in a setting, a bauble
For necklace or crown, or as ivory shines when an artist
Has framed it in boxwood or ebony from Oricia;
His flowing locks lay on his milky-white neck and a circlet
Of soft gold bound it back. You, Ismarus, too, your high-hearted
Peoples could see, as you aimed to make wounds and armed arrows
With poison, a noble of Lydian house, where men till
Fertile fields and the Pactolus waters them with its gold.
And Mnestheus was there, whom yesterday's glory raised high,
For he routed Turnus from earthwork and walls. There was Capys;   150
From him rose the name of Capua, Campania's city.

These men took and gave to each other war's terrible buffets.
Aeneas at midnight was plowing the waters of ocean.
When, leaving Evander, he entered the Tuscan camp,
He came to the king and told him his name and race
And what he was seeking and what he was bringing and how
Large a force had been gained by Mezzentius, how violent was
The nature of Turnus, how little assurance there was
In the fortunes of men (mingled with his own prayers).

          Then King Tarchon
By no means delayed but joined forces and made an agreement. *160*
Free now of its fate, the Lydian folk was entrusted
By command of the gods to a foreign leader. Aeneas'
Ship held the lead; at its beak yoked Phrygian lions
Were shown with Mount Ida above them, a vision most pleasing
To exiles from Troy. Here sat great Aeneas and pondered
The varied events of the war. Pallas, close to his left side,
Now questioned him as to the stars which were guiding their path
Through dark night, or what he had suffered on land and on sea.

 Spread Helicon wide now, you goddesses, and inspire
My poem to describe what forces companioned Aeneas *170*
From Tuscan shores, arming the fleet that sailed over the sea.

First, Massicus cut through the waves with his bronze-clad Tigress.
His group was one thousand young men who had left the walls
Of Clusium and of Cosa; their weapons were arrows,
With light quivers on their shoulders and death-dealing bows.
Grim Abas sailed with him. His soldiers were splendid in arms.
At his stern shone a statue in gold of Apollo. Six hundred
Men his mother-city, Populonia, had given him,
Experienced at warfare, and young. The island of Ilva,
Abounding with limitless metals, sent three hundred fighters. *180*
Asilas came third, the prophet who gave out his answers
Between men and gods, whom the entrails of cattle obeyed,
And the stars of the sky and the songs of the birds and the lightning
As well, in their prophecies. He brought one thousand men,
Close-packed in a line, and their spears made a blood-curdling sight.
Pisa, their city, Etruscan in soil but Alphaean
In origin, gave them their orders. There followed Astur
Most handsome; he trusted his horse and his rainbow-hued armor.
Three hundred were added from Caere, their home, all determined

As one man to follow, from fields by the Minio river,   *190*
From Pyrgi the ancient and Gravisca, unhealthful in climate.
    I should not omit you, Cynaras, the bravest Ligurian
Leader in war, and Cupavo, whose comrades were few.
Your crest was of swan-feathers rising from helmet-peak,
The sign of your father's mutation from man to bird,
And a crime that was yours, O Love, and your mother's.

                                             They say
That Cycnus, your father ("the swan"), lamented the death
Of his beloved Phaethon while he was singing among
The boughs of the poplars and shadow cast by the sisters
Of the dead man, consoling sad love with his muse;   *200*
Then, singing, drew over his body the whiteness of age
With the white plumes of swans, till he rose from the earth and followed
The stars with his cry. The son, in a crowd of age-fellows
On deck, pushed the great ship Centaur ahead with oars.
Its figurehead hung over water and from high above
Threatened the waves with a rock of enormous size,
While the long keel which carried the image was plowing deep seas.
    That leader named Ocnus was also leading his column
From paternal shores, the son of the prophetess Manto
And the river god Tuscus. He gave you your walls and the name   *210*
Of his mother, O Mantua, rich in your ancestors. They
Were not of one stock. Three-fold are your clans and four
The townships of each, but you are the chief of the peoples,
Your strength from Etrurian blood. Mezzentius armed
These people against him, five hundred from this place as well.
As figurehead, Mincius, river god son of Benacus
The lake, crowned with grey reeds, was leader of these in their warship
Of pine on the waters. Aulestes the stately moved onward,
Striking the waves with a hundred oars as they lifted
His ship, and the shallows foamed up to the stricken surface.   *220*
Huge Triton was figurehead for him; he frightened the ocean
With his sea-blue horn. He looked like a man with a shaggy
Trunk to the waist in the water; his belly became
A sea monster. Under his half-savage chest the sea foamed
And murmured. So many picked leaders in three-times-ten
Ships sailed to reinforce Troy, cutting salt fields with bronze.
    Now daylight had gone from the sky and the bountiful Moon
In her night-wandering chariot was stamping the middle of heaven.
Aeneas—for care gave no rest to his limbs—sat holding

The tiller and guiding the ship and adjusting the sails,   230
When, look, there came toward him a chorus of his companions
During his journey: nymphs whom the generous Cybele
Had granted the power of sea-change from ships into nymphs.
They swam side by side and cut through the waves, just as many
As the bronze prows which first lay anchored on shore.
They recognized him from afar and danced round their king.
Cymodocea, ablest at speaking, held on to the stern
Of his ship with her right hand, while lifting her shoulder above
The water, and rowed with her left under silent waves.
Then she spoke to him in his bewilderment: "Are you awake,   240
Aeneas, offspring of the gods? Wake up and give slack
To your sails. We are pines from the sacred slope of Mount Ida,
Now nymphs of the ocean, your fleet. The perfidious Turnus
With sword and with flame pursued us in headlong flight
Until we broke hawser unwillingly and over ocean
Came looking for you. The great Mother gave us new faces
In pity, allowed us as goddesses to live under sea.
But your son Ascanius is hemmed in by wall and ditches
As a target of weapons and Latins terrific in war.
Arcadian cavalry mingled with brave Etruscans   250
Already are holding objectives you gave them. Yet Turnus
Intends to send troops to oppose them and cut off their access
To camp. Hurry, rise, and when Dawn comes, first order the allies
To arms and take up your shield which the Mighty-With-Fire,
Invincible Vulcan, gave you, surrounding its border
In gold. With morning light, you will see huge masses of slaughtered
Rutulians, if you will think of my words as effective."
She spoke and, departing, pushed his tall ship with her right hand,
Well knowing just how. It fled through the waves more swiftly
Than a thrown javelin or arrow that flies like the wind.   260
The other ships gathered more speed. The Trojan Aeneas,
The son of Anchises, was numb with astonishment. Still,
His courage arose with this omen. Then, gazing a while
At the vault of the sky, he spoke, praying: "O bountiful Mother
Of Ida and gods, the lover of Dindyma mountain,
Of tower-crowned cities and lions twin-yoked with their bridles,
Be now my leader in battle, and duly fulfill
This omen, be present to Trojans with favoring feet."
This was his prayer, and meanwhile the daylight returning
Had risen full circle and put the darkness to flight.   270

First he gave orders his allies should follow the signals,
Fit courage to weapons and ready themselves for a fight.
Now he had sighted the Trojans and his own camp
As he stood high up on the stern; then he gave them the signal
By raising his left arm and shield with the sunlight upon it.
The Dardans alert on the walls raised a shout to the stars.
Hope added to anger revived them; they hurled missiles by hand,
As Strymonian cranes give their signals beneath the black clouds
While they sail through the sky with a clamor and flee from the South
Winds with a trailing cry. This was strange to the king   280
Of the Rutuli and to his leaders until they could see
The sterns turned toward shore, the whole sea rolling in with the ships.

The top of his head and his crest were alive with flames
And the golden boss on his shield poured out fiery reflections,
Just as sometimes in velvet night the comets are shining
A baleful blood-red, or Sirius burning; it brings
Sickness and thirst to poor suffering mortals whenever
It rises, and saddens the sky with a sinister glow.
      But confidence did not depart from bold-hearted Turnus
To capture the beach and drive the invaders from land.   290
Beyond that, he cheered them with words; beyond that, he ranted:
"What you have desired in prayer is at hand for destruction
Under your right arm. The war is now in your strong hands.
Let each man remember his wife and his home and remember
The great deeds and praise of his father. Now let us run down
To the waves while they hesitate and, when they land, let their footsteps
Falter. Fortune helps those who are bold."
He spoke thus and turned in his mind the men he should lead
In attack and the men he might leave in charge of the siege.
      Meanwhile, Aeneas had landed his men from the high   300
Ships upon gangways. Many had waited for tides
To retreat in the ebbing waves and then trusted to leap
Into shallows, but others had landed by use of their oars.
Tarchon, his eye on the beaches where no shallows heaved,
No broken waves echoed but ocean swell rolled to the land
With the tide as it rose, of a sudden tacked sharply and called
To his comrades: "Now, band of the chosen, lean hard on your oars.
Rise up, drive her forward, and split this unfriendly land
With your prows, let the keel dig a furrow, let her crash at the stern
On the beach just so long as we reach it." After such orders,   310

His companions rose up on their oars, drove the foaming ships
Onto fields of the Latins until the prows held the dry earth
And the keels came to rest all unbroken—but, Tarchon, not yours.
For, dashed upon shoals, while it hung on a dangerous reef,
Sustained at a balance for long, and wearied the waves,
Tarchon's ship broke at last and tossed its crew overboard
Into mid-ocean; the splinters of oars and the floating
Thwarts blocked their way while the ebb tide dragged away footholds.
    No sluggish delay held back Turnus, but swiftly he led
His whole line against Trojans and took up position on shore.   320
The trumpets rang out. Aeneas first charged the detachments
Of farmers, an omen of battle, and scattered the Latins.
He killed Theron, a very large man who had singled Aeneas
Out for attack. The sword cut through joints in his brazen
Breastplate and tunic stiff with gold thread till it drained
The lifeblood from his side now laid open. Then he struck Lichas,
Once cut from the womb of his mother already dead,
And sacred, O Phoebus, to you, for in infancy he
Had been granted escape from his death by the surgeon's knife.
Not long after he hurled to destruction hard Cisseus and huge   330
Gyas, who laid low the lines with their weapon, a club.
It helped not at all that they fought with Hercules' side arm,
That their hands were strong or that their father was Melampus,
The comrade of Hercules while earth still offered stern labors.
As Pharo was emptily boasting, Aeneas took aim
With a javelin and threw it straight into his clamoring mouth.
You too, luckless Cydon, while you followed your recent delight,
Clytius, whose cheeks had grown yellow with man's first beard,
Struck down by the Dardan right hand without care for the love
Which young men were always displaying to you, would have lain   340
A sight to stir pity if you had not had a dense body
Of brothers to guard you, the offspring of Phorcus; these men were
Seven in number and hurled seven javelins. Some of these
Rebounded from Aeneas' helmet and shield without danger,
Others good Venus deflected; they barely grazed him.
To faithful Achates, Aeneas said: "Pile up some javelins
For me; not any of those which killed Greeks on the fields
Of Troy shall be twisted in vain by my right hand
Against the Rutulians." He grasped a tall spear and he hurled it,
Piercing the bronze of Maeon's shield till it broke   350
Through his breastplate and chest. Alcanor, his brother, rushed up

To sustain him from falling with his right hand; at an instant
A thrown spear plunged into his shoulder and, covered with blood,
Went flying upon the same course, while Alcanor's right arm
Hung dead from the shoulder by sinews. Then Numitor charged
On Aeneas, extracting the spear from his brother's body.
But he was not permitted to wound him; the spear grazed the thigh
Of Achates the great. Then trusty young Clausus from Cures
Advanced and struck Dryops under the chin from a distance
With a stiff spear; with great force it snatched in a moment   360
His life and his voice as it pierced his throat; he fell
On his face to the ground, and thick blood gushed out of his mouth.
Clausus killed three men of Thrace from high Borean stock,
And three who were sent by their father Idas from Ismara,
Each by a different death. Halaesus advanced
With the bands from Aurunca to fight with the offspring of Neptune,
Messapus, who drove a fine team. Now these men, now those
Tried hard to drive back the Trojans; they fought on the very
Threshold of Ausonia. As contrary winds in the wide
Heavens make war when their spirits and power are equal,   370
Nor yield to each other, nor clouds nor the ocean yield,
And the battle is doubtful a long time, all standing at firm odds,
Not otherwise did battle lines of the Trojans and Latins
Run together in combat, feet and men gripped closely together.
     In another part of the field, where a torrent had scattered
Rolling boulders about and torn the brush from its banks,
Pallas observed the Arcadians, untrained for close action
On foot, in full flight from the Latins, who were pursuing,
Because the rough country had made them dismount from their horses.
One measure alone remained for their rescue: now pleading,   380
Now kindling their courage with harsh words: "Where are you
Running, my comrades? By your own brave deeds, by the name
Of your leader Evander, the wars you have won, by the prospect
I have of attaining the praise which my father won, trust not
To flight. You must cut through the enemy with your swords
Where the mass of the fighters is thickest. Your proud fatherland
Calls you and your leader Pallas. No powers of gods
Press upon you. We mortals are under attack by a mortal
Enemy. As many lives as they have, we have,
And as many hands. Look, the ocean now hems us in   390
With its expanse of water. There is no more land for flight.
Shall we run for the sea or for Troy?" He spoke and hurled

Himself in the midst of the hostile group. First to meet him
Came Lagus, led on by an unjust fate. While he pulled
At a stone of great weight, Pallas struck him with whirling spear
Where the spine divided his ribs in the middle, then tugged back
The spear while it clung to the bones. Hisbo did not surprise him
Although he had hoped to, for Pallas engaged him beforehand
As he rushed to attack, made reckless by his companion's
Cruel death; Pallas thrust the sword into rage-swollen lungs.   400
Then Pallas rushed down upon Sthenius, and upon Anchemolus
Of the ancient stock of Rhoetus, who had dared to commit
Incest with his stepmother. You twins, Larides and Thymber,
Identical offspring of Daucus, fell dead in Rutulian
Fields, hard to separate even for kinfolk, affection's
Delightful confusion. But Pallas now made stern distinction
Between you; the sword of Evander's son cut off
Your head, Thymber. Your right hand when it was severed,
Larides, looked for its master; the fingers, half-living,
Spasmodically twitched and groped for the sword again.   410
Sorrow mingled with shame armed the Arcadian fighters,
Kindled by Pallas' reproof and the sight of his exploits.
Then Pallas slew Rhoeteus as he was running away
In his two-horsed chariot. This was a breathing-space
And so much delay to Ilus, for from a distance
Pallas had levelled against him his powerful spear,
Which Rhoeteus received in his flight as he ran from you,
Teuthras the best, and your brother Tyres. He rolled
From the chariot, kicking Rutulian soil with his heels,
Half-living. As when, at his will, in summer where winds   420
Have arisen, a shepherd sets fires in different parts
Of a forest, which suddenly scatter among all the trees,
And the bristling spear-tips of Vulcan spread out through the wide
Fields, while the victor sits looking and cheering the flames,
So all of his comrades' valor came together as one
And aided you, Pallas. But Halaesus, eager for war,
Rushed to oppose him and tensed himself under arms.
Now he killed Ladon and Pheres and Demodocus.
With his shining sword he cut off Strymonius' right hand,
Raised to strike at the throat of Halaesus. He crashed   430
A big stone on the mouth of Thoas and scattered his bones
Mingled with bloody brains. His father foretold
His fate as he hid him, Halaesus, away in the forest.

But when the old man had loosened his eyes, grown glazed,
In death, the Fates grasped Halaesus and made him subject
To die by Evander's weapons. So Pallas went for him
After he offered prayer: "Grant now, Father Tiber,
Good chance to this spear I balance before I hurl it,
And passageway into the chest of the tough Halaesus.
These arms and the spoils of the man your oak tree shall have."   440
The god heard these words; while he was protecting Imaon,
Halaesus unluckily turned a bare chest to the Arcadian
Missile. Lausus, redoubtable bulwark in war,
Did not leave his ranks panic-stricken by such great slaughter.
First he killed Abas, who challenged him, the knot and hindrance
Of battle. The offspring of Arcadia died, the Etruscans
Were laid low, and you, O Trojans, whose bodies were saved
From destruction by Greeks. The battle lines clashed together
With leaders and men who were matched. The rear guard pushed forward,
Jamming the front lines in one; the massing allowed   450
No freedom for weapons or hands. Here Pallas pressed onward,
There Lausus fought opposite: both differed slightly in age
And both were quite handsome to view. But Fortune refused them
Return to their fatherland. He who rules mighty Olympus
Nonetheless did not let them meet face to face in the battle.
Their Fates were awaiting them under a more fearful fighter.

　　　　Turnus' dear sister meanwhile was urging that he should
Take Lausus' place, who was cutting the center of battle
In his swift chariot. When he saw his comrades, he shouted:
"It's time to stop fighting; I'll charge upon Pallas alone.   460
He is due me alone. I wish that his father could see him."
He spoke, and his friends left the battlefield under his orders.
As the Rutuli retired, young Pallas, astonished to witness
Such insolent dictates, turned eyes upon Turnus' huge body
And scanned every detail with glances quite fierce from a distance,
Then countered the words of the tyrant with words such as these:
"I shall either be praised for the best spoils I take in a moment
Or for my great death; my father is steadied for either
Great lot. Down with threats!" So speaking, he moved into mid-field.
Chilly blood gathered close round the hearts of the Arcadians.   470
Turnus jumped down from his two-horsed chariot, ready
To fight him on foot. As a lion, who sees from a lofty
Point of advantage a bull standing far in the fields
And practicing battle, flies toward him, not otherwise

Was the vision of Turnus advancing. When Pallas considered
His enemy fully in spear-range, he made the first move,
Hoping that Fortune might help him who took a bold gamble
When odds were uneven, and spoke to high heaven above:
"By my father's guest-friendship and table, at which you were present,
A stranger, I beg you, Alcides, be here now to aid my   480
Tremendous attempts. Let Turnus look on me as victor
With eyes that are dying, while I pull his arms from a bloody
And half-dead corpse." Hercules heard the young man, as he stifled
A long sigh of heart-felt sorrow and shed empty tears.
Then Jupiter spoke to his offspring with friendly words:
"His day stands and waits for each man. The time they may live
Is brief for all men and never to be restored.
But to lengthen his fame with his deeds is the task of man's courage.
So many sons of the gods have fallen where lofty
Troy lifts her walls. Yes, Sarpedon, my offspring, has fallen.   490
His Fates also call to Turnus; he has reached the goal line
Of the age he was given." He spoke and turned back his eyes
From Rutulian fields. But Pallas sent forth his spear
With a powerful heave and drew his bright sword from its hollow
Scabbard. The spear flew on and struck where the shoulder
Was covered above and passed through the rim of the shield
To glance at last from the body of giant Turnus.
Next, Turnus took up an oak shaft with a sharpened blade
At its end and poised it a long time before he spoke,
And threw it at Pallas: "Look here, see whether my missile   500
Will penetrate farther than yours." He spoke and the spearpoint
Pierced with a vibrating stroke the shield in the middle,
Through so many layers of tough steel, so many of bronze
Bound together with circling bull-hide, and made a deep hole
Through the breastplate's resistance and into his mighty chest.
In vain Pallas tugged the warm weapon from out of the wound;
His blood and his life passed together along the same path.
He fell on the wound, and his armor rang out all around him,
And, dying, he struck hostile earth with a bleeding face.
Then Turnus, standing above him: 510
"Remember, Arcadians, carry my words to Evander:
I send him back Pallas just as he deserved to receive him.
I give him largess of whatever the tomb may bestow
Of honor, whatever the solace of burying him.
No little price shall he pay as a host to Aeneas."

So speaking, he pressed his left foot down on the lifeless
Body and tore away the huge weight of his sword-belt
With an evil picture upon it: a band of young bridegrooms
Done to death foully upon one wedding night—
Clonus, the son of Eurytus, had carved it in gold.   520
Now Turnus rejoiced in these spoils and their welcome possession.
Men's minds are unwitting of fate and the doom to come
Or how to keep balance when prosperous days elate them.
A time there shall be for Turnus when he shall wish
That Pallas untouched had been ransomed at heavy cost,
And when he shall hate these spoils and the day he won them.
But the comrades of Pallas, in throngs, with a great lament
And tears, bore him off on a shield. O sorrow, O great
Honor about to return to your father! This day
Was the first that gave you to war, and it took you away,   530
Although you left heaps of Rutulians behind on the field.
        Not yet had the rumor of such a disaster arrived.
But a messenger more trustworthy flew up to Aeneas:
His men were upon the slender edge of destruction;
It was time to bring aid to defeated Trojans. Whatever
Was nearest he mowed down in anger and cut a wide swath
With his sword-blade of steel through the lines in his search for you,
O Turnus, now boasting of recent slaughter. Pallas,
Evander, the banquets he ate as a newcomer, pledges
Struck with a handclasp—all these now rose to his eyes.   540
He seized the four sons of Sulmo, the four whom their father
Ufens had reared, all alive, to offer as victims
To the shades of the dead and to pour the blood of the captives
Upon the flames of the pyre. From a distance he hurled
A dangerous spear at Magus, who cleverly dodged it
As the quivering weapon flew past. He embraced the knees
Of Aeneas, in suppliance spoke: "By the shade of your father,
The rising hope of Iulus, I beg you, preserve
My life for my son and my father. There lie in my tall
Home, buried deep in the earth, chased talents of silver.   550
I have also a burden of gold, both worked and unworked.
The victory of the Trojans does not turn on me.
One life will not make a great difference." He spoke, but Aeneas
Spoke in return: "Save up for your children the many
Talents of silver and gold you mention. The first
To dispense with such commerce of war was Turnus when he

Killed Pallas: my father's ghost and Iulus declare this."
So speaking, he grasped with his left hand the helmet of Magus
And bent back his neck as he pleaded, and up to the hilt
He buried his sword in the man. Not far off was Haemon's   560
Son, who was priest of Apollo and of Diana.
His sacred fillet was bound round his temples, he shone
All splendid in vestments of white with his emblems white.
Aeneas rushed at him and chased him over the field,
Then towered above his victim in ritual slaughter
And shaded him with his huge body. Serestus collected
That armor so fine on his shoulders, a trophy for you,
O Mars, king of marchers. Caeculus, born of Vulcan,
And Umbro from Marsian mountains renewed the conflict.
Aeneas, descendant of Dardanus, raged out against them.   570
His sword-blade had cut off the left arm of Anxur and with it
The round shield as well—the man in his pride had been making
Big boasts and believing that strength could be found in mere words,
Allowing his spirit to soar, and had promised himself
Grey hair and old age—when Tarquitus, in shining armor,
A man whom the nymph Dryope had borne to Faunus
Woods-dweller, exultantly crossed before angry Aeneas.
The latter with spear drawn back pinned both breastplate and weighty
Burden of shield together and cut off his head,
Sent it whirling to earth with the trunk of his body, still warm,   580
Though he pleaded in vain and thought of the many words
He might utter. Aeneas stood over his body and spoke
With hostile heart: "Lie there, who thought you were to be dreaded.
Your excellent mother will never lay you in earth
Or heap your remains in an ancestral tomb. I shall leave you
To wild birds of prey or plunge you into running water
Where, tumbled by waves, hungry fish shall nibble your wounds."
Then instantly he pursued Antaeus and Luca
Of Turnus' front line, and brave Numa and yellow-haired Camers,
Born of great-hearted Volcens, the richest in land   590
Of all the Ausonians, who ruled over silent Amyclae.
As Aegaeon, who had, as they say, fifty arms and a hundred
Hands and who burned with fire from fifty mouths
And fifty breasts, clashing against the lightnings of Jove
With so many similar shields, drawing fifty swords,
So victor Aeneas raged madly across the whole field,
When once he had dipped sword in blood. Look, he strained toward
     the chests

Of Niphaeus' four-horse team; but when they saw him striding
From a distance and roaring with rage, they turned tail in terror,
Ran away, threw their driver, and dragged the chariot down   600
To the seashore. Meanwhile Lucagus and his brother Liger
Drove into the midst of the battle their team of white horses.
Liger was handling the reins while Lucagus fiercely
Was whirling the sword he had drawn. But Aeneas would not
Put up with their furious rage. His huge figure loomed upward
With a spear pointed toward them. "It is not Diomedes' horses,"
Said Liger to him,
"Nor the chariot of Achilles nor fields of the Phrygians
That you see; now the war and your life shall be ended in these lands."
Such words flew abroad from mad Liger. The Trojan hero   610
Did not prepare words in reply, but he twisted a javelin
At his enemy. Lucagus bent forward, urging his horses
With the flat of his sword, while with left foot advanced he was ready
For battle. The spear plunged through the rim of the shining
Shield at the bottom and pierced him in the left groin.
Knocked out of the chariot, he rolled on the field to die.
Then loyal Aeneas addressed him with bitter words:
"No cowardly flight of your horses, Lucagus, betrayed you,
Running from bodiless shadows of your assailants.
You jumped from the chariot yourself and abandoned your wheels." 620
So speaking, he seized the horse-bridles. Antaeus, the brother
Of unhappy Liger, stretched upward his unarmed hands,
Felled from the same chariot: "For yourself, for the parents
Who created a man like you, Trojan, spare me this life
And pity a suppliant." He would have said more, but Aeneas
Replied: "This is not how you boasted a moment ago.
Die! Do not desert your brother." With sword-point he opened
His chest, where the breath lies hidden. Such deaths did the Trojan
Leader produce through the field, like a torrent of water
Or a black tornado. At last the young men and Ascanius   630
Broke out from the camp and left it, besieged all in vain.

        Jupiter meanwhile, unprompted, spoke as follows to Juno:
"O sister of mine, at the same time my dearly beloved
Wife, as you thought (your opinion did not deceive you),
Venus, not their lively valor, supports Trojan power
In war, not their spirit so fierce and so patient in peril."
Juno replied to him meekly: "Most handsome of husbands,
Why do you trouble me, sick and in fear of your orders
So grim? If there were in my love the force it once had

And still ought to have, you would not deny me now,   640
All-mighty, the power to take Turnus out of the battle
And keep him unharmed for his father Daunus. Now let him
Perish and pay with his loyal blood to the Trojans.
Nonetheless he was given his name from my family line.
Pilumnus was his father's great-grandfather, and often
With generous hand he heaped many gifts on your altars."
     The king of ethereal Olympus spoke briefly as follows:
"If you ask a reprieve for the present from death, a delay
For the young man, who still must die, and you understand clearly
The condition I make, then save him by flight and remove him   650
From hurrying fate: thus far there is room to indulge you.
But if any mercy is what you are hinting at under
These pleadings, some thought that the entire war can be altered,
You nourish vain hope." Then Juno in tears replied:
"What if the favor you now begrudge with your voice
Should be granted in your heart, and life should continue for Turnus?
Now grievous destruction remains for an innocent man,
Or I wander away from the truth. May I be deluded
And may you in your power change your design for the better."
When she had said this, she sent herself down from high heaven,   660
Surrounded by clouds and driving a storm through the air,
And made for the Ilian lines and the Laurentine camp.
Then the goddess provided a thin, strengthless shadow of hollow
Cloud with the face of Aeneas, a marvellous vision,
Equipped it with Trojan weapons and copied the crests
And shield of that godlike man, gave it unreal words,
Sound without mind, and made it walk just like Aeneas.
Like those shapes which they say flit about after death, or the dreams
Which delude our senses in sleep, so this joyous image
Pranced about in the front lines and stirred up the hero by shaking 670
Its weapons and mocking him. Turnus attacked it and hurled
His whistling spear from a distance. It rounded and fled.
Then Turnus believed that Aeneas had turned and was fleeing;
In confusion he drank up an empty hope in his mind.
"Where do you run, Aeneas? Do not desert
A marriage arranged. This right hand will give you the land
You came searching for over the waves." He shouted these words
And followed, his drawn sword gleaming; he did not see
That the winds were carrying his joyous dream away.
It happened a ship lay moored to a pier of rock,   680

With ladders in place and a gangway already prepared;
King Osinius had sailed in her from the shores of Clusium.
The image of trembling Aeneas had fled in its fear
To the hold of this ship, where Turnus arrived just as quickly,
Surmounting all obstacles, leaping across the high gangway.
Scarce had he touched her prow when Saturnian Juno
Parted the hawser and sent her, torn free, through the ebb
Of the tide out to sea. Aeneas called out for the vanished
Turnus in battle and sent many bodies of men
Whom he met down to death. Then the light image sought
No longer for hiding-place; flying aloft, it was mingled   690
Within a black cloud. When Turnus, borne out in a whirlwind,
Looked back from mid-ocean, bewildered by his situation
And ungrateful for safety, he raised both his hands to the stars
And spoke: "Mighty father, do you consider me worthy
Of such a great punishment, and am I so great a wrongdoer?
Where am I carried? Whence did I come? What flight
Pulls me back? Who am I to run? Shall I see once more
The Laurentine walls or my camp? What of that band
Of men who followed me and my arms, what of those
Whom I left, all abandoned to an unspeakable death?   700
I can see them now, straying about! They groan as they fall!
What am I to do? What earth can yawn deep enough
To swallow me up? O rather have mercy, you winds.
On the cliffs, on the rocks, on the savage reef of a sand bar
Drive the ship—I, Turnus, implore you with all my heart!
There neither Rutulians nor my ill fame shall find me."
Saying such things, his mind wavered here, now there,
Whether to stab himself madly in such a disgrace
And drive the bare sword through his ribs or to dash himself
Into mid-ocean and swim to the curving shore,   710
Return to the Teucrian battle and face their weapons.
Three times he tried each way, three times mighty Juno
Restrained the young man and pitied him in her soul.
Cutting the deep he glided with favoring tide
And wave and was borne to the ancient city of Daunus.
       But Mezzentius, burning for war meanwhile, was warned
By Jove. He came back to the fight and attacked the rejoicing
Trojans. The Etruscan battle lines merged and against one,
One man with their hatred and showering missiles they pressed.
He, like a rock that rises from the broad sea   720

Exposed to the fury of winds in the midst of the ocean,
Endures all their strength and the threats of heaven and water,
Remaining unmoved. He struck Dolichaon's son,
Hebrus, to earth; with him Latagus and Palmus,
Speedy in flight. He crushed Latagus on the mouth
And face with a rock, a gigantic fragment of mountain.
He hamstrung Palmus and left him to roll on the ground
With his feet now sluggish, then gave his weapons to Lausus
To wear on his shoulders and fix the man's crest on his head.
He killed Euanthes the Phrygian and Mimas, age-fellow   730
And comrade of Paris, whom his mother Theano bore
To his father Amycus upon the same night when Cisseus'
Daughter, Queen Hecuba, pregnant with a torch of fire,
Gave birth to Paris. He sleeps in his father's city.
The coast of Laurentum holds Mimas, a stranger to it.
Like a boar driven out by the biting of dogs from high mountains,
Whom pine-bearing Vesulus defended for many years
And the Laurentine swamp fed on reedy growth,
When he has come among snares stands and growls fiercely,
His shoulders a-bristle, so none has the courage to vent his   740
Anger on him and approach, but safe at a distance
They press upon him with javelins and shouts, but unfrightened
He stands, facing in each direction, and grinds his teeth,
Shaking the spears from his back; in a similar way
Not one of the fighters righteously angry against
Mezzentius dared to attack him with a drawn sword.
They harassed him only with missiles and shouts from a distance.
Acron, a Greek, had come from the ancient borders
Of Corythus, a fugitive forced to abandon his wedding.
From afar Mezzentius saw him disrupting the center   750
Of battle, adorned with red feathers and a purple cloak
His sweetheart had given him. Just as a ravenous lion
Who often goes ranging through deep forest coverts, while hunger
Makes him more fierce, perhaps sights a bounding she-goat
Or a stag towering to his antlers, rejoices and opens
Wide his huge mouth, his mane bristling up as he crouches,
Clinging upon the beast's entrails as hideous gore
Bathes his cruel jaws,
Thus eager Mezzentius attacked his close-ranked opponents.
Unhappy Acron was killed and he beat the black earth   760
With his heels as he died and bloodied the broken spear.

Mezzentius did not even deign to chase fleeing Orodes,
Or give him an unseen wound with a thrust from behind.
He ran to meet him, as man to man he attacked him,
By no means the better with stealth but with strength of arms.
Then he planted his foot on the prostrate man, leaned downward
And pressed on his spear; he said: "My companions, the lofty
Orodes, a power in war not to be despised,
Lies here." His comrades echoed his victory cry.
But Orodes said as he died: "Whoever you are,   770
My victor, you will not rejoice over me unavenged
For long; a similar fate is watching for you
And soon the same earth will hold you." Mezzentius laughed;
Yet his laughter was mingled with anger: "Now die. For me,
The father of gods and the king of men will decide."
As he said this, he pulled his weapon out of the body.
For Orodes, harsh peace and an iron sleep pressed down
On his eyes, and their glow was extinguished in endless night.
Caedicus killed Alcathous, Sacrator killed Hydaspes,
Rapo killed Parthenius and Orses, very tough in strength;   780
Messapus slew Clonius and Erichaetes, son of Lycaon,
The first as he lay on the ground, thrown from his unbridled
Horse, and the second a footsoldier. Agis the Lycian,
Footsoldier as well, had come forward. But Valerus, sharing
His grandfather's valor, brought him to earth. Meanwhile Salius
Slew Thronius, and Nealces in turn slew Salius,
The first from an ambush with javelin, the second by shooting
An arrow deceptive through distance.
                              Now Mars made the struggle
Equally heavy with mutual slaughter. Both victor
And vanquished slew and were slain in an equal exchange,   790
And neither one side nor the other decided to run.
The gods in the palace of Jupiter pitied the fruitless
Anger of both, the terrible suffering of mortals.
Venus on one hand looked down and Saturnian Juno
On the other, while pallid Tisiphone raged in the middle
Of thousands. Mezzentius, shaking a giant spear,
Advanced on the field like a whirlwind, as tall as Orion,
Who paces on foot through the deepest shallows of Nereus,
Cutting his towering way through the waves with his shoulder,
Or when bringing an ancient ash tree down from the mountain   800
Top, he walks on the soil and hides his head among clouds:

So Mezzentius bore himself forward beneath heavy armor.
Scouting aslant the long line of battle, Aeneas
Saw him and readied to meet him. The man remained fearless,
Awaiting his great-hearted foe, and stood firm in his huge mass;
With his eyes he measured the space he would need for his spear.
"Now, right hand, my god, and the missile I balance, be with me.
I vow that you, Lausus, shall wear the spoils torn from this brigand's
Body, my trophy against Aeneas." He spoke, then
Threw at long range the whistling spear, but it glanced from   810
The shield of Aeneas and struck the outstanding Antores
Between his side and his groin, Antores the comrade
Of Hercules. Exiled from Argos, he clung to Evander
And settled in an Italian city. Unlucky,
He fell with a wound intended for someone else;
He looked at the sky as he died and remembered sweet Argos.
Then loyal Aeneas hurled his spear; through the hollow
Circle of triple brass, through three layers of linen
And three of bull-leather it passed till it planted the point
In the lower groin but did not carry its force   820
Through to the end. Aeneas was happy to see
The Etruscan blood. He drew the sword from his thigh
And swiftly dashed at his confused enemy.
Lausus groaned loudly with love for his dear father
As he saw him wounded; the tears rolled down his cheeks.
The sorrow of your harsh death, your deeds nobly done,
If antiquity shall lend credence to such great adventure,
I shall not pass over in silence nor you, young man,
Worthy to be remembered.
                          Mezzentius retreated,
Disabled, impeded; he dragged the enemy's weapon   830
Stuck in his shield. The young man flung himself forward
And mixed in the fight, when Aeneas lunged upward
To strike a blow. With his right hand Lausus restrained him
By grasping the swordpoint and checked him with this delay.
His comrades followed with mighty shouts till his father,
Protected by his son's shield, could make an escape.
They cast their spears for a cover and confused the Trojans
With missiles thrown from afar. Aeneas, though raging,
Kept himself well concealed. And just as when storm clouds
Fall in descending hail, every plowman deserts   840
The open fields, and each farmer and wayfarer

Seeks a safe shelter, perhaps the bank of a river
Or hollow of some tall rock as long as the rain falls,
So that they may follow their tasks when the sun returns,
Thus Aeneas with spears raining on him from every side
Endured the storm cloud of war till the last thunderclap.
Then he burst into rage against Lausus and threatened him thus:
"Why do you hasten to die, daring deeds quite beyond you?
Your loyalty tricks you to recklessness." No less did Lausus
Continue his insane attack. Now savage defiance   850
Rose higher within the Dardanian leader. For Lausus
The Fates spun his ultimate threads. Aeneas unsheathed his
Strong sword and buried it up to the hilt in the belly
Of the young man. The point of it passed through his little
Shield, thin protection for such heavy threats; it passed through
The tunic his mother had woven with pliant gold,
Filling its folds with blood. Then his spirit departed
Sadly through air to the Manes and left his body.
But while the son of Anchises gazed on the dying
Features and face of the man grown wondrously pale,   860
He gave a deep groan in pity and stretched out his right hand,
Gripped to the heart by this vision of love for a father,
Recalling his own: "O pitiful boy, what can I,
Loyal Aeneas, now give you befitting your action
So brave and worthy of such a character? Keep
The weapons in which you delighted. I give you release
To join the dead spirits and ashes of your ancestors,
If this is your wish. But even in miserable death
You may find consolation in knowing you fell by the right hand
Of mighty Aeneas." Moreover, he scolded the comrades,   870
Reluctant to aid, and lifted him up from the earth,
Where he lay in the blood that was soiling his neatly cut hair.

      Meanwhile, his father was staunching his wounds in the Tiber
With water and leaning his body against the trunk
Of a tree. At a distance his helmet of bronze was hanging
From the branches; his heavy armor lay on the meadow.
Round him there stood picked young men. He, in his weakness,
Was panting and resting his neck; his combed beard flowed down
On his chest. He kept asking questions about his son Lausus
And sending off messengers with the commands of a father   880
In sadness, to call him back. At that very moment
The comrades of Lausus in tears were bringing his body

Upon his own shield, a great man downed by a great wound.
Mezzentius' mind, foreboding some evil, had noted
Their groans from afar. He smeared his white hair with handfuls
Of dust, raised both palms to the sky, and clung to the body.
"My son, did so great a desire for living possess me
That I should allow you to die in my place by the right hand
Of the enemy, you I created? And am I, your father,
Preserved by your wounds? Ah, now at last death is bitter,   890
My wound driven home. It was I, son, who sullied your name
With my guilt, for banished from throne and paternal scepter
Through hatred against me, I should have been punished long since
By my country and people and should of my own accord
Have yielded my guilty soul to all kinds of death.
I live, and not yet do I leave the light of day
And of men. But I shall!" As he said this he raised himself
On his injured leg and although his strength was failing
Because of his dangerous wound, he was not disheartened
But ordered his horse to be brought. The horse was his glory,   900
His consolation; as victor, he rode him away
From every war; he spoke to the grieving horse:
"Rhaebus, we have lived long, if length can be reckoned
In human affairs. Today in victory you will
Carry off bloody spoils and the head of Aeneas, avenging
The sufferings of Lausus with me; or, if no force can
Open the way, you shall die with me, for I think
You will not, my bravest, obey another man's orders
Or a Trojan master." He spoke and, mounting his back,
Settled his legs in the place to which they were accustomed,   910
Loading sharp javelins in both hands. His head flashed with bronze
Under its plume of shaggy horsehair. He charged
Full-speed at the midst of the enemy. Shame in a tide
Mingled with madness and grief swept over him now,
And love driven onward by fury, and self-conscious courage.
Three times he shouted his challenge aloud to Aeneas.
Aeneas recognized him and prayed in delight:
"So may the father of gods, may Apollo on high
Grant! Now begin the fight!"
Thus much he spoke and advanced with his terrible spear.   920
Mezzentius said: "How can you frighten me,
Most savage of men, now that my son has died?
This was the only way by which you could ruin me.

I have no horror of death, no regard for a god.
Stop, for I come to die and I bring these gifts to you
Before." He spoke and hurled a missile against him,
Another and still another he flung as he rode
A wide circle around him; the golden boss of the shield
Held firm. Three times he rode round Aeneas standing,
To reach his unshielded left, still throwing his weapons.   930
Three times the Trojan hero turned round him an endless
Forest of spears that clung to his bronze-covered shield.
Then, weary of so much delay and weary of pulling
So many darts from his shield, he was forced by unequal
Combat to think of a plan of attack; at last
He burst forward and planted a spear in the hollow temples
Of Mezzentius' war horse. The beast reared upward and pawed
The air with his hoofs, tossed his rider, and then fell upon him,
Pitching headfirst as he dislocated a shoulder.
Trojans and Latins set heaven aflame with their shouting.   940
Aeneas flew up and ripped his sword from the sheath.
He spoke as he stood over him: "Where now is that eager
Mezzentius, where that fierceness of mind?" The Etruscan
Spoke in reply as he looked up at air and drank in
The sky and recovered his senses: "O bitter foeman,
Why do you taunt me and threaten with death? There is nothing
Sinful in slaying me; I did not come into battle
On any such terms. My Lausus made no such agreement
Between you and me. One thing, if whatever favor
May be granted to enemies conquered, I beg. Let my body   950
Be covered in earth. I know that the bitter hatred
Of my people surrounds me. I charge you, fend off their fury
And allow me to rest as his comrade in my son's tomb."
He spoke and, still conscious, accepted the sword in his throat
And poured out his life in a torrent of blood on his weapons.

BOOK ELEVEN

End of War

Meanwhile, the Dawn in her rising had left the ocean.
Aeneas, although he was troubled by thoughts of the killing
Of comrades and anxious for respite to bury their bodies,
At earliest light paid his vows to the gods. A large oak tree,
Its branches lopped off on all sides, was set up on a mound.
He hung there the shining weapons, the spoils of the leader
Mezzentius, trophy to you, O Mighty-in-Warfare.
He fitted thereon the blood-dripping crests and the broken
Darts of the man and his breastplate, battered and pierced
Twelve times, fastened his shield made of bronze on the left side,   10
And hung up his ivory-hilted sword on the tree-neck.
Then he began to encourage his comrades. The thronging
Staff of commanders encircled him, pressing up closely:
"The greatest part of our task is completed, my men.
Have no fear for the rest. Look at these spoils and the first-fruits
From a proud king! Here is Mezzentius at my
Hands. Now our pathway leads on to the king and the walls
Of the Latins. Get ready your weapons with courage. Be hopeful
To forestall the war, lest delay hold you back in amazement
When the gods give the signal to pluck up the standards and lead   20
The young men from camp, or a cowardly purpose retard you.
Let us commit in the meantime these unburied bodies
To earth, their sole honor when they have reached Acheron's gulf."
"Go," he said, "pay the last tribute to these noble spirits
Who gained us this fatherland at the price of their blood.
First to Evander's sad city let Pallas be sent,
Whom a black day has taken and plunged into bitter death,
Lacking no valor." He spoke and in tears turned back
To his dwelling where lay the lifeless body of Pallas,
With the old man Acoetes on vigil, a man who had been   30

Arms-bearer to Parrhasian Evander, not equally happy
In auspices when he was given as comrade to Pallas.
Around him there gathered the entire band of the Trojans,
Of servants and Ilian women, their hair hanging down
In ritual sorrow. As Aeneas walked through the high entrance,
They raised loud lament to the stars and beat on their breasts;
The palace re-echoed with anguish. When he saw the head
And pale face of Pallas propped up and the gaping wound
From a spear of Ausonia on his smooth breast, he began,
With tears welling up: "O pitiful boy," he said,   40
"When Fortune came happily, did she begrudge me the pleasure
That you might survey our kingdom, be borne as a victor
To your ancestral home? I made to your father
No pledge about you when I left. He embraced me and sent me
Forth to great empire; he told me how much he dreaded
These fierce enemies, that the battle would be with a hardened
Race. Even now, enchanted by baseless hope,
Perhaps he is making his prayers and heaping his altars
With sacrifice, while we are bringing the lifeless young man
Home with his fruitless honor, no longer in debt   50
To any immortals. Unhappy man, you will see
The cruel last rites of your son. This is our return,
The triumph we waited for, the great trust you placed in me!
But, Evander, you shall not look on your son, a defeated
Soldier with shameful wounds, nor shall you, his father,
Prefer an accursed death for him, safe though a coward.
Ah, what a bulwark Ausonia loses in him,
And, Iulus, you lose as well!" When he had lamented
The dead, he gave orders the miserable body be lifted,
And commissioned one thousand picked men from the entire line   60
To serve as an honor escort and take part in his father's
Lament, a small solace for such a great grief but befitting
A father's sorrow. Rapidly, others entwined
A bier of soft wicker-work from arbutus twigs and the offshoots
Of oak trees and shaded the high-piled couch with a cover
Of leafy boughs. They placed him high on this rustic
Bed, like a flower plucked off by a virgin's thumb,
Whether soft violet or drooping hyacinth,
The bloom not yet lost and all its beauty unfaded
Although mother earth no longer strengthens or feeds it.   70
Then Aeneas brought forward twin garments stiff with embroidered

Purple and gold, which Dido of Sidon had made
Once with her own hands, pleased with her labor for him,
Dividing the web with gold thread. He placed one of these sadly
Round the young man as a final honor; the other
He used to cover the hair that was soon to burn.
Many besides of the spoils from Laurentian battle
He piled up with the booty and ordered to be led forward
In a long line, adding horses and weapons which he had
Stripped from the foe. Then he tied the hands of the captives   80
(Whom he was to slay in sacrifice to the spirits
Below earth) behind their backs, now ready to scatter
Their blood on the pyre. He ordered the leaders to carry
Tree trunks with enemy weapons attached to them
And the enemies' names inscribed. Unlucky Acoetes,
Worn out with age, was led in procession, defiling
Now his breasts with fists and now his face with his nails.
He fell, and his entire body lay stretched on the ground.
They drove chariots stained with Rutulian blood.
Behind them walked Aethon, the war horse, his trappings removed;   90
He wept, and his features grew wet with abundant tears.
Other men carried his spear and his helmet; the rest
Turnus the victor possessed. Then followed a sad
Long line of Tyrrhenians, Trojans, Arcadians, all
With spears in reverse. When the procession of comrades
Had passed on ahead, Aeneas stood still. With a heavy
Groan he added: "The same dreadful Fates of war
Recall us to other tears. Eternally hail
And eternally fare you well, my Pallas the great!"
No more. He turned to the high walls and entered the camp.   100
    Ambassadors now were at hand from the Latin city,
Veiled with the boughs of the olive and seeking this favor:
That he should return the bodies that lay in the fields,
Felled by steel, and allow them to rest in the earth;
There could be no quarrel with the dead now deprived of the light.
He should spare those who once were called hosts and his parents-in-law.
Aeneas the good conceded the favor they asked,
One not to be spurned, and followed it with these words:
"What unworthy fortune, O Latins, enmeshed you in war
So great that you flee from us friends? You are asking a peace   110
For those who are dead, who have perished by chance of war.
I would grant it to them even if they were still alive!

I should not have come here if fate had not given a place
For my home; I wage no war with your people; your king
Gave up his guest-friendship with me and entrusted himself
To the weapons of Turnus instead. It would have been fairer
For Turnus to face this death. If he is preparing
To finish the war with his strength and to drive out the Trojans,
He should have attacked me with weapons like these. That man would
Have survived to whom god or his own right hand gave his life.   120
Now go and set fire beneath your poor citizens."
Aeneas had spoken. They stood in bewildered silence,
Turning their eyes and their faces to stare at each other.
Then Drances, an old man who always pursued the young Turnus
With hate and denouncements, thus opened his mouth to reply:
"Trojan, O mighty in fame, more mighty in arms,
What praise shall I use to make you the equal of heaven?
Shall I marvel first at your justice or toughness in battle?
We are happy to carry these words to our paternal city,
And link you, if Fortune shall give us the way, to Latinus,   130
Our king. Let Turnus seek his own treaty of peace.
We shall be pleased to heave Trojan stones on our shoulders
And build up the mass of those walls which are destined to rise."
When Drances had spoken they all roared approval as one.
They struck up a truce for twelve days, with peace as stake-holder.
Trojans and Latins together went wandering freely
Through woods and the mountain ridges. Tall ash trees rang out
Under the strokes of a two-edged axe. Pine trees
That soared to the stars they cut down. Oaks and the fragrant
Cedar they split unceasingly with their wedges;   140
On wagons that groaned they carried the mountain ash.
      And now Rumor flying, the messenger of great sorrow,
Filled Evander, the home of Evander, and his walled city—
Rumor, which lately had brought news of Pallas the victor
In Latium. The Arcadian people rushed to the gates
And in ancient fashion they snatched up funeral torches,
Lighting the way with their flares and dividing the fields
By a long streak of light. The Trojan procession
Moved forward to join them in mourning. The mothers came after
As soon as they saw them arrive and kindled the city   150
With their own sad clamor. No force could restrain Evander
From running among them. When they set the bier down before him,
He crouched over Pallas and clung to him wailing and weeping;

Scarcely at length was his sorrow relaxed into speech:
"O Pallas, not this was the promise you gave to your father
Who begged you to trust yourself cautiously to savage Mars.
I knew very well what a young man's ambition for glory
Could bring, and how sweet to win fame in your first encounter.
These are the first-fruits of miserable youth, the harsh training
Of war near your home! Not one of the gods heard my vows   160
Or my prayers. And you, wife, most worthy of my adoration,
Are blessed in death since you were not preserved for this sorrow.
But I, since I live, have conquered my fate as a father
And survived you. I should have been overcome by Rutulian
Spears, I who followed the allied arms of the Trojans.
I should have surrendered my life and this funeral journey
Should have carried me, not you, Pallas, back to my house.
I would not lay blame on the Trojans, our pact, or agreements
Made by our right hands in friendship. This lot is inherent
Within my old age. Yet if early death was awaiting   170
My son, it will help to know he has fallen a leader
Of Trojans who come into Latium, having killed thousands
Of Volscians before. I would not have held you worthy,
Pallas, of funeral rites other than those which loyal
Aeneas, than those the great Phrygians, the Etruscan leaders,
And all the Etruscan army have chosen for you.
Great are the trophies they bring from those killed by your right hand.
You also, Turnus, would be standing there now, a monstrous
Trunk hung with arms, if you had been equal in years
And the same in your strength by those years. But why does my   180
    sorrow
Delay the Trojans from war? March on and remember
To carry these words to your king: the reason I linger,
Though life is now hateful with Pallas destroyed, is your right hand
Which owes, as you see, to my son and to me, his father,
The slaying of Turnus. This way is the only one open
To your fortune and merits for valor. I seek satisfaction
Not in this life—that is wrong—but to carry the joyful
Tidings down under the earth to the ghost of my son."
        Meanwhile, for miserable mortals Aurora had lifted
Her fostering light, bringing back their tasks and their troubles.   190
Now Father Aeneas, now Tarchon set up on the curving
Beach the death-pyres. Here each man carried by custom
Of his ancestors the bodies of kith and kin.

The smoke from the fires beneath them sent upward a pall
Of darkness to heaven. Three times, arrayed in their shining
Armor, they marched round the pyres aflame; on their horses
Three times they rode round the sad fires of death in a ritual,
And uttered three times a lament. The earth with their weeping
Was sprinkled, their weapons were sprinkled: the clamor and clangor
Of men and of trumpets rose skyward. Here some threw on the fire   200
The plunder torn from the Latins they slew, the helmets
And beautiful swords and the bridles, the glowing wheels.
Others threw things which the dead men had owned and loved,
Their shields and the weapons unlucky. They slaughtered the hulks
Of many an ox round the bodies, an offering to Death,
And bristly boars and cattle dragged out of each field,
They slew on the flames. Then down the entire shore
They looked at their burning comrades and tended the pyres
Half-burned. They could not be torn from the place until moist
Evening inverted the sky with its shining stars.   210
     No less did the sorrowing Latins build numberless pyres
In another direction; some of the many dead bodies
They buried in earth, while others they lifted and carried
Away to the neighboring fields and sent back to the city.
The rest, a huge mass of slaughter commingled, they burned,
Unreckoned, unhonored; then everywhere fires, both frequent
And eagerly lit, burned over wide fields. The third morning
Had driven the chilly shadows from heaven: still grieving,
They drew the deep ashes and masses of bones from the pyres
And heaped over them a mound of warm earth. In the city   220
Of wealthy Latinus, inside of the walls, a great lament
Arose and the loudest of wailing, the longest. Here wretched
Mothers and daughters-in-law, dear hearts of the mourning
Sisters, and children bereft of their parents who cursed
The terrible war and the wedding of Turnus. They bade him
To make a decision himself with arms, with the sword,
Since he claimed for himself the kingship and the first honors
In Italy. Angrily Drances increased the effect
Of their words, saying Turnus alone was called out by Aeneas,
Who demanded him only in combat. Opposing opinion   230
Was expressed through various pleas in defense of Turnus,
While the queen's great name cast a sheltering shadow upon him.
His great fame and well-deserved trophies supported the man.
     Amid this excitement, while tumult was flaming among them,

To cap all, sad envoys arrived from Diomedes'
Great city to bring this reply: not a thing was accomplished
By all the expense of large efforts; the gifts and the gold,
Their long prayers availed nothing. The Latins must seek other arms
Or ask peace from the Trojan king. King Latinus himself
Had lost heart under his huge sorrow. The anger of gods,   240
The graves of the dead freshly buried before their eyes,
Gave warning with manifest power that Aeneas was guided
By destiny. Thus at Latinus' command a great council
Of chiefs was collected within his high palace. They gathered,
Rushing through crowded streets to the royal dwelling.
Latinus, the eldest, the first, sat there with his scepter
In hand and no smile on his face. He commanded the envoys
Sent back from the Aetolian city to tell him their message.
He bade them to speak in reply and report every detail
In order. Then silence of tongue was proclaimed and, obeying   250
Command, Venulus commenced to deliver harangue:
    "We have seen, O citizens, Diomedes and the Argive
Encampment, completed the route, overcome every hazard.
We have shaken the hand which once crushed the Ilian land.
The victor by Garganus mountain in fields of Apulia
Was founding the city of Arpi, named after the race
Of his ancestors. When we had entered, he gave us permission
To speak; giving gifts, we told him our names and our country,
Who waged war against us and why we had come to Arpi.
He listened to us and calmly replied in this manner: 260
'O fortunate peoples, the kingdom of Saturn, you ancient
Ausonians, what fortune disturbs your repose and persuades you
To create unknown dangers of war? Those among us who ravaged
The Ilian fields with our swords—I say nothing about those
Sufferings endured under Troy's lofty walls in the fighting,
Those men whom the Simois drowned, our unspeakable anguish,
And all of the penalties paid for our crimes—are a band
That Priam himself might pity: the sinister star
Of Minerva knows this, and the Euboean headland, Caphereus
The vengeful. From that campaign they were driven to different   270
Shores—Menelaus to Protean Pillars, Ulysses
Saw Aetnaean Cyclopes. What shall I say of the kingdom
Of Neoptolemus, the household of Idomeneus
In ruin, of Locrians living on Libyan shores?
Agamemnon himself, of Mycenae, the leader of famous

Argives, was killed when he entered his house, by the hand
Of a queen who was foul, her adulterer lying in wait
For the downfall of Asia to strike. To think that the gods
Have begrudged me return to my father's altars, the sight
Of the wife whom I longed for, and beautiful Calydon!   280
Now followed still omens revolting to look at; my comrades
Are lost; they seek heaven on wings, and they wander by rivers
As birds—what disaster for us! With their sorrowful voices
They fill the rock cliffs. Yet these horrors I should have expected
From that very time when, attacking the heavenly bodies
And Venus with steel in my madness, I wounded her right hand
In sacrilege. No, do not drive me to any such battles!
Since Troy was destroyed, I have had no warfare with Trojans,
Nor do I remember those bygone evils with pleasure.
Give to Aeneas the gifts which you brought from the shores   290
Of your homeland for me. I have withstood his harsh missiles
And grappled him hand to hand. Believe me, I know him,
How huge he springs up with his shield, in what a great whirlwind
He levels his spear. If the Idaean land had created
Two heroes like him, the Trojans would have invaded
The cities of Inachus freely and Greece would have mourned
Her fates in reverse. Whatever the time that we spent
Before the hard walls of Troy, Greek victory wavered
Beneath Hector's hand and Aeneas'; they forced it to linger
Until the tenth year: both noble in spirit, both expert   300
With excellent weapons, Aeneas more loyal than the other.
Join your right hands in a treaty as it is permitted;
Beware lest your arms clash with arms.'
                                        You have at one hearing,
O excellent king, his reply and the king's own opinion
About this great war."
                        Scarcely had the ambassadors spoken,
When varied disturbance of protest ran swiftly among
The troubled Ausonians, as when rapid rivers are hindered
By boulders, a gurgle is made in a throttled whirlpool
And the river banks murmur nearby with the splashing of waves.
As soon as their spirits were calm and their eager mouths quiet, 310
The king from his lofty throne first prayed to the gods,
Then addressed them: "Latins, I wish we had settled the matter
Of public safety before, that would have been better,
And not at a time like this to summon a council,

With the enemy at our walls. We wage a completely
Unseasonable war with the race of the gods and unconquered
Men. No combat wearies them; even defeated,
They can lay down no sword. If you had any hope of alliance
With arms of Aetolia, put it aside. Each man has
His hope: but you see how narrow a margin we have   320
And into what ruin the rest of our fortunes lie fallen:
All the facts are before your eyes and within your hands.
I do not accuse anyone. The greatest that courage
Could do has been done; the fight has been fought with all forces
Of our body politic. I shall explain my opinion,
Though doubtful in mind, and briefly: give me your attention.
I have an old piece of land near the Tuscan river,
Far to the west, just beyond the Sicanian border.
The Aurunci and Rutuli till it and plough up its rugged
Hillsides and use the roughest parts for their pasture.   330
Let all of this region with pine slopes of lofty mountains
Be granted in friendship to Trojans, and let us declare
Just terms for a treaty and call them our allies in ruling.
Let them settle, if so they desire, and found city walls.
But if to seek other borders and another people
Is their wish—and, of course, they are able to leave our soil—
Let us build for them twenty good ships of Italian oak wood
Or as many as they can man, since all of the timber
Lies close to the shore. Let them tell us the number and model
They wish for their keels. Let us give them the labor, the bronze,   340
And the shipyards they need. Moreover, it is my pleasure
That one hundred Latin envoys of noblest descent
Should carry our message, and ratify treaties, and wear
The olive branches of peace, bring talents of gold,
And ivory gifts, the throne of our kingdom, the robe
Of our royalty. Plan for the public welfare, assist
Our depleted resources."

            Then Drances arose with the same
Hatred of old. The glory of Turnus disturbed him
With bitter pin-pricks of side-glancing envy, the master
Of lavish wealth and more lavish speech; yet his right hand   350
Was sluggish for war. His words were not empty in council
But powerful at intrigue. His mother's family
Had given him pride of birth though his father's name
Was uncertain. He heaped up the load of his anger in speech:

"Your advice, O good king, is clear to us all, and it does not
Require my vocal support. Each one of us knows
And admits what course the people's fortune is taking,
But all of us fear to speak out, and we mutter in private.
Let him give freedom of speech and restrain his loud boasting
Because of whose failure as leader and whose awkward nature—   360
I shall speak even though he threaten with weapons and death—
So many of our great commanders have fallen, we see
The whole city beset with grief, while, trusting to flight,
He attacks the camp of the Trojans and frightens the heavens
With weapons. Add one more gift to the sum of those
Which you say should be sent to the Dardans, most excellent king:
Let nobody's violence cow you from giving your daughter,
As a father may do, to an excellent son-in-law
In honorable marriage, or from establishing peace
With eternal agreement. But if such a terror possesses   370
Our minds and our hearts, let us plead with him, beg his permission:
Let him grant and return *his* just rights to both king and country!
Why do you so many times throw your miserable fellow
Countrymen into sheer dangers, O both chief and the cause
Of those evils for Latium? There is no salvation in war.
You, Turnus, we ask for peace and the single unbroken
Pledge of that peace. I first, whom you fancy am hostile
To you—though whether or not I am does not matter—
Come as a beggar. Take pity upon your people!
Lay by your anger; now conquered, retreat from the battle.   380
We have seen enough deaths in defeat and have ravaged wide fields.
Or if fame stirs you, if courage is so strong within you,
And if a royal dowry is so very close to your heart,
Be bold and with confidence turn your own breast to the foe.
Surely, that Turnus may win him a royal bride,
We, lives that are worthless, unwept and unburied a throng,
Must not lie on the field of battle! If any
Strength is within you, if you have your ancestors' valor,
Look him in the face who gives challenge!"

                              At speech such as this
Turnus' violence flamed.   390
He rumbled; these words burst from the depths of his chest:
"You, Drances, at any rate always have much to say
At a time when war demands action. As elders are summoned,
You are the first to be present. The meeting must not be

Filled with your words that go boastfully flying in safety
As long as the moat and the walls hold the enemy back
And the ditches not running with blood. Then thunder ahead
With your eloquence after your custom. You, Drances, accuse me
Of fear when your right hand has heaped up as many piles
Of dead Trojans as mine has and dotted the fields here and there   400
With trophies. Go test for yourself what a lively courage
Can achieve. I am sure that you need not go far to seek
Our enemies; everywhere they stand round the walls.
Are we attacking? Why pause? Or shall Mars exist
Forever upon your windy tongue and flying
Feet? Have I been repulsed? Or shall anyone charge
With justice (the scoundrel!) that I have been driven back,
When he sees Tiber river swollen with Trojan blood
And Evander's household destroyed from its very root,
The Arcadians stripped of weapons? Not thus did Bitias   410
And gigantic Pandarus know me, or a thousand others
I as a victor sent in one day to Tartarus,
Shut up in their walls and fenced by a hostile rampart.
'There is no salvation in war.' You madman, prate
Such words at the Trojan's head and your own misfortunes!
Then do not cease to confuse all things with great fear
And to praise a people twice conquered, to belittle the arms
Of Latinus. Even now the Myrmidon leaders are trembling
Before Phrygian power, now both Diomedes and Achilles
Of Larissa, now even Aufidus river flows back   420
In flight from the waves of the Adriatic. Or when,
Again, he pretends he is fearful of my upbraiding,
The artful villain, and uses this fear to embitter
His charge against me—you never will lose such a life
At my right hand, so do not shrink back! Let it dwell
Within your breast. Now, father, to you and to your
Great plans I return. If you place no hope any longer
In weapons of ours, if we are deserted thus,
If we are completely crushed this time and our battle
Line has been routed and fortune cannot return,   430
Let us ask for peace and offer our limp right hands.
If only something of our old valor remained!
For me, that man is blessed beyond all others
In his undertakings ,and noble of heart, who preferred
To bite the earth and to die than to see such events.

But if we have resources left and a manhood intact,
And cities and peoples of Italy in full support,
And if by the Trojans as well their glory is won
With great spilling of blood, as with us, and they have their deaths 440
As all of us have and a similar storm of war,
Why do we fail in dishonor upon the first threshold,
Why does a trembling seize our limbs before
The trumpet of war is blown? The passage of time,
The changing travail of varied age has brought
Much to a better pass. Fortune in shifting
State has sported with many, then placed them again
On a solid foundation. No rescue will come from him,
The Aetolian, or from his Arpi. Messapus will help,
And lucky Tolumnius; so will those leaders whom many   450
A people sent to the war. No little the glory
Won by the flower of Latium's troops and Laurentian
Fields. There is noble Camilla from Volscian stock,
Leading her squadrons of horsemen a-blossom with bronze.
But if I am called by the Trojans in single combat,
And this is your pleasure and I stand so much in the way
Of the common good, Victory has not fled from my hands
In such hatred that I should refuse to make any attempt
For the sake of so great a hope. I shall meet him with courage
Even though he should play great Achilles and wear equal armor   460
Made by the hands of Vulcan. I, Turnus, devote
This life to you and Latinus, my father-in-law,
I second in valor to none of the ancient heroes.
'Aeneas calls me alone.' I ask that he call me;
Nor, whether the gods shall be angry, would I rather that Drances
Appease them with his own life, or whether the glory
Of valor awaits us, bear it away as his own."
        These in disagreement discussed their uncertain position.
Aeneas moved camp and his battle line. Look, a swift message
Rushed through the palace with mounting excitement and filled   470
The city with widespread terror, to say that the Trojans
Were drawn up in battle array; the Etruscan army
Was descending through all the fields from the Tiber river.
At once their spirits were stirred and the hearts of the people
Were shocked, their anger aroused with the sharpest spurs.
Excited, they asked for their weapons, the young men shouted
For war, their elders wept and complained in murmurs.

Here on all sides a huge clamor of discord rose upward,
As when flocks of birds have settled by chance in a lofty
Grove or beside the fishy stream of Padusa,   480
Or swans with their strident voices give sound through the echoing
Marsh. Turnus seized his moment and called: "Citizens,
Now don't keep debating but gather a council, sit down
To praise peace. Those people are rushing with arms to the kingdom."
Saying no more, he sprang up and ran out of the lofty
Palace. "You, Volusus, order the Volscian detachments
To arm and lead out the Rutulians," he shouted.
"Messapus, stand to! With your brother, Coras, go lead
The cavalry through the wide fields. Let guards take position
Upon each approach to the city and man the watch-towers: 490
The rest of you, follow with me, to attack where I order!"
They hurried throughout the whole city at once to the walls.
Father Latinus himself abandoned the council,
Postponing its weighty transactions, disturbed by the anxious
Moment, with much self-abuse because without waiting
He had not accepted Dardanian Aeneas and made him
His citizen son-in-law. Others in front of the gates
Dug trenches or carried up stones and stakes. The harsh bugle
Blared out bloody signal for war. Then children and matrons
Made a ring of defenders upon the walls. The last struggle   500
Called everyone. Also the queen with a throng of the mothers
Rode up to the temple, the citadel stronghold of Pallas,
Carrying gifts; beside her there rode her companion,
The virgin Lavinia, cause of such terrible troubles,
With her decorous eyes looking downward. The mothers came after,
Filling the temple with incense and lifting sad voices
From the high threshold: "Tritonian virgin, decisive
In war, strong in weapons, break with your hand the javelin
Of the Phrygian bandit and stretch him out prone on the soil.
Under the high gates destroy him." The furious Turnus   510
Was first of them all to prepare himself for the battle.
And now in his shining red breastplate he bristled with brazen
Scales, he had greaves of gold; his temples were naked
As yet; he had buckled a sword to his side. In a golden
Glitter he ran from the fortress, already exulting
In spirit and hope of forestalling the enemy,
As when a horse who has broken his halter runs freely
Away from his stall and has reached the wide-open field,

And either bolts after the mares who are feeding in pasture
Or darts toward a river where he is accustomed to swim　　　520
Leaping up high as he neighs, and lifts his proud head
In simple delight while his mane sports on neck and on shoulders.
Camilla came riding to meet him with Volscian detachments.
Close to the gates the queen leaped down from her horse,
While all of her company followed her lead and dismounted,
Gliding to earth. Then she uttered the following words:
"Turnus, if those who are brave can be confident also
With reason, I dare and I promise to meet all alone
Aeneas' group and the cavalry of the Etruscans.
Allow me to test with my hand the first perils of war.
You remain on foot near the walls and guard the defenses."　　　530
Turnus said, fixing his eyes on the frightening virgin:
"O maiden, Italy's pride, what thanks or what payment
Can I even begin to express or return? Since your spirit
Soars above every reward, now share the tense struggle.
Aeneas, as rumor and scouts who are worthy of trust
Report, has remorselessly sent his light cavalry forward
To harass the fields. He himself, crossing over the ridge
Through wilderness trails of the mountain, approaches the city.
I am preparing a stratagem in an arched pathway
That runs through a wood, to block off both ends of the pass　　　540
With armed soldiers. Be ready to catch the Etruscan horsemen
When standards advance. Brave Messapus and the Latin units
Will be with you, as well as Tiburtus' group: take command."
So he spoke and with similar orders encouraged Messapus
And his fellow commanders to battle. Then he moved toward the foe.

There lies a low valley with curving terrain that is suited
For ambush and armored deception, slopes dark with thick branches
Confining a pass on both sides. The brief path that leads to it
Runs through a narrow ravine with a grudging approach.
Above this, among look-outs high on the top of a mountain,　　　550
There is a plateau which cannot be seen from below,
Secure and secluded, whether you wish to attack
On right or on left or to stand on the ridge and roll boulders
Down on the enemy. To this place the young man hurried
Over familiar ground, took position in cover
Of lowering woods.
　　　　　　Meanwhile, in the palace of heaven,

Diana was holding swift Opis, a maiden among
Her holy band of companions, in sad conversation:
"O virgin, Camilla advances to mortal combat
And binds on our weapons in vain. She is dear beyond others   560
To me. For this love comes not freshly nor does it disturb
My heart with a sudden sweetness. When Metabus left
The old city Privernum because of the hatred aroused
Toward his rule by his insolent power, and fled among battles,
He carried his infant daughter as comrade to exile,
And called her Camilla by changing a part of her mother
Casmilla's name. Hugging her close he sought the long ridges
Of groves in the wilderness. Weapons were flying about him;
The Volscian soldiers were scouring the country to find him.
Look, in the midst of his flight he came to the river   570
Amasenus with flood water foaming up both of its banks,
So heavy a downpour had burst from the clouds in a rainstorm.
He, ready to swim, was delayed by love of the infant
And feared for his tender charge. Turning every plan over
In mind for escape, he suddenly settled on this one:
The warrior carried by chance in his strong right hand
A spear that was grotesquely huge, with knots on its solid
Well-seasoned oak wood: to the middle of this he tied
His small daughter, rolled up in the bark of a wild cork tree,
Handily. Hefting the spear in his right hand he spoke   580
Thus to the heavens: "Latona, nourishing virgin
Who cherish the groves, I devote my child as her father
To your service. Your weapons are the first she holds;
As your suppliant she flies from the enemy through the air.
Accept her as yours, I beg you, O goddess; she now is
Committed to doubtful air." He spoke and drew back
His arm to send forward the whirling missile. The waters
Resounded, unhappy Camilla fled over the rapid
River upon the whistling javelin. Her father
Metabus, with a large throng now pressing him closely,   590
Jumped into the stream and triumphantly pulled up the javelin
And girl, a gift to Diana, from the green turf.
None of the cities received him into their houses
Nor into their walls, nor would he, so fierce, have surrendered
To any; he lived among shepherds on lonely mountains.
There among thickets and lairs of wild animals,
He nourished his daughter on milk from a mustang mare,

Squeezing it out of the udder to her tender lips.
And when the child had taken her first baby footsteps
He placed a sharp javelin in her hands, from her shoulder   600
So little he hung a bow and a quiver of arrows.
Instead of a golden hair-clasp, in place of the cover
Of a long gown, the skin of a tiger hung downward
From the back of her head. Soon at her tender age
She threw little javelins and whirled a sling of smooth leather
Around her head and killed a Strymonian crane
Or a white swan. In vain through Etruscan cities
Many a mother wished her as a daughter-in-law.
She was content with Diana alone and, a virgin,
Cherished her love for weapons and chastity   610
Without end. I could wish she had never been caught in such
A campaign nor had tried to attack the Trojans. Dear
She would be to me as one of my comrades now.
But come, since we are pushed onward by bitter Fates,
Glide downward, nymph, from the pole and visit the land
Of the Latins, where grisly battle is joined under omen
Malign. Take these, and draw an avenging arrow
Out of the quiver. Whoever shall mar her sacred
Body shall pay for that wound in blood,
Whether Italian or Trojan. I shall afterward carry   620
Her pitiful corpse in a hollow cloud with her weapons
Unspoiled and shall place them within a tomb in her country."
She spoke and Opis slipped lightly down from the sky
Through the air. Her weapons rattled, her body was covered
In a black whirlwind. Meanwhile the Trojan contingent
Was approaching the walls, both the Etruscan leaders
And the entire cavalry army, drawn up with their squadrons
In orderly number. The horses were prancing and charging
All over the field and chafing against tight reins,
Neighing and lunging this way and that. The plains   630
Bristled with spears and steel, ablaze with their weapons
Held upright. Messapus came out to meet them, the swift
Latins, Coras and his brother, the virgin Camilla's
Detachment, right arms drawn far back for spear-thrust. They brandished
Javelins. The marching of men and the snorting of horses
Grew livelier. Each side now came to a stop within spear-range.
Suddenly each of them burst into shouts and urged on their
Furious horses and fired their missiles on all sides

At once like a heavy snow, while a shadow came over
The sky. In an instant Tyrrhenus and fierce Aconteus   640
Made the first charge, their spears at the ready, with impact
Of crashing sound as their horses met breast to breast.
Thrown from his horse like a thunderbolt or a siege-engine
Driving a weight with its ropes, Aconteus fell
And scattered his life to the breeze. The line of battle
Was broken, the Latins retreated, their shields turned over
Their backs for protection, and wheeled their mounts toward the walls.
The Trojans pursued, Chief Asilas leading his group;
They came near the walls, the Latins again raised the war-cry
And turned back the yielding necks of their horses. The army   650
That rushed in pursuit now fled with loose reins to a distance:
Just as the swell of the ocean with alternate billows
Now rushes to land and dashes its waves on the cliffs,
Foaming and spreading far up the sand of the beach,
Now swiftly runs back as it swallows the rolling stones
With a backwash of water, retreating at last from the shore
In a dwindling shallow, two times did the Etruscans drive backward
The Rutuli toward the walls; twice checked, the Etruscans
Looked behind them in fear and covered their backs with their shields.
But after they clashed for the third time in battle, the whole line   660
Was locked in one combat, and man picked his man. Then the groaning
Of those who were dying, and weapons, and bloody bodies
Were mingled in slaughter, half-dead horses rolled over;
A bitter struggle arose. Orsilochus whirled
A spear at the horse of Remulus, since he was frightened
To attack its master, and struck it beneath the ear.
The war horse went wild with the blow and reared upward in pain,
His feet high above his chest. His rider rolled over
To earth. Catillus struck Iollas and then Herminius,
Huge in their spirit and arms and body. Herminius   670
Rode with his blond head bare and his shoulders naked,
Without fear of wounds, so tall he stood forth against weapons.
The spear driven through his broad shoulders trembled and stuck there;
He doubled with pain as it pierced him, his dark blood flowed
Everywhere. Fighting, they killed with the sword and sought handsome
Death with their wounds. But there in the midst of the slaughter
Camilla rejoiced like an Amazon, baring one breast
For the fight as she carried her quiver, and now with her hand
She scattered tough spears in a shower, now snatched with untired

Right fist a strong axe with two edges. There hung from her shoulder 680
A bow made of gold, the weapon of goddess Diana.
Also, whenever repulsed, she fled and directed
Her arrows with back-bent bow. But around her were chosen
Companions, Larina the virgin, Tulla, Tarpeia
Swinging a brazen axe, the Italian daughters
Divine Camilla herself had selected to honor
Her, faithful attendants in peace and in war; as when Thracian
Amazons beat the Thermodon river with horse-hoofs
Or fight with their painted weapons, Hippolyta's escort,
Or when Penthesilea the warlike rides in her chariot,   690
With a great howling tumult of women who cheer her procession,
Waving their crescent-shaped shields. Who was the first,
Who was the last you struck with your weapon, fierce virgin,
Or how many dying bodies did you beat to the ground?

Euneus, the son of Clytius, was first: she pierced him
With a long pinewood spear through his naked chest.
Dying, he poured out his blood in rivers, bit earth
Red with his gore; then he twisted and turned on his wound.
Then Liris fell, Pagasus on him: the first while he gathered
The reins of the horse shot under him, as he was rolling   700
To earth; the second came up and extended his hand
Without weapon to save him. Together they fell headlong.
To these she added Amastrus, the son of Hippotas.
Leaning toward them with her spear, she went after Tereus
And Harpalycus and Demophoon and Chromis.
As many the darts that were flung from the hand of the virgin,
So many Phrygians fell. At a distance Ornytus,
Unused to his weapons, was riding a horse from Apulia.
The hunter's broad shoulders were covered with hide from a fighting
Steer, and his huge head wore for protection the yawning   710
Face and jaws of a wolf with white teeth. He held
With his hands a countryman's spear. He turned in the middle
Of his contingents, a head taller than the rest.
She caught him—it was not hard when the line was turned—
Pierced him, and spoke in addition with hostile heart:
"Did you think, Tyrrhenian, that you were hunting beasts
In the forest? That day has come when a woman's weapons
Will refute your boasts. You shall carry this fame to the spirits
Of your fathers, no trivial one: you fell by the spear

Of Camilla." She killed Orsilochus next and thereafter   720
Butes, two very strong men of the Trojans; but Butes
She struck with her spear as he turned, between helmet and breastplate,
Baring his neck to the light while his shield hung down
From his left arm. She fled from Orsilochus in a wide circle,
Eluding him with a small swoop to pursue her pursuer.
Then, rising higher, she struck him again and again
With the powerful axe through armor and bones while he pleaded
And prayed for mercy; his wound oozed warm brains and blood
Down on his face. The warrior son of a dweller
On Apennine heights, named Aunus, not the least of Ligurians   730
While fate still allowed his deceit, chanced suddenly on her
And stopped dead with fear at the sight. When he could not avoid
The fight by running nor turn the queen from her onset,
He tried to be clever and crafty, beginning this way:
"What is so strange in being a female fighter
If you rely on a powerful horse? Don't run but entrust
Yourself to a single combat with me on an equal
Footing; prepare for a battle upon the ground!
Soon you will know to whom windy vanity brings
A bitter deception." He spoke, and her anger was heightened   740
With a sharp indignation at insult. She handed her horse
To one of her comrades and faced him with similar weapons
On foot, with a naked sword and an unblazoned shield,
Without terror. The young man, supposing his trick had succeeded,
Fled off without waiting and, fleetly reversing the reins,
He goaded his horse to a gallop with iron spurs.
"Foolish Ligurian, exalted in vain by your spirit
Of pride, you have tested your slippery national cunning
Fruitlessly. Tricks will not bring you safe to your father,
A trickster himself." The virgin spoke. Swifter than lightning   750
She darted across the path of his horse, seized its bridle,
And engaged him in combat, exacting his hostile blood
As penalty for his deceit, like some hawk, that sacred
Bird from a lofty rock that easily catches
A dove high above in a cloud, then grasps it and holds it,
Scratching its entrails out with the claws of his feet,
As ripped out blood and feathers float down from the sky.
      Meanwhile the creator of men and gods who sits
On the top of Olympus had eyes to observe all this.
The Father urged on the Tyrrhenian Tarchon to savage   760

Battle and goaded his anger with pricks that were stinging.
So Tarchon rode amidst slaughter and yielding battalions
And cheered on the cavalry wings with a varied appeal.
He called every man by his name and restored to the battle
Those who were routed: "What fear has come over you, always
Sluggards, Tyrrhenians, never ashamed to be cowards?
A woman has put you to flight and has scattered these columns.
To what purpose do we wear swords and carry these useless
Weapons in our right hands? But you are not sluggish
For love and its nightly combat nor when the curved flute   770
Announces the Bacchic dance. Be eager for feasts
And wine on a groaning board—this is love, this you long for—
Until the soothsayer says omens are good and fat victims
Invite you to sacred groves." Having spoken, he spurred his
Horse into battle, prepared for his death. Like a whirlwind
He charged upon Venulus, grappled him from his horse
With his right hand and held him in front of himself, a huge effort,
And carried him off. Their shouting arose to the heavens,
While all of the Latins looked on. Tarchon flew like lightning
Over the plain, bearing arms and the man. Then he broke   780
Away the spear-point and groped for an unarmored region
Where he might inflict a death wound. Venulus, fighting back,
Held off Tarchon's hand from his throat and tried to avoid
Force with his force. As when a grey eagle flies skyward,
With a snake in his talons wound round the bird's feet; while he clings
To the wounded creature which writhes with its sinuous coils
And bristling scales erect, its hissing mouth
Rising on high; the eagle strikes back nonetheless
With hooked beak at the struggling snake and beats heaven with wings;
Not otherwise Tarchon, the victor, carried off booty   790
From the battle line of Tiburtians. Maeonian men
Followed their leader's example and his success.
Then Arruns, pledged to the Fates, ran round Camilla
The swift, much better at throwing her javelin, and tried
What fortune might be the easiest. Wherever the raging
Virgin would dash in the midst of the battle line, there
Arruns would turn and silently follow her steps.
Where she returned victor and retreated away from her foe,
Here the young man would stealthily twist his swift reins.
He tried this approach, now that, on every side   800
All around her, remorselessly shaking his fatal spear.

It happened that Chloreus, devoted to Cybele, once
Her priest, glittered in distinctive Phrygian armor.
He urged on his foaming war horse, covered with scales
Of bronze set like feathers to form a coat which was buckled
With gold. Chloreus, brilliant in foreign and deep purple garments,
Was using his Lycian bow to shoot Cretan arrows:
Gold was the bow which he slung on his shoulder, his helmet,
A priest's, was golden. He gathered the rustling linen
Folds of his saffron cloak with a knot of tawny   810
Gold, his tunic was pictured with gold, and heathen
Breeches he wore on his legs. The huntress virgin,
Whether to hang up his Trojan arms in the temples
Or to display herself dressed in his captured gold,
Followed him alone of the combatants heedlessly, blindly,
Aflame with a feminine love for plunder and booty.
Then, seizing his chance at last as he lay in wait,
Arruns snatched up his weapon and prayed to the gods:
"Highest of gods, Apollo, who guard Mount Soracte
The sacred, whom we worship first, for whom the pine fire   820
Is fed from a heap of wood where, sustained by our faith,
We worshippers walk through the flames on many a live coal,
Allow us, great father, to wipe from our arms this dishonor.
I seek not the spoils of the virgin defeated, no trophy,
No other booty; what deeds I have done will bring
Fame; but so long as this evil plague falls defeated
By my wound, I shall go back to my father's city, contented
Without any glory." Phoebus heard and gave permission
For part of the vow in his mind, part of it he scattered
On the swift breeze. He nodded assent to the suppliant,   830
That he should strike down a bewildered Camilla with sudden
Death; he denied the request for return to his noble
Fatherland. Storm gusts diverted his speech to the South Winds.
Thus as the spear let loose from his hand gave a whistle
Through air, all the Volscians paid close attention and turned
Their sharp gaze on the queen. She was mindful neither of air
Nor sound of the weapon that came from the sky, until
The spear driven hard beneath her bare breast clung there drinking
Deep of her blood. Her anxious comrades ran to her
To raise up their mistress now falling. Arruns, amazed,   840
Ran before all of them, joy mixed with dread in his heart,
No longer trusting his spear or daring to meet

The maid and her weapons, just like that wolf, before hostile
Missiles pursue him, who kills a large bullock or shepherd,
Then hides straightaway on the pathless mountain, well knowing
How reckless his exploit; he lowers his trembling tail,
Drawing it back to the belly between his legs
And makes for the woods, so Arruns hid in confusion
From everyone's eyes and made an eager escape
Through the midst of the army. Camilla pulled at the weapon   850
As she died, but the iron point stood deep in her ribs
With its wound. She sank down, bloodless; her eyes drooped shut
In a chilly death; her color, once rosy, departed.
Then, dying, she spoke to Acca, one of her maidens
Faithful beyond all others to Mistress Camilla,
Sharing her sorrows; and these are the words she said:
"Acca, my sister, I have done what I could thus far:
Now this bitter wound destroys me and everything round me
Grows black in the shadows. Escape and carry to Turnus
My last orders. Tell him to move to my place and hold   860
The Trojans off from the city. And now goodby."
So speaking, she dropped the reins and glided, unwilling,
To earth. Then little by little, grown cold, she released
Herself from her entire body, laid down in death
Her nerveless neck and her conquered head, with her weapons,
And her life with a groan fled indignantly down to the shadows.
Then truly an endless lament struck the golden stars
As it rose; the battle grew grim when Camilla fell.
At once all the Trojan force, the Tyrrhenian leaders,
The Arcadian cavalry wings of Evander fought closely.   870
    But Opis, the guard of Diana, had sat all the while
High up on a mountain top surveying the battle,
Unfrightened. Amid the clamor of angry young men,
She saw from afar Camilla's sad punishment—death.
She moaned and heaved up these words from the depths of her breast:
"Alas, too cruelly, O virgin, too harshly you pay
The penalty for your attempts to harass the Trojans
In war. No profit for you to worship Diana
Among the wilderness-thickets, to carry our arrows
Upon your shoulder. Your queen has not left you without   880
Some honor, however, now in extremes of death.
Nor shall your demise be nameless among the world's nations,
You shall not be scorned, unavenged; whoever has marred

Your body with wounds shall pay with a death deserved."
The grave of Dercennus, an ancient Laurentian king,
Lay at the high mountain's base, heaped high with a mound
Of earth, shaded by dark oaks: the beautiful goddess
Alighted here first in her sweeping descent and examined
Arruns from the lofty mound. When she saw him all shining
In armor and swelling with empty pride, she said: 890
"Why do you run away? Turn your steps this way.
Come here to your death, to receive fit reward for Camilla.
You also shall die by Diana's weapons." The Thracian
Nymph spoke and took a swift arrow from golden quiver.
Fiercely she stretched the bow and pulled it far back
Till each of the curving ends of it came together
And her hands drawn apart were touching at equal distance,
With the left the steel arrow-head, with the right hand her breast
At the bowstring. Arruns could hear in a single moment
The whizz of the arrow and whir of the air as the arrow   900
Buried its point in his flesh. His comrades, forgetful,
Left him to die and to moan last words in the unknown
Dust of the fields. Opis flew up to lofty Olympus.
    Camilla's light cavalry fled, having lost its commander,
The panicking Rutuli fled, keen Atinas fled,
And leaders torn from their men, their abandoned troops,
Went looking for safety, and wheeling their horses around
They ran for the walls. No one was able to bear
The deadly attack of the Trojans with weapons or stand
Against them, but slinging their unstrung bows to slack shoulders,   910
With four-footed thud horses' hoofs struck the crumbling field.
A turbulent cloud of black dust rolled up to the walls,
And mothers from watch-towers, striking their breasts, raised a cry
To the stars of heaven. An enemy crowd pressed hard
On the first disorganized groups who burst from the open
Gates to the city. They did not escape sore death,
But on the threshold itself, within sight of their fathers'
Walls and the safety of homes, they breathed out their lives.
Some of them closed the gates and did not dare open
The way to their friends nor receive them within the walls,   920
Though they begged. There arose a most miserable slaughter of men
Who defended approaches with arms and men rushing against
Those arms. Excluded before the eyes and the faces
Of their weeping parents, some rolled headlong to the moat

With ruin behind them; some, blindly loosing the reins,
Rode hard as a ram at the gates and the strongly barred doors.
Mothers themselves from the walls at the height of the conflict,
Showing true love for their country and seeing Camilla's
Example, with trembling hands hurled javelins and quickly
Made objects that looked like weapons from solid oak   930
And stakes pointed up in the fire to serve as steel:
They were first in their ardor to die in their place on the walls.
    Meanwhile in the forest the tragic report reached Turnus,
Absorbing his thoughts, while Acca described the huge tumult:
The lines of the Volscians destroyed, Camilla fallen,
The dangerous foemen advancing, and all gone to ruin
With Mars to increase it, and panic now brought to the walls.
He in his rage—savage power of Jove made him do so—
Deserted the hills he had held, left the wilderness woodland.
He had scarcely gone out of sight to gain level fields   940
When Father Aeneas, after entering the open valleys,
Mounted the ridge and came out of the shadowy forest.
Thus both to the walls were rapidly borne with entire
Columns of battle, nor were they far distant apart.
At the moment Aeneas could spy the fields smoking with dust.
He saw the Laurentian columns far off, and Turnus
Himself recognized him, so fierce in his gleaming armor,
And heard the advancing of feet and the snorting of horses.
At once they might have begun to fight and join battle
If Phoebus the rosy had not already bathed weary   950
Horses in Spanish waters, while day, slipping outward,
Brought back the night. They camped and made wall by the city.

BOOK TWELVE

Turnus against Aeneas

When Turnus could see that the Latins were broken by hostile
Mars and were sick at heart, that his promises now
Were asked for as due, that the eyes of the men were upon him,
His unappeased spirit rose up in a furious flame.
Like that lion in fields of Carthage whose chest has been wounded
Severely by hunters, who at last moves in to attack,
Rejoicing to shake the mass of his mane and, unfrightened,
Breaks off the fixed lance of their leader and roars with a bloody
Mouth, so with violence Turnus glowed in his anger.
Then he addressed the king in disordered fashion: 10
"There is no delay in Turnus, no reason why cowards
Who follow Aeneas should swallow their words or break pledges.
I go forth to fight. Prepare sacrifice, father, and draw up
The agreement. Either I send down to Tartarus
This Dardan deserter from Asia with my right hand—
Let the Latins sit down and look on—and all alone
With my sword shall refute his charge against all my people,
Or let him possess us as conquered, let Lavinia yield
To him as his wife." Latinus replied to him calmly:
"O young man of noble heart, the more you excel me   20
In ferocious courage, the more it is right that I counsel
You earnestly, weighing with caution all chances of danger.
Yours is the realm of your father Daunus and yours are
The many cities you captured; in addition, Latinus
Has gold and is generous. There are other unmarried maidens
In Latium and lands of Laurentum, nor are they ignoble.
Allow me to speak hard words, all flattery absent,
And drink them into your soul. It was right that I give my
Daughter to none of her earlier suitors, and all
The gods and the human soothsayers have prophesied this.   30

I was conquered by love of you, by our kinship of blood,
By the tears of my grieving wife: so I broke every bond.
I snatched her away from Aeneas, my son-in-law,
To whom she was promised; I took up unholy arms.
You see from that day to this my misfortune, the wars
That have plagued me, Turnus, the troubles that you first have suffered.
Conquered in two great battles, we scarcely preserve
Italian hopes with our city. The Tiber flows warm
With our blood, and the endless plains are still white with our bones.
Why do I backslide so often, what madness is this   40
That changes my mind? If I am prepared to greet allies
When Turnus is dead, why do I not stop the fight
While he is uninjured? What will the Rutulians say,
My kinsmen? What will the rest of Italy say
If I betray you to death—may fortune forbid it!—
Seeking my daughter and marriage within my house?
Gaze on war's fickle fortunes and pity your aged
Father whom now in his sadness his fatherland holds
Far off in Ardea." Turnus' violence scarcely
Was touched by these words; it rose higher, grew sick with its healing. 50
As soon as he could, he spoke, beginning as follows:
"This care that you have for me, O best ruler, I beg you,
Lay by and allow me to barter my death for glory.
Father, my powerful right hand can still scatter missiles,
And blood issues out of the wounds I inflict. Far from him
Will be his mother, the goddess, who covers him fleeing
In a womanish cloud, and he hides himself in vain shadows."
        But the queen, in terror at the new peril of fighting,
Wept, and as one on the point of death she embraced
Her fiery son-in-law: "Turnus, I beg you by these   60
Tears, by whatever grace in Amata which touches
Your spirit: you now are my only hope and my solace
In miserable age; Latinus' glory and power
Are both in your hands. On you rests our whole sinking household.
One thing I beg: hold off your hand from the Trojans.
Whatever chances are waiting for you in this combat,
Turnus, are waiting for me; when you die I abandon
The hateful light of the day; I shall never see
Aeneas, my son-in-law, when I am captured." Her daughter
Lavinia heard, as she wept, what her mother had said,   70
Wetting her cheeks where a fiery blush ran deeply

Over her feverish face, as when someone stains
Indian ivory with blood-red dye or mingles
Many white lilies with roses, thus tinting them red,
Such were the colors the virgin showed in her face.
Turnus, disturbed by his love, fixed his gaze on the maiden;
He burned all the more to fight and spoke to Amata
Briefly: "O mother, do not pursue me with tears
Or with such an omen as I go into the combat
Of Mars the harsh god: there is no freedom for Turnus   80
To delay his death. Idmon, carry these words to the Phrygian
Tyrant; they will not please him; as soon as tomorrow
Aurora rides red in the sky on her crimson wheels,
Let him send no Trojans against Rutulians; both
Should rest on their weapons. Let us break off the war with our blood:
Let Lavinia be wooed as a wife upon that field."
    So speaking, he swiftly turned back into the palace,
Demanded horses, was pleased as he saw them neigh
Before him, the horses Orithyia herself gave Pilumnus
As a treasure for him. They were whiter than snow, they ran   90
Faster than winds. Brisk charioteers stood around them,
Slapping their chests with hollow hands to arouse
Their spirits, and combing their flowing manes. Then Turnus
Put a mail-coat with scales of gold and white brass on his shoulders,
Took up for wearing a sword, a shield, and a helmet
With horns of red feathers, a sword which Mighty-With-Fire,
The god, had made for Daunus, his father, and tempered
Glowing in waves of Styx. Then mightily seizing
The strong spear which leaned against a great pillar within
The heart of the palace, spoil from Actor of Aurunca,   100
He shook it, all quivering, and shouted: "O never in vain
Have I called on you, spear of mine, and now is the time!
Great Actor carried you, now Turnus carries you in his
Right hand. Grant me to lay low his body and pierce
His breastplate with my strong hand and tear it away
From the Phrygian half-man and dirty his hair in the dust,
Curled with hot iron and dripping with perfume of myrrh."
This was the madness that drove him. Sparks leaped from his face,
All burning, his eyes were shining with furious fire.
As when at beginning of battle a bull starts to bellow,   110
Strikes terror and tries to throw anger into his horns,
Charging the trunk of a tree and wounding the winds

With his blows, or scattering sand as a prelude to battle.
Meanwhile, Aeneas, no less fierce in the arms his mother
Caused to be made for him, sharpened his ardor for fighting
And roused up his anger, rejoicing to settle the warfare
By a pact. He comforted comrades, and the dread of sad Iulus,
Describing their destinies, and ordered a definite answer
To be given to King Latinus, which stated conditions
Of peace. Morning scarcely was spreading its first light on hill tops,   *120*
As soon as the horses of Sun arise from the ocean
And puff out the light with their nostrils distended, when the Trojans
And Rutuli measured the field for the combat beneath the
Walls of the mighty city, made fires, and set up
Altars of turf to the gods who were worshipped by both sides.
Others, dressed in priestly aprons, brought water and firewood,
Binding their temples with wreaths. The Ausonian legion
Poured out its closely packed ranks through the crowded gates.
Opposite them rushed the Trojan, Tyrrhenian army,
With their different armor, not otherwise weaponed for war   *130*
Than if Mars' bitter battle were calling; so there in the middle
Of thousands the leaders themselves moved swiftly and proudly
In purple and gold, both Mnestheus, son of Assaracus,
And brave Asilas and Messapus, the tamer of horses,
The offspring of Neptune. When signal was given, each fighter
Fell in at his post, stuck spears in the ground and leaned
On his shield. Then, eagerly streaming, the mothers and unarmed
Civilians and powerless old men sat down on the towers
And roof tops while others took stand on the towering gates.
But Juno looked down from the top of the mountain Albanus,   *140*
As it is called now—for then neither a name nor an honor
Nor glory it had—out over the plain toward both armies,
The lines of Laurentians and Trojans, and Latinus' city.
At once goddess spoke to goddess, the sister of Turnus,
Who presides over echoing rivers and pools—this honor
High Jupiter, lofty in heaven, had given to soothe her
For taking her maidenhead: "Nymph, the pride of the streams,
Most dear to my heart, you know I have favored you only
From all of the Latin virgins who climbed the ungrateful
Bed of large-spirited Jove, and I placed you quite gladly   *150*
In your part of the heavens. Discover your sorrow, Juturna,
But do not upbraid me. Where Fortune had seemed to permit
And the Fates allowed triumph to Latium, I guarded your walls

And Turnus. I see now the young man engaging in battle
Under unequal advantage. The day of the Fates
And an enemy's power draw near. With my own eyes I cannot
Look on at this fight or this pact. If you dare to defend your
Brother more capably, do so, that's fitting. Perhaps
Better things will turn up for the wretched." The goddess had scarcely
Spoken this way when Juturna poured tears from her eyes,   160
Struck her hand on her beautiful breast three times and four.
"This is no time for tears," said Saturnian Juno.
"Run to your brother and snatch him from death if you can.
Either cancel the compact that's made or stir up the fighting.
Be bold at my order!" Encouraging thus, Juno left her
Uncertain, distraught in her mind with its grievous wound.
        Meanwhile the kings: Latinus came riding a chariot,
Four-horsed, enormous, with twelve gilded rays shining round his
Temples, the sign of his grandfather Sun; in a chariot
Pulled by two white horses came Turnus, who brandished   170
Two spears of broad iron. Then Father Aeneas, the founder
Of the Roman race, bright with star-flashing shield and celestial
Armor, beside him Ascanius, the second hope
Of great Rome, came forth from the camp. The priest in his spotless
Robes brought the young of bristling swine and an unclipped
Two-year old sheep, and drove cattle to fiery altars.
Turning their eyes to the rising sun, they scattered
Salt meal, marked the beasts on the temple with iron blade,
And poured wine from their bowls on the altars. Loyal Aeneas,
Drawing his sword, prayed thus: "Now, Sun, be my witness,   180
And Earth, as I pray; for your sake I was able to suffer
So many great trials, and Almighty Father, Saturnian
Wife—now kinder, now, goddess, I pray—and you, glorious
Mars, father, who sway every war under your divine power:
I call on the fountains and streams, whatever we worship
With dread in high heaven, and spirits that rule the blue sea:
If victory passes by chance to Ausonian Turnus,
We agree that the conquered shall go to Evander's city.
Iulus shall leave these fields, nor shall men of Aeneas
Take arms in rebellion or harass this realm with the sword.   190
But if victory favors our war effort, as I assume
(And may the gods strengthen that favor with all their power),
I shall not command that Italians be subject to Trojans
Nor seek an empire for me. Let both peoples unconquered

Submit under justice of law to eternal treaties.
I shall give holy things and gods; let my father-in-law
Latinus have arms and the power to govern by custom.
The Trojans shall build walls for me, and Lavinia shall
Give her name to the city." Thus first Aeneas. Then followed
Latinus with this, looking up at the sky and extending   200
His right hand to the stars: "I swear by the same things, Aeneas,
By earth and the sea and the stars and Latona's twin children,
And Janus two-faced, by the power of gods under earth,
And the sacred land of harsh Dis; let the Father hear this,
Who ratifies treaties with lightning. I touch the altars
And call to these fires and powers between us for witness.
No day shall destroy this peace for Italians, this treaty,
Whatever befalls; nor shall any compulsion avert
My will, not if earth is poured into ocean and mingled
In deluge and heaven be broken and thrown into hell.   210
Just as this scepter"—by chance he was holding a scepter
In his right hand—"will never sprout twigs with light leafage nor shade,
Since once for all cut in the woods from its lowest root
It misses the parent stock and has laid aside foliage
And branches beneath the axe; once a tree, now an artist's
Hand has enclosed it in bronze decoration and given
It to Latin fathers to carry." With such confirmation
They strengthened the pact in full view of the army commanders.
Then, rendering them sacred with flame, they slaughtered the victims
In ritual fashion and tore out the entrails from living   220
Carcasses, heaping the altars with loaded platters.
        But truly the Rutuli saw for sometime that the combat
Was one-sided, their hearts were in turmoil with varied emotions,
Especially when, on a closer inspection, they noticed
The unequal strength of the two. This impression was heightened
By Turnus' silent tread as he reverenced the altars
With suppliant downcast eyes and cheeks that were downy,
His young body pale. As soon as his sister Juturna
Saw whispers increasing and confidence leaving the crowd,
Their hopes in collapse, she took on the appearance of Camers;   230
Descended from a great family, his own name was famous
For ancestral valor, and he was most zealous in arms.
She threw herself into their midst and she knew what to do.
Scattering different rumors, she spoke: "Are you not
Ashamed, Rutulians, that one life for all is exposed

In defense of an army like ours? Is our strength or our numbers
Not equal to theirs? Look, there are the Trojans, Arcadians,
All of that fate-guided band of Etruscans, hostile
To Turnus. We'd scarcely have enemy troops to fight
If alternate men on our side should attack them. The fame   240
Of Turnus at least shall rise to the gods, to whose altars
He devotes himself as a victim, and it shall be carried
On lips of the living. We, quietly settled now
In these fields, shall be forced to obey proud masters when we have
Lost our fatherland." She fired the wills of the young men
With statements like these. Now more and more quickly a murmur
Crept down the long lines; Laurentians themselves and Latins
Were changed. Those who hoped at last for rest from the battle
And salvation from death now called for their weapons and pleaded
The treaty be broken and pitied the unequal lot   250
Of Turnus. To these Juturna added inducement
Much greater by sending an omen from lofty heaven
Than which no sign could more powerfully stir the Italian
Minds and deceive them with portent. Jove's golden bird,
An eagle, flew past in red heavens, pursuing some shore birds
And a clamorous flock in their wing-bearing line; then swooping
Suddenly down to the water, it fiercely snatched up
A leader of swans in its claws. The Italians lifted
Their spirits, when all of the birds in a clatter reversed
Their flight—a thing wondrous to see—and darkened the upper   260
Sky with their wings and, forming a mass like a cloud,
They drove the marauder through air till their strange attack
And the weight of the swan itself made the eagle give way,
Dropping the bird from its claws to a stream below
And fleeing completely through clouds. Then the Rutuli greeted
The augury with their shouting and readied their weapons.
The augur Tolumnius spoke first: "This, this is what often
I prayed for. I welcome and recognize gods. Wretched fellows,
With me, me as leader, take sword, you whom a rascal
Newcomer affrights in war like strengthless birds   270
And whose shoreline he ravages. He shall take flight and give sail
On the ocean. Close ranks with one spirit, in battle defend
Your king who is seized." He spoke and whirled spear at his foemen,
Running forward. The hissing cornel-wood shaft cut the air,
Flying straight. At the same time a great shout arose, all the wedge-formed
Divisions were troubled, and hearts were made warm with excitement.

The spear as it flew struck one of nine handsome brothers
Who stood opposite; a faithful Tyrrhenian wife had borne them
To Gylippus of Arcadia. It pierced him close to his middle
Where the belt stitched in gold and its brooch gripped the joints at   280
  each end,
A young man of noble appearance and shining weapons.
The spear plunged through ribs and he died on the yellow sand.
But his brothers, a phalanx of courage, now kindled with sorrow,
Seized, part of them swords in hand, part missiles of iron,
And rushed blindly. Against them the line of Laurentians pressed
  forward,
Then waves of dense Trojans and men from Agylla and men
From Arcadia in emblazoned armor rolled forth: thus all
Were gripped by one passion: to settle the battle with swords.
They broke down the altars, a whirling tempest of missiles
Filled the whole sky, and an iron rain came bursting down.   290
They carried off bowls and fire-braziers. Latinus himself
Ran away with his conquered gods since the treaty was broken.
Others gave rein to their chariots or leaped on their horses
And, drawing their swords, came up. Messapus, desiring
To break the agreement, spurred horse and frightened the king
Of Etruscans, Aulestes, wearing his royal badge.
He retreated and fell back, poor man, on head and shoulders
Over altars directly behind him. But eager Messapus
Rode up with his spear and, high on his horse, looked down,
With his shaft like a beam of wood, and wounded him gravely   300
While he was praying and pleading, then spoke as follows:
"He has it! This worthier victim I offer the great gods!"
The Italians clustered upon him and stripped his warm body.
While Ebusus came up to strike, Corynaeus before him
Snatched a hot brand from the altar and thrust it into his
Face; his huge beard flashed up into flame and the odor
Of singeing arose. Then, following up, he grasped
The hair of his bewildered foe with his left hand and pressing
His knee on him bore him to earth: he struck with a stiff sword
In his side. Podalirius, chasing a shepherd named Alsus   310
Running through weapons in first line of battle, loomed over
His foe with a naked sword. But Alsus with an axe-blow
Split chin and forehead in two and flooded his armor
With blood spattered widely. Harsh quiet and iron slumber
Possessed him: he closed his eyes in eternal night.

But loyal Aeneas extended his right hand unarmed,
Baring his head, and called to his men with a shout:
"Where do you rush? What sudden discord now arises?
O restrain your anger! The oaths have been struck and agreement
Is made. I alone have the right to join single combat.   320
Allow me, and lay aside dread. I shall conclude the compact
With a firm hand. These sacred rites now make Turnus
A debt to my credit." In the midst of this speech, as he said
Such words as these, look, a whistling arrow slid down
With its wings on the man. None knew what hand had despatched it,
What whirlwind gave impulse, what chance or what god brought such
        high praise
To Rutulians: the deed's great glory was kept as a secret,
Nor did any man ever boast he had wounded Aeneas.
When Turnus could see that Aeneas was leaving the battle,
His commanders dismayed, he ardently glowed with swift hope.   330
He asked for his horses and arms and at once he leaped
To his chariot, proudly shining, and grasping the reins
He dashed along, gave many brave bodies of fighters
To death and rolled many half-dead, either striking the army
Under his chariot or throwing the spears he had gathered
At men who were running, as bloody Mars, roused near the icy
Stream of the Hebrus, makes noise with his shield and drives horses
Furiously, stirring up wars; they fly over the open
Plain before South Wind and West Wind, and farthest Thrace
Groans with the thud of their feet, while around him black faces   340
Of Dread and of Anger and Treachery, the god's own retainers,
Are driven, so agile Turnus in the midst of the battle
Drove his horses smoking with sweat over enemies fallen,
Trampling them pitilessly. Rapid hoofs scattered the blood-drops,
And trod the sand mixed with gore. He killed Sthenelus, Thamyrus,
And Pholus, the first from a distance, the last two at close range.
From afar he slew Imbrasidas, Glaucus, and Lades,
Whom Imbrasus himself had raised in Lycia and fitted
With arms all alike to fight hand-to-hand combat or outstrip
The winds upon horseback. Elsewhere, Eumedes was carried   350
Into the contest, renowned for his fighting, the offspring
Of old Dolon, in name recalling his grandfather, in spirit
And deeds his father, who once when he came to the camp
Of the Greeks as a spy dared to demand for himself
The chariot of Achilles as reward. Diomedes rewarded

Him quite otherwise for such daring, nor did he desire
Achilles' horses in death. Turnus saw him afar on
The open field and pursued him through a long space
With a light javelin, then stopped his horses and jumped
From his chariot and stood above the half-dying man   360
Where he fell. Pressing foot on his neck he tore the sword
From his right hand and dyed it gleaming deep in his throat,
Saying: "Lie there and measure Hesperian fields,
Trojan, the fields which you sought in war: this prize
They receive who dare to cross swords with me; these are
The walls that they build." Then hurling a spear at Asbytes,
The comrade of Eumedes, Turnus killed him, and Chloreus,
Sybaris, Dares, Thersilochus, and Thymoetes,
Thrown from the neck of his restive mount. As when Thracian
Boreas roars on the deep Aegean and follows   370
The waves to the shore, where the winds settle down and the clouds
Flee from the sky, so the columns yielded to Turnus
Wherever he cut his way and the battle line fled.
His impetus bore him along while the breeze shook his flying
Crest as his chariot met it. Phegeus could not bear him
Driving along and raging. He ran at right angles
To the chariot, twisted aside the mouths of the hurrying
Horses that foamed at the bits. While he hung to the yoke
And was dragged along, the broad lance-head of Turnus pierced him
Exposed and, thrust deep, it went through his two-linked breastplate, 380
Grazing his body's surface, just tasting its wound.
Nevertheless, he turned with his shield as cover
And attacked his enemy, looking for help with the weapon
Drawn forth, when the wheel and the whirling axle hurled him
Headlong to the ground. Pressing on, Turnus cut off his head
Between the base of the helmet and edge of the top
Of the breastplate, and left his trunk upon the sand.

     But while Turnus the victor spread corpses all over the fields,
Mnestheus and faithful Achates and Ascanius,
His comrade, brought Aeneas to camp with his bleeding wound,   390
Supporting each alternate step with a long spear. He raged
And struggled to pull out the arrowhead with its broken
Shaft and demanded the shortest way to relief:
To cut the wound with a broad sword and open the hiding
Place of the weapon and send him back into the war.
Iapyx, the son of Iasus, beloved by Phoebus

Beyond any other, was there, to whom once Apollo,
Captured by love, gladly gave his arts and his powers:
Prophecy, playing the lyre, and swift-flying arrows.
In order to postpone the fate of his dying father,   400
He preferred to know powers of herbs and the practice of healing
And to follow mute arts without glory. Aeneas stood chafing
Bitterly, propped on a huge spear, a large group of youths
And grieving Iulus around him, unmoved by their tears.
Old Iapyx, his gown twisted up in the manner of Paeon
The healer, tried hard with his medical skill and Apollo's
Powerful herbs, but in vain. In vain with his fingers
He worried away at the steel, and with grip of his forceps.
No fortune guided his way nor did patron Apollo
Assist him. Meanwhile in the fields the horror of warfare   410
Increased more and more, and its danger came closer. Already
They saw the sky clouded with dust. The horsemen rode nearer
And missiles fell thick in the camp. An ominous clamor
Of warring young men falling under harsh Mars reached the heavens.
Here Venus, his mother, distressed at the pain which her offspring
Undeservedly suffered, plucked dittany plants on Mount Ida
In Crete, with their stalk of soft leaves and a purple flower,
A food not unknown to wild goats when swift arrows have clung
To their backs. This herb Venus brought, her face covered up
With a dark cloud. She mixed it in gleaming cauldrons   420
Of water, in medical secrecy, sprinkled the healing
Strength of ambrosia with it and sweet panacea,
The flower that heals all. Old Iapyx bathed the wound
In this water, not knowing its value, and suddenly all
Pain left Aeneas' body, all blood-flow stopped from the wound.
And now the arrow fell out as it followed Iapyx' hand,
Without any forcing. New strength came back as of old.
"Quickly! Bring arms to our man! Why are you standing
Motionless?" cried Iapyx, and was first to rekindle
Their spirits for fighting. "This healing is not from our human   430
Resources, nor from the guidance of medical art;
My right hand does not preserve you, Aeneas; a greater
God is at work, and he sends you to mightier deeds."
Aeneas eagerly wrapped his legs in gold greaves,
Loathed the delay and brandished his spear, but after
His shield had been fitted against his side and the breastplate
Upon his back, in armor he embraced Ascanius

Tightly and gave him the lightest of kisses between
The lips of the helmet and said: "Learn courage, my boy,
And true labor from me, but fortune from others. My right   440
Hand will defend you in war and lead you among
War's marvelous prizes; later, when you have grown up,
Let it be yours to recall the exciting example
Of your father Aeneas and uncle Hector, your kinsmen."
     When he had given this speech, he went out of the gateway,
Huge, with huge weapon to brandish. At the same time,
In a dense line Antheus and Mnestheus rushed forward
With all of the crowd from their abandoned camp. The field
Was blinding in dust, earth shook with the thud of feet.
From the opposite mound Turnus saw the enemy coming,   450
The Ausonians saw, a cold tremor ran through their bone-marrow.
First before all, Juturna heard and distinguished
The Latins, and, knowing their sound, she trembled and fled.
Aeneas flew over the plain and urged on his dark army.
As a storm cloud when bad weather strikes from the middle of ocean
Moves to the land, and the hearts of the luckless farmers,
Fore-knowing, are terrified; it will destroy their trees
And ruin sown crops and everything else far and wide;
The winds fly ahead and carry its thunder to shore:
So the Rhoeteian leader led out the line of his army   460
Against the enemy, each of them massing himself
In a thick wedge closely packed. Thymbraeus struck heavy
Osiris with sword, Mnestheus struck Arcetius, Achates
Killed Epulo, Gyas killed Ufens; the augur himself,
Tolumnius, fell, who was first to hurl spear at the foemen.
A clamor arose to the sky, and the Rutuli swung
Back in their turn to retreat, showing dust-covered backs
Over the fields. Aeneas himself did not stoop
To lay low in death the fleeing or those who attacked
On an equal footing, nor follow the flingers of weapons.   470
In a dense cloud of dust he hunted for Turnus alone,
Challenging him to lone combat. Juturna, a man-like
Maiden, struck to the heart with this dread, knocked Metiscus,
The driver of Turnus, standing among his reins,
Out of the chariot and left him fallen afar
From its pole. She sprang up and handled the wavering reins,
Taking on all his appearance, voice, body, and weapons.
As when a black swallow flies through the great house of a wealthy

Master and wings through its lofty halls picking crumbs
For its noisy nestlings, and now through the empty porches   480
Twitters, and now round the water tanks, so Juturna
Was borne by her horses through enemy ranks and flew over
The entire plain in her rapid chariot. Now
Here, now there she showed her triumphant brother,
Nor allowed him to fight but flew far away from the path.
No less did Aeneas pick up her tortuous flight;
He hunted the man and shouted aloud through the shattered
Battle lines. But just as often as he caught sight
Of his enemy, trying on foot to match flight of winged horses,
So often Juturna twisted the chariot away.   490
Ah, what to do? He was tossed on a shifting tide
In vain. Varied cares called his spirit in different directions.
Messapus by chance carried two tough spears in his left hand
As he ran. They were tipped with iron. He threw one with force
And good aim. Aeneas stood still and gathered himself
Behind his shield, sinking on one knee. The driven spear
Struck the peak of his helmet and knocked off the crest from the top.
Then rose his anger, forced by this treachery,
Seeing the horses and chariot driven away,
He called Jove for witness near the altars of treaty   500
Now broken. At last he invaded the lines in the middle.
Fierce with a favoring Mars, he made terrible slaughter
Without any distinction and loosed all the reins of his wrath.

        What god could disclose so many harsh conflicts, what epic
Describe so much slaughter and deaths of the leaders, whom now
First Turnus, then Trojan Aeneas drove over the plain?
Was it your pleasure, O Jupiter, that future races
Should live in eternal peace at the cost of such struggles?
Aeneas struck Sucro, the Rutulian, in the side—
This first fight held the attacking Teucrians back—   510
Without much delay and, where fate came the swiftest, he plunged
His pitiless sword through the ribs and the thoracic cage.
Turnus killed Amycus, thrown from his horse, and Diores,
His brother, attacking on foot, the first with a long spear
As he came, the next with his sword, and suspended their heads,
Dripping with blood, on his chariot and carried them off.
Aeneas killed Talos and Tanais and brave Cethegus,
Three in one fight, and Onites the sad, with a Theban
Name from Echion's city; his family was noble

Through his mother Peridia. Turnus killed brothers from Lycia   520
And fields of Apollo, then the Arcadian Menoetes, who hated
Wars but in vain: a skilled fisherman from the rivers
Round Lerna, of humble home, he knew nothing of rich mens'
Thresholds or largesse. His father sowed seed as a tenant
In land that he rented. As fires let loose in the forest
From different directions go crackling through thickets of laurel,
Or when in their rapid descent from the lofty mountains
Rivers go foaming and splashing and run to the sea,
Each wrecking its path, so swiftly Aeneas and Turnus
Rushed on into battle. Now, now their anger rose wave-like;   530
Their hearts, never knowing defeat, were bursting within them.
With all of their might they went to the making of wounds.
        Aeneas here struck Murranus, who boasted of ancient
Names of his forefathers, descended from Latin kings,
Headlong with a stone, a whirlwind of massive rock,
And stretched him upon the ground. The wheels rolled over
Him under the reins and the yoke. The hoofs of his horses,
Forgetting their master, struck him again and again.
Turnus met Hyllus, rushing and raging immensely,
And threw a spear at the gilded helmet that covered   540
His temples; the weapon passed through it and lodged in his brain.
Your right hand, Cretheus, the bravest of Greeks, could not save you
From Turnus. Nor could gods protect Cupencus, who served them,
From Aeneas' attack; his breast faced the sword. The delay
Of his brazen shield was no help to the miserable man.
The fields of Laurentum saw death come upon you, Aeolus;
You covered the earth with your back as you fell. The Argive
Phalanxes could not down you, nor Achilles, destroyer
Of Priam's kingdom. Here was the goal of your death.
Your tall house was under Ida, at Lyrnessus, and   550
In the earth of Laurentum your tomb. Then the battle lines met,
All the Latins and all the Trojans. Mnestheus, fierce Serestus,
And Messapus, tamer of horses, and brave Asilas,
The phalanx of the Etruscans, the Arcadian wings
Of Evander's cavalry, each man with utmost strength
Struggled to do his best; no delay, no rest,
In tremendous conflict they struggled.
                                    Here Aeneas' most lovely
Mother prompted his mind to advance toward the walls
And divert his line to the city more swiftly, to frighten

The Latins with sudden destruction. Looking here, looking there,   560
Through the army, seeking Turnus on all sides, he saw
The city untouched by such war, and quiet, unpunished.
The thought of a greater attack burned at once in his mind.
He called upon Mnestheus, Sergestus, and brave Serestus,
The leaders, and stood on a mound where the rest of the Trojan
Army was closely collected, laying down neither shield
Nor spear. In their midst from the top of the mound, he spoke:
"Let my orders be followed at once. Jove stands on our side.
Let no one advance more slowly because of this sudden
Change in our plans. Today I shall root up their city,   570
The cause of the war, the kingdom itself of Latinus,
Unless they accept my rein and agree to obey me
As subjects, and level their smoking roofs with the ground.
Should I wait till it pleases Turnus to suffer a battle
With us and, conquered, be willing to fight again?
Citizens, this is the head, this the heart of a cursed
War: bring torches quickly, demand the return
With fire of treaties they broke." He uttered these words,
And all with a spirit of rivalry formed in a wedge,
And in a dense mass were borne to the walls. The scaling   580
Ladders and fire suddenly appeared in a moment.
Some ran up to the walls and killed the first guards;
Others hurled iron javelins and clouded the sky
With weapons. Aeneas himself in the vanguard stretched
His right hand to the walls, calling out in reproach to Latinus,
And swore by the gods he was forced to fight once again.
Two times already the Italians were enemies; this
Was a second truce they had broken. Discord arose
Among the cowed citizens. Some ordered him to throw open
The city and fling wide the gates to the Trojans, they dragged   590
The king himself to the bulwarks; while others brought weapons
And pressed on to defend the walls; as a shepherd who hunts
For bees where they hide in the honey-combed pumice and fills
Their nest with sharp smoke, and they, terrified over their safety,
Run through the waxen camp and whet up their anger
To a loud buzzing; black odor rolls through their home,
The stone within rings with blind murmurs, the smoke rises up
Into open air.
                    This fortune befell the worn Latins
As well: and it shocked the whole city with grief to its base.

When the queen from the roof of her palace saw the enemy coming,   600
Approaching the walls, fire flying upon the houses,
And nowhere a Rutulian line to oppose them, no army
Of Turnus, the unhappy woman believed he had fallen
In combat; distressed by this sudden sorrow of mind,
She cried that she was the cause and the guilt and the fountain-
Head of these evils, and babbling much in her madness
And sorrowful fury, she ripped off her purple garment,
Resolved upon dying, and tied the knot of her loathesome
Death from a lofty beam. Afterward, when the wretched
Women of Latium heard of her tragedy, Lavinia,   610
Her daughter, tore at her flowery tresses and scratched
Her rosy cheeks. Then the rest of the group raged around her
With grief; the queen's palace resounded throughout with their wails.
Hence the unhappy news was spread over the city.
Their spirit was crushed; Latinus walked round in torn garments,
Stunned by the fate of his wife and the city's disaster,
Befouling his grey hair with dirty dust thrown upon it,
Reproaching himself for his faults, for he had not accepted
Dardanian Aeneas as son-in-law willingly, freely.

     Meanwhile the warrior Turnus at the end of the plain   620
Pursued a few stragglers, more sluggish and less and less gay
In the rush of his horses. The breeze brought the confused clamor
With a feeling of terror to him. The noise of the city
In uproar impinged on his pricked-up ears with its joyless
Murmur: "Ah me, why are the bulwarks in turmoil
With so great a lament? what cry from the distant city?"
He spoke thus and madly drew in the chariot reins.
His sister replied in the form of Metiscus, the driver,
Who managed the chariot, horses, and reins, in these words:
"This way let us follow the Trojans, Turnus, where first   630
Victory showed us the road. There are others who can
With their weapons protect our homes. Aeneas is charging
Against the Italians and mingling in battle. Let us
With fierce hand bring deaths to the Teucrians. You shall not retreat
With less kills to your credit, less fame in the honors of war."
Turnus to these words:
"O sister long since discovered when first with your cunning
You broke up the truce and committed yourself to this war,
Even now it is vain to disguise your divinity. But
Who wished you, sent down from Olympus, to suffer so much?   640

Or was it that you might see your poor brother's death?
What shall I do? What fortune now promises safety?
I saw with my own eyes Murranus dying and calling
Upon me—no other was dearer to me than him—
And falling, huge victim brought down by a wound as huge.
Unhappy Ufens died, not to see my dishonor.
The Teucrians hold possession of his body and armor.
Shall I suffer our homes to be ruined, the one thing that was lacking
For our misfortune, nor challenge the insults of Drances
With my right hand? Shall I run and shall this land see   650
Turnus in flight? Is it so wretched to die?
Be kind to me, deified spirits below, since the will
Of the gods above has turned hostile. I shall descend
To you with a soul that is pure and guiltless of these
Reproaches, never unworthy of my great ancestors."
  Hardly had Turnus spoken when Saces came flying
Through enemy ranks on a foaming horse, with an arrow
Wound in his face, and rushed up to supplicate Turnus,
Calling his name: "Turnus, supreme salvation abides
In you, take pity on us. Aeneas is thundering   660
In arms and threatens to topple the highest defenses
Of Italy and give them to ruin. Now torches are flying
Around our roofs. To you the Latins are turning
Their faces and eyes; King Latinus himself is muttering
Whom to call son-in-law or to what treaty to bind his
People. The queen, furthermore, who trusted so greatly
In you is dead by her right hand and fled in her terror
From the light of day. Only Messapus and eager Atinas
Are holding the line at the gates. Around them their squadrons
Stand closely ranked, their drawn swords like an iron crop   670
Of wheat in the field; you are driving your chariot over
The deserted grass." He was stunned and confused at the image
Of varying fortune thus painted; he stood still and was silent.
An enormous shame burned his strong heart, a madness now mingled
With grief, love driven by fury, and valor self-conscious.
When first to his mind light returned as the shadows were scattered,
He rolled ardent eyes to the walls and, distraught, from his chariot.
Looked back at the city so great.
                      But see, through the floorings
A whirlwind of flame rolled up to the sky from the tower
In a wave and gripped it, the tower which he had constructed   680
High with a framework of beams and set it on rollers

And equipped with drawbridges: "Now, now, sister, Fates overcome us.
Cease your delay: where god and harsh Fortune are calling,
Let us follow. My mind is made up to fight with Aeneas,
To suffer whatever death's bitterness. My sister, you shall not
See me dishonored further. I beg you, allow me
To rage before death's last madness." He spoke and jumped down
To the ground from the chariot and swiftly rushed through the army
Of enemies and through their weapons, deserting his sister.
Just as a boulder torn loose from the top of a mountain   690
Rolls down with the wind or a violent rainstorm that washes
It out of the ground, or age loosens it with the years,
And the massive menace with power behind it is carried
Hurtling over the earth, involving the forests
And flocks and men in its fall, so Turnus went raging
Through scattered lines to the walls of the city, where earth
Was dripping with blood, and the air whistled with thrown weapons.
He made a sign with his hand and began to speak loudly:
"Let up now, Rutulians, and, Latins, hang on to your weapons!
Whatever the fortune of war, that is mine; it is more fitting   700
That I should atone for the truce in your place and decide
The issue with swords." All those in the center moved back
And gave them a space.
                    Then Father Aeneas abandoned
The walls when he heard Turnus' name, and abandoned the fortress,
Laying aside all delay, and broke off all labors.
Jumping for joy, he made thunderous sounds with his armor,
As huge as Mount Athos or Eryx or Father Apennine
When, lifting his snow-covered head, he roars among shining
Oak trees, rejoicing. Now Rutuli, Trojans, Italians
All turned their eyes from the lofty walls where they stood;   710
Some stopped their ramming of walls, laid down arms from their
        shoulders.
Latinus himself was astonished to see these great heroes
Born in two parts of the world wide apart thus agreeing
To settle the matter with steel. As they appeared on the empty
Expanse of plain, they attacked with spears at a distance
On the run, while the earth gave a groan that re-echoed the sound
Of their shields dashed together; they struck with their swords again
And again and again: chance and courage are mingled in one
Furious combat. As when in the forest of Sila
Or on the mountain Taburnus, two bulls run together   720
In bitter attack horn to horn, and the terrified herdsmen

Run off, all the herd stands silent in dread and the heifers
Wonder which bull will be king of the woodland, whom all
Of the cattle will follow, the bulls with all of their might
Slash at each other and butt with their horns and bathe shoulders
And necks with their blood; all the woodland sounds with their bellows:
Not otherwise Trojan Aeneas and the Daunian hero
Clashed with their shields; a huge uproar resounded in heaven.

    Jupiter himself lifted up the two scales with their balance
Made even, imposing a different fate on each of the pair,   730
Which one the struggle would doom and which side destruction
Would cause to descend with its weight. Turnus flashed forward,
Thinking himself to be safe, and with his whole body
He rose on his sword lifted high to strike. There was shouting
From Trojans and frightened Latins, while both battle lines
Grew rigid with tension. The treacherous sword was broken,
Abandoning him in mid-blow although he was burning
To fight, had not rescue come up in the form of retreat.
He fled more swiftly than East Wind when he had discovered
The unknown hilt in his unarmed right hand. The story   740
Tells that when first he mounted the chariot with its
Horses just hitched, in his headlong haste he forgot
His father's sword and snatched the blade of Metiscus,
His chariot driver. This long sufficed while the Trojans
Showed him their backs in retreat, but when it opposed
The divine weapons made by Vulcan, this sword from a mortal
Hand became useless as if it were fashioned of ice,
And broke in one blow; the fragments gleamed on the yellow
Sand. Then crazed Turnus ran for a different part
Of the plain, weaving circles now here, now there in his flight.   750
For everywhere Trojans surrounded him in a thick ring,
And on this side loomed the vast marsh, on that the high walls.

    No less did Aeneas pursue him, although he was hampered
By an arrow wound, slowing his knees, that kept him from running,
And foot to foot feverishly he followed the frightened
Turnus, as when a hunting dog has discovered
A deer that is trapped in a river or fenced by its fear
Of crimson feathers on ropes that force it toward nets,
He runs and barks at the deer, who is frightened by snares
And by the high river bank, gallops and gallops a thousand   760
Times on its trails, but the tireless Umbrian hound
Clings to him open-mouthed, reaches him now and now does not,
And, deluded, snaps shut his jaws as he bites upon nothing.

Then truly rose clamor, the banks of the lake round about him
Resounded, all heaven re-echoed the tumult. So Turnus
Cried as he fled in reproach to people he ran past,
Calling each one by his name, and demanded his well-known
Sword. Ever-present Aeneas, if anyone tried
To approach Turnus, threatened with instant death and destruction,
And terrified him as he trembled with promise to root up   770
Their city, and, wounded, pressed on. They ran in a circle
Five times, unweaving, unwinding their steps now here
And now there, for they sought no slight and trivial prize:
They fought for the life blood of Turnus. There stood here by chance
A bitter wild olive tree sacred to Faunus, once worshipped
By sailors, since they were accustomed to hang up their votive
Garments to the god of Laurentum when saved from the sea.
But the Trojans had taken it off, not respecting its holy
Stock, to be able to have an unimpeded field.
Here stood the spear of Aeneas; the force of its hurling   780
Had fixed it within the tough stump of the olive tree.
Aeneas bent over and tried to pull out the spear
With his hand and hurl it at Turnus, whom he could not
Overtake by running. Then Turnus, crazy with fear:
"Faunus, I beg you, have pity!" he said, "Dear land,
Hold the iron, if I have ever cherished your honor,
As the men of Aeneas have not, but profaned you with war!"
He spoke, nor with empty prayer did he call for aid
From the god, for although Aeneas struggled, the spear
Still clung to the tough old stump nor did all of his strength   790
Avail to pry loose the weapon from the tree's grip.
While he was eagerly straining, the Daunian goddess,
Changed once again to the form of the charioteer
Metiscus, ran up and gave her brother his sword.
Venus, in anger because this permission was given
To the bold nymph, approached and pulled out the weapon
From the deep root. Towering up in renewal of spirit
And arms, this man trusting his sword, the other man eager
With spear raised high, they stood breathless in contest of Mars.
  Meanwhile the king of all-powerful Olympus addressed   800
Juno, who looked at the fight from a golden cloud:
"What end will arise, my wife? What at last remains?
You yourself know that Aeneas will be after death
A patron god of this country; you admit that you know it,
And that he is fated to rise to the stars in heaven.

What are you planning? What hope do you cling to above
In those cold clouds? Was it fitting a mortal should wound
One of the gods in sacrilege or that the sword—
For what power without you could Juturna wield?—which was torn
From Turnus she could restore and increase the strength   810
Of the conquered? Cease now at the end and be swayed by my prayers,
Lest such great sorrow gnaw you in silence and sad
Cares from your sweet lips come again and again to me.
We have come to the end. You were able to harass the Trojans
On land and on sea and to kindle unspeakable war,
To make a home hideous and trouble a wedding with sorrow.
I forbid you to try something further." So Jupiter spoke.
Thus with submissive face the Saturnian goddess
Replied: "I know, great Jupiter, that this is your will,
And indeed I have left both Turnus and earth, though reluctant.   820
Else you would not now see me alone in the airy
Seat of the sky enduring both good and bad treatment,
But girdled with flames I should stand in the line of battle
Drawing the Trojans to hateful struggles. I counselled
Juturna to rescue her miserable brother, and freely
Confess it, approving her boldness in daring still greater
Deeds for his life, but not to contend with her arrows
Or bow. I do solemnly swear by the head of Styx river,
The single unpardoning object of awe which is given
To gods of the sky and earth. And now I give over,   830
Withdraw from the battles I hate. Yet this I implore you:
Bound by no law of fate, for Latium's sake
And for the majesty of your people: when these
Settle the peace with a happy marriage (so be it!)
And join laws and treaties, change not the ancient name
Of the Latins, nor let them become or be called either Trojans
Or Teucrians, nor change their language or alter their clothing.
Let there be a Latium, let there be kings who are Alban
Forever, let Roman stock be strong with Italian
Manhood: Troy fell; let it fall with the name of Troy."   840
Smiling at her, the creator of men and of all things:
"You are the sister of Jove and the second of Saturn's
Children, you roll such great waves of anger within your
Breast! But come, check this passion you need not have harbored.
I grant what you wish, and I willingly yield to your conquest.
Their speech and their ancestral customs Ausonians shall
Retain, and their name as it is; only blood shall they mingle

With Trojans, while Trojans sink into the mass of the people.
Custom and ritual I shall impose. I shall make
Them Latins of single speech. From them shall arise   850
A people of mixed Ausonian blood; you shall see
Them rise above men, above gods, in their loyalty, nor
Shall any folk give you worship with equal honors."
To this Juno nodded assent and happily changed
Her intention, and at the same moment left sky and the cloud.
     This done, the great Father revolved something else in his mind
And prepared to dismiss Juturna from her brother's defense.
Twin pests there are called the Furies, which Night the untimely
Bore at one birth with Megaera, who dwells in Tartarus,
Wrapping them equally in serpent coils and then adding   860
The wings of the wind. These Furies attend the throne
Of Jupiter, near to the threshold of the grim ruler,
And sharpen the dread of sick mortals whenever the king
Of the gods prepares horrible death and diseases or frightens
With war cities which deserve it. Jupiter sent
Down from the top of the sky one of these swift Furies
And ordered her off to Juturna to serve as an omen.
She flew to the earth and was carried within a swift whirlwind;
Like an arrow impelled through a cloud by a bowstring and armed
By some Parthian with dreadful poison of gall, either Parthian   870
Or Cretan, whirling the dart that no drug can heal,
And it passes unknown as it whistles with speed through the shadows,
So this creature of Night bore herself and went down to the lands.
When she had seen the Ilian lines and the army
Of Turnus, she suddenly took on the form of a little
Bird which often perches on tombstones or empty
Roof-tops at night and sings late and unseasonably.
Changed to this shape, the pest flew back and forth
Past Turnus' face and beat on his shield with her wings.
A new numbness made all of his limbs go limp with fear.   880
The hair on his head stood stiff; his voice stuck in his throat.
But unhappy Juturna, his sister, noticed the whir
Of the Fury's wings from afar and tore at her hair
All dishevelled, defiling her face with the scratching of nails
And her breasts with her fists: "What now can your sister do
To assist you, Turnus? What harshness remains for me?
By what skill can I lengthen your life? Can I stand and attack
Such a monster? Now, now, I am leaving the line of battle.
Evil birds, do not frighten me, I am afraid

Already. I notice the beating of your wings   890
And their lethal sound. The proud orders of great-hearted Jove
Do not deceive. Is this the exchange that he makes
For my maidenhood? Why did he give me eternal life
And remove the condition of death? Otherwise I could
Now certainly end so much sorrow and go through the shadows
As my brother's companion. Am I immortal? Is there
Anything sweet that is mine without you, my brother?
O that the earth might yawn sufficiently deep
And send me, a goddess, deep down to the ghosts of the dead!"
Saying this much, the goddess covered her head   900
With a blue robe, groaned often, and hid in the deep
Stream. Aeneas pressed on and shook a big spear
Like a tree trunk and spoke from out of his savage breast:
"What is your delay now, Turnus? Why do you retreat?
Not with running but with fierce weapons you must struggle now.
Turn yourself into all shapes and gather together
All strength of spirit or cunning! Wish you had wings
With which to fly up to the stars or hide in the hollows
Of earth: you cannot escape." Turnus, shaking his head,
Replied: "Your hot words do not frighten me, fierce though you are. 910
The gods frighten me and Jupiter hostile." Saying
No more, Turnus looked round at a gigantic rock,
An old giant of rock, which lay by chance on the field,
Set there as boundary settling a quarrel of possession.
Scarcely could twelve picked men hoist it up to their shoulders,
Such bodies of men as the earth produces today.
Turnus the hero snatched it up in his trembling hand
And hurled it against his foe, rising higher and running.
But he did not know it was he who was running or moving
Or lifting the stone with his hand or throwing the huge thing: 920
His knees buckled under him, his blood was frozen with chill.
Then the stone which was hurled by the man across empty air
Did not cover the space nor deliver a total blow.
As in dreams, when the languid quiet of night bears down
On the eyes and we seem to desire to stretch our run
Eagerly but in vain, and we fail in the midst
Of our efforts, as sick men; the tongue cannot speak and our body
Lacks its accustomed strength, and the sound of words
Does not follow our voice, thus to Turnus; wherever he tried
To find a way for his courage, the terrible goddess   930
Denied him success. Then various feelings revolved

In his breast. He saw the Rutulians and the city.
He paused with dread and trembled to see the spear
That threatened him: nowhere to run, no force to attack
The enemy, nowhere his chariot, driver, or sister.
Aeneas brandished his shaft at the hesitant Turnus,
The fate-bringing weapon, selecting the fortunate spot
With his eyes where to strike, and leaned forward with all of his body.
Never did stone hurled from siege-engine made to break walls
Roar so loudly, nor thunder from lightning that leaps in the sky.   940
The spear like a whirlwind of darkness flew onward and bore
Dread disaster; it passed through the edge of the outermost circle
Of his seven-hide shield. It screeched and went through the center
Of his thigh. Huge Turnus doubled his knee and fell
To the earth with the blow. The Rutulians rose with a moan,
And all the hills echoed around, and the groves full of tall trees
Gave back the sound. Then Turnus, humble and pleading,
Lifted his eyes, stretched out his right hand, and spoke:
"This is what I have deserved; I ask for no quarter.
Make use of your fortune of war. If love for your father   950
Can touch you, I beg—you had once Anchises for parent
Such as I have—take pity on Daunus, an old man,
And give me to him, or my body when stripped, if you wish,
To my people. It's you who have won, the Ausonians see
That I lift up my palms in defeat. Lavinia now is
Your wife. Carry hatred no further." Aeneas stood fiercely
Rolling his eyes and drew back his right hand from striking.
Now, now Turnus' prayer had begun its effect on Aeneas
As he faltered. An unlucky sword-belt appeared on the shoulder
Of Turnus, high up; its buckle shone brightly with bosses   960
Well-known; Turnus stripped it from Pallas, the boy, when he
    killed him,
And wore on his shoulder the enemy's ensign. Aeneas,
When he had absorbed with his eyes the spoils and reminder
Of his bitter sorrow, afire with fury and anger,
Spoke terribly: "Shall you escape me with spoils you have taken
From those I have loved? Pallas with this wound shall slay you
In sacrifice, Pallas exacts from your villainous blood
His penalty!" Saying this, burning with anger, he buried
His sword in the enemy's chest. Then Turnus went slack
In his arms and his legs with the chill of death, and his life   970
Fled with a groan indignantly down to the shadows.

The Life and Works of Vergil

Publius Vergilius Maro (70-19 B.C.), known as Vergil from the name of his clan, was born at Andes, a *pagus* or country district not far from Mantua in northern Italy. The place is now tentatively identified either with Pietole or with Calvisano near Brescia. It should be noted at the outset that Vergil, not Virgil, is the correct spelling of his name, as he himself records it in *Georgics*, IV. 563. The error is medieval in origin and was discussed and corrected at least as early as 1498 by Johannes Faber de Werdea. The chief source for Vergil's biography is the life by Aelius Donatus, a grammarian of the fourth century A.D., which he drew, probably in its entirety, from a life by Suetonius, who lived in the first and second centuries A.D. at Rome; the more famous works of Suetonius are the *Lives of the Twelve Emperors*. Donatus has been translated by J. C. Rolfe in the Loeb Classical Library, *Suetonius*, Vol. II. There are other short and less detailed lives of Vergil, all similarly descended from Suetonius; see the stemma in the article on Vergil by Karl Büchner.[1] Several of these Latin texts have been conveniently collected by Walter Janell in his text of Vergil,[2] and published recently by Colin G. Hardie,[3] along with Robinson Ellis' edition of the *Appendix Vergiliana* in the Oxford Classical Library.[4] An admirable brief account of Vergil's life is that by Mary L. Gordon.[5]

Scholars have not yet been able to amplify to any considerable degree the basic facts given in the ancient lives of Vergil or to agree on their interpretation. His parents were apparently of moderate means, his father first a potter and then the hired man of a public official. Later he had his own farm, with woods and bee hives; here the boy Vergil absorbed that love of nature so evident in all his works. His mother, the daughter of Magius, the employer of Vergil's father, was named Magia Polla. Vergil's racial origin has been held to be Celtic or more probably Etruscan. His mother was "apparently of Etruscan blood; his cognomen,

---

[1] Pauly-Wissowa-Kroll-Mittelhaus-Ziegler, eds., *Realencyclopädie der Classischen Altertumswissenschaft*, VIII (1955), 1: 1027.

[2] *P. Vergili Maronis Opera post Ribbeckium tertium recognovit Gualtherius Ianell*, editio major iterum recognita (Leipzig: B. G. Teubner, 1930). (Hereafter referred to as *P. Vergili Maronis Opera*.)

[3] *Vitae Vergilianae Antiquae* (Oxford: 1954).

[4] (Oxford: Clarendon Press, 1907).

[5] *Journal of Roman Studies*, 24 (1934), 1-12.

Maro, can be traced in addition to the title of an Etruscan magistracy, transmitted through the Umbrians and Faliscans."[6] Karl Büchner, however, in view of the widespread occurrence of the name Vergilius, as shown by inscriptions and other sources, and the race mixture of centuries in the region of Mantua, considers it unwise to make firm conclusions about Vergil's ethnological origins.[7]

Vergil assumed the *toga virilis*, the symbol of manhood for a Roman boy, at about the age of fifteen at Cremona, where he seems to have had his early education, which, like that of Horace (who also had a father of modest means), appears to have been the best available. He spent some time at Mediolanum (modern Milan) and then went to Rome. He lived much at Naples in later years; here he probably first met Horace, with whom he formed the firm friendship reflected in Horace's phrase *animae dimidium meae* ("half of my soul").[8] Vergil's education included readings of archaic poets such as Ennius, and of the new poets, the "neoterics," as modern criticism calls them. His philosophic bent was toward Epicureanism; Lucretius was one of his favorite authors. Octavian, the ruler of Rome later known as Augustus, became Vergil's protector and benefactor from the time Vergil sought and received from him the return of his father's estate, which had been expropriated during the unsettled period after the battle of Philippi. Vergil is said to have studied both medicine and mathematics and to have pleaded one case at law before judges; none of these professions became his own. Through the liberality of friends, as Donatus says, he acquired a house on the Esquiline Hill at Rome near the gardens of Maecenas; but he preferred to live in seclusion in Campania and Sicily.

Vergil was tall, dark, and rustic in appearance, with uncertain health, suffering much from stomach and throat disturbances as well as from headaches. Since he often threw up blood, he may have suffered from bleeding ulcers or tuberculosis. His shyness was acute, causing him to avoid crowds and to dodge into doorways to escape the ancient counterparts of autograph hunters. At Naples he was commonly called "the Virgin" for his chaste character, speech, and habits. He is accused in the life of Donatus of being rather too fond of young boys. In embarrassing contradiction, a rumor also existed that he had carried on an affair with a certain Plotia Hieria, Leria, or Egeria, when invited to do so by his friend Varius. Both charges may be mere calumnies by his detractors; like all great men, he had his share of these: *Obtrectatores Vergilio numquam*

---

[6] Paul Linde, cited in *The Classical World*, 51 (1958), 237.

[7] *P. Vergilius Maro, der Dichter der Römer* (Stuttgart: 1956), pp. 1037-1038.

[8] *Odes*, I. 3. 8.

defuerunt, nec mirum, nam nec Homero quidem ("Vergil never lacked detractors; no wonder, for not even Homer lacked them").[9] Hermann Broch makes a good deal of the supposed love affair with Plotia;[10] Broch's impressive prose poem, with the same theme of fate as that of the *Aeneid*, is a recreation of the poet's last days at Brundisium, when he was mortally ill, perhaps in the last stages of tuberculosis, after returning with Augustus from a trip to Greece. Hermann J. Weigand has a useful analysis of this book with a long letter from Broch.[11]

Vergil's works include the collection of early poems called the *Appendix Vergiliana*, which is divided into two parts. First, there is a group of short, sometimes racy lyrics known as the *Catalepton* (Greek for "in small bits"), fifteen in all. Second, there is a series of longer and more colorful poems with fall into two categories: the *epyllion*, or short romantic epic, and the didactic poem (*Lehrgedicht*). They are the *Culex, Ciris, Dirae, Lydia, Aetna, Copa, Moretum, Priapea*, and *Elegies to Maecenas*. Most of these were once accepted as Vergil's; most of them now are attributed instead to other poets from Ovid to Propertius, and even to poets of later times.

With the *Eclogues*, ten pastoral poems written between 43 and 37 B.C., Vergil became famous and demonstrated for the first time his full power as a poet. With them he also entered the charmed circle of one of the most influential patrons of literature in the world: Maecenas, the prime minister of Augustus. The *Eclogues* contain some biographical details and an atmosphere of Arcadian fancy. Their model was the *Idylls* of Theocritus, but with many differences. The bucolic world of shepherds and shepherdesses becomes through the transforming power of Vergil's imagination a world in which man's fate is observed with a touching melancholy from the perspective of a century of civil war and political chaos in Italy. For further comments on these poems, I refer the reader to my introduction in this book and to the notes to Geoffrey Johnson's verse translation, *The Pastorals of Vergil*.[12]

The *Georgics*, which Maecenas urged Vergil to write, and which were published in 29 B.C., the year when the *Aeneid* was begun, would certainly be sufficient alone to establish Vergil's reputation for posterity. Four long didactic epics on agriculture, the raising of crops, vines and

[9] Donatus, 43. In *P. Vergili Maronis Opera* (Leipzig: 1930), xvi.

[10] *The Death of Virgil*, translated by Jean Starr Untermeyer from the German (New York: Pantheon Books, 1945). (Includes charming hexameter versions of selections from Vergil's Latin.)

[11] "Broch's Death of Virgil: Program Notes," *Publications of the Modern Language Association*, 62 (1947), 525-554.

[12] (Lawrence, Kansas: University of Kansas Press, 1960).

olives, cattle breeding, and bee keeping—they are a magnificent confirmation of his genius. The philosophic and reflective basis of these carefully
polished poems is one of their essential traits, causing them to rise above
the often prosaic details of the subject matter. Smith Palmer Bovie's verse
translation of the *Georgics* is an exquisite rendering;[13] a version in imitation of the hexameter is that by C. Day Lewis.[14]

The *Aeneid*, upon which Vergil worked from at least 29 B.C. until
his death in 19 B.C., was a natural development from his other poems,
deeply rooted in the Italian countryside and love of his fatherland. The
descriptions of nature are part of a continuous hymn of praise which
begins with the early poems of the *Appendix* and would gradually have
become pure philosophy, probably in prose, if Vergil had lived to fulfill
the dream which Donatus describes:[15]

> In his fifty-second year he decided to retire to
> Greece and Asia to put the final touches to the
> Aeneid and to spend three years doing nothing more
> than removing the blemishes from it so that he could
> devote the rest of his life to philosophy alone.
>
> Donatus, 35

In my introductions, both to this translation and to Geoffrey Johnson's translation of the *Eclogues*,[16] I discuss this deep longing for the life
of the mind which makes Vergil one of the world's great philosophic
poets, although he never realized his ambition to become a philosopher.
He seems always to have followed the Epicurean doctrine of a quiet life;
he held no public office and did not serve in the army.[17]

Vergil died at Brundisium in October, 19 B.C., leaving an estate
reckoned by Büchner at about $250,000, which he left to Valerius Procu-
lus, his half-brother, to Augustus, and to Maecenas. Lucius Varius and
Plotius Tucca became his literary executors. They did not, of course, destroy the manuscript of the *Aeneid*, as he wished them to if anything
happened to him. Varius edited the book at the suggestion of Augustus
and it was finally published after the ten-year period during which it had
been slowly composed and parts of it read to groups of friends.

The story of the *Aeneid* is the story of the hero Aeneas (the story
of a man; while the *Iliad*, whose title forms an analogy to the *Aeneid*, is

---

[13] (Chicago, Ill.: University of Chicago Press, 1956).

[14] *The Georgics of Virgil* (London: 1940).

[15] In *P. Vergili Maronis Opera*, XV (Leipzig: 1930).

[16] *The Pastorals of Vergil* (Lawrence, Kansas: University of Kansas Press,
1960).

[17] See L. R. Lind, "Vergil's Military Service," *Classical Philology*, 30 (1935),
76-78.

the story of a city). Aeneas escapes from Troy, or Ilium, with a few hundred followers when his city is captured by the Greeks. He sails westward to find the land where, according to a well-known oracle, he must create a new home for his shattered people. This land is variously called Italy, Hesperia, or Ausonia; from it in remote legendary antiquity came the earliest Trojans; Aeneas is simply returning to the ancient home of the Trojan folk—if he can find it.

The *Aeneid* recounts the hazardous adventures of Aeneas as he gropes his way over the Mediterranean. One peril is the great storm raised by Aeolus, god of the winds, at Juno's bidding; Juno had always hated the Trojans because Paris, son of Priam of Troy, had passed her over in awarding the prize to Venus in the first famous beauty contest of European legend. Aeneas is driven to the shores of Carthage; there, in Dido's palace, he tells about his seven years of wandering, included in the first three books of a twelve-book epic. At the beginning of the fourth book, Aeneas ends his tale, just at the point where Venus, his mother, causes Dido to fall in love with him. What follows includes, among other adventures, Aeneas' descent to Hades and the story of his conquest of Italy.

A Reading List for Vergil

Bailey, Cyril. *Religion in Vergil*. Oxford: 1935.

Boemer, F. *Rom und Troia: Untersuchungen zur Frühgeschichte Roms*. Baden-Baden: 1951.

Bowra, C. M. *From Virgil to Milton*. London: 1945. Ch. II.

Büchner, K. P. *Vergilius Maro, der Dichter der Römer*. Stuttgart: 1956.

Buxton, C. R. *Prophets of Heaven and Hell*. Cambridge: 1945.

Camps, W. A. "A Second Note on the Structure of the Aeneid," *The Classical Quarterly*, 53 (1959), 53-56.

Cartault, A. *L'art de Virgile dans l'Enéide*. Paris: 1926. 2 vols.

The Classical Journal, 26 (1930): The Bimillennial Anniversary of Vergil (articles).

Comparetti, Domenico. *Vergil in the Middle Ages*. New edition by G. Pasquali. Florence: 1943-46. 2 vols. The English translation of 1895 was reprinted in 1929.

Conway, R. S. "The Architecture of the Epic," in *Harvard Lectures on the Vergilian Age*. Cambridge, Mass.: 1928.

———. *New Studies of a Great Inheritance*. London: 1921.

———. "Vergil as a Student of Homer," in *Martin Classical Lectures*. Cambridge, Mass.: 1931.

———. *Vergil's Creative Art*. London: 1931.

Coussin, P. "Virgile et l'Italie primitive," *Revue des Cours et Conférences*, 33, 1

(1932), 385-402, 495-512, 714-732; 2 (1932) 45-63, 147-165, 355-373, 557-576, 612-631.

Cowles, F. H. "The Epic Question in Vergil," *The Classical Journal*, 36 (1940-41), 133-142.

Crome, Johann Friedrich. "Das Bildnis Vergils," *Atti e Memorie della Reale Accademia Virgiliana di Mantova, R. Deputazione di Storia Patria per l'Antico Ducato*, Nuova Serie 24, (Padova, 1935), 1-71, with 62 plates.

———. "Il volto di Virgilio," in *Accademia Virgiliana di Mantova*. Mantova: 1959.

Crump, M. M. *The Growth of the Aeneid*. Oxford: 1920.

Cruttwell, R. W. *Virgil's Mind at Work*. Oxford: 1946.

Curtius, E. R. *Kritische Essays zur europäischen Literatur*. Bern: 1950. Ch. I.

Drew, D. L. *The Allegory of the Aeneid*. Oxford: 1924.

Duckworth, George E. "The Aeneid as a Trilogy," *Transactions and Proceedings of the American Philological Association*, 88 (1957), 1-10.

———. "The Architecture of the Aeneid," *The American Journal of Philology*, 75 (1954), 1-15.

———. "Mathematical Symmetry in Vergil's *Aeneid*," *Transactions and Proceedings of the American Philological Association*, 91 (1960), 184-220.

———. "Recent Work on Vergil, 1940-1956," *The Classical Weekly*, 51 (1958), 89-92, 116-117, 123-128, 151-159, 185-193, 228-235.

———. "Turnus and Duryodhana," *Transactions and Proceedings of the American Philological Association*, 92 (1961), 81-127.

Eliot, T. S. "Vergil and the Christian World," *The Sewanee Review*, 61 (1953), 1-14.

———. *What Is a Classic?*, Address before the Virgil Society. London: 1944.

Espinosa Pólit, Aurelio. *Virgilio, el poeta y su misión providencial*. Quito: 1932.

Fowler, W. W. *Vergil's Gathering of the Clans*. Oxford: 1918.

———. *Aeneas at the Site of Rome*. Oxford: 1918.

———. *The Death of Turnus*. Oxford: 1918.

Frank, Tenney. *Vergil: a Biography*. Oxford: 1923.

Glover, T. R. *Virgil*. 6th edition. London: 1930.

Gordon, Mary L. "The Life of Vergil," *Journal of Roman Studies*, 24 (1934), 1-12.

Gosse, Edmund. *Father and Son*. London: 1907. Ch. 6.

Guillemin, A. M. *L'originalité de Virgile*. Paris: 1931.

———. *Virgile: poète, artiste et penseur*. Paris: 1951.

Haecker, Theodor. *Vergil, Father of the West*. London: 1934.

Heath-Stubbs, John. "Tasso's Gerusalemme Liberata as Christian Epic," *Nine*, 7 (1951), 138-152.

Heinze, Richard. *Virgils epische Technik*. 3d edition. Leipzig: 1915.

Henry, James. *Aeneidea*. London and Dublin: 1873-1889. 4 vols.

Hügi, M. *Vergils Aeneis und die hellenistische Dichtung*. Bern: 1952.

Johnson, Geoffrey. *The Pastorals of Vergil*. Lawrence, Kansas: University of Kansas Press, 1960. Introduction by L. R. Lind.

Knight, W. F. J. *Roman Vergil*. London: 1945.

Knoche, U. "Zur Frage der epischen Beiwörter in Vergils Aeneis," in *Festschrift Bruno Snell*. Munich: 1955.

Lewis, R. W. B. "Homer and Vergil: the Double Themes," *Furioso* (Spring, 1950), 47-59.

Lind, L. R. "Vergil's Military Experience," *Classical Philology*, 30 (1935), 76-78.

Mambelli, G. *Gli annali delle edizioni virgiliane*. Florence: 1954.

———. *Gli studi virgiliani nel secolo xx: Contributo ad una bibliografia generale*. Florence: 1940.

Mandra, Raymond. *The Time-Element in Vergil's Aeneid*. Williamsport, Pa.: 1934.

Montenegro Duque, A. *La onomástica de Virgilio y la antigüedad preitálica*. Salamanca: 1949.

Paratore, E. *Virgilio*. 2nd edition. Florence: 1954.

Peebles, Bernard M. "Vergiliana Nova et Vetera: a Lanx Satura," in *Teaching Latin in the Modern World*. Edited by Martin R. P. McGuire. Washington, D.C.: 1960.

Peeters, F. *A Bibliography of Vergil*. New York: 1933.

Perret, J. *Les origines de la légende troyenne de Rome*. Paris: 1942.

———. *Virgile, l'homme et l'oeuvre*. Paris, 1952.

———. *Virgile*, in the series Écrivains de Toujours published by Aux Éditions du Seuil. Paris: 1959.

Pöschl, Viktor. *Die Dichtkunst Virgils: Bild und Symbol in der Aeneis*. Innsbruck and Vienna: 1950. Translation, U. of Michigan Press, 1962.

Prescott, H. W. *The Development of Vergil's Art*. Chicago, Ill.: 1927.

Rand, E. K. *The Magical Art of Virgil*. Cambridge, Mass.: 1931.

Rostagni, A. *Da Livio a Virgilio e da Virgilio a Livio*. Padova: 1942. Reprinted in *Scritti minori*. Torino: 1956. Vol. II, No. 2.

Royds, T. F. *The Beasts, Birds and Bees of Virgil*. Oxford: 1914.

Sargeaunt, J. *The Trees, Shrubs and Plants of Virgil*. Oxford: 1920.

Saunders, Catherine. *Vergil's Primitive Italy*. Oxford: 1930.

Schröder, Rudolf Alexander. *Gesammelte Werke*. Berlin: 1952. 5 vols. Vol. II: *Die Aufsätze und Reden* ("Der Sänger der Aeneis").

Sellar, W. Y. *Roman Poets of the Augustan Age*. 3rd edition. London: 1897. Vol. I: *Virgil*.

Spargo, John. *Vergil the Necromancer*. Cambridge, Mass.: 1934.

Sparrow, John. *Half-Lines and Repetitions in Virgil*. Oxford: 1931.

Stadler, T. W. *Vergils Aeneis: eine poetische Betrachtung*. Einsiedeln: 1942.

Sullivan, Francis A., S. J. "The Spiritual Itinerary of Vergil's Aeneas," *American Journal of Philology*, 80 (1959), 150-161.

Tilly, B. *Vergil's Latium*. Oxford: 1947.

Tracy, H. L. "The Pattern of Vergil's *Aeneid* I-VI," *Phoenix*, 4 (1950), 1-8.

"Virgilio nel medio evo," a series of articles in *Studi medievali, Nuova serie*, 5 (1932).

Westendorp Boerma, R. E. H. *Vergilius*. Groningen: 1955.

Zabughin, Vladimiro. *Vergilio nel rinascimento italiano da Dante a Torquato Tasso*. Bologna: 1921-1923.

Notes

These notes are designed to give essential information for the general reader. References to the Latin text are given in parentheses to avoid confusion with the line numbering of this translation, which is not line for line but somewhat longer than the original. Vergil's text runs to 9,895 lines; mine to 10,217, a total of 322 lines more than Vergil used. I have made it a point to translate each of the half-lines which stand in Vergil's text as "props" (*tibicines*: Donatus) and which he was forced to leave unfinished at his death; they are clearly shown in my translation. The words *fate* and *fortune*, which occur so often in the poem, have also been carefully preserved everywhere in my text. They are the *Leit-motif* of the *Aeneid* and extremely important.

BOOK ONE

I print here the first eleven lines of the *Aeneid* in order to display Vergil's Latin and his verse form: the dactylic hexameter. It is based on quantity, with some stress as well on the first syllable of each foot. The six metrical feet in the line consist of either three syllables (– ∪ ∪, a dactyl) or two (– –, a spondee). After the first syllable of the third foot there is a pause called *caesura*, or cutting. The spondee rarely occurs in the fifth foot and the last foot is usually a trochee (– ∪) or a spondee. Vowels at the end of words and the syllables -am, -em, -um, and -om are elided before words beginning with a vowel or h. Sometimes two vowels not forming a diphthong are made to "sit" on the same syllable by synezesis.

> Arma virumque cano, Troiae qui primus ab oris
> Italiam fato profugus Laviniaque venit
> litora, multum ille et terris iactatus et alto
> vi superum saevae memorem Iunonis ob iram,
> multa quoque et bello passus, dum conderet urbem
> inferretque deos Latio, genus unde Latinum
> Albanique patres atque altae moenia Romae.
> Musa mihi causas memora, quo numine laeso
> quidve dolens regina deum tot volvere casus
> insignem pietate virum, tot adire labores
> inpulerit. Tantaene animis caelestibus irae?

1 (1). *Arms and the man:* an imitation of Homer (*Odyssey*, I. 1). See also further on: "much tossed." The phrase is repeated but in a different context in IX. 55 (57: *viros*) and XI. 780 (747). The theme of the poem is very succinctly stated in these words, as is the "wrath of Achilles" in the opening line of the *Iliad*.

2 (2). *fate's fugitive:* the *Leit-motif* of the *Aeneid* is emphasized early in the poem and repeated about 125 times. Fate indicates the fate of an individual or city, destiny in general, or divine providence. *Lavinium:* a city founded by

Aeneas after his landing in and conquest of Italy, named for Lavinia, daughter of King Latinus of the Latins.

6 (6). *Latium:* the area immediately around Rome, where the Latins lived.

7 (7). *Alban:* the word refers to the "long white hills" about fifteen miles southeast of Rome, the settlement made at Alba Longa by Ascanius, son of Aeneas, about thirty years after the founding of Lavinium. See Livy (*History of Rome*, I. 3. 4), who began to write his great history about the same time as Vergil began the *Aeneid*, 29 B.C.

8 (8). *Muse:* the typical epic invocation of the Muse, unnamed here but called Erato in VII. 38 (37) and Calliope in IX. 541 (525); there is a fourth invocation of the Muses in X. 169 (163), and she is questioned once more in IX. 74.

14 (13). Carthage was actually founded in 814 B.C., 370 years later than the fall of Troy (1184 B.C. is the traditional date).

17 (16). *Samos:* a Greek island off the coast of central Asia Minor.

24 (23). *ancient war:* the Trojan War.

28 (27). *judgment of Paris:* Paris, son of Priam, was asked to serve as judge in a beauty contest which was held after Eris, the goddess of discord, had tossed a golden apple inscribed "For the fairest" into the banquet hall of the gods at the wedding of Peleus and Thetis; Eris had not, of course, been invited. The chief contestants were Juno, Venus, and Minerva. Paris chose Venus, who had promised him the most beautiful of women, Helen, for his wife. Her seduction by Paris from her husband, Menelaus of Sparta, brought on the Trojan War.

30 (28). Ganymede, brother of Priam, was kidnapped by Jupiter to become his cupbearer and take the place of Hebe, who was Juno's daughter.

42 (39). Athena (Minerva) sank the ship of Ajax, son of Oileus, and killed him with a stroke of lightning (she alone of the other gods was allowed to handle Jove's thunder bolts) because he had seized Cassandra, Priam's daughter and the priestess of Athena, before the goddess' temple at Troy.

63 (60). *almighty father:* Jupiter.

70 (67). *Tyrrhenian:* another name for Trojan, from their supposed origin on the shores of the Tyrrhenian sea in western Italy.

104. (101). used again in VIII. 553 (539); Vergil likes to repeat lines and phrases.

139 (130). Jupiter was the brother as well as the husband of Juno.

144 (135). *whom I: quos ego,* an example of the rhetorical figure called aposiopesis, a breaking-off into silence. The most famous quotation of the passage is that by Gustave Flaubert in the early pages of *Madame Bovary*, where Charles Bovary enters the schoolroom and by his appearance and awkwardness causes a tumult which is quelled by the schoolmaster.

205-214 (198-207). One of Aeneas' best-known speeches and a much-quoted passage. There is occasionally an epigrammatic quality in Vergil's style which, unfortunately, can be reflected only with dimness in a translation.

248 (241). *quem das finem rex magne laborum?:* the epigraph and source of

Allen Tate's poem, "The Mediterranean," which, together with his "Aeneas at Washington," shows the strong influence of Vergil on his work. These poems are among the many distinguished reworkings of ancient myths in modern poetry, fusing both history and myth within one perspective. John Peale Bishop, a contemporary of Tate, shows even greater Vergilian influence. In his "Experience in the West," he attempts somewhat the same fusion or synthesis of Trojan and American pioneer history as Tate does in "Aeneas in Washington"; although Bishop's poem is much slighter and more diffuse. *Antenor:* a Trojan who came from Troy before Aeneas and settled at modern Padua in northern Italy.

272 (266). *Rutulians:* the chief enemies of Aeneas in Italy; they were led by Turnus.

274 (268). *Ilus:* a play on the name Iulus (later Julius) and Ilium, connecting Julius Caesar with Iulus and with Troy.

298 (294). During peace the gates of the temple of Janus at Rome were closed; but this occurred only in the times of Numa, T. Manlius, and Augustus, 29 B.C.

331 (327). *O—quam te memorem virgo?* This is the epigraph of T. S. Eliot's *La figlia che piange*, a significant quotation in the writings of a poet who has worked, as Vergil did, so much with verbal and literary associations, echoes, and reminiscences.

377 (367). *Byrsa:* Greek word for bull's hide, later mixed up with the Carthaginian for citadel, *bosra*. The tale arose that the Libyan natives promised to sell the Tyrians as much land as they could cover with a bull's hide. Dido or her companions cut the hide into strips and gained more territory by this device. (See Appian, *Roman History*, VIII. 1. 1.)

444-454 (430-436). Compare the *actual* description of Spring activity among bees in the *Georgic* devoted to them (IV. 52-66), as a parallel to the simile here.

478 (462). Duckworth ("Recent Work on Vergil, 1940-1956," *The Classical World*, 51 [1957-1958], 153-154) cites some recent studies of this line.

485 (471). The event described is related in *Iliad*, X. 435 ff. *Tydeus' son:* Diomedes.

489 (472). According to an oracle recorded by Servius in his commentary on the *Aeneid*, these horses could not be captured if they tasted the grass or drank the water of the region around Troy. (See *P. Vergili Maronis Opera. The Works of Virgil with a Commentary by John Conington*, in George Long, ed., Biblioteca Classica, 4th edition, II [London: 1884], p. 55. A 3rd edition of the *Opera*, Vol. III, was published in 1883. This work is hereafter referred to as Conington, *The Works of Virgil*.)

490 (474). Troilus is briefly mentioned in *Iliad*, XXIV. 257, but his death is not described in the poem. Apparently Vergil draws on other sources, doubtless post-Homeric.

497 (480). *peplos:* the embroidered saffron-colored robe offered by Athenian matrons to Athena as part of the Panathenaic festival each year.

505 (489). *East:* the Indian Ethiopians, allies of Troy, led by Memnon. He is called black here because of his Ethiopian suntan, but is described as beautiful in *Odyssey*, XI. 521.

587 (570). *Eryx:* a promontory in western Sicily. When the Trojans landed there before the storm blew them to Carthage, King Acestes welcomed them.

591 (574). Dido's democratic treatment of Trojans and Tyrians foreshadows the action of Aeneas in Italy, where he made no distinction between Latins and Trojans after his victory; Juno had urged this and Jupiter had supported her: XII. 823-842 (807-840).

626 (607). Repeated from *Eclogues*, V. 78. It is interesting to examine the contexts of repeated lines for the use to which Vergil puts them, usually as contrasted associations. Compare V. 471 (441) and XI. 800 (766), where Entellus and Arruns respectively engage in violent action.

636 (619). Teucer, a Greek fighter at Troy, was rejected by his father Telamon on his return to Salamis in Greece, because he had not brought his brother Ajax home with him. Ajax had gone insane and killed himself when he did not receive the armor of the dead Achilles. Teucer then established a new Salamis in Cyprus, where he met Belus (compare the Phoenician *Baal*, on the same stem), Dido's father. This Greek Teucer should not be confused with Teucer who was the first king of Troy and son of the river god Scamander and the nymph Idaea.

654-660 (637-642). Compare Catullus, LXIV. 43-51. It may be pointed out that Dido has placed her own family history on her embossed silverware but Troy's story on her buildings, a great distinction indeed.

666-678 (650-660). These lines show a curious resemblance in certain phrases to VII. 360-380 (344-355), not only in words but in their place in the line and in the general purpose of both passages: *hymenaeos* (651) and *hymenaeis*, VII (344); *colloque monile* (654) and *tortile collo*, VII (351); *pectore versat* (657) and *pectora lapsus*, VII (349); *furentem* (659) and *furentem*, VII (350); *ossibus inplicet ignem* (660) and *ossibus inplicat ignem*, VII (355). According to a recent theory, Books VII-XII were written before Books I-VI. If so, then Vergil is reworking here the earlier description of Allecto the Fury. Whichever passage Vergil wrote first, he probably recalled the first when he wrote the second. Both contexts involve the description of garments and personal ornaments, and madness (that of Dido's love for Aeneas incited by Venus, which is described throughout Book IV as bordering on insanity, and that of Amata incited by Allecto the Fury). Both Dido and Amata, to complete the parallel, are queens.

683 (665). *Typhoean:* so-called because Jove's thunderbolts killed the giant Typhoeus; he was buried under Mount Etna in Sicily, where his rumblings may be heard to this day.

694 (677). *prince:* Ascanius is again called prince in IX. 244; his dynastic position is carefully emphasized by Vergil.

759-764 (742-746). This curious song about cosmology and materialism seems inappropriate at a banquet but obviously springs from Vergil's admiration for philosophy, which for him seems to have been largely Epicurean materialism. The passage may also have been imitated from the song of Orpheus in Apollonius Rhodius (*Argonautica*, I. 495-511). The song of Iopas is considered by Viktor Pöschl (*Die Dichtkunst Virgils: Bild und Symbol in der Aeneis* [Innsbruck and Vienna: 1950], 246-257 to symbolize the wanderings and labors of Aeneas and Dido, as referred to elsewhere: I. 10, 241, 341, 373, 628; IV. 211; VI. 451. The passage is similar also to the song of Silenus in *Eclogues*, VI. 31-42 and *Georgics*, II. 475-492 (note *lunae labores* in l. 478), the first at least equally inappropriate in context: it seems that Vergil was determined to bring in philosophy even where it did not fit the setting. The Libyans worshipped, as the Persians did, both the sun and moon: see Herodotus, I. 131; IV. 188. For a useful discussion of Iopas' song, see W. Kranz, "Das Lied des Kitharoden von Jaffa," *Rheinisches Museum*, 69 (1953), 30-38. T. T. Duke suggests that "Vergil appears in the character of Iopas in 740-747 and sings from his own Georgics" (*The Classical Journal*, 45 [1949-1950], 191-193, quoted by Duckworth, "Recent Work on Vergil, 1940-1956," *The Classical World*, 51 [1957-1958], 153).

762 (744). Repeated in III. 548-549 (516).

769 (751). *son of Aurora:* Memnon.

BOOK TWO

10-11 (10). Dante clearly echoes these lines in *Inferno*, V. 124-125:

> Ma se a conoscer la prima radice
> Del nostro amor tu hai cotanto affetto

16 (15). According to Euripides (*Trojan Women*, 9-10), Epeios of Phocis (see l. 274 (264): *Epeus*) built the wooden horse, with the help of Pallas Athena. The wood is called pine, 17 (16); later maple, 112 (112); then pine again, 268 (258); and finally oak, 270 (260).

36 (35). *Capys:* the name of the grandfather of Aeneas and the son of Assaracus, who is mentioned in I. 289 (284); but here he is a companion of Aeneas who bears the same name. He is mentioned again in IX. 600 (576), and in X. 150 (145).

41 (40). The scene of Laocoon and his sons and the serpents was the subject of a famous statue now in the Vatican Museum; a giant reproduction has recently been unearthed in Italy and is being restored from many fragments. Gilbert Highet (*The Classical Tradition* [New York: Oxford University Press, 1957], p. 665) discusses the relationship between Vergil's account and the statue, which was made between 32 and 22 B.C. but is thought by Blinkenberg not to have been known to Vergil: see *Mitteilungen des deutschen archäologischen Instituts, römische Abteilung*, 42 (1927), 177-192. It is described by

Pliny (*Natural History*, XXXVI. 37). H. Kleinknecht ("Laokoon," *Hermes*, 79 [1944], 66-111, quoted by George E. Duckworth, "Recent Work on Vergil, 1940-1956," *The Classical World*, 51 [1957-1958], 153) explains the story of Laocoon (II. 40-56, 199-245) as "a *prodigium* of the wrath of the gods."

58-202 (57-195). The episode of Sinon is cleverly devised as the third part of the psychological series: 1. the hesitation of the Trojans to open the horse, take it into the city, or throw it into the sea; 2. the slaying of Laocoon and his sons; 3. Sinon's appearance and his story.

81 (82). This Belus was the father of Danaus (whose daughters were the Danaids), great-grandfather of Palamedes whose father was Nauplius. For the details of Palamedes' story, see Robert Graves, *The Greek Myths*, II (Middlesex, Eng.: 1955), pp. 299-300. *Belidae* in the Latin is a patronymic.

104 (104). *Ithacan:* Ulysses of Ithaca, who hated and plotted against Palamedes (and Sinon, so he says).

210 (203). *Tenedos:* a small island off the coast of Troy.

324 (312). *Ucalegon:* his name is a pun in Greek: "not caring."

429-430 (404-405). Cassandra raises her eyes to heaven because she cannot raise her bound hands: a baroque touch.

450 (425). *goddess:* Pallas Athena.

533 (501). *daughters:* the Latin word *nurus* really means daughter-in-law, but the difficulty involved in the fact that Priam had fifty sons, all presumably married (with Paris adulterously allied to Helen), was resolved in the hands of later commentators by adding Priam's fifty daughters to his fifty daughters-in-law.

642 (602). *gods:* in fact, four of them, all mentioned in the following lines: Neptune, Juno, Athena, and Jupiter.

688 (649). The story was told that Anchises had been struck by lightning for revealing his intimacy with Venus.

747-751 (721-725). Note the precise degree of *pietas* with which Aeneas arranges his family group for flight in relation to himself. A somewhat obscene painting in the Naples museum caricatures the scene, showing Aeneas and his relatives as bears. See A. Maiuri, *Roman Painting* (Zurich: Skira Editions, 1953), p. 109, for comment; and Jacques Perret, *Virgile*, in the series entitled Écrivains de Toujours aux Éditions du Seuil (Paris: 1959), p. 144, for a black and white picture. This beautiful little book has a large number of excellently chosen illustrations of interest for Vergil's life and works, including mosaics, paintings, statues, manuscript-illustrations, woodcuts, and bas-reliefs: note especially the handsome portrait bust of Vergil in the Museum of the Patriarchate at Venice. One should add to the list of representations of Vergil not included by Perret the statue by Benedetto Antelami(?) in the Palazzo ducale at Mantua, circa 1215 (photo in Erwin Panofsky, *Renaissance and Renascences in Western Art* [Stockholm: 1960], fig. 84). Johann Friedrich Crome has written about Vergil's portrait: see my bibliography.

829 (788). Cybele, the Phrygian mother-goddess, was worshipped on Mount Ida near Troy; she is the *magna deum genetrix* of the Latin text.

842 (801). *morning star:* Lucifer, the star of Venus: see VIII. 604-605 (599-590).

BOOK THREE

On the structure of the book it is useful to read Robert B. Lloyd, "Aeneid III and the Aeneas Legend," *American Journal of Philology*, 78 (1957), 382-400.

16-17 (13-15). Note the resemblance of these lines to I. 13-14 (13-14), 546-548 (530-532); and to III. 186-189 (163-165). Mars is connected with Thrace by Homer (*Iliad*, XIII. 301).

41 (35). The Getae of the western coast of the Black Sea are here confused with the Thracians, the same as in *Georgics*, IV. 463.

84 (75). *Archer God:* Apollo, who showed affection for the island of Delos because it was his birthplace.

96 (85). *Thymbraean:* from Thymbra, a city in the Troad with a temple to Apollo; hence an adjective used to describe the god.

137 (122). When Idomeneus was caught in a storm, he vowed to the sea gods that he would sacrifice the first object he met on land. This was his son. After he fulfilled his vow, a plague came to Crete and Idomeneus was driven out by the Cretans. He then settled in Calabria in Italy, leaving room in Crete for Aeneas to settle if he chose.

150 (131). In Crete the Curetes, often associated with the Corybantes, accompanied and celebrated the birth of Jupiter by dancing and clashing cymbals.

160 (139). The plague in Crete is reminiscent of the hardships of the first American settlement at Jamestown, Virginia, in 1607.

206 (180). *twin lines:* Iasius was the brother of Dardanus; hence the ambiguity of Trojan descent.

212 (240). Phineus was king of Salmydessus in Thrace. He put out his son's eyes and thus gained the hatred of the gods, who sent the Harpies, half-human female birds of a foul nature, to snatch away his food as he was about to dine each day. They were at last driven off by the Argonauts, Zetes and Calais, to the islands of the Strophades.

292 (256). Celaeno's prophecy is fulfilled in VII. 123-126 (125).

357 (319). Both Helenus the prophet, son of Priam, and Hector's wife Andromache were given to Pyrrhus or Neoptolemus, son of Achilles, after the sack of Troy. Helenus warned Pyrrhus of dangers on the sea voyage to Greece and thus won his respect. Pyrrhus then gave Andromache to Helenus with a part of his realm in Epirus.

359 (321). *daughter of Priam:* Polyxena, who was sacrificed at the tomb of Achilles.

377 (340). The single line of incomplete sense in all of Vergil's works: see Donatus, *Life of Vergil*, 41. It has not been satisfactorily explained.

585 (553). The coast near modern Squillace in Italy, known for its gales.

BOOK FOUR

1 (1). The Dido episode has a Greek predecessor in the story of Jason and Medea, as told by Apollonius Rhodius in his *Argonautica*. It accounts for the historical hatred between Carthage and Rome in a figurative manner, tests the constancy of Aeneas to his purpose, and is something of a parallel to the description of Penelope, also beset by suitors but faithful to an absent love, in the *Odyssey*. It is most of all an opportunity for Vergil to display his keen understanding of human emotion and behavior in one of the world's best love stories. Naevius mentioned Anna in his *Bellum Punicum;* hence we infer he brought Dido also into his history of the Punic War. (264 B.C.).

251 (244). Maia, daughter of Atlas and Pleione, was the mother of Mercury by Jupiter.

259 (252). *Cyllenian:* from Cyllene, a mountain in northeastern Arcadia where Mercury was born and reared; the present Zyria.

335 (335). *Elissa:* Dido's Phoenician-Semitic name; Dido is her Libyan name, just as Alexander is the Greek name of Paris, and Paris his pre- or at least non-Greek name.

344 (345). *Grynean:* from Apollo's temple at Grynium on the coast of Aeolia. *Lycia:* a region of southeastern Asia Minor, favored by Apollo.

346 (347). *hic amor, haec patria:* compare VI. 141 (129): *hoc opus, hic labor;* XI. 772 (739): *hic amor, hoc studium;* VI. 272 (261).

372 (371). *at a loss:* the magnificent rhetoric and length of her speech belie these words.

414 (412). Compare the same phrasing in III. 63 (56), concerning the "cursed hunger for gold."

448-449 (445-446). See the same statement about the actual, not figurative, roots of the Italian oak tree in *Georgics*, II. 291-292. Compare the image of Tartarus, VI. 587-588.

470 (470). *Pentheus:* as king of Thebes he resisted the entry there of Dionysus. His mother Agave, a follower of the god of wine and revelry, in her madness on Mount Cithaeron tore Pentheus to pieces. He too was driven mad and saw double. The story is best told in the *Bacchae* of Euripides, of which lines 918-919 are quoted here in lines 470-471 (470-471). The career of Orestes, who killed his mother Clytemnestra, who had killed his father Agamemnon when he returned from Troy, is also told in a play by Euripides. The Furies pursued

Orestes until in a trial on the Areopagus hill at Athens he was finally acquitted of his crime.

509 (508). *image:* probably a small clay statuette of Aeneas. With the help of the Massylian (African) priestess, Dido is practicing voodoo against Aeneas. For a somewhat similar description, compare *Eclogues,* VIII, and Theocritus, *Idylls,* II.

516 (515). *love-charm:* hippomanes, an excrescence of flesh on the forehead of a new-born foal. According to common belief this could be used for the preparation of a love philtre if the mare did not bite it off before it could be obtained by the lovelorn.

524-534 (522-528). Scholars like to point out what they regard as a parallel passage, even one copied by Vergil, in Apollonius Rhodius (*Argonautica,* III. 744-751). Actually, it is not at all like Vergil's conception except for the first few words. Vergil emphasizes the unified peace of nature at night, with a few elements drawn entirely from the world of birds, animals, and the heavens. Apollonius Rhodius, on the contrary, mentions sailors looking at the stars, a traveller longing for home and sleep, a mother grieving for her dead children, the fact that no dogs are barking, etc., while Medea, like Dido, is wakeful. His description, unlike Vergil's, is so full of activity that it startles the reader instead of calming him. Vergil's beautiful description probably owes more to Alcman's famous little poem on sleep than it does to Apollonius Rhodius. For a recent verse translation, see Dorothy Burr Thompson, *Swans and Amber: Some Early Greek Lyrics Freely Translated and Adapted* (Toronto: University of Toronto Press, 1948), p. 146.

621 (614). *fates of Jove:* compare IV. 660 (650): *fata deosque;* V. 809 (784): *Iovis imperio fatisque;* VI. 392 (376): *fata deum;* and *Iliad,* XV. 117: *moira Dios.*

649 (640). *the life:* that is, the effigy of Aeneas which is now to be burned with Dido on the pyre, just as fire will burn Aeneas in the flesh by magic.

BOOK FIVE

1 (1). The funeral games for Anchises described in this book have their Homeric parallels in the funeral games for Hector in the *Iliad* and in the athletic contests on the island of the Phaeacians in the *Odyssey.*

26 (24). *half-brother Eryx:* Eryx, the king of the Elymans in Sicily, was the son of Venus by Butes. Hercules killed Eryx in a boxing match by lifting him high in the air and hurling him to the ground. Erice in western Sicily survives as a place name.

76 (64). The *novemdiale* was a festival held on the ninth day after a death when mourning had ended.

95 (95). The snake at the tomb of Anchises is a chthonic symbol of good

fortune as well as a representative of the spirit of the dead. The "genius of the place," the phrase used here in Latin, was often pictured as a snake.

115 (105). *horses of Phaethon:* the sun's chariot.

123 (114). The events of the funeral games are, in order: (1) boat race; (2) foot race; (3) boxing match; (4) archery contest; (5) display of horsemanship called the labyrinth game.

128 (120). Triremes were not invented until about 700 B.C., at Corinth, according to Thucydides (*History of the Peloponnesian War*, I. 13. 2).

206-207 (192-193). *Gaetulan:* a people of North Africa. *Cape Malea:* a promontory on the southern coast of the Peloponnesus in Greece.

229 (214). *hollows of pumice stone:* compare XII. 583 (587).

344 (328). The ludicrous mishap of Nisus is copied from *Iliad*, XXIII. 774, which is also copied by Nonnos (*Dionysiaca*, XXXVII. 653-666).

571 (548). The display of intricate horsemanship known as the labyrinth game is thoroughly discussed by John L. Heller, ("Labyrinth or Troy Town?" *The Classical Journal*, 42 [1946], 123-139, especially 130 ff., with copious bibliography). T. E. Page has in his school edition of the *Aeneid* (*The Aeneid of Virgil*, I [New York: St. Martin's Press, 1960], p. 428) a diagram in illustration. The game, introduced by Sulla and revived by Julius Caesar, was encouraged by Augustus.

593 (568). Atia, mother of Augustus, daughter of M. Atius Balbus and Julia, and sister of Gaius Julius Caesar, was of the Atian clan; the reference is no doubt a compliment to her.

595 (571). Iulus' horse must have been transported from Carthage to Sicily, giving some idea of the size of Aeneas' boats.

666 (639). *four altars:* evidently each of the four ship captains had erected one, according to Servius (see Conington, *The Works of Virgil*, II [London: 1884], p. 396).

754 (731). In Book VI Anchises gives Aeneas a brief glimpse of what he is to see on his descent to Hades.

827 (801). Venus was born from the sea foam, which is the meaning of her name in Greek, Aphrodite. Her portrait, showing her en route to Cythera, is seen in a painting from Pompeii (see A. Maiuri, *Roman Painting* [Zurich: Skira Editions, 1953], p. 7) from the new excavations, region 11, insula 6, no. 3. Botticelli could not have seen it, although his "Birth of Venus" bears much resemblance. His conception of the Graces, however, in the "Primavera," goes back to antiquity; its closest parallel is to be found in the paintings of the Seasons from Herculaneum: see also Kenneth Clark, *The Nude: a Study in Ideal Form* (New York: 1959), p. 150.

841 (814). He refers to Palinurus the helmsman, soon to be drowned.

850 (825). The ancients were fond of such lists of beauties. I refer to the list of the loves of Zeus in *Iliad*, XIV. 312-328; the Nereids in *Iliad*, XVIII. 39-49;

the catalogue of heroines in *Odyssey*, XI. 235-332; in Hesiod, *Theogony*, 226-360; in Quintus of Smyrna, *Posthomerica*, I. 42 ff; in Nonnos, *Dionysiaca*, vii. 117-128; and the Ocean Nymphs in Vergil's *Georgics*, IV. 336-345. Nikaenetos of Abdera (and Samos) wrote love stories which were compared by Athenaeus (XIII. 509b) with Hesiod's catalogue of fair women. For information on this subject, see F. Susemihl, *Geschichte der griechischen Literatur in der Alexandrinerzeit*, I (Leipzig: 1891), pp. 381-382; W. Schmid, *Geschichte der griechischen Literatur*, I. 1 (Munich: 1929), pp. 259-269. See also Schmid's *Geschichte*, I, p. 292, for references to Pausanias, X. 38. 11 and IV. 2. 1; J. A. K. Thomson, *Studies in the Odyssey* (Oxford: 1914), pp. 26-28; H. M. and N. K. Chadwick, *The Growth of Literature* (Cambridge, Mass.: 1932), pp. 276 ff, 532 ff; Konrad Schwenck, "Drei griechische Mythen," *Rheinisches Museum*, 10 (1855), 369-392; Otto Dingeldein, *Der Reim bei den Griechen and Römern* (Leipzig: 1892), pp. 30-34; H. L. Lorimer, *Homer and the Monuments* (Cambridge, Eng.: 1950), p. 472, n. 1. Modern adaptions of the theme of fair women extend, of course, from Chaucer to Tennyson.

894 (867). *sailing aimlessly:* the ship adrift is symbolic of Aeneas' helplessness at this point in the narrative, and another instance in a long series of disappointments on the interminable journey to Italy.

BOOK SIX

12 (12). *Delian:* Apollo.

20 (17). *Chalcidian:* because Cumae was a Greek settlement in Italy made by people from Chalcis in Euboea.

22 (20). Androgeos was the son of Minos, king of Crete. He was killed by Aegeus, king of Athens, who sent him against the bull of Marathon. From this developed the Athenian tribute of young men and girls sent to the Minotaur in Crete; it was ended by Theseus, who killed the Minotaur with the help of Ariadne, daughter of Minos.

24 (22). *the vase:* used to hold the lots by which selection of the boys and girls was made.

25 (23). *Cnossian:* Cretan, from Cnossus, the city of King Minos of Crete. The frieze described here is comparable to that at Carthage and the pictures on the shield of Aeneas in Book VIII. It is another indication of Vergil's interest in art. See E. L. Highbarger, "Vergil and Roman Art," *Classical Weekly*, 36 (1942-1943), 87-89.

48 (42). The cave of the Sibyl at Cumae is almost as awe-inspiring today as it was in Vergil's day, although the temples are in ruins. It is hewn out of the soft tufa rock for a distance of 131.50 meters. The archaeologist's description should be read in A. Maiuri's little book, *The Phlegraean Fields from Vergil's Tomb to the Grotto of the Cumaean Sibyl* (Rome: 1947), which is one of the excellent Guidebooks to Museums and Monuments in Italy published by the

Ministry of Public Instruction. The book also contains pictures of Vergil's tomb as it was pointed out to travellers in the eighteenth century at the northern approach to Naples.

71-73 (63-65). All three names of Troy are used here.

78 (69). Phoebus Apollo and Diana (also known as Trivia or Hecate under another aspect of her powers) were the favorite divinities of Augustus. Upon this line Servius comments (see Conington, *The Works of Vergil*, II [London: 1884], p. 435):

> As usual, he mixes in history. For this temple was built on the Palatine Hill by Augustus [in 28 B.C.] But since Augustus was related to Julius, who drew his origin from Aeneas, he means therefore that Augustus as his relative fulfilled the vow.

80 (72). The Sibylline books of prophecy were removed from the Capitol and placed by Augustus under the statue of Apollo on the Palatine.

98 (89). *another Achilles:* Turnus. Compare IX. 769 (742) and George Duckworth's discussion of the equation of Turnus with Achilles in "Turnus and Duryodhana," *Transactions and Proceedings of the American Philological Association*, 92 (1961), 81-88.

103 (93). Vergil equates Lavinia with Helen in one of his numerous Homeric parallels.

107 (97). *Greek city:* Pallanteum, the city of Evander.

130 (119), 132 (121). The references are to the well-known tales of Orpheus and Eurydice and the brothers Castor and Pollux. Theseus and Hercules also made the journey to and from Hades.

176 (164). *son of Aeolus:* not the king of the winds. Aeolus occurs as a name several times in the *Aeneid* in reference to different people. Misenus' father is probably the Aeolus mentioned in XII. 536 (542).

215 (204). On the golden bough, see A. K. Michels, "The Golden Bough of Plato," *The American Journal of Philology*, 66 (1954), 59-63; R. A. Brooks, "Discolor Aura: Reflections on the Golden Bough," *The American Journal of Philology*, 74 (1953), 260-280. It was from this Vergilian symbol that Sir James G. Fraser took the title of his famous book.

247 (234). The promontory is called Punta di Miseno today.

275 (264). Homer also steps into his narrative *propria persona* in this fashion, just before the catalogue of ships in *Iliad*, II. 484-493.

280-285 (268-272). William Abbott Oldfather, the American classical scholar, once remarked that these were the five most beautiful lines in Vergil:

> ibant obscuri sola sub nocte per umbram
> perque domos Ditis vacuas et inania regna:
> quale per incertam lunam sub luce maligna
> est iter in silvis, ubi caelum condidit umbra
> Iuppiter, et rebus nox abstulit atra colorem.

E. L. Highbarger (*The Gates of Dreams: An Archaeological Examination of Vergil, Aeneid* VI. 893-899, Johns Hopkins University Studies in Archaeology,

No. 30 [Baltimore, Md.: 1940], p. 109) classifies the apparitions described in this passage thus: 1. personified abstractions—common diseases, physical and mental; 2. passions in time of war, external and internal; 3. misleading dreams sent by infernal messengers; 4. sinister, opposing forces of life which only heroes can overcome. The soul must put aside all four evils as it goes to Orcus for purification, in an allegory of the soul's passing from heaven to earth and back to heaven again.

375 (361). Another Homeric parallel may be intended here, since the Laestrygonians, who attacked Odysseus and his men, were localized on the coast of Campania in Italy.

382 (366). *Velia:* a Phocaean colony on the coast of Lucania, now Castellamare della Bruca.

397 (380). The region where he was buried has kept the name Punta di Palinuro to this day.

414 (398). *Amphrysian:* from her connection with Apollo, who pastured the flocks of Admetus near the river Amphrysus in Phthiotis.

418 (402). Proserpina was the daughter of Ceres by Jupiter, Pluto's brother.

429 (413). As Dante casts a shadow in Hell, being a living mortal, so Aeneas has weight in Charon's ferryboat.

447 (433). See C. Murley, "The Classification of Souls in the Sixth Aeneid," *Vergilius*, 5 (1940), 17-27; F. Norwood, "The Tripartite Eschatology of Aeneid 6," *Classical Philology*, 49 (1954), 15-26.

459-464 (445-450). Phaedra, stepmother of Hippolytus of Athens, killed herself because he rejected her love. Procris was killed by her husband Cephalus in a hunting accident. Eriphyle, who was bribed with a necklace to convince her husband Amphiaraus to join the Seven against Thebes, was killed by her son Alcmaeon. When Capaneus, one of the Seven against Thebes was killed there by Jove's lightning, his wife Evadne threw herself upon his funeral pyre; the scene may be read in my verse translation of Euripides' *Suppliants*, in L. R. Lind, ed., *Ten Greek Plays in Modern Translations* (Boston, Mass.: Houghton, Mifflin, 1957). Pasiphae loved the beautiful bull sent to Minos by Neptune; she gave birth to the Minotaur, which was later killed by Theseus. Caeneus had been changed by Neptune from a girl into a young man. Dido, rejected by Aeneas, is the latest to join these tragic women of legend. One may point out some of the musical compositions inspired by her tragic legend: Joaquin des Prez's setting of *Aeneid*, IV. 660-672 (651-685) in 1450; the secular motets of Jean Mouton; Henry Purcell's opera (1689), now in an RCA Victor album; and Hector Berlioz, *Les Troyens à Carthage* (1858), based on *Aeneid* II and IV.

490-492 (479-480). These men were members of the ill-fated expedition of the Seven against Thebes led by Adrastus of Argos in favor of Polynices, son of Oedipus, against his brother Eteocles; this was the most famous war before the Trojan War.

516 (505). *Rhoetean:* from a promontory on the shores of Troy; hence Trojan.

523 (511). Deiphobus married Helen by force at Troy, quarrelling for her with Helenus: see Euripides, *Trojan Women*, 955-960. There are three un-buried heroes thus far—Palinurus, Misenus, and Deiphobus.

540 (529). Aeolus I is an ancestor of Ulysses; Aeolus III is the king of the winds. See Charles Gayley, *Classic Myths in English Literature and Art* (Boston, Mass.: 1911) for a genealogical table, opposite p. 514.

583 (571). *sisters:* Tisiphone is one of the Furies.

608 (601). *Lapiths:* Ixion and Pirithous were punished in Hades for assaults against Dia, daughter of Eioneus and a priestess of Thetis, and against Persephone.

624 (618). Theseus joined his friend Pirithous in kidnapping Persephone, but their attempt failed. Phlegyas, father of Ixion, was punished for burning Apollo's temple at Delphi.

706-708 (700-703). Repeated from II. 833-835 (792-794), the meeting with Creusa after her death at Troy.

729-756 (724-751). Vergil's theory of the *anima mundi*, the life of the universe, ultimately Orphic, Pythagorean, Platonic, and Stoic in its mingled origins, with the transmigration of souls, involved a process of death, purgation, and purification through a period of a thousand years. It is an eloquent and beautiful passage in which Vergil reaches the greatest height of all his specifically philosophic passages; but it contains unphilosophic inconsistencies pointed out by scholars: see Büchner, in Pauly-Wissowa-Kroll-Mittelhaus-Ziegler, eds., *Realencyclopädie der Classischen Altertumswissenschaft*, VIII (1955), 1: 1393; and Brooks Otis, "Three Problems of *Aeneid* 6," *Transactions of the American Philological Association*, 90 (1959), 165-179.

790 (784). Cybele was worshipped on Mount Berecyntus in Phrygia.

801 (794). *Garamantes:* a people in Africa.

808 (801). *Alcides:* Hercules, grandson of Alceus.

832 (824). The Decii and Drusi were famous Roman consuls, heroes, and generals. Torquatus killed a huge Gaul in 361 B.C. and wore the dead man's gold chain (*torques*) around his neck. M. Furius Camillus beat the Gauls at the Allia river and recovered Roman standards lost to them in 390 B.C.

837 (830). *father-in-law:* Julius Caesar. Pompey married Caesar's daughter Julia.

838 (830). *Monoecus:* modern Monaco. Caesar came from Gaul and the Gallic Wars to take power in Italy in 49 B.C. Pompey was leader in the East, 66-61 B.C.

844 (837). L. Mummius destroyed Corinth in 146 B.C.

846 (838). L. Aemilius Paullus conquered Perseus, king of Macedonia, at Pydna in 168 B.C. and brought Roman power to Greece.

850-854 (841-845). M. Porcius Cato, the famous Roman censor, died in 149 B.C. Cornelius Cossus killed Lars Tolumnius, king of Veii, winning the "best spoils" in 428 B.C. The Gracchi brothers, Tiberius and Gaius, who attempted to bring economic reforms to Rome, were killed by senatorial mobs in 133 and 122 B.C., Gaius being stabbed by a slave at his own request. T. Sempronius Gracchus fought in the Second Punic War and was twice consul, in 215 and 212 B.C. The Scipios were Publius Cornelius Scipio Africanus Maior, who defeated Hannibal at Zama in Africa in 202 B.C., and his adopted son, Publius Cornelius Scipio Africanus Minor, who destroyed Carthage in 146 B.C. C. Fabricius Luscinius was consul in 282 and 278 B.C., fought against Pyrrhus, and was noted for his sturdy moral integrity. C. Atilius Regulus Serranus, consul in 257 B.C., defeated the Carthaginians in a sea battle; he, like Fabricius, left the plow to take command. The Fabian clan was famous for its national leaders and heroes. Quintus Fabius Maximus Cunctator, dictator after 217 B.C., fought Hannibal in Italy with delaying tactics.

856 (846). Taken from Ennius, *Annales*, IX. fr. 8, quoted by Cicero, *De Officiis*, I. 24.

856-862 (847-853). See my comments on this passage in the Introduction. Several recent articles dealing with this famous statement are listed by Duckworth in his article "Recent Work on Vergil, 1940-1956," *The Classical World*, 51 (1957-1958), 156. Another article by Duckworth (*"Animae Dimidium Meae:* Two Poets of Rome," *Transactions of the American Philological Association*, 87 [1956], 281-316) analyzes the passage (pp. 304-308) and compares its ideas with those of Horace (*Odes*, III. 1-6).

864 (855). M. Claudius Marcellus, as consul in 222 B.C., killed the king of the Insubrian Gauls, thus winning the *spolia opima* given to the victor when the Roman general killed the enemy general with his own hand. They were given three times in Roman history: to Romulus, to Cossus (428 B.C.), and to Marcellus.

868 (859). *Quirinus:* a name for the god Janus or the deified Romulus.

892 (883). The young man named Marcellus was the son of Octavia, sister of Augustus, and C. Marcellus. He was adopted by Augustus in 25 B.C. and married the emperor's daughter, Julia. He died in 23 B.C. in his twentieth year. Donatus (*Life of Vergil*, 32) says that Octavia fainted with grief and was revived with difficulty when she listened to Vergil reciting these lines about her son.

903 (893). *twin gates of sleep:* the source is *Odyssey*, XIX. 562 ff. A much-discussed passage; the most recent explanation is that by Brooks Otis ("Three Problems of Aeneid 6," *Transactions of the American Philological Association*, 90 [1959], 176):

> his Hades vision is a dream and a 'false dream' in the sense that it is not to be taken as literal reality. . . . Vergil is telling us that the whole *catabasis* is a dream and that in fact sleep and death are alike in their revelation of an underworld unknown to the waking consciousness yet exerting upon it the most powerful effect, precisely because it is only in such a realm that the meaning of time—of past and future, of history and its climax in Rome's eternal empire—can be found.

BOOK SEVEN

An excellent discussion of Books VII-XII has been written by William S. Anderson: see "Vergil's Second Iliad," *Transactions of the American Philological Association*, 88 (1957), 17-30.

2 (2). Caieta's name survives in modern Gaeta.

11 (10). Circe, daughter of Helios and Perse, lived on an island, later the promontory of Monte Circeo on the coast of Latium.

38 (37). Erato was the muse of love poetry but is used here to signify muse in general.

57 (56). A bibliography of the best general discussions of the character of Turnus is given by Stuart G. P. Small in his article "The Arms of Turnus," *Transactions of the American Philological Association*, 90 (1959), 243. Viktor Pöschl has written the most stimulating and original recent book on Vergil: see *Die Dichtkunst Virgils: Bild und Symbol in der Aeneis* (Innsbruck: 1950).

66 (63). Another example of Vergil's fondness for etymologies, one of the facets of his broad scholarship.

77 (73). The portent of fire on Lavinia's hair has its parallel in the fire around Iulus in II. 721 (684).

86 (81). This oracle was probably at Tibur (modern Tivoli), thirty miles from Laurentum, where the nymph Albunea lived near her sulphur spring; but there is no certainty in the identification. See the note for line (82) by Conington (*The Works of Virgil*, III [London: 1883], pp. 9-10). The genealogical descent is from Saturn to Picus to Faunus to Latinus.

90 (85). *Oenotrian:* a synonym for Ausonian, Italian, or Hesperian.

125 (115). T. E. Page compares these cakes to hot crossbuns: see Page, *The Aeneid of Virgil*, II (London: 1884), p. 157.

134-137 (122-125). Vergil is in error: it was Celaeno the Harpy, not Anchises, who prophesied the eating of their tables in III. 293 (257).

168 (159). The Roman camp is, of course, an anachronism, as are the fasces in l. 184 (173) and the statues of ancestors in l. 189 (177); Vergil is thinking of the *imagines* of his own day.

199 (187). *Quirinal:* a reference to the deified Romulus; his attributes were a toga and a staff. (See Livy, I. 16 for Romulus' death.)

202 (189). Picus is the woodpecker; this is still his scientific name.

218-222 (205-211). The story of the Italian origin of the Trojans is now told by the indigenous Latinus, reinforcing the various oracles and information given earlier to Aeneas on the subject. Corythus is modern Cortona in Etruria. The museum of Etruscan antiquities there is well worth seeing.

362 (343). Amata is queen of the Latins.

383 (363). Amata is here comparing Lavinia and Aeneas to Paris and Helen

as the cause of a new war; the difference lies in the fact that Helen was a married woman who committed adultery with Paris, while Lavinia is merely engaged to Turnus. This passage describing Amata's Bacchantic frenzy contains obvious parallels with Euripides' description of Agave's madness in the *Bacchae*. Amata's madness, however, is contrived by means of a snake (the chthonic symbol of death and hence a foreshadowing device), while Agave is driven mad by the young stranger who has arrived at Thebes. Amata's state of mind is pictured with a keen psychological analysis heightened by the extremely apt simile of the spinning top in ll. 401-407 (378-383). There is the possibility that Vergil had in the back of his mind the suppression by Senate decree of the Bacchanalian worship; at any rate that worship was outlawed and it is thus another example of un-Roman *violentia*, which was Turnus' great flaw of character, here shared by Amata.

394 (372). Inachus was the first king of Argos; Acrisius, father of Danäe, was the fourth king. Danäe came to Italy, where she built the town of Ardea and married Pilumnus, a forebear of Turnus.

438 (411). According to Conington (*The Works of Virgil*, III [London: 1883], p. 43), Ardea was desolate in Vergil's day.

544 (516). The lake of Diana is near Aricia, not far from modern Albano.

637 (606). *standards of Parthia:* lost by Crassus in 53 B.C., they were recovered through political negotiation by Augustus in 20 B.C. The scene of their restoration is shown on his breastplate in the Prima Porta statue of the emperor in general's uniform which stands in the Vatican Museum. The campaigns mentioned took place in the time of Augustus.

643 (612). *cincture:* the part of the toga which was bound tightly around the waist; the rest fell over the head.

755 (717). *Allia:* the Gauls defeated the Romans at the Allia river in 390 B.C.

827 (762). Virbius means "as if a man twice"; this is Servius' commentary on the passage: see Conington, *The Works of Virgil*, III (London: 1883), p. 80. See also the story of Virbius in Ovid, *Metamorphoses*, XV. 497 ff; and *Fasti*, VI. 737 ff.

834-845 (783-792). The symbolism of the arms of Turnus is carefully discussed by Stuart G. P. Small: see note on l. 57.

853 (799). *Anxur:* modern Terracina, near the shore of the Mediterranean sea.

BOOK EIGHT

22 (18). Laomedon was the father of Priam, descended from Tros, the eponymous hero of Troy, through Ilus II. Assaracus, brother of Ilus II, was the grandfather of Anchises. Hence Laomedon was the granduncle of Aeneas. See the table of descent among the Trojan kings in Charles Gayley, *Classic Myths in English Literature and Art* (Boston, Mass.: 1911), p. 529.

96 (81). Helenus had prophesied this portent of the pigs in III. 425 (390).

155 (130). *Atreidae:* Agamemnon and Menelaus, sons of Atreus.

249 (228). *Tirynthian:* either because Hercules was born at Tiryns in Greece or because he served Eurystheus there: compare VII. 691 (662).

314 (294). *Cretan monster:* a wild bull killed by Hercules.

316 (296). *gate-guard:* Cerberus; one of Hercules' labors was to bring him up from Hades.

318 (298). *Typhoeus:* a giant thrust down to Tartarus or buried under Mount Aetna after the war between the gods and the giants.

340 (322). *Latium:* Vergil supposes the name to come from *lateo,* "I lie hidden," rather than from *latus,* "broad."

345 (329). *often changed:* because it took in succession the names of the newcomers who took power.

348 (332). The river Albula became known as the Tiber when an early Latin leader named Tiberinus was drowned in crossing it: see Livy, I. 3.

350 (333). The reasons for Evander's exile from Arcadia are not clear.

362 (345). *Argiletum:* a district running from the south side of the Quirinal Hill to the Roman Forum; Cicero owned some shops there: see *Ad Atticum,* XII. 32.

363 (346). I can find no useful information on this particular Argus or the manner of his death.

396 (379). She owed a great deal, for example, to Paris, who had chosen her as the most beautiful goddess.

426 (409). Minerva was goddess of spinning and weaving.

433 (416). The island is supposed to be Hiera (now called Volcano), in the Aeolian group northeast of Sicily.

445 (429). The thunderbolt of Jupiter was represented with rays projecting in all directions.

467 (454). *Lemnian:* from the island of Lemnos, where Vulcan was thrown from Olympus by Jupiter: see *Iliad,* I. 590-595.

492 (479). Agylla is the ancient Caere, now Cerveteri; Mezzentius led a thousand men from there: VII. 680 (652).

557 (542). Aeneas had evidently sacrificed to the household gods of Evander the day before as part of the ritual of guest-friendship. Conington (*The Works of Virgil,* III [London: 1883], p. 138) thinks the gods may be those of either Aeneas or Evander or of both.

614 (600). *Pelasgians:* a most excellent survey which includes a brief report on these shadowy people is by Sterling Dow, "The Greeks in the Bronze Age," *Eleventh International Congress of the Historical Sciences* (Stockholm, 1960), 27, n. 10:

> the Pelasgoi were perhaps in reality fragments of Neolithic peoples displaced or partially submerged by the Anatolian and later invaders. Greek tradition, which made them very ancient, may well have lumped together quite different peoples under one name.

640-678 (625-665). The events and figures described in these lines are those of Rome's earliest and most famous legends, as told by Livy in his Book I.

679-686 (668-677). With Catiline, Vergil's description moves from legend to actual history; Catiline was the Roman revolutionary immortalized by Cicero's orations against him in 63 B.C. Cato was the Stoic statesman of Rome who committed suicide after the battle of Thapsus in 46 B.C. Actium was the sea battle fought by Octavian against Antony and Cleopatra in 31 B.C. off the coast of western Greece; his victory brought him to power at Rome.

672 (682). Marcus Vipsanius Agrippa was the minister and son-in-law of Augustus.

697 (688). *Egyptian wife:* Cleopatra.

738 (727). *Morini:* a people who lived in Belgium near Calais.

740 (728). The bridge was built by Augustus.

BOOK NINE

299 (294). T. E. Page makes the apt observation that Vergil is using *imago* here in the Lucretian sense of thin films rapidly and successively giving off objects in the phenomenon of sight, according to the Epicurean theory of sense perception: see Page, *The Aeneid of Vergil*, II (London: 1894), 270.

515-516 (503-504). This line is imitated from Ennius, *Annales*, 8: *At tuba terribili sonitu taratantara dixit.*

527 (514). *testudo:* a military formation composed by overlapping shields under attack from above: see IX. (518).

613 (588). Vergil shared the ancient belief that lead bullets melted as they flew through the air: see Aristotle, *De Caelo*, II. 7; Lucretius, *De Rerum Natura*, VI. 177; Seneca, *Quaestiones Naturales*, II. 57.

710 (684). *Quercens* recalls *quercus*, oak; *Aquiculus* means "waterman": appropriate names for a passage which describes oak trees beside the Po or Adige rivers.

737-740 (710-715). Anyone who has seen Baiae can imagine the construction jutting out on the black volcanic sand. Horace (*Odes*, II. 18, 20-22) chides the rich man who "pushes out the shore" with such building operations in order to have a larger seaside resort.

832-841 (806-813). This description of Turnus in battle is remarkably similar in detail to Ennius' description of the tribune (fragment in Warmington, *Remains of Old Latin*, I, p. 154, translated in my *Latin Poetry in Verse Translation* [Boston, Mass.: 1957], p. 5).

BOOK TEN

11-14 (11-13). Jupiter is speaking of the Punic Wars. *Alps broken open:* Hannibal crossed them in 218 B.C. and campaigned in Italy for sixteen years.

78-80 (75-76). The taunt is that Turnus, like Aeneas, has a goddess as mother. Venilia was a sister of Amata and was descended from Pilumnus, ancestor of Daunus.

118 (111). *misfortune or fortune:* the thought resembles the Greek saying by the pre-Socratic philosopher Heraclitus: "Character is fate for a man"; see H. Diels, *Die Fragmente der Vorsokratiker griechisch und deutsch*, 6 verb. Aufl. hrsg. von Walther Kranz, I (Berlin: 1951-1952), p. 177.

157 (151). The *violentia* of Turnus is his most significant characteristic. He is often accompanied by flames in both his action and the imagery which enhances it. See the following articles on imagery in the *Aeneid:* B. M. W. Knox, "The Serpent and the Flame," *American Journal of Philology*, 71 (1950), 379 ff; Francis L. Newton, "Recurrent Imagery in *Aeneid* IV," *Transactions and Proceedings of the American Philological Association*, 88 (1957), 39 ff; B. Fenik, "Parallelism of Theme and Imagery in *Aeneid* II and IV," *American Journal of Philology*, 80 (1959), 12 ff.

163 (157). The figurehead of the ship is being described.

192-202 (186-193). Cycnus was in love with Phaethon. When the latter was destroyed as he drove the chariot of his father, the sun god, Cycnus was changed into a swan, in which shape he grieves for his friend. The sisters of Phaethon were in their turn changed into poplar trees, whose sap is their tears for him. The "crime of Love" was the metamorphosis of a man into a bird: see Ovid, *Metamorphoses*, II. 333 ff.

210 (200). Manto is invented to give Mantua, Vergil's city, a patronymic legendary origin. There was a strong Etruscan element in the region, and it is hard to believe that Vergil did not have some Etruscan blood.

216 (205). *Benacus:* Lago di Garda; the Mincio river flows out of it.

283 (270). *top of his head:* of Aeneas. Vergil does not repeat his name throughout this passage from l. 261, where he is merely *Tros Anchisiades;* I have supplied "Aeneas."

322 (311). *omen:* Aeneas was first to charge and to win.

327 (315). Evidently an example of Caesarean section before Caesar. Those who were thus brought into the world were consecrated to Apollo, apparently in his role as god of medicine, according to Servius (quoted by Conington, *The Works of Virgil*, III [London: 1883], p. 265).

402 (388). Rhoetus was king of the Marsian tribe of Marrubii, and his wife was Casperia, the stepmother of Anchemolus. The latter committed incest with her and, when pursued by his father, fled to Daunus, the father of Turnus.

456 (438). Later in this book Pallas is killed by Turnus, Lausus by Aeneas.

480 (461). *Alcides:* Hercules.

518 (497). *evil picture:* the story of the Danaids, who murdered their husbands, the sons of Aegyptus, on their wedding night.

565 (541). *ritual slaughter: immolat quasi victimam, ut ille consueverat* ("he

sacrifices him as a victim according to his custom"), says Servius: see Coning-ton, *The Works of Virgil*, III (London: 1883), p. 285. Compare Achilles' speech to Lycaon before he kills him (*Iliad*, XXI. 122 ff), and that of Odysseus to Socus (*Odyssey*, XI. 452 ff), which are copied here.

590 (564). *Amyclae:* a town between Terracina and Gaeta (Caieta), named for Amyclae in Laconia. It is described as silent because, according to legend, a law was passed there forbidding the report of approaching enemies after false alarms had been given frequently. As a result, the town was captured for lack of proper warning. See the reference to Amyclae in the last stanza of the *Pervigilium Veneris*, translated by Allen Tate and printed in my anthology, *Latin Poetry in Verse Translation* (Boston, Mass.: 1957), p. 312.

643 (617). Turnus is here called "loyal," as Aeneas usually is called. *Pius* may be derived from *piare*, "to placate with sacrifice," hence with pure hands; the irony is obvious if Vergil is calling Turnus "pure."

663 (637). In *Iliad*, V. 449, Apollo also makes an image of Aeneas, although its purpose is less clear and well-motivated than that of its parallel in the *Aeneid*.

674 (643). *drank up: hausit:* a vivid figure of speech; see again in l. 944 (899).

715 (688). *city of Daunus:* Ardea, in Latium.

732 (704). Hecuba, daughter of Cisseus, king of Thrace, dreamed while preg-nant with Paris that she was to give birth to a firebrand, as she almost literally did, since Paris brought fire and ruin to Troy.

826 (791). Vergil once more, as in l. 528 (507) and elsewhere, steps *propria persona* into his narrative, as Thackeray does into his novels.

858 (820). *Manes:* spirits of the dead, worshipped as gods by the Romans.

924 (880). Mezzentius, like Turnus, is a scorner of gods. (I prefer to spell his name with two z's as the earliest manuscripts do: see Janell's text, *P. Vergili Maronis Opera* [Leipzig: B. G. Teubner, 1930], p. 6.)

BOOK ELEVEN

7 (8). *Mighty-in-Warfare:* Mars.

31 (31). *Parrhasian:* from Parrhasia, a town in Arcadia; Evander came from Arcadia.

70 (71). *mother earth: mater ... tellus* (71).

91 (90). The horses of Achilles also weep for the dead Patroclus in *Iliad*, XVII. 426 ff., and Zeus pities them.

232 (223). Amata was the aunt of Turnus, the sister of his mother Venilia.

235 (226). *Diomede's great city:* he built Argyripa, later known as Arpi. He was once king of Argos.

248 (239). *Aetolian:* that is, of Arpi: see note for l. 235.

269 (260). There was a legend which told how Nauplius, to be revenged for the death by treachery of his son Palamedes, put up false beacon lights on Cape Caphereus on Euboea in order to wreck the Greek ships on their return from Troy.

271 (262). *Protean Pillars:* Egypt and the island of Pharos, where Proteus was king: see *Odyssey*, IV. 354.

286 (277). Diomedes wounded Venus in *Iliad*, V. 318 ff.

301 (292). The loyalty of Aeneas is in particular filial piety and a deep fellow-feeling for his comrades, traits not distinguished in him by Homer, although he is described as faithful in making sacrifices: see *Iliad*, XX. 298. See also note on X. 643: *pius*-pure.

367 (354). The violence by which Latinus is cowed is, of course, that of Turnus. In 372 (359) the just rights belong to king and country but are spoken of by Drances, who hates Turnus, as if Turnus had usurped the right to Lavinia's hand.

390 (375). The half-line is really *qui vocat*, merged with 389 (374); its substitute in the translation is 390 (375). Turnus' speech is carefully designed with rhetorical skill to refute Drances point by point.

450 (429). Tolumnius is called lucky by euphemism, since he is an augur who, it is hoped, will have only good luck to report.

480 (457). Padusa is the name of one of the four mouths of the Padus (Po) river, now extinct.

563 (540). Some ruins near Piperno in Latium are all that remain of the ancient Privernum.

748 (715). According to authorities mentioned by Servius on (701), the Ligurians were noted for their falsehood and cunning (see Conington, *The Works of Virgil*, III [London: 1883], p. 384); compare Cicero's *Pro Cluentio*, 26, where Staienus chooses his cognomen from the Aelii, a noble clan, in order to obscure his Ligurian origins.

753 (721). *sacred:* to Mars; the hawk is also called the bird of Apollo.

791 (759). *Maeonian:* the Etruscans were believed by the ancients (except Diodorus Siculus) to have come from Lydia in Asia Minor; Maeonia stands here for Lydia.

812 (777). Trousers were regarded as effeminate Oriental clothing by the kilted Roman soldiers and by the "race that wears the toga."

820 (787). The ritual is fire-walking, like that of the Hindu fakirs, practiced by the Hirpi among the Faliscans on Mount Soracte: see Pliny, *Natural History*, VII. 2. 19; Silius Italicus, V. 178; and Varro (quoted by Servius), who says the Hirpi put some medicament on the soles of their feet before they walked across the live coals (see Conington, *The Works of Virgil*, III [London: 1883], p. 392).

866 (831). This line is repeated in XII. 961 (952), where Turnus dies.

911 (875). This line is repeated from VIII. 610 (596).

BOOK TWELVE

2 (2). *promises:* to meet Aeneas in single combat.

28 (26). *drink:* compare note to X. 674.

88 (83). Orithyia was the wife of Boreas, master of the horses which belonged to the royal house at Troy. She gave some of these horses to the Italian god Pilumnus, brother of Picus and grandfather of Latinus, who gave them to Turnus.

127 (121). *legion:* the Latin has *legio* which in historical times meant, of course, the Roman legion. Here its use also includes, no doubt, the meaning of group or gathering, but I have translated it "legion" to preserve the double meaning which it may have had in Vergil's subtle mind.

144 (138). *sister of Turnus:* Juturna, who is not named until 141 (146). She was a nymph of lakes and rivers. Six miles from the spring of Numicus was Lake Juturna. A temple of Juturna stood in the Campus Martius and the *lacus Iuturnae* lay near the temple of the Dioscuri in the Roman Forum. Ovid (*Fasti*, II. 583-616) relates the tale of her love affair with Jupiter.

169 (164). *grandfather Sun:* Hyginus (*Fables*, 127) makes Latinus the son of Telemachus and Circe: see the first English translation of Hyginus' fables, *The Myths of Hyginus*, translated and edited by Mary Grant, Humanistic Studies, No. 34 (Lawrence, Kansas: University of Kansas Publications, 1960), p. 107. In *Aeneid*, VII. 47-51 (45-48), Latinus is the son of Faunus and Marica, the grandson of Picus, and the great-grandson of Saturn. In 169 (164) Vergil probably follows Hesiod (*Theogony*, 1011 ff.), who says that Circe, daughter of the Sun, gave birth to both Agrius and Latinus, with Odysseus their father.

242 (235). Imitated from Ennius' epitaph: *volito vivu' per ora vivum.*

390 (385). The healing of Aeneas recalls that of Godfrey of Bouillon, which is the subject of a painting by Francesco Solimena (now accession No. 54. 153, Francesco Solimena, 1657-1747, The Art Museum, University of Kansas, Lawrence, Kansas). This painting is inspired by a passage from Tasso (*Gerusalemme Liberata*, XI. 68-77) in which Erotimus heals the wounded hero of the epic. Godfrey led the first Crusade, 1096-1110 A.D. In a note discussing the further relation of the painting to Vergil ("Francesco Solimena and Tasso," in *The Register of the Museum of Art of the University of Kansas*, No. 7, [May, 1956], pp. 17-18), I write as follows:

> Tasso's Christian epic mingles chivalry and romance within a framework borrowed from Vergil's *Aeneid*. Historical fact and pure invention; reality, magic, and mystery are combined in it with a languorous lyricism unique in the epic tradition. The source of Solimena's picture is Tasso, but Tasso's own source is Vergil, *Aeneid* XII. 383-440, where Aeneas,

wounded by an arrow from an unknown hand, is instantly healed by his
mother, Venus. She mingles dittany, ambrosia, and panacea in the com-
pounds with which Iapyx, the old Trojan physician, had until her arrival
been vainly trying to cure his master.

Tasso follows Vergil very closely. The wounded Godfrey, like
Aeneas, is surrounded by his comrades as he breaks the arrow, leaving
the head within his flesh. He too leans upon a spear as he thrusts his leg
forward to the ministrations of Erotimus, a fictitious character who takes
the place of Vergil's Iapyx. Erotimus cannot draw forth the arrowhead;
his herbs are useless until an angel brings dittany from Mount Ida, as
Venus had done for Aeneas, to accomplish the magical cure. The angel
is unseen by the comrades of Godfrey: *e non veduto entro le mediche
onde/de gli apprestati bagni il succo infonde* (Canto XI, stanza 73, lines
583-584). Venus is, in the *Aeneid*, enshrouded in a cloud: *Venus, ob-
scuro faciem circumdata nimbo* (XII. 416). . . .

Solimena's painting is one more illustration of the Renaissance humanist's theory of painting, *ut pictura poesis*, which Prof. Rensselaer W.
Lee has so thoroughly discussed in his article, "Ut Pictura Poesis: the
Humanist Theory of Painting"; *Art Bulletin* 22 (1940) 197-269. The
quotation from Horace, which, according to Plutarch, goes back in somewhat amplified form to Simonides, became firm classical doctrine. It was
elaborated upon at length by the sixteenth-century writers of treatises on
poetry, Vida, Daniello, Robortello, Fracastoro, Minturno, J. C. Scaliger,
Castelvetro, and by Torquato Tasso himself.

According to this theory of imitation, painting was, in effect, a kind
of poetry; and poetry in turn was regarded as a form of painting; the
echoes of this curious confusion of genres (so stoutly castigated by Irving
Babbitt in *The New Laokoon*) linger in the use of the term "word-pic-
ture." Gradually the painter came to be regarded, in the development of
this theory, as a learned person, like the poet. He too followed the same
principles of poetic expression: *decorum; docere et delectare; si vis me
flere dolendum est primum ipsi tibi*, all drawn from Horace's *Art of
Poetry*, an immensely influential document in the history of art as well as
of literature.

550 (547). I prefer Homer's spelling Lyrnessos (-us) and have used the double
s also in X. 134. Lyrnessos was a city sacked by Achilles in *Iliad*, II. 691; XIX,
60; XX. 92, 191.

596-597 (591). The images here are a form of synesthesia, or what Conington calls "an artificial confusion between the impressions on different senses"
(*The Works of Virgil*, III [London: 1883], p. 456).

618-619 (612, 613). These lines, almost identical with XI. 495-496 (471,
472), do not appear in the best manuscripts; Servius and Donatus ignore
them.

729 (725). Zeus in the *Iliad*, XXII. 209 also balances the scales to decide that

Hector must die. He lifts the balances three times in the *Iliad:* VIII. 69; XVI. 658; XXII. 209; but Jupiter does so only once in the *Aeneid.*

852 (839). *loyalty:* as usual, *pietas.* There is still no comprehensive and satisfactory study of this great Roman moral idea, as I have discovered in preparing a 55-page unpublished bibliography on the history of Roman ideas. Chester G. Starr's statement: "The rise of Rome can best be explained in terms of Rome's piety" (*The Classical Weekly,* 50 [1956], 73) still requires a full-length analysis to substantiate it. T. E. Page says in his commentary (*The Aeneid of Virgil* [New York: 1960], p. 467):

> This is in Virgil the special Roman virtue. The ideal Roman is *vir pietate gravis* (I. 151), and it is as the type of his race, not merely as the saviour of Anchises, that Aeneas is everywhere *pius.* The word expresses dutiful regard for natural obligation either to the gods, kinsfolk, or country.

Page also points out that the gods were obliged to display reciprocal *pietas* toward man, and when they failed to do so, man might exceed them in this virtue without risking the charge of "rhetorical exaggeration," which is all that Conington (*The Works of Virgil,* III [London: 1883], p. 476) can contribute to the passage in his note on (839). It is *pietas,* of course, which Ezra Pound mistakes for that stuffiness he ridicules by way of the anecdote borrowed from Yeats (see Pound, *ABC of Reading* [New York: New Directions, n.d.], p. 44— an immensely stimulating little book):

> The gulf between Homer and Virgil can be illustrated profanely by one of Yeats' favourite anecdotes.
>
> A plain sailor man took a notion to study Latin, and his teacher tried him with Virgil; after many lessons he asked him something about the hero.
>
> Said the sailor: 'What hero?'
>
> Said the teacher: 'What hero, why, Aeneas, the hero.'
>
> Said the sailor: 'Ach, a hero, him a hero? Bigob, I t'ought he waz a priest.'

Yet Pound's great affection for Gavin Douglas' translation of the *Aeneid* makes me wish he could read Latin with greater facility; he might then read Vergil's text with more sympathy.

875-876 (862). *little bird:* the melancholy owl, bird of ill-omen.

908 (892). The ideas expressed here are curiously similar to a favorite idea of Euripides in passages where the speaker longs for escape: see *Hippolytus,* 732-734, 836, 1290-1292; *Hercules Furens,* 1157; *Lon,* 796, 1238-1240; *Hecuba,* 1100; *Medea,* 1296-1297. See also my discussion, "A Note on Euripides, *Hippolytus* 732-734," *The Classical Weekly,* 29 (1936), 87-88.

Glossary of Proper Names

This glossary is highly selective; it lists only those proper names not easily identifiable from the context or for which information is needed for other reasons. The reader should also consult handbooks of mythology and of classical antiquities for additional knowledge. Certain names are used for more than one person or place and are therefore confusing; they are presented in the order of their appearance in the *Aeneid*. The notes deal with some items.

Abas: (1) a friend of Aeneas; (2) a king of Greek Argos; (3) an Etruscan.

Acheron: one of the four rivers of the Underworld.

Achilles: the central character of Homer's *Iliad*, its great hero.

Acrisius: the father of Danae and king of Argos.

Actium: a promontory in western Greece near which Octavian beat Antony and Cleopatra in a famous sea battle, 31 B.C.

Adrastus: a king of Argos, who survived the expedition of the Seven against Thebes.

Aeacus: the ancestor of Achilles, son of Peleus and Thetis, leading warrior in the *Iliad;* the name is used in reference to Ajax, son of Telamon, and to Pyrrhus, son of Achilles, and to Perseus. It is also used in reference to Circe, whose home was Aea in Colchis.

Aeolia: some islands off the west coast of Italy, now called Lipari.

Aeolus: (1) god of the winds; (2) a comrade of Aeneas.

Agamemnon: king of Mycenae and leader of the Greek army against Troy.

Agrippa: the son-in-law and minister of Augustus Caesar.

Ajax: a chief character in the *Iliad;* he attacked Cassandra, daughter of Priam, and was punished for his sacrilege.

Allia: a tributary of the Tiber river six miles distant from Rome, where the Romans were defeated by the Gauls in 390 B.C.

Alpheus: a river in Elis, Greece, which legend held arose in Sicily after having passed under the Aegean sea.

Amphitryon: ruler of Thebes; his wife Alcmene gave birth to Hercules by Jupiter.

Anchises: the son of Capys and the father of Aeneas.

Ancus Martius: the fourth king of Rome.

Androgeos: (1) a Greek leader at Troy; (2) the son of Minos, king of Crete, killed by the Athenians.

Andromache: wife of Hector of Troy.

Antonius: Mark Antony, who was defeated by Augustus at Actium, 31 B.C.

Apollo: the god of culture and music, son of Jupiter and Latona, and twin-brother of Diana.

Arcadia: a region of the Peloponnesus in Greece, famous for pastoral simplicity.

Ardea: the capital city of the Rutulians and home of Turnus.

Arethusa: a famous fountain or spring at Siracusa (Syracuse) in Sicily.

Argos: a city in the Greek Peloponnesus; the adjective Argive usually refers to Greece in general.

Argiletum: a street between the Forum and the Subura in Rome.

Argus: (1) the hundred-eyed guardian of Io, who was killed by Mercury; (2) one of Evander's guests.

Arpi: also known as Argyripa, the city of Diomedes of Argos in Italy.

Ascanius: son of Aeneas and Creusa; he is also called Iulus, with accent on the first u.

Assaracus: the son of Tros and the father of Capys, the father of Anchises.

Atlas: the son of Iapetus, changed by Perseus through the use of Medusa's head into Mount Atlas.

Aurora: goddess of the dawn; daughter of Hyperion, wife of Tithonus, mother of Memnon.

Ausonia: an ancient name for Italy.

Aventinus: a son of Hercules and Rhea; the Aventine hill at Rome.

Bacchus: the son of Jupiter and Semele; the god of wine.

Bellona: goddess of war; sister of Mars, the god of war.

Belus: (1) the father of Dido; (2) the founder of Dido's family.

Brutus: Lucius Junius Brutus, who drove out the last Tarquin at Rome and became the first consul.

Butes: (1) son of Amycus, king of the Bebrycians; (2) the armor-bearer of Aeneas and attendant of Ascanius.

Cacus: son of Vulcan; he was a giant defeated by Hercules.

Caesar: Caius Julius Caesar Augustus, also known as Octavianus, grandnephew of Julius Caesar and adopted by him as his son and heir.

Calliope: the muse of sacred poetry, invoked by Vergil.

Caphereus: a promontory on the island of Euboea in Greece.

Capreae: modern Capri, an island in the bay of Naples.

Capys: (1) a comrade of Aeneas, who gave Capua his name; (2) the eighth king of Alba Longa.

Cassandra: prophetess and daughter of Priam, who was believed by no one.

Catilina: a conspirator at Rome exposed by Cicero in 63 B.C.

Cato: (1) Marcus Porcius Cato, the author and moralist; (2) a man of the same name called Uticensis because he killed himself at Utica.

Ceres: the goddess of agriculture and grains.

Chalybes: a people who lived in Asia Minor, noted for their production of iron and steel.

Ciminus: an Etrurian lake, now Lago di Ronciglione.

Circe: daughter of the Sun, and a witch, who came to Italy from Colchis.

Cisseus: (1) father of Hecuba and a king of Thrace; (2) a Latin fighter.

Claudius: a famous clan at Rome with two branches, one patrician, the other plebeian.

Cloelia: a Roman girl who ran away from Porsenna the Etruscan and swam the Tiber.

Clusium: now Chiusi, in Etruria.

Corynaeus: (1) a Trojan priest; (2) a Rutulian.

Cossus: A. Cornelius Cossus, consul in 428 B.C.; he won the *spolia opima*, "the best spoils," when he killed the king of Veii.

Creusa: daughter of Priam and wife of Aeneas.

Cures: a town of the Sabine people.

Cybele: (1) the great mother-goddess of Phrygia in Asia Minor; (2) the mountain on which she lived.

Daedalus: the architect and artist who built the Labyrinth for the king of Crete.

Danae: the daughter of Acrisius, king of Argos; she founded Ardea, the city of the Rutulians.

Dardania: a synonym for Troy, from Dardanus, son of Jupiter and Electra, who founded the line of Priam.

Dares: (1) a Trojan boxer; (2) a Trojan soldier.

Decius: the name of two famous Roman patriots who sacrificed themselves for Rome, one at the battle of Veseris, the other at Sentinum.

Diana: sister of Apollo, goddess of the moon, and a famous huntress; she had other attributes too.

Diomedes: son of Tydeus, a great Greek hero at Troy and founder of Argyripa (Arpi) in Italy.

Dis: god of the lower world, also known as Pluto.

Drances: a Latin, the great enemy of Turnus the Rutulian.

Egeria: a nymph in Latium who became the adviser and wife of Numa, the second Roman king.

Entellus: a boxer from Sicily who fought Dares.

Eryx: (1) the son of Venus, and a king of Sicily, killed by Hercules in a boxing-match; (2) a town and a mountain in Sicily.

Evadne: she killed herself on the funeral pyre of her husband Capaneus after the expedition of the Seven against Thebes.

Evander: king of the town of Pallanteum, who welcomes Aeneas at Rome's site.

Fabius: a famous Roman clan or *gens* which contributed many generals and statesmen to Roman history.

Feronia: a goddess of the Italians.

Gabii: a town in Latium.

Ganymedes: the son of Laomedon of Troy, whom Jupiter carried off to become his cup-bearer.

Geryon: a monster with three bodies in Spain; Hercules stole his oxen.

Gorgo: sister of Medusa, a creature with snakes for hair; one of the Gorgons.

Gracchus: a Roman family name, of the clan Sempronia.

Halaesus: (1) a follower of Agamemnon; (2) a Rutulian soldier.

Harpy: a mythical monster with the body of a bird but a human head.

Hector: the most famous of Priam's sons, leader of the Trojans.

Hecuba: wife of Priam of Troy.

Helen: wife of Menelaus, seduced by Paris of Troy; the cause of the Trojan War.

Hercules: son of Jupiter and Alcmene; a hero famous for his Twelve Labors.

Hesperia: the land of the West, a name for Italy.

Hippolytus: son of Theseus of Athens and Hippolyte; his stepmother Phaedra contrived his death because he refused her love. He reappears in Italy as Virbius (see note on VII. 827), after his restoration to life by Aesculapius.

Iapyx: (1) a wind which blows from Apulia in Italy toward Greece; (2) the son of Iasus.

Iarbas: king of the Gaetulians in Africa near Carthage, the son of Jupiter Ammon.

Ida: (1) a mountain in Phrygia near Troy; (2) a mountain in Crete; (3) the mother of Nisus.

Ilium: a name for Troy.

Inachus: the father of Io and king of Argos in Greece.

Janiculum: a hill on the west shore of the Tiber at Rome.

Juno: wife of Jupiter.

Jupiter: the greatest god of the sky, king of the gods, and the son of Saturn.

Juturna: a nymph who is the sister of Turnus; she was loved by Jupiter and made a goddess by him.

Laocoon: the priest of Neptune at Troy.

Laomedon: father of Priam and king of Troy.

Latinus: king of Latium and father of Lavinia.

Latona: the mother of Diana and of Apollo.

Laurentum: chief city of Latium, capital of Latinus, king of the Latins.

Lausus: son of Mezzentius, the Etruscan leader exiled from his home.

Lavinia: daughter of King Latinus and future wife of Aeneas.

Libya: a region in northern Africa not far from Carthage.

Lycurgus: a king of Thrace.

Lydia: a region of Asia Minor from which the Etruscans were supposed to have come to Italy.

Maia: the mother of Mercury; she was the daughter of Atlas, son of Iapetus.

Manlius: M. Manlius Capitolinus, a Roman general who fought the Gauls and rescued Rome from them.

Marcellus: a family name belonging to the clan of Claudius.

Mars: the Roman god of war.

Memnon: the king of Ethiopia and son of Aurora and Tithonus.

Mercury: the messenger of the gods and son of Jupiter and Maia.

Messapus: a hero from Messapia or Iapygia in the southern part of Italy.

Mezzentius: a king of the Etruscans.

Minerva: goddess of arts and crafts and of wisdom among the Romans.

Mycenae: the city of Agamemnon in the Peloponnesus in Greece.

Neptunus: god of the sea.

Numa: (1) the second Roman king after Romulus; (2) a Rutulian.

Numicus: a river in Latium now called Rio Torto.

Ocnus: the founder of Mantua.

Oenotria: in the southern part of Italy; a synonym for Italy.

Orestes: the son of Agamemnon and Clytemnestra.

Ortygia: (1) the island of Delos; (2) an island in the harbor of Syracuse.

Palinurus: the pilot of Aeneas' fleet.

Pallas: (1) another name for Minerva; (2) a king of Arcadia, ancestor of Evander; (3) the son of Evander.

Paris: the son of Priam of Troy who seduced Helen of Sparta.

Parthenopaeus: a member of the Seven against Thebes, the son of Atalanta and Meleager.

Pasiphae: the wife of Minos, king of Crete, and mother of the Minotaur, a monster half-man, half-bull.

Peleus: father of Achilles, husband of Thetis, and the son of Aeacus.

Pentheus: the king of Thebes who was torn to pieces by his mother Agave while she was under Bacchic influence.

Phaedra: wife of Theseus of Athens and daughter of Minos; see Hippolytus.

Phaethon: (1) Helios, the god of the Sun; (2) a son of Helios who tried in vain to drive the chariot of the Sun.

Phineus: son of Agenor; he was a king of Thrace blinded by the gods and plagued by the Harpies because he blinded his own sons.

Phlegethon: the river of fire in the underworld (Tartarus).

Phoebus: another name for Apollo.

Pilumnus: son of Daunus and forebear of Turnus the Rutulian leader.

Pirithous: son of Ixion, the king of the Lapithae, who was the great friend of Theseus of Athens.

Polyphemus: the Cyclops of Sicily whom Ulysses blinded.

Priam: king of Troy and father of Hector and Paris, among numerous other children.

Proserpina: daughter of Ceres and wife of Pluto, god of the underworld.

Pyrrhus: the son of Achilles; he is also named Neoptolemus.

Quirinus: the name given to Romulus when he became a god.

Rhadamanthus: the brother of Minos and son of Jupiter; he is one of the three judges in the underworld.

Rhoetus: (1) a Rutulian; (2) a king of the Marsians.

Romulus: the first king of Rome, according to legend.

Salmoneus: son of Aeolus, ruler of Elis in Greece, punished for imitating Jupiter.

Sarpedon: son of Jupiter and king of Lycia; he was killed at Troy.

Saturn: a legendary king of Latium during the Golden Age; he was the father of Jupiter and other gods and goddesses.

Sidon: a city in Phoenicia.

Silvia: daughter of Tyrrhus, a Latin.

Soracte: a mountain in Etruria, now Mount S. Oreste.

Styx: a river of the lower world.

Sychaeus: husband of Dido, killed by her brother Pygmalion.

Tarquin: also called the Proud, the last king of Rome.

Tartarus: the place in the underworld where the sinful abide.

Tatius: Titus T., the king of the Sabines; Romulus divided his kingship with him.

Teucer: (1) first king of Troy; his daughter Batea married Dardanus, an eponymous hero of Troy; (2) founder of Salamis in Cyprus and half-brother of Ajax.

Theseus: king of Athens; he killed the Minotaur in Crete.

Tiber: the river that flows through Rome; also the river god of the same name.

Tibur: now Tivoli, about twenty miles northeast of Rome on the Anio river.

Tithonus: the son of Laomedon, husband of Aurora, and father of Memnon.

Trivia: a name given to Diana as goddess of the crossroads.

Turnus: son of Daunus and the nymph Venilia; he was king of the Rutulians and fiancé of Lavinia, daughter of Latinus.

Typhoeus: a son of Earth and Tartarus; he had a hundred heads; he was struck by lightning and was buried under the island of Ischia or under Mount Aetna.

Tyre: a city in Phoenicia.

Ulysses: Latin name of Odysseus, hero of the *Odyssey*.

Venus: goddess of love and beauty, daughter of Jupiter.

Vesta: goddess of the Roman hearth.

Virbius: the name by which Hippolytus was known when Aesculapius brought him back to life.

Vulcan: god of the forge, son of Jupiter and Juno, who made armor for Aeneas.

Zephyr: the West Wind personified.